THE RIGHT TO WORK

The value of work cannot be underestimated in today's world. Work is valuable because productive labour generates goods needed for survival, such as food and housing; goods needed for self-development, such as education and culture; and other material goods that people wish to have in order to live a fulfilling life. A job also generally inspires a sense of achievement, self-esteem and the esteem of others. People develop social relations at work, which can be very important for them. Work brings both material and non-material benefits.

There is no doubt that work is a crucial good. Do we have a human right to this good? What is the content of the right? Does it impose a duty on governments to promote full employment? Does it entail an obligation to protect decent work? There is also a question about the right-holders. Do migrants have a right to work, for example? At the same time many people would rather not work. What kind of right is this, if many people do not want to have it? The chapters of this book address the uncertainty and controversy that surround the right to work both in theoretical scholarship and in policymaking. They discuss the philosophical underpinnings of the right to work, and its development in human rights law at national level (in jurisdictions such as the United Kingdom, Australia, Japan, France and the United States) and international level (in the context of the United Nations, the European Social Charter, the International Labour Organization, the European Convention on Human Rights and other legal orders).

The Right to Work

Legal and Philosophical Perspectives

Edited by
Virginia Mantouvalou

·HART·
PUBLISHING

OXFORD AND PORTLAND, OREGON
2017

Hart Publishing
An imprint of Bloomsbury Publishing Plc

Hart Publishing Ltd
Kemp House
Chawley Park
Cumnor Hill
Oxford OX2 9PH
UK

Bloomsbury Publishing Plc
50 Bedford Square
London
WC1B 3DP
UK

www.hartpub.co.uk
www.bloomsbury.com

Published in North America (US and Canada) by
Hart Publishing
c/o International Specialized Book Services
920 NE 58th Avenue, Suite 300
Portland, OR 97213-3786
USA

www.isbs.com

First published in hardback, 2014
Paperback edition, 2017

British Library Cataloguing-in-Publication Data
A catalogue record for this book is available from the British Library.

ISBN: PB: 978-1-50991-378-7
HB: 978-1-84946-510-6

Typeset by Compuscript Ltd, Shannon
Printed and bound in Great Britain by
Lightning Source UK Ltd

To Ross

FOREWORD

'Everyone has the right to work'. So states the Universal Declaration of Human Rights of 1948 and other international instruments as well as some national constitutions. What does this mean and what is its significance? A generation ago I was one of those scholars who tried to find answers to these questions.[1] I did so in the context of English and comparative European law in response to the proposal by Professor Peter Townsend, a distinguished sociologist, that there should be a 'legally enforceable right to work'. This suggestion was made at the end of his massive study of poverty in the United Kingdom.[2] His research showed that there is a systematic association between the likelihood of poverty and greater discontinuity of employment, that there are not two broad states of employment and unemployment but a hierarchy of ranks from whole-time secure employment to continuous unemployment, and that there had been a tendency since the 1970s for inequality to grow between these ranks. He believed that there could be an enlargement of access to jobs through a legal 'right to work'.

There was little interest in the debate sparked by Peter Townsend during the periods of relatively full employment in the economically advanced countries until the crisis of financial capitalism starting in 2007. According to the ILO by 2012, 197 million work seekers worldwide were without jobs and another 39 million had left the labour market. There was an increase in unemployment in the advanced countries of 28 million between 2007 and 2013. Depressed growth and unemployment has spread to the developing countries. In all countries there has been an exponential growth in the 'precariat' – those without formal full-time, indefinite, secure employment. The ILO estimates that some 70 per cent of the world's population is not adequately covered by social protection – so even in the restricted sense of a right to social assistance a universal right to work does not exist. It is still a 'noble lie'[3] – a well-meant promise that seems to be incapable of fulfilment. In its current proposal for an ILO Recommendation on 'Facilitating transitions from the informal to the formal economy' the International Labour Office speaks of 'rights *at* work' but not a 'right *to* work.' The ILO seeks to promote the creation, preservation and sustainability of decent jobs in the formal economy by various means but not through a legally enforceable right to work.

It is in this depressed situation that the debate about a right to work has once again assumed enormous importance. This is a debate no longer confined to the

[1] B Hepple, 'A Right to Work?' (1981) 10 *Industrial Law Journal* 65.

[2] P Townsend, *Poverty in the United Kingdom: A Survey of Household Resources and Standards of Living* (California, University of California Press, 1979) 926.

[3] O O'Neill, 'The Dark Side of Human Rights' (2005) 81 *International Affairs* 427.

rather narrow focus of my own early study. It embraces philosophical, sociological and legal questions that are both global and national. In this exciting and significant book a new generation of scholars examine the right to work in these multidisciplinary dimensions. The book is both timely and important to the development of social and legal policy.

Professor Sir Bob Hepple QC FBA
Clare College
Cambridge

ACKNOWLEDGMENTS

This book represents the culmination of a project on the 'Right to Work: Legal and Philosophical Perspectives', which started with a workshop at University College London (UCL) in May 2012. I am very grateful to everyone who took part and contributed to the great success of the workshop. The UCL Faculty of Laws has provided both great intellectual stimulation and practical support from the moment that I proposed the project. The workshop was also kindly supported by the *Modern Law Review*, the Human Rights Consortium of the University of London, as well as the UCL Human Rights Institute and the Labour Rights Institute. Some colleagues participated in the workshop but did not contribute to the book, and I would particularly like to thank Diamond Ashiagbor, Anne Davies, Andrew Lang and John Tasioulas. Many of the contributors met again and participated in a session on the topic at the Labour Law Research Network inaugural conference in Barcelona, in June 2013. I would like to thank the organisers of this conference, Chelo Chacartegui, Guy Davidov and Julia Lopez for hosting our session, as well as all participants for their excellent comments and their enthusiasm.

I have benefited from the help and support of a number of other friends and colleagues. I am deeply grateful to Hugh Collins for endless discussions on the project from its first stage in summer 2011 until now, and Guy Mundlak for his warm encouragement and support throughout. Einat Albin, Alan Bogg, Nicholas Hatzis and Charlie Webb have also patiently listened to me and advised me on numerous occasions. My UCL colleagues have been a source of support. I'd particularly like to mention Nicola Countouris, Ronan McCrea, Colm O'Cinneide and Prince Saprai, as well as my UCL students who have been a source of inspiration. I am also very grateful to Eleni Frantziou and Inga Thiemann for their excellent editorial work. Finally, I need to thank George Letsas for his critical insights, his patience and his constant support.

CONTENTS

LIST OF CONTRIBUTORS

Dr Einat Albin is Lecturer in Labour Law and Human Rights at the Hebrew University of Jerusalem and Academic Director of the Clinical Legal Education Centre.

Professor Kenji Arita is Professor of Labour Law at Seinan Gakuin University.

Professor Alan Bogg is Professor of Labour Law at the University of Oxford, and a Fellow and Tutor in Law at Hertford College, Oxford.

Professor Hugh Collins FBA is Vinerian Professor of English Law, All Souls College, Oxford.

Professor Mark Freedland QC (hon) FBA is Emeritus Professor of Employment Law at the University of Oxford and an Honorary Professor in the Faculty of Laws, University College London.

Dr Joanna Howe is Lecturer in Law at the University of Adelaide.

Dr Nicola Kountouris is Reader in Law at University College London.

Dr Virginia Mantouvalou is Reader in Human Rights and Labour Law and Co-Director of the Institute for Human Rights, University College London.

Professor Guy Mundlak is Professor of Law at the Faculty of Law and Department of Labor Studies, Tel-Aviv University.

Professor James Nickel is Professor of Philosophy and Law at the University of Miami.

Colm O'Cinneide is Reader in Law at University College London and General Rapporteur of the European Committee of Social Rights.

Dr Amir Paz-Fuchs is Senior Lecturer in Employment Law at the University of Sussex.

Professor James Penner is Professor of Law at the National University of Singapore.

Professor Kerry Rittich is Professor of Law, Women and Gender Studies, and Public Policy and Governance at the University of Toronto.

Professor Sophie Robin-Olivier is Professor of Law at La Sorbonne School of Law (University Paris I) and a member of the Research Institute in European and International Law (IREDIES).

Professor Katherine VW Stone is the Arjay and Frances Fearing Miller Professor of Law and Director of the Globalization and Labor Standards Project at the University of California School of Law at Los Angeles (UCLA).

Professor David Wiggins FBA is Wykeham Professor of Logic Emeritus and Emeritus Fellow of New College, Oxford.

Introduction

VIRGINIA MANTOUVALOU

Is there a human right to work? If so, is it a universal right that everyone should have or is it only a right of citizens within and against a particular state? There is also disagreement about what duties the right entails. Does it encompass a positive right to obtain the job of one's choice or a negative right not to be forced to work? Is exploitative work compatible with it? Against whom is the right held: an employer, the state, trade unions? And what types of conflicts does it generate with other rights? This book investigates questions such as these in light of both law and philosophy. Whether there is a right to work at a moral level is to a certain degree a different enquiry from whether there is a right to work in various legal orders, and particularly how it is and how it should be protected there: through legislation, constitutions, international treaties or soft law. But the legal and philosophical analyses inform each other. By combining legal and philosophical perspectives, this book explores both the nature of the right and its normative implications.

I Why the Right to Work?

Most people will agree that work is a crucial good. It is valuable because productive labour generates goods that each person needs for him or herself, as well as for those for whom he or she cares: goods needed for survival, like food and housing; goods needed for self-development, like education and culture; and other material goods that people wish to have in order to live a fulfilling life. In a market economy, productive labour benefits not only those who produce goods by bringing them income, but also those who purchase and consume these goods. But work is not only valuable for the income that it generates; it is crucial for a person's feeling of membership in society. In addition, a job generally inspires a sense of achievement, self-esteem, as well as the esteem of the others. Through work people also develop social relationships. The possibility of developing such relations, then, is another reason why most people value work. Work brings both material and non-material benefits.

Yet two key paradoxes emerge when thinking about a right to work. First, work, unlike other basic goods such as housing or health care, is not something that everyone desires to have. Many people would rather not work, in order to have more time for other activities that they value, such as spending time with their friends, attending artistic events, playing sports and other such things. What kind of right is this, if many people do not want to have it? Is there a hidden agenda, namely a duty to work in disguise, because of the need for productive labour in a market economy?[1] The second paradox involves the idea of full employment. The example of former communist regimes shows that it is unsustainable to provide jobs for everyone because this system would be very inefficient. So, many would think that we should not talk about a right to work at all. 'It would be a splendid thing for everyone to have a job',[2] but there can be no such human right. To say that there is such a right would be to 'remove whatever follows from the region of what is immediately and unequivocally compelling into that of distant aspiration'.[3]

Despite these paradoxes, the Universal Declaration of Human Rights of 1948 (UDHR) placed the right to work and other social rights, such as housing and education, next to civil and political rights, like the right to life and freedom of expression. Article 23(1) of the UDHR states: 'Everyone has the right to work, to free choice of employment, to just and favourable conditions of work and to protection against unemployment'. Later on, though, the international community and some national legal orders decided to separate the two groups of entitlements. The UN included civil and political rights in the International Covenant on Civil and Political Rights (ICCPR, 1966), and economic and social rights in the International Covenant on Economic, Social and Cultural Rights (ICESCR, 1966). The Council of Europe and the Organization of American States adopted a similar approach, drawing a sharp dividing line between categories of human rights. The right to work was classified as a social right by the international community.

The classification of the right to work as a social right had implications both for its symbolism and for its legal protection. Social rights were viewed as different in nature from civil and political rights. They were typically presented as positive, resource-demanding and vague, and these supposed features were said to distinguish them from civil and political rights. Today it is well established that social rights have much more in common with civil and political rights than was once suggested, and that there is no sharp division between the two groups of entitlements.[4] Social rights were also typically presented as rights of secondary importance, which is something that the wording of the Treaties that protect them

[1] G Mundlak, 'The Right to Work – The Value of Work' in D Barak-Erez and A Gross (eds), *Exploring Social Rights: Between Theory and Practice* (Oxford, Hart Publishing, 2007) 341, 356.

[2] Here I am paraphrasing Maurice Cranston, *Human Rights To-day* (London, Ampersand, 1962) 44.

[3] ibid, 45.

[4] See V Mantouvalou, 'In Support of Legalisation' in C Gearty and V Mantouvalou, *Debating Social Rights* (Oxford, Hart Publishing, 2010); B Hepple (ed), *Social and Labour Rights in a Global Context* (Cambridge, Cambridge University Press, 2002); S Fredman, *Human Rights Transformed: Positive Rights and Positive Duties* (Oxford, Oxford University Press, 2008).

reflects.[5] Most importantly, the monitoring machinery of social rights has traditionally been weaker than that of civil and political rights which are generally enforceable by individual petition and justiciable in courts. Against this background, the right to work was insufficiently analysed by monitoring bodies.

A few decades ago, leading law and philosophy scholars started to examine the human right to work. More than 30 years ago, Bob Hepple published an essay on the legal right to work, which explored its meaning as a right against the state, an employer and trade unions in English law.[6] At about the same time, James Nickel analysed the right to work as a philosophical issue, addressing in particular the objection raised in scholarship that it is a social right, which is and must be treated differently from civil and political rights,[7] and Jon Elster critically examined some possible justifications of the right.[8] In recent years, efforts to develop a justification and explore the content of the right to work have been relatively scarce.[9] For this reason, the analysis of the right to work that this book attempts is a genuine intellectual enquiry. Like other areas of human rights, which are frequently invoked by activists and others in everyday discourse, but infrequently analysed in depth, the right to work needs to be investigated.

But, in addition to the intellectual merit of the endeavour, it is particularly timely to analyse the right to work today for strategic reasons. Following the fall of communism in Europe, it is crucial to assess the meaning of the right to work afresh, as part of a unified list of human rights. At times of high levels of unemployment in Europe and elsewhere, and as the right to work is sometimes used as a slogan in favour of deregulation of the labour market, as well as a slogan against immigration and unionisation, the purpose of this book is to reclaim the right to work and, hopefully, develop a research agenda for the future.

II Why Legal and Philosophical Perspectives?

I have argued elsewhere that there are three approaches to the question whether labour rights are human rights, which are sometimes conflated in the literature: a positivistic approach, an instrumental approach and a normative approach.[10] This division of perspectives captures the analysis of the right to work, as well as other

[5] cp Art 2(1) ICCPR with Art 2(1) ICESCR.

[6] B Hepple, 'A Right to Work?' (1981) 10 *Industrial Law Journal* 65.

[7] J Nickel, 'Is there a Human Right to Employment?' (1978–79) X *Philosophical* Forum 149.

[8] J Elster, 'Is There (or Should There Be) A Right to Work?' in A Gutmann (ed), *Democracy and the Welfare State* (Princeton NJ, Princeton University Press, 1988) 53.

[9] With some notable exceptions: see particularly G Mundlak, 'The Right to Work – The Value of Work', above n 1; G Mundlak, 'The Right to Work: Linking Human Rights and Employment Policy' (2007) 146 *International Labour Review* 189; V Schultz, 'Life's Work' (2000) 100 *Columbia Law Review* 1881; P Harvey, 'The Right to Work and Basic Income Guarantees: Competing or Complementary Goals?' (2005) 2 *Rutgers Journal of Law & Urban Policy* 8.

[10] V Mantouvalou, 'Are Labour Rights Human Rights?' (2012) 3 *European Labour Law Journal* 151.

labour rights. On the view of the positivists, the right to work is a human right if it is protected as such in human rights documents. On the view of the instrumentalists, the right to work is a human right if courts or civil society organisations are successful in using it in order to promote their goals. Finally, on the normative approach, the right to work is a human right if there is a sufficiently strong justification for it to be treated as such.

The positivistic, the instrumental and the normative approach to the question whether the right to work and other labour rights are human rights, are all valuable. The positivistic approach not only serves as a starting point in the analysis of the legal protection of human rights, it may also reflect democratic legitimacy, if a democratically elected body has decided to include the right to work in a legal document. The instrumental analysis reflects a neo-Marxist approach to human rights,[11] which seeks to utilise legal tools in order to promote aims that its proponents deem valuable. Finally, the normative analysis is the one that brings the legal and philosophical discussions together most. This is because it assesses the theoretical justification of the right to work and has implications for its legal protection.

The view taken in this book, which explores legal and philosophical perspectives next to each other, is that these should both be assessed separately, but above all should inform each other. It rests on the belief that lawyers and philosophers exploring the questions have shared concerns. It is based on the idea that if there is a moral right to work, this should inform what the law provides and how it should be interpreted.

The range of jurisdictions covered in the book is broad – from the Council of Europe and the European Union (Freedland and Kountouris, Mantouvalou, Mundlak, O'Cinneide, Rittich); to the United States (Mantouvalou, Stone); Japan (Arita); Australia (Howe); the United Kingdom (Bogg, Collins, Howe, Mantouvalou); the international human rights system (Albin, Arita, Collins, Mantouvalou, Nickel, O'Cinneide); as well as other international law regimes (Mundlak, Rittich). Even though several legal orders are covered, the book is by no means exhaustive. It contains certain common law legal orders and certain civil law legal orders; certain legally binding documents (European Convention on Human Rights, European Social Charter, American Convention on Human Rights, International Covenant on Economic, Social and Cultural Rights) and certain soft law systems (European Union Open Method of Co-Ordination). There is no chapter that compares the different jurisdictions, so the readers can draw their own conclusions. What emerges, though, is that the right to work has a legal effect both when it is explicitly mentioned in a legal document, and when not explicitly mentioned, through interpretation of other human rights.

The range of theoretical analyses is also broad, reaching from ancient Greek philosophy (Wiggins, Penner); to liberal political theory (Albin, Bogg, Nickel,

[11] On the Marxist approach towards legal rights, see H Collins, *Marxism and Law* (Oxford, Oxford University Press, 1982) 142 ff.

Paz-Fuchs, Penner, Stone); Marx (Collins, Mantouvalou); critical theory (Albin, Rittich); deliberative democratic theory (Mundlak); labour and industrial relations theory (Arita, Stone). What is common in all the analyses, both those that explicitly rely on philosophical texts and those that do not do so, is that they are normative throughout. The authors develop normative concerns that are, in most contributions, used to assess the position of the law.

III The Value of Work – The Right to Work

The value of work cannot be underestimated, and David Wiggins explores the ethical meaning of work in chapter one, 'Work, its Moral Meaning or Import'. He begins from Aristotle's account of the conceptual connection between human happiness, virtue and ergon. Encouraged by the etymology and semantic affinities of the Greek word traditionally translated as 'function', he makes the case for understanding ergon as 'work', and aligns the Aristotelian position that results with the thoughts about work that he finds in some subsequent philosophers. Yet he leaves open the question whether there is a *right* to work.

A right exists when an aspect of the individual's circumstances is such that it imposes duties on others. A possible justification for the right to work is explored in the contribution of Hugh Collins. Having addressed the challenges faced by the proponents of the right to work – challenges such as imprecision and impracticability of the right and the duties that it imposes – he turns to the value of self-realisation, examines the meaning of it and explores what aspects of the right to work it supports (chapter two). Following this, my analysis rests on the belief that if the right to work is to be a valuable addition to a list of human rights, it must be viewed as a right to non-exploitative work. I take the example of the right to work of undocumented migrants, and develop a conception of exploitation that captures their situation, to explore whether human rights law tolerates their treatment (chapter three). An alternative justification of the right to work, based on equality and dignity, is offered by Einat Albin who investigates the right to work in the United Nations Convention on the Rights of Persons with Disabilities. She explores the question whether the approach of this Convention to the right to work should also be adopted in other human rights documents, and grounds her analysis on critical disability studies and the theory of human capabilities (chapter four). James Penner looks at how valuable social activity, including work, is remunerated. He draws on Arendt's distinction between labour, work and action, which he considers against the background of Western societies, and suggests that the way that we think about remuneration reflects on the way that we think about work itself (chapter five).

The right to work is protected in international human rights documents, such as the ICESCR, and the European Social Charter (ESC) of the Council of Europe. By way of an example, Article 6(1) ICESCR provides:

> The States Parties to the present Covenant recognize the right to work, which includes the right of everyone to the opportunity to gain his living by work which he freely chooses or accepts, and will take appropriate steps to safeguard this right.

The monitoring bodies of the ICESCR and the ESC, namely the Committee of Economic, Social and Cultural Rights and the European Committee of Social Rights respectively, have their own, detailed jurisprudence, which sheds light on components of the right to work. Colm O'Cinneide presents and critically analyses these rulings in his contribution, including General Comment No 18 on 'The Right to Work' of the Committee on Economic, Social and Cultural Rights. He emphasises that these materials are 'highly authoritative' and play a role also in the interpretation of other documents, such as the European Convention on Human Rights (chapter six).

Many of the authors in this volume admit that different components of the right to work may be in tension with each other, an issue that is not always sufficiently acknowledged. Tensions and conflicts between rights or components of the same right are not unique in the right to work. In the context of the right to work, the matter is of fundamental importance because it highlights, among other issues, conflicts that may arise *between* workers or between the workforce and the unemployed. This is particularly discussed in the piece by Mark Freedland and Nicola Kountouris, who explore the right to work at the level of the European Union. They stress that international human rights law does not always appreciate conflicts between the right to work and rights to decent working conditions. The tensions that they analyse are particularly complex and acute, because they sometimes involve cross-border situations of the kind that we find at EU level. The authors urge us to think carefully about the application of aspects of the right beyond its declaratory framings, in the 'real world' (chapter seven).

Revisiting the right to work almost 40 years after he published his seminal essay, James Nickel diagnoses and explains that the right to work viewed as a right to access employment, has failed. He expresses scepticism both about the theoretical justification of the right and its legal protection in the ICESCR, and considers the question whether, as an alternative, we should view 'work' as a goal, rather than a legal right. Yet Nickel explains that his analysis of the right to work should not be taken as a rejection of the whole category of social rights (chapter eight). Further sceptical reflections are offered by Alan Bogg who does not question the nature of the right to work as a moral and legal right. He analyses duties of governments to promote decent work, which are not grounded on the right to work, but on the general duties of governments to promote human well-being. Bogg raises concerns about the effect of the legal right to work on workers' solidarity and distributive justice. Yet his main scepticism revolves around the role of the judiciary, particularly given common law approaches to the right to work in the United Kingdom that have, on his analysis, failed to address the complexities that arise (chapter nine).

Rights are correlative to duties. Human rights law, which traditionally imposed obligations on states, has over the years developed so as to impose direct or indirect obligations on private individuals too.[12] All chapters in the volume that examine the right to work reflect on the duties that governments, employers, trade unions and others may have. Yet there is another way in which the right to work brings about questions of duties, and this has to do with welfare-to-work programmes. In modern societies, welfare support is sometimes made conditional on a duty to accept suitable work. As Amir Paz-Fuchs explains, the right to work becomes a duty to work in this way. The unemployed have a duty to work in order to be entitled to welfare support. Is this justified on the basis of human rights theory? In addressing this question, Paz-Fuchs explores the theoretical conflation of rights and duties. He then turns to justifications of the right to work (citizenship and individual well-being), and finds that these do not necessarily ground a legal duty to work (chapter ten). The duty to work is also touched upon in several other chapters of the book on national law and on theory.

Some national legal orders protect the right to work explicitly in their constitutions (France and Japan, for instance). The interpretation of the right to work by French courts is developed by Sophie Robin-Olivier, who notes that the constitutional right to work is frequently invoked in French courts, and has an effect on judicial decision-making. Her analysis of French law presents the impact of the constitutional provision, the delicate balance of powers (between the judiciary and legislature in particular) and the conflicts of the right with the right to free enterprise. It examines both the challenges and limitations of the provision (chapter eleven). The Constitution of Japan also contains explicit recognition of the right to work. Against this background, there has been considerable academic debate on the meaning of the constitutional provision, which we find in the chapter by Kenji Arita. Arita first presents and analyses right to work theories in Japan, before comparing these approaches with theories on the right to work in other national and international legal orders (chapter twelve).

The United Kingdom, with a common law tradition and no written constitution or Bill of Rights, does not contain explicit protection of the human right to work. In the chapter on the United Kingdom, Hugh Collins revisits the questions asked by Bob Hepple in 1981 and traces elements of the right to work in both transnational sources of labour law that are binding on the United Kingdom (the European Convention on Human Rights that has been incorporated in national law through the UK Human Rights Act, the EU Charter of Fundamental Rights and other areas of EU law), and goes on to examine several areas of national law, such as hiring decisions and termination of employment, to assess whether they are compatible with the right to work (chapter thirteen).

If a right to work were explicitly included in the European Convention on Human Rights, the European Court of Human Rights might rule that a right to reinstatement in cases of unfair dismissal would be an essential component of it, for it would provide an effective remedy for the person whose right has been violated. The remedy of reinstatement would make the right to work 'practical and

[12] I use the terms 'duties' and 'obligations' interchangeably.

effective'. In his 1981 essay, Bob Hepple argued that the right to work must encompass a right to be reinstated in cases of unfair dismissal. Joanna Howe builds on this aspect of Hepple's analysis, and assesses the protection of the right to work in Australia and in the United Kingdom, in light of how often employees return to their jobs. She finds that the remedy is very rarely used nowadays, explores the reasons why this is happening and compares the current situation with the past, before suggesting ways to improve the use of this remedy in the future (chapter fourteen).

The US approach to the right to work is, famously, the opposite from other jurisdictions. Right-to-work laws are used there to outlaw 'closed shop' arrangements, namely agreements between an employer and one or more unions, according to which an individual needs to become a member of a particular union or unions, in order to obtain or retain his or her job. Yet the contribution from the United States by Katherine Stone leaves aside this 'misleadingly termed' right to work, and takes a different line of enquiry, exploring visions of the right to work in US industrial relations theory and policymaking. Building on these insights, Stone develops a normative proposal for the right to work today, as a right to livelihood security, which should encompass a right to be supported during transitions (chapter fifteen).

The final two chapters examine the right to work against the background of globalisation, on the one hand, and economic crises, on the other. Having presented established territory on the right to work and its interpretation, Guy Mundlak explores the extent to which process-based, deliberative, approaches to constitutional review are appropriate in dealing with it at national level. Turning to the globalised legal order and the challenges that it sets to the right to work – challenges such as the distribution of jobs – he suggests that cosmopolitan approaches are needed, and process-based solutions are the way forward in order to maintain the right to work on the political agenda in the context of globalisation (chapter sixteen). Kerry Rittich, finally, views the right to work as the end product of changing processes and circumstances. She places it in the post-war social contract to assess how it has been shaped, explores the effects on it of ideologies and policies of labour market flexibility, as well as the recent financial crises and examines the challenges ahead. In doing so she stresses that the right to work cannot do all the work that progressive scholars may expect it to do, when confronted with today's context of international economic and financial institutions, and emphasises that consideration of the links between the law, the power of the market and the dynamics of the labour market is also essential (chapter seventeen).

This volume does not exhaust the potential for an analysis of the right to work, nor does it conclude the debates around it. At the same time, the analysis of the right to work or rights at work does not exhaust the domain of labour law, just as human rights and the duties that they impose do not exhaust the domain of morality.[13] An inflation of rights can harm the ideals to which their supporters are

[13] J Raz, *The Morality of Freedom* (Oxford, Oxford University Press, 1986) 194 ff.

committed.[14] Yet human rights, including the right to work, incorporate moral and legal claims of high priority, and the purpose of this book is to highlight areas of importance and themes that need to be further explored. There is no doubt, for instance, that there are legal orders that are not discussed here, which can offer further insights on the interpretation of the right and the institutions that are appropriate for its monitoring. Further theoretical analysis of the justification and content of the right is also needed. Specific areas, like domestic work or the right to work of asylum seekers, are particularly challenging. The tensions between components of the right need to be further carefully analysed. This book seeks to underline areas of importance and suggest further avenues for research.

[14] O O'Neill, 'The Dark Side of Human Rights' (2005) 81 *International Affairs* 427.

1

Work, its Moral Meaning or Import

DAVID WIGGINS

Before lawyers, political scientists and other experts settle down to the questions awaiting them of rights and the putative right to work, I am to say something about work itself – its moral meaning or import. Such is the behest of the editor. But, proceeding by indirection, I shall reach that destination by a detour.

Long before the Universal Declaration of Human Rights (1948) asserted a right to work and a right to just and favourable remuneration for work, the Virginia Declaration of Rights (1776) and the American Declaration of Independence (1776) each asserted a human right to the pursuit of happiness. 'All men are created equal, they are endowed by their Creator with unalienable rights . . . among these are life, liberty and the pursuit of happiness'. No one is uninterested in happiness, or the right to pursue it, but how does the pursuit of happiness connect with work? Well, if you look hard enough, you will find one part of an answer to that question in Aristotle. Or so I shall claim.

Aristotle says that happiness is activity of the soul in accordance with virtue in a complete life. In order to understand this properly we must gloss *virtue.* To judge from book I, chapter VII and book II, chapter VI of the *Nicomachean Ethics,* Aristotle thinks that the *arete* or virtue of a human being is the disposition by whose exercise that being carries out the *ergon* that is proper to man and engages in activities and acts of the soul that arise from reason:

> We state the ergon of man to be a certain kind of life and this to be activity or actions of the soul applying a rational principle . . . the ergon of man is the good and noble performance of such activity or actions.[1]

So the next thing we need to know is what *ergon* is.

Traditionally, *ergon* is translated as *function.* But can we really say that man has a function? In this connection, Aristotle suggests that man is to his *ergon* as a flute player is to flute-playing, a builder to building, an eye to seeing, a hand to the things that we do with a hand, a foot to walking or running. Our difficulty here, however, is that, as explained in terms of function, none of these analogies is very illuminating or even plausible. It is not as if Aristotle is party to the thought that

[1] Aristotle, *Nicomachean Ethics* 1098–a14.

man is to be compared to a cog or spindle in a machine, or compared to a limb or an organ that serves some larger creature or organism. Aristotle is no more party to such thoughts than we are. Nor, moreover, is it easy to model virtue in a human being on the functional or technical or executant goodness of a craftsman or musician. That was the other idea Aristotle had. But, you can't be a builder without possessing some training, skill or aptitude; and it is hard to conceive of a builder or musician in the complete absence of the framework that creates such roles, crafts or métiers. You can, however, be a human being or *anthropos* without having any special skill or aptitude at all. Nor is any particular framework presupposed to simple human beinghood.

Before we throw up our hands or simply let go of Aristotle's conception of the pursuit of happiness, let us make an experiment. In the spirit of Richard Bentley who was prompted when studying the Homeric hexameter, its prosody and metre, to supply the letter digamma, a disused letter of the archaic Greek alphabet, to certain words at certain places in Homer's text, let us restore digamma, as Bentley did, to the word *ergon*. At once we catch sight of an Indo-European root. As it figures in *Nicomachean Ethics* book I, chapter VII, isn't *ergon* what in English we call *work* and the Germans *Werk*? A human being pursues the human good that is happiness, Aristotle will now appear to suggest, by doing the *work* (as we may now say) that is proper to a human person. Loosening the tie to Aristotle, one might say we pursue happiness by doing well the work that is proper to the particular person we are, given our abilities, our reasonable predilections, our situation and our commitments. It is by doing this well that we pursue true happiness. It is in doing that sort of work that a man or woman has a life worth living.

Or so one might aver. But at this point in the argument it becomes necessary to allow for the evident fact that our everyday conception of work – the calling, occupation or employment by which one earns one's living etc – embraces less than the whole of *ergon* as Aristotle understands *ergon*.[2] What a shame it would be though, given the huge portion of life that is consumed in labour, to see their imperfect fit as amounting to the total separateness of workaday labour and the human happiness that Aristotle seeks to understand by reference to the *ergon* that is proper to any creature with the *phusis* of *anthropos*.

What is to be expected of human activities or action that come with (*meta*, as Aristotle says) a rational principle? Well, *in extenso*, we may get the hang of what this means by reading Aristotle's account of human life in its involvement with vice or virtue, with base or noble, injurious or useful and painful or pleasant. Acts or activities that apply what he calls a rational principle aim at something worthwhile by drawing upon faculties and dispositions whose exercise gives pleasure (a distinctive, associated pleasure) to the doer and enlarges also – here I reach beyond Aristotle – the doer's understanding of the realities we inhabit. That is to say that the exercise of these faculties or dispositions affords both practical under-

[2] Nor (one should one remark) do the virtues as Aristotle conceives them correspond exactly either in extension or in conception to those recognized in moral philosophy as we now have it.

standing of those realities and the satisfactions that we attain by learning to wrestle or struggle with them.

On these terms – with or without their culmination in Hegel's further claim that it is only by man's own work that man can leave his image upon the world or attain to full consciousness of himself as a free agent – engagement with the human *ergon*, taken as I am suggesting we take this, must appear as important to a person as anything can be to him or her. In one way or another, it will embody or embrace or organize most of everything (but not of course everything) that *means anything* for him or her.[3] Not least it will shape our understanding of life, leisure and repose, and mould our aspirations for the calling or occupation by which we shall subsist and get the necessities of life itself.

It is most of this and more that one hears when, at the moment of his final defeat, Shylock cries out to Portia, Antonia and the Duke of Venice:

> Nay take my life and all, pardon not that.
> You take my house when you do take the prop
> That doth sustain my house: you take my life
> When you do take the means whereby I live.

If there is a right to work it is not a right like any old other right. It is a right to something momentous.

One who agrees to speak about the ethical meaning of work might be expected to say something about its religious significance. Given limitations of time and competence, let me simply offer two remarkable utterances from the closing chapter of Simone Weil, *The Need for Roots*:

> Death and labour are things of necessity and not of choice. The world only gives itself to Man in the form of food and warmth if Man gives himself to the world in the form of labour. But death and labour can be submitted to either in an attitude of revolt or else one of consent. They can be submitted to either in their naked truth or wrapped in lies . . .
>
> Man placed himself outside the current of Obedience. God chose as his punishment labour and death. Consequently labour and death, if Man undergoes them in a spirit of willingness, constitute a transference back into the current of Supreme Good which is Obedience to God.

If you prefer this over the quasi-Aristotelian account I have offered of the meaning of work – if you prefer to meditate here upon the person who undergoes labour and death in a spirit of acceptance – well, you arrive by another route at something not altogether alien to the conclusion that we reached before. On both accounts, the power and the possibility to do proper work is something that is central to the life and being of a human person. To have no work to do – to find nothing one can do that makes any difference to anyone or anything – is among

[3] For a variant upon this, see Joseph Conrad, *Heart of Darkness*, ch 1 (two pages from the end of the chapter): 'I don't like work – no man does – but I like what is in the work, – the chance to find yourself. Your own reality, – for yourself, – not for others – what no man can ever know. They can only see the mere show, never tell what it really means'.

the very worst things that can befall someone, even if he or she can escape starvation. There is, however, at least one notable difference between the Aristotelian and the Weilian outlooks. One who acts in the spirit that Weil enjoins upon us has to accept whatever labour presents itself and be ready to adjust his or her expectations and putative satisfactions to the way things have to be. They must deploy their talents as best they can wherever it falls to them to labour. For others that may be more difficult. What these others may look for (in something of the spirit still of Aristotle, see *Rhetoric* 1367–a32) is work or occupation which, however hard it presses upon them, is not felt as an external constraint or alien compulsion upon them. In the world as it is they will often lament the shortfall between the work they find to do and the ideal we have described, according to which work at once reveals reality and places demands upon their best powers and faculties. Something important will disappear from the world when human beings no longer even lament this shortfall but simply acquiesce in it.

Anticipating now the deliberations that will preoccupy this book, I cannot pass over the question (framed in terms of the everyday conception) *what if there is no work*? You will decide, I am sure, whether, even then, you want to say that there can be a right to work. Deferring to the experts on that matter, the thing that I am eager to say concerns not so much the right as the *special strength* of the demand (however that is to be described) that there be some possibility, some opening, some opportunity or other, for each and every one of us to engage and engage cheerfully in labour that makes some – however slight – difference to something that we can care about and by which we can also sustain our own being and that of those who depend on us.

Suppose now that the government of a given country constantly encourages Taylorist research into ways of dispensing so far as humanly possible with human labour and assiduously promotes automation, robotics, IT and all other means there are to uttermost productivity. Suppose that this government is so obsessed also with the economic theory of comparative advantage – and so taken up with the increase of GDP that is promised by unrestricted free trade and the struggle for the survival of the (globally) fittest – that it applies free trade policies not only without regard to humane animal husbandry, the long-term fertility of the soil or the long-term resilience of the country they govern, not only without regard to the effects of such a policy on the life and livelihoods of countless previously more or less contented citizens, but also without regard to the distributional effects of its policies. A government of this sort inflicts a mortal injury. Even if the losers *could* be compensated for the harms they suffer, we know by now (2012) that even in material terms they never will be. Indeed in many cases there is difficulty in the very idea of compensation. For everything that I have tried to spell out quasi-analytically is known to almost every human being on the level of feeling and of *amour-propre*; and in *amour-propre* (as Rousseau so clearly perceived) lies one other ineradicable need. Such is the power and significance of the idea of a human being seeking out a place and an occupation where what they are and want to be is part and parcel with what they do. On what terms could a rational person possibly want to accept something quite else in exchange or compensation for *that*?

A government of the sort I have described disregards the most important kind of duty a government can have – a momentous negative duty *not* to ignore the risk of doing what I am representing as a fundamental harm to its citizens. The strength of this condemnation does not depend on whether we want to say that the human need to work can amount to a *right* to work. Let us bear always in mind the awful possibility that not every morally momentous demand can be harmlessly or plausibly transposed, or transposed without loss, into the language of rights.

2

Is There a Human Right to Work?

HUGH COLLINS

Introduction

Mohamed Bouazazi set himself on fire in Sidi Bouzid, Tunisia on 17 December 2010. His self-immolation turned out to be the tipping point for the 'Arab Spring', a political earthquake that toppled governments in North Africa and that reverberates throughout the Middle East to this day. Mohamed was 26 years old, trying frantically to support his extended family. Like a high proportion of his contemporaries, he was unemployed with no realistic prospects of ever securing a job in a country with persistently high levels of unemployment. To scrape a living, he purchased fruit and vegetables on credit and sold them from a rented wheelbarrow on street corners. Local officials demanded money from him, ostensibly for a licence for street vendors, though since no such licence was officially required, this demand was plainly extortion. Unable and unwilling to pay the bribe, Mohamed's scales were confiscated by a local official. Heavily in debt with no means to feed his family, in despair at official intransigence, Mohamed set himself on fire outside the local town hall when crying out his last reported words: 'How do you expect me to make a living?'[1]

His fraught cry demands a right to work. It demands a way to make a living to feed oneself and one's dependants. The cry is addressed to a government, which is held responsible for high levels of unemployment and for obstructing an individual's efforts to earn a living through the market. The right is concerned with economic deprivation, but it is also directed against degradation. The denial of the right humiliates a person and undermines a sense of self-worth and dignity, so much so that, for Mohamed, life was no longer worth living. The right to work therefore addresses simultaneously basic human necessities for survival, such as food and shelter, and values that are frequently associated with the foundations of human rights such as human dignity, freedom and self-esteem.

[1] Mohamed Bouazazi died some weeks later in hospital. Ten days later the President fled the country. Bouazazi was posthumously awarded the Sakharov Prize, and the new government in Tunisia chose him as 'the person of the year'. The events are fully reported on CBS News, *60 Minutes* (20 February 2011), available at: www.cbsnews.com/stories/2011/02/20/60minutes/main20033404.shtml.

Despite this pivotal role of the right to work at the intersection of social and economic rights and of civil liberties, it is rarely examined or included in philosophical investigations of the foundations of rights. In discussions of social and economic rights, though satisfaction of basic necessities such as food, clothing and shelter are regarded as fundamental rights of every person, the manner by which these goods can be obtained is rarely considered. Yet in most countries, for most of the population, the income to purchase these necessities derives from work, either through employment or self-employment. For these people, securing the right to work is a necessary precondition for securing the necessities of life. Similarly, in discussions of civil and political liberties, though respect for human dignity and liberty are generally regarded as essential conditions of justice, little attention is paid to the importance of work as a means for securing those values. If a person has to beg or live on handouts from others, he or she is unlikely to be treated with respect, to have a sense of self-esteem, or to experience the value of autonomy. Although 'sturdy beggars' and 'benefits cheats' may suggest counter-examples to the value of possessing a job, in my opinion most people would not trade paid work for a life hustling on the streets or for petty criminality. Work can be hard, unpleasant and unrewarding, of course, but most prefer employment for a wage to the restricted alternatives that are available to everyone except the extremely wealthy, both because jobs satisfy basic needs and at the same time give individuals a basis for self-respect, respect from others and the possibility of autonomous choices in life.

If work is so central to most of the valuable features of life that are protected through appeals to human rights, why does the right to work scarcely receive any attention in discussions of human rights? Five reasons can be advanced for justifiable hesitation before embracing a right to work as a fundamental human right. The right to work can be criticised as being imprecise, impracticable, inconsistent, instrumental and incoherent. Criticisms of this kind may be voiced against any proposed human right and indeed the very idea of human rights. But the right to work attracts particularly vehement challenges, even from those who may in general be sympathetic to claims for human rights.

1. *Imprecise meaning.* There is certainly a damaging lack of consensus about the meaning of the right.[2] In particular, disagreement arises over the question whether the right to work possesses both negative and positive dimensions. The negative aspect concerns the duty on a government not to interfere unjustifiably with a person's opportunities to obtain work, as in the example of the extortion by local officials in the case of Mohamed. The positive aspect concerns the right to have a job rather than being unemployed or being supported by welfare benefits or charity. Does the right to work include both the negative and positive aspects? Furthermore, to add to the lack of consensus regarding the content of the right, it

[2] The importance of consensus to construction and validity of human rights is recognised in J Gardner, '"Simply in Virtue of Being Human": The Whos and Whys of Human Rights' (2008) 2 *Journal of Ethics & Social Philosophy* 1, 9; J Raz, 'On the Nature of Rights' (1984) 93 *Mind* 194, 208–09.

is often suggested that there are other dimensions to the right, such as the right to decent work or just conditions of employment. Are all these dimensions integral parts of the right to work or does the special moral claim of the human right apply only to some aspects? The force of the right often seems seriously compromised by disagreement about its core ingredients.

2. *Impracticable.* If the right to work includes a positive aspect that imposes on governments and perhaps others a duty to find a job for everyone who wants one, the question arises whether in a market society this right can be regarded as a feasible proposition. To create jobs for everyone who wants one is almost certainly beyond the financial and technical capacity of any government in the long term. If the positive claim for a job is therefore merely an aspiration for full employment, which can never be achieved completely, does it make sense to rank it as a human right rather than a widely supported social and economic policy? This doubt about the feasibility of the right to work leads either to proposals to confine its content narrowly to its negative dimension, or to the rejection of the existence of the right altogether.

3. *Inconsistency.* Another off-putting feature of the right to work is that it appears to be a mixture of two kinds of rights. It contains in its negative aspect a civil liberty that protects individuals against unjust exclusions from the labour market by the law or discriminatory employers. By emphasising also the importance of full employment for all who wish to work, it also presents the features of being a social and economic right. Since these two species of rights are commonly regarded as being different in kind, if nevertheless linked in important ways, and are frequently protected through different international conventions with diverse enforcement mechanisms, the question arises whether a hybrid right like the right to work can exist in any consistent and comprehensible form. In particular, the two kinds of rights are often presented as differing in their strength: negative rights issue a prohibition from which only powerful reasons can provide justifiable exceptions; positive rights typically are framed as goals that need only be met to the extent that available resources permit. Can these two kinds of rights be united into a single composite right and, if so, what is its force?

4. *Instrumental.* Another reason why the right to work may not have been regarded as significant or worth deeper investigation by philosophers and advocates of human rights is that it can be dismissed as at most an instrumental right. An instrumental right is (as defined here) one that has to be enjoyed in order to achieve a more fundamental right. The right to work can also be described as derivative in the sense that, given the existence of other important human rights such as liberty and subsistence, the right to work can be derived from those rights in a particular social context. For instance, if it is correct that having a job usually gives a worker dignity, self-esteem and respect from others as well as the means of subsistence and a degree of autonomy, the right to work can be regarded as a practical implication of those fundamental rights without it being a human right

itself. Those fundamental rights such as dignity, liberty, or subsistence can be regarded as ends in themselves and are therefore treated as the sort of right worthy of the name of being a human right. Philosophical justifications for human rights therefore typically search for fundamental ends that are upheld by human rights. Instrumental rights are acknowledged to be useful for achieving those fundamental ends, but not essential, because there may be alternative routes to achieve the enjoyment of human rights. From that instrumental point of view, the right to work can be important as a contribution to liberty, dignity and the enjoyment of social and economic rights, but since other routes are possible, such as possessing considerable wealth, the right to work is not essential, and therefore does not have to be a universal human right. Is the right to work an instrumental right of this kind, one that is useful but not essential to an adequate theory of human rights?

5. *Incoherent value of the right.* Human rights are usually regarded as protecting interests that all humans value. Does work qualify as such an interest? In particular, is there such a vital human interest in boring, monotonous, dangerous jobs that are badly paid? Similarly, does the right to work apply to jobs that many regard as demeaning, such as prostitution? Few people are lucky enough to have a job that they really enjoy doing all the time, and even the most satisfying jobs will present moments of frustration and disappointment. If they could still make ends meet, many people would rather trade less work for more leisure time, though it seems that, even with an unexpected windfall of great wealth, few would give up working altogether.[3] In short, is work a necessary evil rather than an interest that all human beings value?[4] This last question forms the core of the discussion below, for unless convincing reasons can be supplied for valuing the right to work in itself, rather than valuing its instrumental benefits such as subsistence, it is dubious that the right deserves to be regarded as a human right. Before considering that core issue of the intrinsic value of the right to work, however, the previous four issues need to be addressed.

I Imprecise Meaning – A Composite Conception of the Right to Work

First, we require a serviceable conception of the right to work. The Universal Declaration of Human Rights (1948) declares in Article 23(1): 'Everyone has the right to work, to free choice of employment, to just and favourable conditions of work and to protection against unemployment'. This formulation apparently dis-

[3] S Sayers, 'The Need to Work: A Perspective from Philosophy' in RE Pahl (ed), *On Work: Historical, Comparative and Theoretical Approaches* (Oxford, Blackwell, 1988) 722, 724, quoting from, inter alia, Department of Health, Education and Welfare Report, *Work in America* (Cambridge, MA, 1973) 9.

[4] B Russell, *In Praise of Idleness and Other Essays* (Abingdon, Routledge, 1935).

tinguishes four related rights, though an alternative possible reading regards the right to work as the summary declaration, which is then fleshed out in three dimensions: (a) free choice of employment; (b) decent work; and (c) protection from unemployment. Other international declarations of human rights, such as the European Social Charter,[5] separate these rights, though they include similar protections. We will consider the meaning of those three elements before returning to the initial declaration of the right to work itself and how, if at all, these various elements fit together.

(a) Certainly the right to work is often interpreted as including (and perhaps being synonymous with)[6] the right to free choice of employment or occupation.[7] This latter liberty-right consists at least of the freedom of each individual to pursue an occupation of his or her choice without unjustified restrictions or discrimination. This must be a key right for liberal political theories that regard equal opportunities as a central principle of justice. As part of a strong principle of fair equality of opportunities to achieve the benefits of a society, free choice of employment can only be limited by compelling reasons, such as the requirement that, in order to pursue the career of being a surgeon, appropriate qualifications should have been obtained. This aspect of the right may also include the right not to be enslaved or to be coerced into working for another, though this right is recognised independently in Article 4 of the Declaration and the very notion of employment implies the voluntary consent of the worker. Of course, economic necessity usually forces most people to look for a job, but this structural compulsion is not the same kind of interference with liberty as a deliberate enslavement as a result of human agency.[8] The correlative of this right to free choice of occupation is the inability of governments and private actors to place unjustified restrictions on this freedom.

The importance of this negative aspect of the right to work helps to explain why the value of work is elevated to the status of a fundamental right. Theories of constitutional rights often explain the selection of rights for independent judicial protection as directed towards a concern that the interest at stake is subject to a special threat from majority behaviour or the government itself. Of course, in general, no one objects to a person working for a living. The problem arises rather from discriminatory preferences imposed by employers or from formal restrictions imposed by governments such as those placed on refugees and migrants who are denied permission to work. The civil rights movement in the United States commenced with the demand of the black minority community for a right

[5] Council of Europe, Revised European Social Charter 1996. Part II, Arts 1–4.

[6] eg, the International Covenant on Civil and Political Rights, Art 8, para 3(a) does not protect the right to work directly but does protect against forced or compulsory labour. The position is the same in the European Convention on Human Rights, Art 4.

[7] International Covenant on Economic, Social and Cultural Rights, Art 6(1), 'the right to work, which includes the right of everyone to the opportunity to gain his living by work which he freely chooses or accepts'.

[8] GA Cohen, *History, Labour, and Freedom* (Oxford, Oxford University Press, 1988) ch 12.

to work without discrimination in the kinds of jobs they could obtain,[9] and subsequently anti-discrimination laws have prioritised unrestricted entry into the labour market for women and other disadvantaged groups. Discriminatory exclusion from the labour market or particular careers was correctly perceived as a special threat to minorities.

However, democratic majorities and autocracies may pose special threats to all kinds of interests of minority groups, including for instance dress codes, lifestyle choices, sexual preferences, cultural artefacts and language. In order to keep a parsimonious list of fundamental rights, it is necessary to identify the key interests of persecuted minorities. To address this problem, in *The Morality of Freedom*, Joseph Raz, for instance, adds to the requirement of a special threat to individual interests the idea that the right concerns an important aspect of the public culture.[10] In accordance with that approach, it could be suggested that work is regarded as an important aspect of the public culture, so much so indeed that it is frequently asserted that there is a moral duty, as well as a right, to work.[11] Given this importance attached to work and the real risk of unjustifiable discrimination and unfair restrictions on employment, the negative aspect of the right to work becomes an essential ingredient of a constitutional order that embraces the protection of fundamental rights.

(b) The right to just and favourable conditions of work, though vague in detail, offers a clear conception that the terms of employment should be just and beneficial to the worker. This right may also qualify or elucidate the right to work itself by insisting that, as the International Labour Organization puts it, it is a right to 'decent work' rather than crude exploitation. Nevertheless, the determination of these minimum conditions is perplexing. For instance, one frequently suggested minimum condition is that the work should be paid. Indeed, the concept of employment under the common law requires remuneration or at least the prom-

[9] J Shim, 'Equality or the Right to Work? Explaining and Justifying Employment Discrimination Law' (PhD, London School of Economics, 2008) ch 6, which examines the history of measures, such as HR 7142, 'A Bill To Prohibit Discrimination In Employment Because Of Race, Color, Creed, Religion, National Origin, Or Citizenship' (20 July 1942, referred to the House Committee of the Judiciary) placed before the US House of Congress prior to the Civil Rights Act 1964, in which the right to work rather than the idea of equality was presented as the justification for the legislation. The principle of the right to work was also invoked as the justification to combat discrimination by trade unions: CW Summers, 'The Right to Join a Union' (1947) 47 *Columbia Law Review* 33, 73. 'The right to work is uniformly recognized as essential, for it involves not only the right to live but the right to follow one's chosen occupation. The right to work includes also the right to work on equal terms free from unreasonable discriminations. But beyond the right to work on equal terms is the element almost uniformly ignored – the right to participate in making decisions'. *cf* K Stone in this volume, ch 15.

[10] J Raz, *The Morality of Freedom* (Oxford, Oxford University Press, 1986) ch 10.

[11] The duty to work is compatible with a right to work, because the duty is framed as a condition for the receipt of a different social right, the right to welfare payments in cases of need. The duty to work therefore does not conflict with a right to leisure, provided the individual does not also seek to claim welfare benefits. Although this conditionality can be criticised as coercive in some respects in its current form of welfare-to-work programmes, it has always been part of social security schemes in order to discourage free-riders: J Fulbrook, 'New Labour's Welfare Reforms: Anything New?' (2001) 64 *Modern Law Review* 243. *cf* A Paz-Fuchs in this volume, ch 10.

ise of payment. And without remuneration, we rightly suspect the presence of forced labour or slavery. As we shall see below, however, even this minimum condition of payment proves troublesome for a precise conception of the right to work when it is applied to unpaid domestic work in the family household or to voluntary work for a charity.[12]

A greater obstacle to a clear conception of the right to work is presented by the question whether the standard of just and favourable conditions requires the job to be meaningful at least to some extent. If a job is reasonably safe, does not involve excessive hours and the rate of pay provides a living wage, are these conditions 'just and favourable' where the job itself is pointless, frustrating and alienating? Does a liberal theory of justice require jobs not only to be freely chosen and materially rewarding, but also psychologically fulfilling or meaningful? A liberal theory of personal autonomy requires a person to have the capacity to choose a meaningful life plan, but that does not necessarily require such meaning to be achieved through work as opposed to other activities such as raising a family, play and leisure activities.[13] Yet, where work occupies a large proportion of our waking hours, for that time to be spent on a completely pointless activity or perhaps even worse in complete idleness seems at least to undermine the capacity to choose a meaningful life plan.[14]

(c) The further right to protection against unemployment contained in Article 23(1) is both vague and conceptually unclear. It could mean that everyone should be given a job, no matter how pointless and exploitative the work may be, or it could mean that all that is required from a government is an adequate social security system for the jobless. But the latter meaning of the right to subsistence payments from the government in cases of necessity is surely not derived from the right to work. It is a failure to uphold the right to work that necessitates a further right to social support. This right to welfare benefits constitutes an independent social right concerned with subsistence or poverty, which is protected separately under Articles 22 and 23(3) of the Declaration of Human Rights. The right to protection against unemployment, as associated with the right to work, therefore suggests that it is having a job that matters, not welfare benefits.

As well as indicating that governments should try to avoid any unemployment, the phrase 'protection against unemployment' could, if applied to decisions made by employers, have a very different meaning. In this context, 'protection against unemployment' could require restrictions on the employer's right to terminate the contract at will or at least require compensation to be paid to the dismissed worker to protect against the economic consequences of unemployment. Another possible interpretation of the phrase 'protection against unemployment' might

[12] G Mundlak, 'The Right to Work – The Value of Work' in D Barak-Erez and A Gross (eds), *Exploring Social Rights: Between Theory and Practice* (Oxford, Hart Publishing, 2007) 341, 352.

[13] W Kymlicka, *Contemporary Political Philosophy: An Introduction*, 2nd edn (Oxford, Oxford University Press, 2001) 190.

[14] B Roessler, 'Meaningful Work: Arguments from Autonomy' (2012) 20 *Journal of Political Philosophy* 71.

include positive action in favour of those who face particular obstacles in obtaining employment, such as people with disabilities.[15]

That leaves the initial declaration of the right to work itself, which may simply summarise the other three rights or it may constitute an additional right. If it is an independent right, what does it add to the other three elements listed in Article 23(1)? If it adds anything at all, it stresses the positive aspect of the right. Its focus is on granting an individual an actual job or some kind of productive activity that qualifies as work. It makes clear that the right is not confined to the negative aspect that protects individuals against unjustifiable discrimination and barriers in the labour market, and nor can it be satisfied by social security unemployment benefits. What matters in the right to work is having a job.

It is not necessary to decide whether the right to work is a composite of the four elements prescribed in Article 23(1) or a group of four severable rights. But a strong case can be made for an integrated approach, with the positive aspect of the right to work at its centre. The other three dimensions listed under Article 23(1) can all be regarded as aspects of other fundamental rights. Free choice of employment could be derived from a more general right to liberty combined with the value of equal respect for the dignity of individuals. Just and favourable conditions of work could be derived from a right to subsistence or a concern that the degree of exploitation in a job should not violate human dignity or degrade a person. Protection against unemployment, as we have noted, may be restricted to minimum welfare benefits and the right to subsistence. If those three elements could all be derived from other, more fundamental human rights, there would be little need to emphasise a further, independent right to work.

It is only when the positive aspect of the right to work is included that the right takes on an independent shape and focus that distinguishes it sharply from the other rights listed in the Universal Declaration of Human Rights. If the right to work exists, therefore, it should contain the positive right to a job at its centre. This composite conception of the right to work would place a positive right to a job at the core of the right, flanked on three sides by the supportive constraints of the negative protections against discrimination in the labour market, the requirement for decent work and perhaps protection against unjustifiable termination of employment. These rights are mutually supportive, but not indivisible.[16] Although these rights can be associated together in ways that complement each other, it should be acknowledged that this composite right also contains internal tensions. For instance, there is likely to be a trade-off between the positive right to a job and good labour standards, because demand for labour by employers is likely to be depressed when wages and conditions are high. It is this composite conception of the right to work that will be examined here.

[15] See E Albin in this volume, ch 4.

[16] JW Nickel, 'Rethinking Indivisibility: Towards a Theory of Supporting Relations between Human Rights' (2008) 30 *Human Rights Quarterly* 984.

II Impracticable

The composite conception of the right to work advances a strong claim that may appear impracticable. The emphasis on the positive claim-right to a job apparently demands a correlative duty placed on government (or someone else) to provide the paid work to be done. This interpretation of the right to work always provokes scepticism,[17] because it is evident that in market economies no government has the power actually to guarantee everyone a job. Governments lack the levers to manage the economy to ensure full employment, and they lack the resources in the long term to provide every unemployed person a job in the public sector. Even if governments enjoyed such powers and resources, the system of patronage that would be created by governments dispensing jobs would be extremely dangerous and unstable, because governments would be unable to make good but unpopular decisions for fear of undermining the patronage system that sustains them in power. In communist countries adhering to the Soviet model governments boasted the attainment of full employment. This result could only be achieved at the price of great inefficiency, because it granted paid jobs even when there was no work to be done. The system also discouraged capital investment since there was a surplus of cheap labour that had to be retained even if it could be replaced efficiently by mechanisation and computerisation. But does the positive aspect of the right to work really require a claim-right of all individuals to full employment?

With regard to all human rights, having established the notion of a particular human right based on a vital human interest, it is then necessary to consider the separate questions of who are the duty bearers and the precise content of those duties. For many social and economic rights, such as the right to health and education, duty bearers may include not only the government but also other actors such as employers, and the content of their respective duties may differ substantially. In the case of the right to work, the duty of governments may be limited to the progressive realisation of the positive right to a job by taking measures that support full employment, whereas for employers the duty may be confined to prohibitions against unjustified discrimination in hiring practices. Does the denial of a claim-right against the government to an actual job take the sting out of the right to work? This is the standard objection voiced against social and economic rights: because they do not have the simple structure of claim right and correlative duty, they cannot be human rights. But there are other kinds of rights, such as immunities and liberties, which can structure moral and legal reasoning. For instance, such a right can play a significant role in assessing the rationality of public policy and the proportionality of governmental measures. Similarly, a

[17] K Drzewicki, 'The Right to Work and Rights in Work' in A Eide, C Krause and A Rosas (eds), *Economic, Social and Cultural Rights*, 2nd edn (Leiden, Martinus Nijhoff, 2001); J Nickel in this volume, ch 8.

social and economic right, such as the positive right to work, plays a vital role in determining the weight and reach of civil liberties, including that negative aspect of the right to work concerning free choice of employment. The allegation of the impracticability of the right to work is no more than a variant of the standard objection made against recognising social and economic rights as human rights, and can be addressed by the standard rebuttals.[18]

III Inconsistency – Hybrid Right

The composite conception of the right to work outlined above puts together what are usually understood as two different kinds of right. The negative aspect of the right concerned with freedom from unjustifiable discrimination and barriers in employment takes the form of a traditional civil liberty. The positive right plainly shares the characteristics of a social and economic right. Does this hybrid character undermine the coherence of the right?

The right to work is not alone in having this hybrid quality. For example, the right to education can be interpreted as both forbidding unjustifiable discrimination in access to an education and imposing a positive duty on governments to provide, in the light of available resources, schools and colleges to educate its citizens.[19] Indeed, one can argue that all rights have this hybrid quality to some extent.[20] For example, the right to a fair trial clearly prohibits measures such as internment without trial or biased courts, but it also requires governments to devote resources to ensuring that citizens have access to justice and legal representatives.

The significance of the hybrid character of the right to work rather lies in the complexity of the moral or legal reasoning when assessing the content of the duties and the justifications for interference with the right. When the negative dimension of the right is at stake, as where a group of the population is excluded from a particular type of job, the moral and legal reasoning must require an extremely strong justification for using such a suspect classification. When the positive dimension of the right is contested, however, the moral and legal reasoning is likely to engage in more of a balancing exercise, weighing the interests of

[18] C Gearty and V Mantouvalou, *Debating Social Rights* (Oxford, Hart Publishing, 2010); with respect to the right to work itself: G Mundlak, 'The Right to Work: Linking Human Rights and Employment Policy' (2007) 146 *International Labour Review* 189.

[19] The European Convention on Human Rights First Protocol, Art 2, only contains a negative right not to be denied an education (see *Belgian Linguistics Case (No 2)* (1968) 1 EHRR 252 (ECtHR), but other charters such as the Universal Declaration of Human Rights, Art 26, and the International Covenant on Economic, Social and Cultural Rights, Art 13, as well as many state constitutions also contain a positive right. The negative and positive right are often linked by attaching a requirement of non-discrimination to the negative right: S Fredman, *Human Right Transformed: Positive Rights and Positive Duties* (Oxford, Oxford University Press, 2008) 215–26.

[20] S Holmes and C Sunstein, *The Cost of Rights: Why Liberty Depends on Taxes* (New York, WW Norton, 1999).

those seeking employment against the costs to others and the taxpayer. Provided this separation in the evaluation of claims for the right is maintained, the hybrid character of the right to work should present no insuperable difficulties and should not lead to incoherence.

IV Instrumental Right

Is the right to work purely instrumental? This question matters because human rights are usually regarded as ends in themselves rather than the means to other rights or goals. The right not to be subjected to cruel and unusual punishment, for instance, is regarded as having a value in itself. This right may also instrumentally protect other rights, such as the right to life, or other welfare values, but those instrumental benefits derived from observance of the right are not regarded as a significant part of its justification. Human rights are self-standing, even if they indirectly contribute to the observance of other rights and contribute to human happiness. If the right to work is a purely instrumental right, which serves to protect or implement other rights and goals, such as the rights to life or subsistence and personal well-being, it becomes less convincing to regard the right to work as a human right as opposed to a particular way of realising human rights. To borrow Raz's example of a derived right,[21] I have the right to walk on my hands if I so choose, but this is a right derived from a general right to liberty in the sense that it is grounded on that general right. The right to walk on my hands is not a human right itself, but rather a justifiable inference drawn from a human right.

This questioning of the validity of instrumental rights or applied rights can lead to intractable problems for theories of human rights, because it is probably possible to argue, though with some difficulty, that nearly all rights that have been identified as human rights can be derived in a loose sense from some fundamental abstract right, such as a right to be free or a right to dignity. Clearly a theory of human rights has to identify a list of rights that has a sufficiently concrete and distinctive application of deeper values such as liberty and dignity that they can be accepted as valuable ends in themselves without further reference to those underlying values. If this test is applied to the right to work, the question becomes whether the value of work, though perhaps grounded in deeper values such as dignity and liberty, is a sufficiently concrete and distinctive application of those values that it can be regarded as representing a valuable end or human interest in itself. To answer that question, we need to turn finally to the question of what constitutes the inherent value of the right to work.

[21] Raz, *The Morality of Freedom*, above n 10, 169.

V The Value of the Right to Work

In theories of the nature of human rights and their justification, one important strand recognises that human rights strive to protect important interests of individuals. These human interests may include individually or in combinations – depending on the theory – liberty, dignity, autonomy, respect and life (including perhaps subsistence, shelter, security, etc). The problem for this kind of theory of human rights then becomes to identify among those interests the ones that are of paramount and universal importance. Furthermore, the selected interests must have the distinctive quality that makes them suitable for inclusion as a human right, with the consequence that others, in particular governments, are subject to a correlative duty to respect and promote the right.[22] For instance, there may be a universal human interest in love or happiness, but these interests seem unsuitable for inclusion as a human right, because the content of the correlative duty to make another happy or fall in love and the identity of holder of that duty seem impossible to identify. Although attempts can be made to identify a single human interest such as dignity or freedom that provides the basis for human rights, here it will be assumed, following John Tasioulas,[23] that a pluralist account of human rights is more plausible, so that different rights may have different underlying interests that they protect. Here, the task is not to provide a complete theory of human rights, but merely to examine the values or interests that lie at the root of the composite right to work. Given the multifaceted character of the right to work, however, it seems likely that we will need to draw on a pluralist account of human rights to provide an explanation of the right to work itself.

The Committee on Economic, Social and Cultural Rights of the United Nations has suggested such a pluralist account of the right to work:

> The right to work is essential for realizing other human rights and forms an inseparable and inherent part of human dignity. Every individual has the right to be able to work, allowing him/her to live in dignity. The right to work contributes at the same time to the survival of the individual and to that of his/her family, and since work is freely chosen or accepted, to his/her development and recognition within the community.[24]

In this formulation, respect for dignity is placed at the core of the right to work, but it is also associated with the right to life (survival), and self-realisation (development). Similarly, in his seminal essay on 'Is there a Human Right to Employment?',[25] James Nickel considers a number of foundational interests of

[22] J Tasioulas, 'On the Nature of Human Rights' in G Ernst and J-C Heilinger (eds), *The Philosophy of Human Rights: Contemporary Controversies* (Berlin, de Gruyter, 2012) 17, 18.

[23] J Tasioulas, 'Towards a Philosophy of Human Rights' (2012) 65 *Current Legal Problems* 1.

[24] Committee on Economic, Social and Cultural Rights, General Comment No 18: The Right to Work, Article 6 of the International Covenant on Economic, Social and Cultural Rights, UN Doc E/C.12/GC/18 (adopted on 24 November 2005).

[25] J Nickel, 'Is there a Human Right to Employment?' (1978–79) X *Philosophical Forum* 149.

this kind with regard to the right to work, which include self-respect and respect from others, and self-development, all of which can contribute to an understanding of the human interest protected by the right to work.

My argument will be that an adequate account of the right to work should put the human interest in self-development or self-realisation at its core, though respect for the dignity of others plays an important role in explaining the remaining dimensions of the flanking rights. Dignity, both in the sense of self-respect and respect from others, it will be argued, fails to capture the central feature of the right to work, its positive aspect of the right to a job itself.

A Dignity, Self-Respect or Self-Esteem

Nickel suggests that the right to work can be grounded in self-respect and respect from others.[26] We might paraphrase this description of the interest at stake as one concerning dignity, both as regards how one is treated by others and how one regards oneself. Nickel observes that exclusion from the labour market by unemployment causes a person to be subject to the 'humiliating trilemma of starvation, a life of crime, or dependence' on welfare benefits or charity. That loss of self-esteem is mirrored in a denial of respect by others, because they have either obstructed a person's opportunity to gain employment or they have not shown concern about the individual's plight of unemployment and therefore have treated the unemployed person with less than equal concern and respect. Though promising, this justification for the right to work in terms of dignity is vulnerable to a number of criticisms. The argument relies on some questionable assumptions about the effect of the receipt of welfare benefits or charity and the contribution of work to the dignity of the individual. The argument also relies on a false dilemma.

The stated dilemma is that one has the choice of work or welfare dependency. There are other choices such as crime or starvation, but there are independent reasons for rejecting those options. It is then argued that since welfare dependency undermines self-esteem, the dignified option must be to have a job. That conclusion does not follow, because the jobs available may also undermine self-esteem. A person may decide that in the choice between evils, welfare dependency is less damaging to self-esteem and respect from others than taking one of the demeaning jobs that are available. Indeed, the linking of welfare dependency to harm to the dignity of an individual can be challenged on a number of fronts.

For a start, in modern Britain, where at least in some parts of the country there is what is described by fretting politicians as a culture of welfare dependency, it seems dubious that living on welfare payments is universally or even generally regarded as humiliating. On the contrary, receipt of welfare payments may be regarded as an entitlement, based on contribution through taxation or simply by

[26] ibid; also RJ Arneson, 'Is Work Special? Justice and the Distribution of Employment' (1990) 84 *American Political Science Review* 1127, 1132.

virtue of citizenship. Consider, for example, the position of the 12 million pensioners who receive a state pension having reached a certain age. Although most of the recipients have contributed to their pension through national insurance payments, the long-term unemployed also qualify. There are many other groups who receive benefits such as the disabled and others who are not able to earn a decent living through the labour market. The aim of such payments is to support dignity and self-respect, and the recipients should not feel humiliated by their treatment by others. To the extent that people are confronted by the choice between work and welfare benefits, therefore, it is unclear that dignity is only achievable by the former and that welfare benefits damage self-esteem and prevent respect from others.

Indeed, modern European government policies with respect to the labour market advocate 'flexicurity', under which labour should become more mobile and adaptable to changing market conditions in return for state support during periods of unemployment or partial employment.[27] The Danish model, for instance, provides little protection for job security in the face of declining demand for labour, but offers relatively generous support for workers who have been dismissed for economic reasons until they obtain a new job. Under this scheme of flexicurity, welfare support is regarded as an essential mechanism for promoting competitiveness in the national economy. Workers, who become dependent on welfare benefits, at least in the short term, are not regarded by the government or others with disrespect, but as rather making their contribution to the safeguarding of the standard of living for everyone.

While welfare dependency may not invariably damage dignity for the reasons given above, it is also questionable whether having a job always supports the dignity of the individual. Jon Elster accepts that that even dull and routine work, provided that it is not completely futile work, produces self-esteem, because the work produces goods or services that others value enough to purchase. [28] His objection to a positive social right to work is precisely that the kinds of jobs that would have to be offered in order to fulfil the right would be artificial creations and futile, serving no recognisable economic purpose. At its core, he is making the controversial argument that if there is no demand for the job to be done, it is not the kind of work from which people can gain self-esteem.[29] This is not a rigid free-market-based principle: Elster recognises that governments can usefully increase demand for products and services on a temporary and artificial basis in order to address the problem of unemployment during the business cycle. His objection is rather to the Soviet-style permanent commitment to full employment by the creation of quantities of pointless jobs. It follows from this argument that although self-esteem is an extremely valuable interest, and although work normally pro-

[27] Council Conclusions on 'Towards Common Principles of Flexicurity' of 5–6 December 2007 (Doc 16201/07); European Commission, 'An Agenda for New Skills and Jobs' COM (2010) 682 final.

[28] J Elster, 'Is There (or Should There Be) A Right to Work?' in A Gutmann (ed), *Democracy and the Welfare State* (Princeton NJ, Princeton University Press, 1988) 53.

[29] ibid, 76.

vides self-esteem as a side effect, a right to work in the sense of providing a job for everyone cannot protect the interest in self-esteem. On Elster's view, it seems that living on welfare benefits is not conducive to self-esteem either, but it is not obviously worse in this regard than performing a pointless job.

While I agree with this general line of argument that not all jobs are conducive to the value of self-esteem, the distinction between proper jobs (for which there is a derived demand and which therefore produce self-esteem) and pointless jobs (where the opposite is true) is hard to identify in practice. Vincent Van Gogh worked hard as an artist, but he never sold a painting, so was his work pointless, thereby producing no self-esteem? More pertinently, a large proportion of our highly educated youth have chosen at present to become interns, performing unpaid services in the hope of obtaining valuable experience, rather than living off welfare benefits. Instead, interns are usually parasitic on their parents, a position which the young people do not in general, I think, find humiliating, but rather as their right. Although unpaid, my sense is that interns do obtain self-esteem from entering the world of work. Of course, their work may not be pointless in the sense that the employer would be prepared to pay for it if it had to, or would pay for it if its balance sheet was healthier, so interns may not straightforwardly demonstrate the inadequacy of the criterion of demand for distinguishing between jobs that provide self-esteem and pointless jobs.

Another troubling example of unpaid work is domestic work within the family.[30] Under the male breadwinner model, the man sought paid employment while the woman stayed at home to do the domestic work and nurture the children. Today, this sexual division of labour can be reversed. Does the person staying at home to do the chores and look after the children feel that this is a source of serious humiliation or loss of dignity? Although the market does not pay for this work to be done, carers and homemakers may not experience a lack of self-esteem or disrespect from others. Not all people regard such domestic work as dignified, however. Vicki Shultz, an American feminist law professor, argues that all domestic work and childcare should be performed as paid work, for she regards paid work as the route to autonomy and self-respect.[31] But I doubt that everyone shares that view, and even granting the possibility that false consciousness may be prevalent among unpaid carers and homemakers, it seems to me probable nevertheless that many people do not find the notion of looking after a home and children a demeaning option for life.

My conclusion is, therefore, that, although Elster is correct that not every job produces self-esteem or dignity as a by-product, the category of demeaning jobs that produce no self-esteem at all is small, and that the criterion of payment of

[30] A similar problem is presented by non-market work, which is work for which some payment is made, but not at market rates, as in the case of a live-in member of the family who helps with caring, or prison labour, where the work may produce self-esteem: see ND Zatz, 'Working at the Boundaries of Markets: Prison Labor and the Economic Dimension of Employment Relationships' (2008) 61 *Vanderbilt Law Review* 857.

[31] V Schultz, 'Life's Work' (2000) 100 *Columbia Law Review* 1881.

wages is inadequate to identify that category.[32] Even so, this argument demonstrates that dignity may not be a sufficient justification for the right to work in its positive aspect, though it is certainly important in explaining the negative aspect of protection from discrimination in the labour market. Nor is unemployment and support from government welfare, parents, partners, or charity necessarily a source of humiliation in many circumstances. As in the example of state pensions, welfare benefits actually contribute to dignity in many instances. Therefore, the argument that poses the dilemma of the choice between work and welfare as a source of dignity is not only false, but it relies on an inadequate description of the choice, because work is not always a source of dignity and nor is welfare dependency always a source of humiliation. It follows that the moral interest in self-esteem or dignity, though contributing an understanding of the importance of work in many people's lives, especially if the job is believed to confer prestige, does not provide a sufficient argument to justify a human right to work in the sense of a positive right to a job (and avoidance of dependence on welfare benefits or charity). The question is why a job is always an important interest for individuals, even in the context of generous welfare benefits for the unemployed or economically dependent and where the jobs available may be regarded as demeaning.

B Self-Realisation

What is this missing moral value or human interest that stresses the importance of work? Both mice and men need food and shelter to survive. Both mice and men work hard to scrabble a living out of the available resources and opportunities. But human beings, unlike mice, have an additional reason to work. That reason concerns the meaning for their lives which men and women can achieve through work. It is not easy to put into words this notion that people find fulfilment or a point to their lives through work. I do not think that the idea is adequately captured by the claim that through work people achieve self-respect or dignity or independence. Nickel and others rightly make a distinction between self-esteem and self-development. I think that the idea of the quest to establish meaning for one's life goes deeper than dignity or independence, because it is trying to answer the question: 'What is the point of my life?' Or perhaps, more fundamentally: 'What is the point of me?' Unless we have some kind of answer to that question, our psychological condition is likely to be very unstable: if there is no point to my life, why not end it all? To believe that there is a point to one's life is the opposite of what Durkheim called 'anomie'.[33] This missing moral value or human interest can be labelled in different ways, such as self-actualisation, personal fulfilment or, my preferred term, self-realisation.

[32] For similar arguments: Arneson, above n 26, 1141–43.

[33] A Giddens (ed), *Émile Durkheim, Selected Writings* (Cambridge, Cambridge University Press, 1979); SR Marks, 'Durkheim's Theory of Anomie' (1974) 80 *The American Journal of Sociology* 329; S Lukes, 'Alienation and Anomie' in P Laslett and RG Runciman (eds), *Philosophy, Politics and Society*, 3rd series (Oxford, Oxford University Press, 1967) ch 6.

In political philosophy, Karl Marx is most clearly identified with this idea that human beings achieve self-realisation through work. His texts, both published and unpublished in his lifetime, are open to a variety of interpretations.[34] In my view, there are two related themes. On the one hand, Marx argued that through work men achieve self-actualisation. They can use their capacities of thought and physical strength to achieve something which is their own creation, thereby fulfilling a need to have a point to one's life. For Marx, this was a crucial aspect of being a human being, which distinguishes us from animals. On the other hand, Marx observed that in most jobs in his society, men strived to achieve something that was defined by and belonged to someone else, the capitalist employer, who in turn chose this product because of demand from a market composed of other people. Marx's theory of alienation, as it has been called, which was never fully developed, and which later on, Marx, having transferred to the emerging discipline of political economy, called 'commodification', seemed to identify the tension between these two themes as explaining the fundamental problem with capitalism. We might summarise the thesis by saying that while work is essential for human self-realisation, almost the only work available in a capitalist society, namely paid employment, is the type of work that seriously obstructs self-realisation because the market system treats labour as a commodity. In this context, what I want to draw out of Marx's philosophy is not his perfectionist critique of capitalism,[35] but rather his insight that finding meaning through work is essential to what it is to be a human being, what he called in an Aristotelean flourish, our 'species-being'.

In his later work in political economy, Marx seems to me to have lost sight of a second aspect of the theory of alienation that had been central to his early work, which is sometimes labelled 'estrangement'.[36] In his reflections on the origins and nature of human society, he always stressed the fundamental importance of the 'relations of production', which concerns the need for human beings to cooperate in order to produce what was necessary for survival or well-being. In his theory of social change and revolution, changes in the relations of production were the engine of history.[37] It was through work or productive activities that human beings came together to form communities or societies. Animals such as bees also cooperate in their relations of production, but they function like cogs in a machine, whereas human beings form social relationships through work, making choices, agreements, plans, friends and organisations. As social animals, human beings create their society around their work relations. So we might say that human beings find meaning for their lives through work, not just from the achievements of what is produced, but also, and importantly, from the establishment of social relations with colleagues, which is also a vital part of our

[34] The central text is: Karl Marx, 'Economic and Philosophical Manuscripts' in L Colletti (ed), *Early Writings* (London, Penguin/NLB, 1975) esp 322–34. For my own analysis of this text and Marx's other writings: H Collins, *Marxism and Law* (Oxford, Oxford University Press, 1984) 115–23.

[35] Kymlicka, above n 13.

[36] Collins, above n 34, 111–15.

[37] GA Cohen, *Karl Marx's Theory of History: A Defence* (Oxford, Oxford University Press, 1978).

species-being. Or, to put the point negatively, being denied social relationships, as in the case of imprisonment under solitary confinement, is inhuman treatment precisely because it negates that fundamental human interest in sociability. Similarly, exclusion from work is a primary cause of social exclusion.

In this theory of self-realisation through work, Marx was not, of course, setting out to provide a justification for the right to work. He was not an admirer of the bourgeois individualism (as he saw it) of rights talk,[38] and thought that talk of a right to work in a market economy was (impracticable) nonsense, though he recognised that the right to work could prove a good rallying cry for revolutionaries and socialists. Nor is Marx unique in recognising the importance of work for self-fulfilment and as an opportunity to create social relationships. As John Rawls acknowledges, there is a close affinity between this idea of self-realisation and his 'Aristotelian principle' of human motivation, which states: 'other things equal, human beings enjoy the exercise of their realized capacities (their innate or trained abilities), and this enjoyment increases the more the capacity is realized, or the greater its complexity'.[39] Where Rawls and other liberals depart from Marx is in their insistence that work is only one occasion when self-realisation may be achieved, whereas Marx insisted that self-realisation through work was essential to being human. Rawls more plausibly recognises that self-realisation might be achieved in many ways, through 'friendship, meaningful work and social co-operation, the pursuit of knowledge and the fashioning and contemplation of beautiful objects'.[40] Rawls also gives the example of becoming an excellent chess player as a route towards self-realisation. As Will Kymlicka argues, Marx fails to make a convincing case for work being the sole source of self-realisation and, in any case, since according to Marx most jobs in a capitalist economy are alienated or commodified and therefore cannot provide an opportunity for self-realisation, in the absence of a credible alternative economic system, work is not even a plausible candidate for an opportunity for self-realisation for most people.[41]

Although Marx was wrong in many important respects, his view that through work men and women can achieve self-realisation is nevertheless plausible in many instances. Jobs can be exhausting and fairly monotonous, but people can feel a sense of achievement at a job well done, fulfilment from the opportunity to use their skills in partnership with others to achieve something and can identify themselves with the outcome of their labours.[42] 'Work, according to Marx, is rewarding *and* painful; moreover, it could not be rewarding without being

[38] For discussion of the view of human rights held by Marx and Marxists, see: S Lukes, *Marxism and Morality* (Oxford, Oxford University Press, 1985) 61–70; Collins, above n 34, 142.

[39] J Rawls, *A Theory of Justice* (Oxford, Oxford University Press, 1971) 424. Rawls notices the affinity with the idea of self-realisation at 431.

[40] ibid, 425.

[41] Kymlicka, above n 13. See also J Elster, *Making Sense of Marx* (Cambridge, Cambridge University Press, 1985) 521–27.

[42] Repetitive work is not necessarily inimical to job satisfaction: W Ronco and L Peattie, 'Making Work: A Perspective from Social Science' in RE Pahl (ed), *On Work: Historical, Comparative and Theoretical Approaches* (Oxford, Blackwell, 1988) 709, 713 (fisherman); 717 (automobile assembly line).

painful'.[43] It is the opportunity for self-realisation through work by meeting its physical and intellectual challenges that explains why the right to work requires a positive aspect, so that having a job matters for its own sake and not simply because it affords material benefits or avoids welfare dependency. Empirical surveys in psychology also identify self-actualisation as well as material rewards and social relationships as primary motivations for work.[44] In this respect, the human interest in self-realisation explains and justifies the positive right to work, while the previously considered justification in terms of dignity or self-esteem seems unable to do so.

Admittedly, it is not always easy to distinguish between, on the one hand, dignity and self-respect and, on the other, the value of self-realisation. Consider the case concerning the entertainment provided in France of dwarf-throwing.[45] The local authorities tried to ban this show on the ground that it was demeaning to the tiny people who were being hurled about in front of the audience, but the entertainers concerned objected that this ban was an unconstitutional interference with their liberty. Considering the facts of this case rather than how it was presented in the courts, it seems to me clear that public authorities correctly formed the view that the performance was demeaning for the participants, so that it denied them dignity as human beings. They were tossed around like a football. Yet the performers themselves insisted on their right to work because the job at least gave some meaning to their lives and material benefits. By putting on an entertaining show for the audience by using their acrobatic skills, the performers were able to use the job to contribute to their self-realisation, even if the authorities were correct that in some respects it diminished the performers' dignity. Similar problems of distinguishing between dignity and self-realisation may arise in respect of other kinds of jobs. A woman who performs a nude table dancing act in a club may not be treated with dignity and may therefore feel a lack of self-esteem, but may find the work rewarding in some respects such as fulfilment from freely using her capacity for dancing and entertaining others.

Elster rejects this view that self-realisation provides the core justification for the right to work. He appears to think that if the right to work were based on the value of self-realisation, 'chaos would ensue'.[46] His argument is that for self-realisation to be achieved, the right to work would have to permit everyone to do the job of their choice. This is plainly unrealistic in any society: as he says, 'No individual can have a right to direct epic color films'. Of course, that is true, but beside the point. In the civil liberty aspect of the right to work, the right requires that there

[43] J Elster, 'Self-Realization in Work and Politics: The Marxist Conception of the Good Life' (1986) 3 *Social Philosophy and Policy* 99, 110, relying on a passage in K Marx, *Grundrisse* (Harmondsworth, Pelican Books, 1973) 611.

[44] eg, M Ross, S Schwartz and S Surkis, 'Basic Individual Values, Work Values and the Meaning of Work' (1999) 48 *Applied Psychology* 49, 55.

[45] UN Human Rights Committee, *Wackenheim v France* (Com No 854/1999) UN Doc CCPR/C/75/D/854/1999 (2002); www.bayefsky.com/docs.php/area/jurisprudence/node/4/filename/france_t5_iccpr_854_1999.

[46] Elster, 'Is There (or Should There Be) A Right to Work?', above n 28, 77.

should be no unjustifiable barriers to the choice of occupation, not an absolute right to the job of one's choice. Merit, in the sense of the ability to do the job well, should always be a justifiable barrier. For the social right aspect of the right to work, the positive right to a job, all that is needed is some kind of job, even if it is not one's dream job. Jobs may be more or less meaningful to the worker, but pretty much any job is better in this respect than none at all.

But is it true that all jobs have this feature of enabling self-realisation? If we seek to ground the right to work in a universal human interest, is it not necessary to establish that every job, no matter what its content, shares the quality that it affords an opportunity for self-realisation?

One way to answer this question is to draw a distinction between work and labour. Work, on this view, is limited to jobs that have at least some opportunity for self-realisation, whereas labour is simply the mechanical performance of a task dictated by someone else. In other words, the right to work is limited by the underlying human interest that justifies the right, namely the potential for self-realisation through work. Jobs that lack any such potential for self-realisation are not regarded as work but mere labour.[47]

Although this way of answering the question may look like simply a device by which by definition the right to work is restricted to meaningful work, there are independent reasons for so restricting the definition of the right to work. If we include mere labouring, being treated as a commodity, in the right to work, it seems doubtful that it would merit the status of a human right. Not only would 'work' be lacking the potential for self-realisation, but the worker would be denied dignity as a human being. Furthermore, the negative right to be protected against discrimination and obstructions to work opportunities would make less sense if the purpose of any prohibition was to protect people against meaningless and undignified work.

This interpretation of the meaning and value of the right to work, which restricts the human interest to work capable of providing an opportunity for self-realisation, depends on being able to distinguish reasonably clearly between mere labour and work. The difference clearly does not depend on payment or demand in the market; the difference lies in the combination of task execution and task definition. In the case of labour, the worker has no choices in the kind of work to be performed, how and when it is done and employs no personal skills to complete the task. Few jobs fit that category. Even in menial jobs, the worker will have some discretion in how the job should be done, the ordering and pacing of the tasks, and will need to have some skills. Human resources management today relies on the insight that workers will be better motivated and more productive if they feel that they have some say about working conditions and discretion about how best to perform the task. This management strategy recognises that by increasing the meaningfulness of work, even at the margins, workers will obtain greater satisfaction from their jobs and display greater commitment to the aims of

[47] See J Penner in this volume, ch 5.

the business. In the context of a radical division of labour, few workers except specialised craftsmen and artists can determine on their own the nature of the task to be performed and how it should be executed. Most employees including professionals and managers must operate within the constraints of accepting at least the broad definition of the tasks to be performed and the operational needs for efficiency in task execution. Nevertheless, within those confines, there is the necessary space for workers to find their jobs to some extent fulfilling.

The need to cooperate with others within the division of labour of organisations further improves the extent to which work offers opportunities for self-realisation. That need for cooperation explains additionally why this human interest in meaningful work should be treated as a right. To ensure that the right to work is achieved, there has to be at least some correlative duties placed on others to cooperate. At the very least, particular groups should not be unjustifiably excluded from the labour market or particular jobs.

VI Conclusion

The central claim advanced here has been that the value or human interest of self-realisation best explains why the right to work should be regarded as a human right with correlative duties. The value of self-realisation proves vital to an understanding why having a job matters and why the positive right to work is regarded as the core of the right. Other accounts of the right to work, particularly those based on dignity and self-esteem, fail to capture this positive dimension of the right to work, though, in this pluralist approach, those other interests help to explain the importance of the negative dimensions of the right to work. The right to work is, however, a social right that requires progressive realisation according to the resources of the community. In some cases, the right to work might require that the government creates jobs for the long-term unemployed, but a better strategy for respecting the right will often be improvements in the supply-side of the labour market through education, training and help with job search. Whatever the means that seem appropriate and effective to achieve an egalitarian distribution of employment opportunities, the central point of acknowledging the human right to work is that guaranteed income through welfare benefits is not an adequate substitute.

The human interest in self-realisation also helps us to understand why not every kind of work satisfies the right, but why most jobs do provide the requisite chance for self-realisation. Unpaid work such as an internship or homemaking can provide opportunities for self-realisation, so that remuneration is not a key requirement of the right to work. But the kind of job where a worker is treated as a cog in a machine, required to work as an automaton without exercising any talents or skills, without collaborating with others, is not the kind of work protected by the right to work. Fortunately, such jobs are not prevalent. Although many kinds of work may be dull and repetitive, there are usually opportunities for self-realisation in the power to determine how the tasks should be completed, exercising skills when performing the task and in the opportunities for collaboration and cooperation with others.

If self-realisation is the human interest that lies at the core of the right to work, that value can guide an interpretation of other aspects of the right. The view that the core of the right is contained in the positive right to a job is, of course, confirmed. The distinct human interest in self-realisation also explains why the right to work is not purely an instrumental right, but represents a basic and independent value. Yet work is not the only way in which humans achieve self-realisation. This value may infuse other human rights such as the right to education and broader protections for autonomy. The emphasis on self-realisation does, however, suggest limits on the scope of the right. It implies that 'decent work' in this context should be a job where there are some opportunities for self-realisation, but it does not provide direct support for such further requirements as a just wage or favourable working conditions. Concerns about fair labour standards and exploitative jobs in sweatshops can be addressed in part by reference to other human rights that can justify minimum standards, but the right to work itself need not be indissolubly linked to such fair labour standards in order to avoid the charge that it is merely a right to be exploited.[48] Like the human interest in welfare benefits for the unemployed, just working conditions represent on this view a different interest that should be protected independently, if necessary, by a separate human right. But protection against unfair dismissal does not seem to be closely tied to the right to work itself except where dismissal from a particular position deprives a person of the opportunity to pursue a vocation or profession.

[48] For the contrary view: Mundlak, 'The Right to Work – The Value of Work', above n 12, 341, 345–51; and V Mantouvalou in this volume, ch 3.

3

The Right to Non-Exploitative Work

VIRGINIA MANTOUVALOU*

Introduction

The right to work is sometimes grounded in values such as human dignity or self-realisation. Individuals need to work in order to make a living that will grant them access to basic material goods that are a precondition to a good life. Work also provides opportunities for self-development through interaction with others.[1] This chapter rests on the belief that if the right to work is to be a valuable addition to a list of human rights, it must be viewed as a right to non-exploitative work. Non-exploitation is an associated value of dignity and self-realisation, but it must be examined separately in order to assess how it complements the foundations of the right to work and to develop its normative implications.

The right not to be exploited at work is probably one of the least controversial aspects of the right to work, but this chapter focuses on a group of right-holders that generates much controversy: undocumented migrants. In the case of these workers, denial of a right to work because of immigration rules often leads to exploitation. International human rights law prohibits this exploitation. Even though my focus is on undocumented workers, the argument that non-exploitation underlies aspects of the moral right to work and their encapsulation in human rights law applies to all workers. In fact, the right to non-exploitative work, both as a moral right and in international human rights law, is a truly universal right that

* Drafts of this chapter were presented at the University of Oxford, Centre for Migration, Policy and Society, the London Labour Law Discussion Group, a staff seminar at UCL, the University Pompeu Fabra in Barcelona and the University of Bristol SLS Conference. Thanks are due to the organisers and all participants of these workshops, as well as Hugh Collins and Prince Saprai for having acted as commentators. I am also grateful to Einat Albin, Alan Bogg, Cathryn Costello, Leda Lakka, George Letsas, Charles Mitchell, Rob Stevens and John Tasioulas for comments and discussions.

[1] On dignity as a foundation of the right to work, see G Mundlak, 'The Right to Work – The Value of Work' in D Barak-Erez and A Gross (eds), *Exploring Social Rights: Between Theory and Practice* (Oxford, Hart Publishing, 2007) 341, 348 ff; and G Mundlak, 'The Right to Work: Linking Human Rights and Employment Policy' (2007) 146 *International Labour Review* 189, 197; J Elster, 'Is There (or Should There Be) A Right to Work?' in A Gutmann (ed), *Democracy and the Welfare State* (Princeton NJ, Princeton University Press, 1988) 53, 77. On self-realisation as a justification of the positive right to work see H Collins in this volume, ch 2.

applies to everyone. This is to be contrasted with the right to access a job, which may legitimately be limited to certain groups of the population.

The argument unfolds as follows: the right to work is a human right that at first glance appears universal in international law, but is in reality conditional on citizenship or immigration status in national legal orders, as sections I and II of the chapter show. Migrants usually need a work permit in order to exercise their human right to work. Undocumented migrants, in turn, have no legal right to work under immigration law. Section III of the chapter turns to two legal orders, the United Kingdom and the United States, which exemplify how no legal right to work because of immigration rules can lead to exploitation. It discusses two judicial decisions that illustrate the social problem and legal regime on undocumented migrant workers. Section IV of the chapter argues that even though those who have no legal authorisation to be in a country have no right to work as a matter of immigration law, they still have a moral right not to be exploited, which constitutes part of the moral right to work and the right to work in international human rights law. This section develops a conception of exploitation, which consists in the abuse of a person's vulnerability that is created or exacerbated by law,[2] in order to make profit. It then examines whether undocumented migrant workers are subject to exploitation. Having found that the undocumented are exploited, the chapter turns to human rights law in section V. In human rights law, we do not find an explicit right not to be exploited. However, the principle of non-exploitation underlies several provisions. The section explores case law on the prohibition of slavery, servitude, forced and compulsory labour, as well as the prohibition of discrimination, to show that these provisions capture and counteract the exploitation of all workers (both migrants and non-migrants). The exploitation of undocumented migrant workers that stems from what in the United Kingdom is termed 'the doctrine of illegality' is in breach of these norms of higher order. The final section concludes that an exploitative job cannot be dignified and cannot lead to self-realisation. It is essential then to approach the right to work as a right to non-exploitative work.

I The Right to Work as a Human Right in International Law

The right to work is protected in international law in several human rights treaties. The UN International Covenant on Economic, Social and Cultural Rights (ICESCR), for example, incorporates the right, which 'includes the right of every-

[2] There are, of course, other definitions of vulnerability that capture situations, which can lead to exploitation. See J Fudge and R Owens (eds), *Precarious Work, Women and the New Economy* (Oxford, Hart Publishing, 2006); and the special issue on 'Precarious Work and Human Rights' (2012) 34(1) *Comparative Labor Law & Policy Journal*.

one to the opportunity to gain his living by work which he freely chooses or accepts', and requires that the authorities 'take appropriate steps to safeguard this right'.[3] Article 7 ICESCR protects rights to fair and just working conditions, and Article 8 trade union rights.

As with other social rights, which were until recently relatively under-explored in literature and in human rights adjudication,[4] in contrast to civil and political rights, the right to work may seem vague at first. Does the provision require that everyone acquires the job of her or his choice? Does it demand that everyone be paid for her or his work? Does it require decent wages for all? In the process of specifying the content of the right to work, the Committee on Economic, Social and Cultural Rights (CESCR), which monitors the ICESCR, has issued a General Comment that provides an authoritative interpretation of the Covenant. General Comment No 18 makes mention of the right to work in Article 6, which is the proclamation of the right in a general manner, and then explains that Article 7 further develops the individual dimension of the right to work and Article 8 develops its collective dimension.[5] It claims that Articles 6, 7 and 8 are interdependent.[6]

The General Comment also discusses the foundation of the right. It states: 'Every individual has the right to be able to work, allowing him/her to live in dignity'.[7] Like other human rights, the right to work here is linked to human dignity, because the General Comment recognises that without work and the income that it generates, most people would not be able to satisfy their basic needs or feel self-fulfilled. From the wording of the General Comment, it is a right that every human being has simply by virtue of being human.

Like other socio-economic rights in the ICESCR, the right to work is not interpreted as imposing on state authorities an immediate obligation to provide a job to everyone. However, it does contain some immediate obligations, which are similar to obligations imposed by civil rights: for example, the right to work contains a right not to be forced to work. In addition, the right also imposes certain duties of progressive realisation. According to General Comment No 3 of the CESCR, '[t]he concept of progressive realization constitutes a recognition of the fact that full realization of all economic, social and cultural rights will generally not be able to be achieved in a short period of time'.[8] The second paragraph of Article 6 ICESCR provides that the steps that the authorities ought to take for the

[3] Art 6 ICESCR.

[4] See V Mantouvalou, 'In Support of Legalisation' in C Gearty and V Mantouvalou, *Debating Social Rights* (Oxford, Hart Publishing, 2010). Some notable exceptions on the right to work include the seminal pieces by B Hepple, 'A Right to Work?' (1981) 10 *Industrial Law Journal* 65; and J Nickel, 'Is there a Human Right to Employment?' (1978–79) X *Philosophical Forum* 149. Both authors revisit the issues in this volume: Bob Hepple in the Foreword and James Nickel in ch 8.

[5] CESCR, General Comment No 18: The Right to Work, Article 6 of the International Covenant on Economic, Social and Cultural Rights, UN Doc E/C.12/GC/18 (General Comment No 18), para 2.

[6] ibid, para 8.

[7] ibid, para 1.

[8] CESCR, General Comment No 3: The Nature of State Parties' Obligations (Art 2 para 1 of the Covenant), E/1991/23, para 9.

full realisation of the right include technical and vocational programmes, and policies that will lead to full employment.

To give another example from international law, at regional level, in Europe, the right to work is protected in the European Social Charter (ESC), which states in Article 1:

> With a view to ensuring the effective exercise of the right to work, the Contracting Parties undertake:
>
> to accept as one of their primary aims and responsibilities the achievement and maintenance of as high and stable a level of employment as possible, with a view to the attainment of full employment;
>
> to protect effectively the right of the worker to earn his living in an occupation freely entered upon;
>
> to establish or maintain free employment services for all workers;
>
> to provide or promote appropriate vocational guidance, training and rehabilitation.

Article 2 of the ESC protects the right to just working conditions, Article 3 provides for health and safety at work and Article 4 protects the right to fair remuneration.[9] In international law, in other words, we find the right to work both at international and regional level in various social rights treaties, which also include other related rights, such as the prohibition of forced labour and the right to decent working conditions. International documents such as the above view the right to work as a right to 'decent work',[10] which brings to mind the agenda of the International Labour Organization (ILO) as well.[11]

II The Conditionality of the Right to Work of Migrants

In theory, in international human rights law, the right to work is a universal right. Universality is a normative concept here, which means that everyone *should* enjoy a particular right (not that everyone *actually* enjoys it).[12] It is an aspiration, not a description of social reality. However, in practice in most national legal orders the right to work is not universal. Very often, it is based on citizenship as legal status, rather than dignity: only a country's nationals or certain categories of migrants have a legal right to work. Immigration law sets restrictions to the universality of the international human right.

[9] On the interpretation of the right to work by the European Committee of Social Rights and the CESCR, see C O'Cinneide, in this volume, Ch 6. For further analysis of the right to work under the ESC and the EU Charter of Fundamental Rights, see also D Ashiagbor, 'The Right to Work', in de Búrca, de Witte (eds), *Social Rights in Europe* (Oxford, Oxford University Press, 2005) 241.

[10] General Comment No 18, paras 7–8.

[11] On the agenda of the ILO, see: www.ilo.org/global/about-the-ilo/decent-work-agenda/lang--en/index.htm.

[12] See V Mantouvalou, 'Are Labour Rights Human Rights?' (2012) 3 *European Labour Law Journal* 151, 166.

The linkage between the right to work and citizenship will appeal to many. Discussing American citizenship, Judith Shklar argued that the right to work is one of its central elements. 'The dignity of work and of personal achievement', Shklar said, 'and the contempt for aristocratic idleness, have since colonial times been an important part of American civic self-identification'.[13] Earning through work (together with voting) are the key components of American citizenship, on this analysis. In the European Union (EU), it is not only citizens of each state that have a right to work within each legal order: citizens of other Member States have this right too, and this is a central tenet of EU citizenship.[14] But third-country nationals, namely those that do not come from a Member State of the EU, most often need a work permit. This group of migrants has a right to work only for so long as her or his visa permits. When the visa expires, there is no legal right to work. A migrant who is undocumented, in turn, namely someone who has come into a country without a visa and a work permit or someone who has entered a country with legal documents that later expired, has no right to work at all. The right to work, in other words, is made conditional on a person's migration status. It is a right of nationals and some (but not all) migrants.

That the right to access work is conditional on citizenship or a valid work permit is not necessarily a violation of the (at first glance universal) right to work. Human rights are sometimes conditional on a particular status and this conditionality can be permissible, unless it is arbitrary.[15] For example, child labour is generally either prohibited or heavily regulated.[16] That children have no right to work is not a breach of their human rights because the reason for the prohibition is the protection of this vulnerable part of the population. This is a legitimate reason, not an arbitrary one. Because the reason for the restriction to the exercise of the right is legitimate, it is hard to argue that it violates the human rights of children.

Contrary to the restrictions on child labour, restrictions on the right to work on the basis of immigration status do not have as an aim the protection of migrants. The reason for placing restrictions on migrants' right to work is viewed as part of the exercise of state power to control immigration and to protect the national labour market. The protection of the national labour market could also be presented as protection of the right to work of the country's nationals. There is no general internationally recognised right to migrate from one country to another,

[13] J Shklar, *American Citizenship: The Quest for Inclusion* (Cambridge MA, Harvard University Press, 1991).

[14] See Art 45 of the Treaty on the Functioning of the European Union, which is also developed by EU secondary legislation.

[15] J Tasioulas, 'On the Nature of Human Rights' in G Ernst and J-C Heilinger (eds), *The Philosophy of Human Rights: Contemporary Controversies* (Berlin, de Gruyter, 2012) 17, 37. Mantouvalou, 'Are Labour Rights Human Rights?', above n 12.

[16] See the 1998 ILO Declaration of Fundamental Principles and Rights at Work. For a brief presentation of the Declaration and its follow-up procedure see H Kellerson, 'The ILO Declaration of 1998 on Fundamental Principles and Rights: A Challenge for the Future' (1998) 137 *International Labour Review* 223.

unless someone is an asylum seeker,[17] and the restrictions placed on the right to work of non-nationals are viewed as a legitimate aspect of the exercise of states' sovereign power that includes a power to regulate their labour market. There will be some who will argue that there should be free movement of workers around the world.[18] But it is likely that most people will accept the statement that undocumented migrants, who do not have the necessary authorisation, do not have a right to access the labour market. Most will not view the restrictions imposed on the basis of citizenship or a work permit as arbitrary.

This chapter will not discuss further the moral and legal justification of restrictions of access to work on the basis of immigration status. It will not discuss whether migrants have a moral or legal positive right to access jobs. It will focus on the treatment of undocumented workers once they are employed, and on what I call a right to non-exploitative work. It is important to appreciate that, despite the legal provision that undocumented migrants have no right to work, the social reality is that there are millions of undocumented migrants the world over, and many of them exercise their human right to work.[19] It is hard to have precise numbers of undocumented migrant workers. According to some estimates, in 2008 between 1.9 million and 3.8 million undocumented migrants resided in the EU, while in the United States, which has a smaller overall population, there was a larger population of undocumented migrants of about 11.2 million people.[20] Many of the undocumented migrants are either jobseekers or workers, because work is a key reason why people migrate. They often concentrate in specific work sectors. Undocumented migrants are usually employed in the informal labour market, in sectors with low union density, such as domestic labour, sex work, agriculture and construction.[21] For these workers, the implications of the statement that they have no legal right to work because of immigration rules are dramatic.

III No Rights at Work for Undocumented Migrants

This section will illustrate the dramatic implications of the lack of a right to work for undocumented workers in some legal orders by looking at two examples: a case from the United Kingdom and another one from the United States. While

[17] See the analysis of the Council of Europe Commissioner for Human Rights, 'The Right to Leave a Country' (Council of Europe, 2013).

[18] J Gordon, 'Transnational Labor Citizenship' (2007) 80 *Southern California Law Review* 503.

[19] For some estimates, see EU Fundamental Right Agency Report, 'Fundamental Rights of Migrants in an Irregular Situation in the European Union' 2011 (hereafter FRA Report 2011).

[20] C Morehouse and M Blomfield, 'Irregular Migration in Europe' (Migration Policy Institute, 2011) 6.

[21] B Anderson, *Us and Them? The Dangerous Politics of Immigration Control* (Oxford, Oxford University Press, 2013) 79 ff. See also E Albin, 'The Sectoral Regulatory Regime: When Work Migration Controls and the Sectorally Differentiated Labour Market Meet' in C Costello and M Freedland (eds), *Migrants at Work* (Oxford, Oxford University Press, 2014 forthcoming).

these two examples serve to illustrate the social problem and related legal issues, they are by no means isolated.[22]

A *Hounga v Allen*

The UK case on the issue of workplace rights of the undocumented is *Hounga v Allen.*[23] Hounga is a Nigerian national who came to the United Kingdom to work as a domestic worker for the Allen family. When she travelled to the United Kingdom, she was either 14 or 16 years old. She would look after the children, and would be provided with accommodation and board. Before arriving in the United Kingdom, she had been promised that she would attend school, would be paid £50 a month and would also have her travel to the United Kingdom paid. In order to come to the United Kingdom, she made false statements so as to obtain a passport and a six-month visa, which she overstayed.

In the United Kingdom she looked after the three children of the family and cleaned the house. During the 18 months that she was employed, she suffered serious physical abuse, and was regularly threatened that should she go to the authorities, she would be imprisoned because she was in the country illegally. At some point, Ms Allen attacked and beat Ms Hounga because the children had not eaten their supper. She was then physically pushed out of the house. She slept in the garden at night, with very light clothes on, and tried to re-enter in the morning, but she was not let in. Eventually someone found her in a distressed state and took her to the social services.

Ms Hounga brought two types of complaints to UK tribunals and courts. The first type were contract claims (unfair dismissal, breach of contract, unpaid wages and holiday pay) and the second type were discrimination claims in relation to her dismissal and to the harassment she suffered while employed, under the UK Race Relations Act 1976. The Employment Tribunal described the case as 'probably one of the saddest case [sic] that has come before this tribunal'.[24] Yet it dismissed her contractual claims for unfair dismissal, breach of contract, unpaid wages and holiday pay. Being an undocumented migrant, Ms Hounga had no right to work in the United Kingdom, so her contract was illegal and could not be enforced. She was also not entitled to loss of earnings. She was awarded £6000 compensation for injury to feelings because of the racially discriminatory dismissal, which was her only claim that was upheld. The Court of Appeal later overturned this, ruling that even her discriminatory dismissal was inextricably

[22] See, for instance, the Irish approach in the decision *Hussein v the Labour Court and Anor* [2012] IEHC 364; FRA Report 2011; M LeVoy and N Verbruggen, *Ten Ways to Protect Undocumented Migrant Workers* (PICUM, 2005).

[23] *Hounga v Allen and Another* [2014] UKSC 47 on appeal from [2012] EWCA Civ 609. See A Bogg and V Mantouvalou, 'Illegality, Human Rights and Employment: A Watershed Moment for the United Kingdom Supreme Court?' UK Constitutional Law Association Blog (13 March 2014) (available at: ukconstitutionallaw.org/).

[24] As cited in EAT decision, para 6.

bound to her illegality; she was therefore not entitled to compensation for it.[25] The finding of the Tribunal was as follows:

> The Tribunal are satisfied that the claimant did know and understand that as her contract was illegal she is not entitled to benefit therefore cannot bring her claim of unfair dismissal or any claims which arise under a contract of employment.[26]

That the employers had initiated the illegality themselves, and also benefited from it, did not trouble particularly the tribunals and courts, because the UK Supreme Court had explained in an earlier case that the defence of illegality (of the contract) is 'not a principle of justice: it is a principle of policy whose application is indiscriminate and can lead to unfair consequences as between the parties' litigation'.[27] The courts 'exist to enforce the law, not to enforce illegality'.[28] Hence this aspect of Ms Hounga's claim failed, as did her claims for unpaid wages. She never had a right to work, so she could have no rights whatsoever on the basis of her illegal contract, on the analysis of the Court of Appeal.

The discrimination claim in relation to the dismissal reached the UK Supreme Court. The Court accepted that the defence of illegality precluded Ms Hounga's contractual claims, but took a different approach towards the tort of discrimination. The discriminatory treatment was not viewed as inextricably linked to the illegal contract, which was only 'the context in which Mrs Allen then perpetrated the acts of physical, verbal and emotional abuse by which, among other things, she dismissed Miss Hounga. . .'.[29] The Court also examined the public policy upon which the defence of illegality is said to rest, namely the preservation of 'the integrity of the legal system'.[30] In this regard, it ruled that the current public policy is to tackle human trafficking and protect its victims. As Ms Hounga was probably a victim of human trafficking, the Court decided to allow her appeal. She was therefore successful in her discrimination claim, but not on the contractual claims, which were ('rightly',[31] as Lord Hughes stressed) not pursued in the Court of Appeal or the Supreme Court.

[25] On a criticism of the Court of Appeal decision on the basis of precedent, see the analysis by A Bogg and T Novitz, 'Race Discrimination and the Doctrine of Illegality' (2013) *Law Quarterly Review* 12. See also A Bogg, 'The Immoral Trap: Migrant Workers and the Doctrine of Illegality' in B Ryan (ed), *Labour Migration in Hard Times* (Liverpool, Institute of Employment Rights, 2013) 119.

[26] As cited in EAT decision, para 31.

[27] *Tinsley v Milligan* [1994] 1 AC 340, 355 (Lord Goff). Cited in EAT decision, para 36.

[28] *Newland v Simons and Willer (Hairdressers) Ltd* [1981] ICR 521, 532. Cited in EAT decision, para 37.

[29] *Hounga*, para 16.

[30] *Hounga*, para 44.

[31] *Hounga*, para 54.

B *Hoffman Plastic Compounds, Inc v National Labor Relations Board*

The second case that illustrates the problem that this chapter addresses, *Hoffman Plastic Compounds, Inc v National Labor Relations Board*,[32] comes from the United States. Jose Castro had been employed by Hoffman, having arrived in the United States and presented the employer with fraudulent identity documents. He was dismissed when his employer found out that he had taken part in union organising activities. The National Labor Relations Board (NLRB) said that the dismissal had been unlawful because it was in response to the exercise of his legal right to organise, and that Jose Castro was entitled to remedies, such as back pay.

The employer appealed against the decision of the NLRB, in a case that went up to the US Supreme Court. The Court was divided. A majority of five judges ruled that the NLRB could not award back pay to the worker who had been unlawfully dismissed, because he had had no right to be employed in the United States in the first place. Awarding back pay to an undocumented migrant worker, who had been unlawfully dismissed for exercising his right to unionise, would undermine immigration policy: it 'not only trivializes the immigration laws, it also condones and encourages future violations'.[33] The NLRB therefore should not have awarded this remedy. In a decision that reflects the position that courts should not condone illegal acts, and that labour laws only apply if immigration rules are respected, the majority ruling endorsed the position that no right to work means no rights at work.[34]

In *Hoffman*, the liberal, progressive members of the Court dissented. Judge Breyer, joined by Judges Stevens, Souter and Ginsburg, issued a separate opinion. They supported the view that back pay is an essential remedy for the NLRB to award in the case of an unlawful dismissal. The dismissal of Jose Castro was unlawful because it occurred in response to the exercise of a fundamental labour right: the right to form a trade union. In terms of the implications of the ruling for immigration policy, the dissenting judges said that leaving undocumented migrant workers without labour rights, such as this, would provide further incentives for employers to employ undocumented workers. The decision of the majority, in the view of the dissenting judges, was not only contrary to the fundamental right to organise; it was also counterproductive for it could lead to an increase in the demand for undocumented migrant workers.

[32] *Hoffman Plastic Compounds, Inc v National Labor Relations Board*, 535 US 137 (2002). For discussion of the issue in the United States more broadly, see M Ontiveros, 'Migrant Labour in the United States: Working Beneath the Floor for Free Labour?' in C Costello and M Freedland (eds), *Migrants at Work* (Oxford, Oxford University Press, 2014 forthcoming). On the right to work in the United States more generally, see K Stone in this volume, ch 15.

[33] *Hoffman*, above n 32, 12.

[34] I further discuss the right to form workers' associations of undocumented migrants in V Mantouvalou, 'Organising Against Abuse and Exclusion: The Associational Rights of Undocumented Migrants' in C Costello and M Freedland (eds), *Migrants at Work* (Oxford, Oxford University Press, 2014 forthcoming).

From the above examples, it emerges that aspects of labour legislation are conditional on compliance with immigration rules. Both UK and US courts found that components of the right to work under international human rights law (the right to organise, protection from dismissal, the right to a minimum wage) are tied to the right to work under immigration rules, which only certain categories of migrants have. Is it correct to say that someone who has no legal right to work because of immigration law should not have human rights at work? Some tribunals and courts have not been troubled by this formulation. If the human right to work is interpreted as a right to non-exploitative work, as this chapter argues, the above decisions pose problems.

The dissent in the US Supreme Court decision highlighted the following issue: 'The policy of *applying* labor laws must encompass a policy of *enforcing* the labor laws effectively. Otherwise, "we would leave helpless the very persons who most need protection from exploitative employer practices"'.[35] The same problem was emphasised in a different context, in the Report of the EU Fundamental Rights Agency on the rights of undocumented migrants: 'An employment relationship where core labour law rights are disregarded becomes exploitative'.[36] Is this correct? In order to address this question, I will discuss the concept of exploitation, which must be central in this setting.

IV The Exploitation of Undocumented Migrants

What is exploitation? Is it correct to say that undocumented migrants are exploited? The concept of exploitation is contested and has been analysed at length in literature.[37] In much of the scholarship it is discussed against the background of the theory of Karl Marx. In the technical sense developed by Marx, exploitation occurs when one class of non-workers appropriates the surplus product of a class of workers.[38] On this analysis, exploitation is a condition that always exists in a capitalist society, so the discussion of the right to work in this context would primarily be viewed as a right to be exploited.[39] This is not necessarily morally wrong, though, because there is a difference between the Marxist conception and other conceptions of exploitation.[40] Here I do not use the Marxist

[35] *Hoffman*, above n 32, dissenting opinion.

[36] FRA Report 2011, 47.

[37] As a starting point, see A Wertheimer and M Zwolinski, 'Exploitation' in EN Zalta (ed), *The Stanford Encyclopedia of Philosophy* (Spring 2013 edn), available at: plato.stanford.edu/archives/spr2013/entries/exploitation/. See also A Wertheimer, *Exploitation* (Princeton NJ, Princeton University Press, 1996); A Wood, 'Exploitation' in K Schaff (ed), *Philosophy and the Problems of Work: A Reader* (Lanham MD, Rowman & Littlefield Publishers, 2001) 141.

[38] See GA Cohen, 'Karl Marx and the Withering Away of Social Science' (1972) 1 *Philosophy and Public Affairs* 182; J Wolff, 'Marx and Exploitation' (1999) *Journal of Ethics* 105.

[39] See the discussion in Mundlak, 'The Right to Work – The Value of Work', above n 1, 345.

[40] R Arneson, 'What's Wrong with Exploitation?' (1981) 91 *Ethics* 202, 203.

conception of exploitation, though the conception that I develop may have certain common elements with it.

The type of exploitation that I want to focus on here is the abuse of a person's vulnerability that is created or exacerbated by law, in order to make profit. So the present conception of exploitation has three central elements: (a) vulnerability of a worker created or exacerbated by law, which I have also called 'legislative precariousness';[41] (b) abuse of this vulnerability that consists in the violation of labour and other human rights; and (c) an aim to make profit. Because this analysis of exploitation is based on taking advantage of someone's vulnerability, it is always a moral wrong that the law should not permit.

A Vulnerability Created or Exacerbated by Law

What do we mean by vulnerability? A person's vulnerability may be due to physical, mental or psychological characteristics. Lovers are vulnerable to those whom they love;[42] people with a disability may become vulnerable because of some physical characteristic which society sees as a weakness;[43] poor homeless people may become vulnerable because of desperate material need. All these people may be exploited because of their weaknesses.

Migrants are generally vulnerable for many reasons, and hence prone to exploitation. Their vulnerability may stem from factors such as poverty, language barriers or social isolation in a country that is not their own. It should not come as a surprise that the international community has recognised the vulnerability of migrants in international law. The United Nations adopted the 1990 International Convention on the Rights of All Migrant Workers and Members of their Families, which in its Preamble emphasises

> the situation of vulnerability in which migrant workers and members of their families frequently find themselves owing, among other things, to their absence from their State of origin and to the difficulties they may encounter arising from their presence in the State of employment.

Even though this Convention does not guarantee the right to access work of undocumented migrants, it protects their rights at work.[44] The UN Commission on Human Rights in a resolution on the 'Rights of Migrants' also emphasised

> the situation of vulnerability in which migrants frequently find themselves, owing, inter alia, to their absence from their State of origin and to the difficulties they encounter because of differences of language, custom and culture, as well as the economic and social difficulties and obstacles to the return of migrants, especially for those who are undocumented or in an irregular migratory situation, to their States of origin.[45]

[41] V Mantouvalou, 'Human Rights for Precarious Workers: The Legislative Precariousness of Domestic Labor' (2012) 34 *Comparative Labor Law & Policy Journal* 133.

[42] Wood, above n 37, 147.

[43] On the right to work of people with disability, see E Albin in this volume, ch 4.

[44] Arts 25 and 26.

[45] UN Commission on Human Rights, Resolution 2002/62, 'Human Rights of Migrant', Preamble.

Yet the focus of this chapter is not on physical, mental or psychological reasons that make someone vulnerable, even though reasons like poverty can also create vulnerability and lead to exploitation. My focus is on vulnerability created or exacerbated through legislation or legislative precariousness. To return to the classic, Marxist account for a moment, for Marx the whole class of workers is vulnerable and prone to exploitation in a capitalist system. For the purposes of this chapter, though, the definition of who is vulnerable is narrower. Workers may often (but not always) be vulnerable to their employers because of the relationship of economic dependency. However, migrant workers are made particularly vulnerable by law, through immigration rules.[46] Here I will not look at the background fairness of specific immigration restrictions; I simply argue that these create vulnerability that can lead to exploitation.

Migrants who have the right to remain in a country are much less vulnerable than the undocumented. However, even documented migrants may be vulnerable depending on the work permit they have. By way of an example of a visa regime that makes workers particularly vulnerable and prone to exploitation, in the United Kingdom since 2012 there has been a system of special visas for migrant domestic workers who accompany their employers from abroad. Under this regime, a migrant domestic worker who leaves her employer will be deported. Domestic workers under this visa have no right to change employer, not even within the same work sector. This makes this group of domestic workers exceptionally vulnerable and prone to exploitation, and it should not come as a surprise that a similar system has been found contrary to human dignity in other legal orders.[47] This type of visa also often leads these workers to irregularity. Other types of work permit are less restrictive, so they do not create the same degree of vulnerability. In other words, vulnerability exists because of various different visa regimes, and has degrees.

It is not only immigration law that makes workers vulnerable. Labour law also makes particular groups of workers prone to exploitation. Domestic workers, like Hounga in the case discussed earlier, are a typical example of a group of workers that are regularly made vulnerable through law in various legal orders.[48] Examples of vulnerability created by law for this group of workers include their exclusion

[46] B Anderson, 'Migration, Immigration Controls and the Fashioning of Precarious Workers' (2010) 24 *Work, Employment and Society* 300. Criminal law also makes migrants vulnerable. See D Guilfoyle, 'Transnational Criminal Law as a Governance Strategy in the Global Labour Market: Criminalizing Migration from Below' (2010) 29 *Refugee Survey Quarterly* 185.

[47] V Mantouvalou, 'What Is to Be Done for Migrant Domestic Workers?' in B Ryan (ed), *Labour Migration in Hard Times* (Liverpool, Institute of Employment Rights, 2013). There was a similar visa regime in Israel, which has been ruled unconstitutional by the Israeli Supreme Court. On this, see Albin, 'The Sectoral Regulatory Regime', above n 21.

[48] Mantouvalou, 'Human Rights for Precarious Workers', above n 41. See also C Murphy, 'The Enduring Vulnerability of Migrant Domestic Workers in Europe' (2013) *International & Comparative Law Quarterly* 599; E Albin, 'From Domestic Servant to Domestic Worker' in J Fudge, S McCrystal and K Sankaran (eds), *Challenging the Legal Boundaries of Work Regulation* (Oxford, Hart Publishing, 2012) 231.

from labour inspections, minimum wage and maximum working hours' legislation.[49]

The undocumented are no doubt more vulnerable than most other groups of migrant workers. Because they have no authorisation to be in the country and no right to work in immigration law, they wish to remain invisible to the authorities, and are less likely than other workers to report abuse. They know that if they do so, they may be arrested and deported, so they prefer to remain hidden from the police. All these characteristics make undocumented workers uniquely vulnerable to exploitation, a situation that is recognised in international and European law. The UN Migrant Workers Convention states already in its Preamble that undocumented workers are employed in less favourable conditions than other groups of workers, and contains several provisions that target this specific group of workers.[50] The EU Fundamental Rights Agency has issued two important reports on the rights of undocumented workers: one involving a comparative study of the fundamental rights of undocumented migrants in the EU, and the other involving undocumented migrant domestic workers in particular.[51] The doctrine of illegality takes this vulnerability to an extreme.

B Abuse of Vulnerability Consisting in the Disrespect of Fundamental Labour Rights and Other Human Rights

The vulnerability of undocumented migrant workers, as illustrated above, makes them prone to disrespect of their labour rights and other human rights. Employers, in turn, regularly take advantage of this situation: they pay them below the minimum wage, disregard health and safety rules, threaten that they will denounce them to the authorities should they attempt to claim their fundamental rights, dismiss them without compensation should they exercise these rights.[52] This is frequently documented in the press:

> The employer knew we were undocumented workers. He hired us knowing that, and took advantage of us by not paying us overtime. He knew we were vulnerable and desperate. He never expected us to stand up for our rights, our human rights.[53]

In fact, such is the vulnerability of these people that employers violate not only their fundamental labour rights, but also other human rights, such as the right to life or the prohibition of inhuman and degrading treatment.[54]

[49] See Mantouvalou, 'Human Rights for Precarious Workers', above n 41.

[50] See, for instance, Arts 25(3) and 28.

[51] FRA Report 2011; EU Fundamental Right Agency Report, 'Migrants in an Irregular Situation Employed in Domestic Work: Fundamental Rights Challenges for the European Union and its Member States' 2011.

[52] For discussion, see FRA Report 2011.

[53] P Harris, 'Undocumented Workers' Grim Reality: Speak Out on Abuse and Risk Deportation' *The Guardian* (28 March 2013) available at: www.theguardian.com/world/2013/mar/28/undocumented-migrants-worker-abuse-deportation.

[54] There are numerous examples of abuse in the press: see, for instance, Amnesty International, 'Greece: Despair Pervades Camps as 33 Migrant Workers Shot in Manolada' (22 April 2013) available

The examples of *Hounga* and *Hoffman* show how undocumented workers are not viewed as holders of fundamental rights, such as freedom of association, protection from unfair dismissal or the right to a minimum wage. Employers often prefer to employ them, rather than other workers, exactly because they know that they can treat them below some basic standards with limited or no accountability for doing so. And this is not only due to the fact that in reality the undocumented will prefer to remain invisible to the authorities for fear of deportation, but also because of the fact that the employers do not have a duty to respect their fundamental labour rights under the law, which leaves them in a legal black hole.

C Employer's Profit

The third element of the conception of exploitation that I develop here is the employer's profit. For a Marxist, this final element, namely the employer's profit, would probably be sufficient for a relationship to be described as exploitative. The previous two elements of the conception of exploitation that I presented would not be necessary for a situation of exploitation to exist. This is because on a Marxist analysis, making profit as an employer through the workers' labour is what constitutes exploitation. On the analysis of this chapter, though, exploitation exists when someone abuses the vulnerability of another, which is due to her legislative precariousness. So on the present analysis the previous two elements are also essential. There is a special moral wrong in abusing vulnerability in order to make profit:

> Proper respect for others is violated when we treat their vulnerabilities as opportunities to advance our own interests or projects. It is degrading to have your weaknesses taken advantage of, and dishonorable to use the weaknesses of others for your ends.[55]

In the situations described in this chapter, the employer takes advantage of the legal vulnerability of the undocumented in order to advance his or her interests. If the employer hired a worker who has a legal right to work in a country, he or she would have a duty to respect labour legislation, which would be costly: paying the minimum wage, respecting health and safety rules, giving compensation in case of unfair dismissal, respecting the right to unionise etc. By employing undocumented workers, the employer can disregard these fundamental labour rights.

Unsurprisingly, in some legal orders making profit by exploiting a worker is not allowed: an undocumented migrant can recover her unpaid salary, for example, under the law of unjust enrichment.[56] UK courts have not examined such a claim of unjust enrichment so far. It could be said that the right to wages is a contractual right that could not be enforced. However, the right to restitution of the

at: www.amnesty.org/en/news/greece-despair-pervades-camps-after-33-migrant-workers-shot-manolada-2013-04-22; The facts of the *Hounga* case, discussed earlier, also illustrate this.

[55] Wood, above n 37, 153.

[56] This is the case, eg, in Germany and in Greece.

value of services in the absence of a valid contract is not a contractual right, but arises by operation of law, and unless the employer can take the benefit of the illegality defence, the employee should be entitled to the market value of her services, which may well be much higher than what the employer promised to pay.[57] Yet the illegality doctrine might still bar this type of claim in UK courts. More importantly, an unjust enrichment claim would not be sufficient for the argument developed in this piece, which is that when someone is employed, she should enjoy all fundamental rights at work, and not only a right to decent pay.

Someone might say that the situation discussed here is not morally reprehensible, because the relationship is mutually advantageous for the migrant worker and the employer. This is because the alternative for the worker (deportation and a life in great poverty) would be worse than being employed in the receiving country. A different way to put this is that the worker was a free agent who decided to cross the border unlawfully in order to get a job or to remain in the country after the expiration of her visa. The worker chose to stay employed in these conditions. Such an argument should be rejected. The choice between two extremely bad alternatives is not genuine choice. As Jeremy Waldron put it:

> If we value freedom in each particular case because of the importance of choice and of not being constrained in the choices one makes, then that value ought to direct some attention to how many choices a person has left after each constraint has been exercised.[58]

As in most of the examples of undocumented workers there is a lack of alternatives (and in some of the examples, like *Hounga*, there may even be elements of human trafficking), it cannot be said that they have exercised genuine choice as free agents. The employer's behaviour is still morally wrong.[59]

The situation that undocumented migrants face because they have no right to work under immigration law is exploitative, as this section has argued. Judicial decisions, such as *Hounga* and *Hoffman*, condone this exploitation through the law. Not only do they accept the exploitative conduct, but they also create further conditions for exploitation by stripping undocumented workers from other key aspects of the right to work. Undocumented workers are exploited. At a normative level the doctrine of illegality is not acceptable for it leads to exploitation. How do international human rights bodies address this situation of exploitation?

[57] I am grateful to Rob Chambers for making this point. On the law of unjust enrichment and exploitation, see P Saprai, 'Unconscionable Enrichment?' in R Chambers, C Mitchell and J Penner (eds), *The Law of Unjust Enrichment* (Oxford, Oxford University Press, 2009) 417. See also, E Dewhurst, 'The Right of Irregular Immigrants to Back Pay: The Spectrum of Protection in International, Regional and National Legal Systems' in C Costello and M Freedland (eds) *Migrants at Work* (Oxford, Oxford University Press, 2014 forthcoming). This is also the position under the EU Employer Sanctions Directive, Directive 2009/52/EC.

[58] J Waldron, 'Homelessness and the Issue of Freedom' in J Waldron, *Liberal Rights – Collected Papers* (Cambridge, Cambridge University Press, 1993) 309, 330.

[59] See further, Wood, above n 37, 153–54.

V Non-Exploitation as a Human Rights Principle

Human rights law does not explicitly recognise a right not to be exploited, which this chapter develops. We do not find such a provision in human rights treaties or constitutional documents. Yet there are aspects of it in international documents that were discussed earlier, and principles in human rights jurisprudence that can counteract the problem of the exploitation of undocumented workers. These principles that capture and prohibit the exploitation that was presented in the previous sections can be found in cases of the European and inter-American human rights systems.

At European level, it was earlier said that the ESC explicitly protects the right to work. However, in its Appendix, the Charter excludes most migrants from its personal scope. For this reason, undocumented migrants would most probably not be able to have a claim heard by the European Committee of Social Rights.[60] That undocumented migrants are generally excluded from the scope of the ESC does not mean that the Council of Europe as an organisation does not recognise the challenges that this group of individuals face. In 2006, for instance, the Council of Europe's Parliamentary Assembly adopted a resolution entitled 'Human Rights of Irregular Migrants'[61] that stated that there were at the time between three and five million irregular migrants in Europe, living and working in deplorable conditions. The Assembly urged Member States to protect at least a 'core minimum' of rights of irregular migrants. The labour and social rights identified included fair wages and working conditions, compensation for accidents, access to justice and trade union rights for all those that work.[62]

Turning to the European Convention on Human Rights (ECHR), its Article 1 protects the rights of everyone within Member States' jurisdiction. It does not distinguish between citizens and non-citizens, documented and undocumented migrants. The ECHR is not primarily about workers' rights. Being a traditional liberal document, it mainly protects civil and political rights. It only contains two labour rights: the prohibition of slavery, servitude, forced and compulsory labour (Article 4) and the right to form and join a trade union (Article 11). It also prohibits discrimination, not as a free-standing right to equality, but in the enjoyment of other Convention rights (Article 14).[63] The American Convention on Human Rights similarly primarily protects civil and political rights. In the jurisprudence of the European Court of Human Rights (ECtHR) and the Inter-

[60] *cf* Complaint No 14/2003, *International Federation of Human Rights Leagues (FIDH) v France*, Decision of 8 September 2004; and Complaint No 47/2008, *Defence for Children International (DCI) v Netherlands*, Decision of 20 October 2009.

[61] Council of Europe, Parliamentary Assembly Resolution 1509 (2006).

[62] ibid, para 13.

[63] The more recent Protocol 12 of the ECHR contains a free-standing equality clause.

American Court of Human Rights, though, we find that these documents can capture certain fundamental interests underlying the right to work.[64]

Of course, human rights law, such as the ECHR, has traditionally addressed the conduct of state authorities, rather than private individuals (employers in this case). Yet human rights law has over recent years been found to give rise to positive state obligations to regulate private conduct in several jurisdictions.[65] Positive obligations can be imposed when there is an imbalance of power between private parties, and state authorities know or ought to have known that one of the private actors abused the position of power. The imbalance of power between parties that requires positive intervention is very familiar in labour law, where it is used to justify unionisation or legislative intervention. The existence of positive obligations, it ought to be explained, does not mean that an individual who has a claim under the Convention can turn against another individual directly. The horizontal effect of the ECHR is indirect: it is the state that may be liable for failing to protect individuals from abuse by other individuals. The Court has frequently ruled that human rights are applicable in the employment relationship because of lack of legislation to protect vulnerable groups or because of judicial decisions (actions of state organs) that misapplied or did not take account of Convention rights.[66] When it comes to the issue that this chapter addresses, the exploitation of undocumented migrant workers, these positive obligations are particularly pertinent. The reason for this is that the situation of vulnerability that employers abuse, as the earlier section argued, is created by law. This direct state action, then, has created legislative precariousness that leads to exploitation. This is an additional reason why the state bears a legal obligation to address the resulting human rights violations in the private sphere.

It was earlier said that human rights can sometimes legitimately be made conditional on a status. This section shows that the right to non-exploitative work should not be made conditional on a right to work granted through a work permit. I will, first, examine the prohibition of discrimination that shows that when it comes to labour rights, like a right to a minimum wage or the right to health and safety at work, conditionality on immigration status is unacceptable. The section will then turn to situations of grave exploitation. In human rights law, these situations have been classified as a breach of the prohibition of slavery, servitude,

[64] See, for instance, R O'Connell, 'The Right to Work in the European Convention on Human Rights' (2012) 2 *European Human Rights Law Review* 176; K Ewing and J Hendy, 'The Dramatic Implications of *Demir and Baykara*' (2010) 39 *Industrial Law Journal* 2; V Mantouvalou, 'Labour Rights in the European Convention on Human Rights: An Intellectual Justification for an Integrated Approach to Interpretation' (2013) 13 *Human Rights Law Review* 529; V Mantouvalou, 'The Protection of the Right to Work Through the European Convention on Human Rights',(2014) *Cambridge Yearbook of European Legal Studies*, forthcoming; R McCrea, 'Religion in the Workplace: *Eweida and Others v United Kingdom*' (2014) 77 *Modern Law Review* 277.

[65] For analysis of positive obligations under the ECHR, see A Mowbray, *The Development of Positive Obligations under the European Convention on Human Rights by the European Court of Human Rights* (Oxford, Hart Publishing, 2004).

[66] *Wilson and Palmer v UK* App nos 30668/96, 30671/96 and 30678/96 (ECtHR, 2 July 2002); *IB v Greece* App no 552/10 (ECtHR, 3 October 2013).

forced and compulsory labour, which imposes duties that are again never conditional on migration status. It will be shown here that in international human rights jurisprudence, there is an implicit, universal right not to be exploited.

A The Prohibition of Discrimination and the Conditionality of Human Rights

The ECHR contains a non-discrimination provision, which is not a free-standing equality right: instead, it prohibits discrimination in the enjoyment of the rest of the Convention rights. It also contains a right of everyone to the peaceful enjoyment of their possessions (Article 1 of Additional Protocol 1). These two provisions were examined in the case of *Gaygusuz v Austria*,[67] which concerned social rights: the social security benefits of foreign nationals. As Article 14 is not a free-standing provision that can be invoked on its own, applicants have to demonstrate that the conduct in question 'falls within the ambit' of some other Convention right.[68] In *Gaygusuz*, the applicant was a Turkish national lawfully resident and working in Austria, who had paid contributions to an unemployment insurance fund in the same way as Austrian nationals. The authorities refused to pay an advance on his pension as an emergency payment under Austrian legislation for the sole reason that he did not have Austrian nationality. He claimed that this treatment was discriminatory, and hence contrary to Article 14 of the Convention in conjunction with Article 1 of Protocol 1, which states that '[e]very natural or legal person is entitled to the peaceful enjoyment of his possessions'.

Reading social rights into the right to property, the ECtHR held that the benefit that Gaygusuz claimed could be classified as 'possessions', so that his situation was within the ambit of Article 1 of Additional Protocol 1. Turning to Article 14, the Court considered whether the difference of treatment between the applicant, on the one hand, and Austrian nationals, on the other, was justified. It ruled that it was not based on an 'objective and reasonable justification'. The Court referred to the possibility of granting state authorities some discretion in the area of the social rights of migrants, by mentioning its margin of appreciation doctrine, but stressed that 'very weighty reasons would have to be put forward before the Court could regard a difference of treatment based exclusively on the ground of nationality as compatible with the Convention'.[69] There was therefore a violation of the prohibition of discrimination in conjunction with the right to property. A similar finding was also made in a case where the authorities refused a non-contributory disability benefit to the applicant who was a documented migrant.[70] The same

[67] *Gaygusuz v Austria* App no 17371/90 (ECtHR, September 1996).
[68] See, for instance, *Thlimmenos v Greece* App no 34369/97 (GC, 6 April 2000).
[69] *Gaygusuz*, above n 67, para 42. On the margin of appreciation, see G Letsas, 'Two Concepts of the Margin of Appreciation' (2006) 26 *Oxford Journal of Legal Studies* 705.
[70] *Koua Poirrez v France* App no 40892/98 (ECtHR, 30 September 2003).

principle was endorsed in cases on maternity and child benefits of foreign nationals with limited residence rights[71] or those that have the status of a refugee[72] under Article 8 (the right to private life) in conjunction with Article 14.

The case law under Article 14 of the ECHR shows that at least documented migrants, even those with limited residence rights, cannot be treated differently in the enjoyment of their social rights for the sole reason of their nationality or residence status. The ECtHR has frequently classified salaries as property,[73] so at least the property-related social rights of migrants would be protected. The justification for different treatment of similar situations has to be strong. It has to satisfy a strict test of proportionality, which state authorities have failed to pass so far. Documented migrants may even establish a right to work under the ECHR, which does not explicitly contain such a provision.[74] Finally, people who enter a country unlawfully, in order to seek asylum, are generally protected under the Convention.[75]

More importantly for the present discussion, following *Hoffman* of the US Supreme Court, Mexico submitted a request for an Advisory Opinion to the Inter-American Court of Human Rights. A key question asked of the Court was whether immigration status can be a legitimate condition for the protection of fundamental labour rights. The Court, in its landmark opinion 'Juridical Condition and Rights of the Undocumented Migrants',[76] stated that workers' rights can *only* be dependent on the status of someone as a worker, and not on the status of someone as a lawful migrant:

> Labor rights necessarily arise from the circumstance of being a worker, understood in the broadest sense. A person who is to be engaged, is engaged or has been engaged in a remunerated activity, immediately becomes a worker and, consequently, acquires the rights inherent in that condition [. . .] [T]he migratory status of a person can never be a justification for depriving him of the enjoyment and exercise of his human rights, including those related to employment.[77]

Some human rights can legitimately be made conditional on a certain status, as was stated earlier in this chapter. However, only certain conditions (and only in respect of certain labour rights) are acceptable, as it emerges from this section.

[71] *Niedzwiecki v Germany* App no 58453/00 (ECtHR, 25 October 2005).

[72] *Fawsie v Greece* App no 40080/07 (ECtHR, 28 October 2010).

[73] P Herzfeld Olsson, 'Every Natural or Legal Person is Entitled to the Peaceful Enjoyment of His or Her Possessions: Article 1, Protocol 1 to the European Convention on Human Rights' in F Dorssemont et al (eds) *The European Convention on Human Rights and the Employment Relation* (Oxford, Hart Publishing, 2013) 381, 400 ff; and T Novitz, 'Labour Rights and Property Rights: Implications for (and Beyond) Redundancy Payments and Pensions?' (2012) 41 *Industrial Law Journal* 136.

[74] *Bigaeva v Greece* App no 26713/05 (ECtHR, 28 May 2009). For an overview of the case law on migrants, see Y Ktistakis, *Protecting Migrants under the European Convention on Human Rights and the European Social Charter* (Strasbourg, Council of Europe Publishing, 2013).

[75] See *MSS v Belgium and Greece* App no 30696/09 (GC, 21 January 2011.

[76] *Juridical Condition and Rights of the Undocumented Migrants*, Advisory Opinion OC-18/03 (17 September 2003), IACtHR (Ser A) No 18 (2003). Noted by SH Cleveland, 'Legal Status and Rights of Undocumented Workers' (2005) 99 *American Journal of International Law* 460.

[77] Advisory Opinion, above n 76, paras 133–34.

Making the right to non-exploitative work conditional on immigration status is illegitimate. Exploitation of a worker because she or he has no right to work under immigration rules violates international human rights law.

The underlying reason why courts in the United States and the United Kingdom make labour rights conditional on immigration status involves immigration policy, as the dissent in *Hoffman* recognises.[78] Yet accepting that labour rights can be violated for immigration policy reasons is contrary to basic values that are central in human rights law.[79] Many will accept that an undocumented migrant may be legitimately arrested and detained with a view to deportation, so his or her right to liberty would be limited.[80] However, an undocumented migrant still has a right to be free from torture, while in detention, as well as a right to expression, association and private life. This would be true even if it were proven that the violation of these rights would discourage migrants from entering a country without authorisation. It is only a limited number of human rights, which can be made conditional on immigration status. The Advisory Opinion of the Inter-American Court of Human Rights shows that the right to non-exploitative work can never be made conditional on immigration status. This approach makes the position on illegality and labour rights of UK, US and other courts very questionable.

B The Prohibition of Slavery, Servitude, Forced and Compulsory Labour

Traditional liberal documents, such as the ECHR, do not only prohibit discrimination, they also capture the gravest forms of labour exploitation as such by prohibiting slavery, servitude, forced and compulsory labour. At the heart of Article 4 of the ECHR lies the idea of exploitation. Looking at the provision, the UK Supreme Court itself recognised that '[f]orced labour is not fully defined and may take various forms, but exploitation is at its heart'.[81]

The ECtHR has examined the link between exploitation and slavery in the context of the exploitation of a domestic worker. In recent years, there has been analysis in judicial decision-making and academic literature of what is sometimes called 'modern slavery'. Some of the debate in Europe at least was triggered by a decision of the ECtHR, in *Siliadin v France*,[82] which involved the living and work-

[78] *Hoffman*, above n 32, dissenting opinion.

[79] On equality as a foundation of the ECHR, see G Letsas, *A Theory of Interpretation of the European Convention on Human Rights*, 2nd edn (Oxford, Oxford University Press, 2008). On dignity as a justification of human rights, see C McCrudden, 'Human Dignity and Judicial Interpretation of Human Rights' (2008) 19 *European Journal of International Law* 655.

[80] Even this has limitations. See C Costello, 'Immigration Detention: The Ground Beneath our Feet' (2015) *Current Legal Problems*, forthcoming.

[81] *Reilly & Anor, R (on the application of) v Secretary of State for Work and Pensions* [2013] UKSC 68, para 81.

[82] *Siliadin v France* App no 73316/01 (ECtHR, 26 July 2005). For analysis, see V Mantouvalou, 'Servitude and Forced Labour in the 21st Century: The Human Rights of Domestic Workers' (2006) 35 *Industrial Law Journal* 135.

ing conditions of a migrant domestic worker, who had faced a situation similar to Hounga (without the element of physical abuse). The applicant submitted an application to the ECtHR, claiming that her situation should be classified as slavery, servitude, forced and compulsory labour, which should in turn constitute a criminal offence in French law. In its ruling, the Court found that the applicant's treatment breached the prohibition of slavery, servitude, forced and compulsory labour under the ECHR.

The ECtHR said that the applicant's situation was not slavery, if defined as 'classical slavery'. It said that 'slavery' ought to be interpreted narrowly, according to the 1927 United Nations Slavery Convention, which provides that 'slavery is the status or condition of a person over whom any or all of the powers attaching to the right of ownership are exercised'.[83] However, the Court said that there was a breach of the prohibition of servitude. The concept of 'servitude', in the Court's view, is somewhat more general and broad. When examining servitude, the Court stated that it prohibits a 'particularly serious form of denial of freedom'.[84] It includes an obligation to provide certain services for someone, an obligation to live in another person's property and the impossibility of changing this condition.[85] The concept of servitude may under some conditions be able to capture the situation of those who are exploited, like Siliadin and Hounga.

The concept of exploitation, as developed in this chapter, is broader than the concept of slavery, servitude, forced and compulsory labour. Undocumented migrant workers may be exploited, but their situation does not always amount to a breach of Article 4 of the Convention, which is about the worst forms of exploitation. However, we can identify two common elements between slavery and servitude, on one hand, and exploitation, on the other: First, a slave/serf cannot claim wages because the contract is illegal. Second, a slave/serf cannot report abuse to the authorities for reasons such as the fear of deportation. She is treated like an object, rather than a subject of rights. This is sometimes the position of exploited undocumented migrants too: they cannot claim wages, and they cannot go to the authorities. The effect of immigration rules in situations such as those discussed here is that they objectify workers in a manner similar to classical slaves. This is contrary to human rights law.

In *Siliadin*, it will be recalled, the Court stated that for grave labour rights violations that can be classified as servitude, forced and compulsory labour, criminal legislation is essential. The thinking underlying the Court's decision was that criminal law is effective in deterring the conduct in question. In its judgment the Court did not examine whether labour legislation is also needed in order to address the problem. Yet there is nothing in the reasoning and decision of the Court that would limit the requirement to criminal law. If immigration law, contract law or labour law rules, such as the doctrine of illegality in English law, create situations of vulnerability that lead to exploitation, the ECtHR may rule that the

[83] *Siliadin*, above n 82, para 122.
[84] *Van Droogenbroeck v Belgium* (Commission Report, 9 July 1980); Series B no 44, 30, paras 78, 80.
[85] *Van Droogenbroeck v Belgium* App no 7906/77 (Commission Decision, 5 July 1979); 17 DR 59.

law in question violates the Convention; it may decide that other protective legislation is needed, and that this may not only be criminal; it may also be labour legislation.

What emerges from this section is that even though in human rights law there is no right not to be exploited as such, there are several provisions which are pertinent to the right to non-exploitative work. These provisions protect a category of workers who are vulnerable because of the law, and indicate that the right to non-exploitative work is universal – as much as other human rights are.

VI Conclusion – The Right to Non-Exploitative Work

This chapter rests on the belief that the right to work should be interpreted as a right to non-exploitative work. In the case of undocumented migrants, denial of a right to work in immigration law guarantees their exploitation. Even though my focus is on undocumented migrants and their special vulnerability (or legislative precariousness), the argument that the right to work should be read as a right to non-exploitative work applies equally to all workers.

As a matter of human rights law, it is crucial to appreciate that the right to work protects against exploitation, for exploitative work fails to satisfy other justifications of the right to work too: workers that are exploited cannot be self-fulfilled or feel dignified. The law in the two legal orders discussed here permits the exploitation of a most vulnerable group of workers. On the courts' analysis, someone who enters a country unlawfully is rightly deprived of the right not to be exploited. This cannot be correct. To the extent that certain labour rights are human rights, these cannot be made conditional on a work permit. International human rights law, as section V of the chapter showed, has supported this position by capturing and prohibiting this exploitation as discriminatory, and as a breach of the prohibition of slavery, servitude, forced and compulsory labour.

Immigration rules cannot and should not be enforced through the exclusion of human rights. This will probably be counterproductive: the more employers know that they can exploit undocumented workers, the more they will seek to employ these workers. Most importantly, it is problematic as a matter of principle, and it breaches the right to non-exploitative work, which is implicit in human rights law.

4

Universalising the Right to Work of Persons with Disabilities: An Equality and Dignity Based Approach

EINAT ALBIN*

What is done in the name of disability today will have meaning for all of society's tomorrows (Irving Kenneth Zola).[1]

Introduction

Rarely do labour law theories draw on disability studies. However, with the growing acceptance that both disability and labour are human rights issues that are concerned with dignity and equality, and that both fields of study tempt to address the social context of disadvantage,[2] an opportunity emerges to bring the two discourses together. In this chapter, I take advantage of this opportunity to discuss the right to work. The interest lies in the new and crucially important direction that Article 27 of the Convention on the Rights of Persons with Disabilities (hereafter the CRPD or the Convention) has taken. Article 27, the latest international human rights instrument that has been adopted regarding the right to work, offers what I consider to be an innovative and welcome approach towards this

* Thanks are due to Guy Davidov, Sagit Mor, Adva Eichengreen, Roni Rothler and Virginia Mantouvalou for their extremely valuable comments. I have also benefited from a discussion with Guy Mundlak.

[1] IK Zola, 'Toward the Necessary Universalizing of a Disability Policy' (1989) 67 *The Milbank Quarterly* 401, 422.

[2] 'Labour law is chiefly concerned with this elementary phenomenon of social power' said Kahn-Freund. See: P Davies and M Freedland, *Kahn-Freund's Labour and the Law* (London, Stevens & Sons, 1983) 14. Since then labour law developed to address the social construction of gender (see S Fredman, *Women and the Law* (Oxford, Oxford Monographs on Labour Law Clarendon, 1997)), race, migration etc. Disability studies have also sprung from exposing the social construction of disability. See generally M Oliver, *Understanding Disability: From Theory to Practice* (Hampshire, Macmillan, 1996); and V Finkelstein, *Attitudes and Disabled People: Issues for Discussion* (New York, World Rehabilitation Fund, 1980) and discussion further below.

right, while addressing some of the main concerns that were raised in the literature regarding the right to work as adopted in other international human rights documents and implemented in practice.

The aim of the chapter is twofold. First, it offers an account of the right to work as it is adopted in Article 27 by drawing on two main theories: critical disability studies and Nussbaum's capabilities theory. In doing so, I claim that the provision adopts an important new approach – one which offers a structural–institutional equality prism, while respecting one's dignity, and that places meaningful obligations on states – stressing how this approach addresses some of the main concerns raised in the general discourse on the right to work. With structural–institutional equality I mean a duty to restructure the social institutions, resulting in proactive structural change, while acknowledging the social contextual causes of inequality.[3] Dignity, as proposed below, is achieved through respect for personal freedom and the idea of inclusion. Second, it leans on that analysis to argue that a reason exists for a universal application of Article 27 to persons that are not considered to experience disability – not only within the field of disability studies, which encompasses Zola's above-quoted words – but also in the field of labour.

A discussion on Article 27 is important for the theory on the right to work due to three main reasons. First, as noted, Article 27 is the latest international human rights instrument adopted regarding this right, and thus its analysis provides a more updated and fuller understanding of the right to work as it manifests in the international legal sphere. Although on a declarative level it has been said that the CRPD did not develop any new human right – for its mandate was only to apply existing human rights adjusted to the situation of persons with disabilities[4] – such adjustment brings to the fore a new and interesting interpretation of those human rights, including the right to work.

Second, it has always been challenging to focus research on persons with disabilities, due to the tension created by the fact that political and social theory has largely neglected them.[5] The focus on persons with disabilities enables scholars to develop a fuller account of society and its members and to think rigorously about theories of justice and of human rights.[6] In the case of the right to work, a rigorous new account of this right emerges due to the analysis offered by critical disability studies, which views the problems of achieving dignity and equality as bound by social context. It is generally accepted today that disability is not attributed to impairment but mainly to social, economic and physical environmental factors. However, disability studies scholars such as Tom Shakespeare point out that despite the importance of the social context to shaping disability, character

[3] On the structural–institutional equality approach see S Fredman, 'Disability Equality: A Challenge to the Existing Anti-Discrimination Paradigm?' in C Gooding and A Lawson (eds), *Disability Rights in Europe: From Theory to Practice* (Oxford, Oxford University Press, 2005) 199, 212.

[4] R Kayess and P French, 'Out of Darkness into Light? Introducing the Convention on the Rights of Persons with Disabilities' (2008) 8 *Human Rights Law Review* 1, 20.

[5] M Nussbaum, *Frontiers of Justice: Disability, Nationality, Species Membership* (Cambridge MA, Harvard University Press, 2006) 2.

[6] ibid.

and impairment can still impact one's choice and feelings.[7] Hence, there is a blurred line between impairment, personal decisions and the environment, which requires delicate theoretical and practical thought on every aspect of life, including employment. For example, some discussions on the right to work of persons with disabilities follow a general line of argument that within the right social–economic and physical environment, disabled persons can reach the goal of full equality in the labour market. In reality, however, the situation is more complex. While most persons with disabilities wish to integrate into the labour market and seek every opportunity to do so, some are capable of working but find personal difficulty entering the market (many times such difficulty is embedded in previous social orders that they ascribe to), and others still experience severe impairments that challenge such entry (a limitation resulting also from the social context, which thus should be assessed carefully).

Drawing on critical disability studies I claim that Article 27 addresses this complex reality, offering a new theoretical direction that deals more adequately with the social context and with personal constraints. Because the situation described above is true for other persons in society as well, such a direction can also be fruitful for discussions of the right to work regarding different groups. Discussions on the implications of the social context have been central to labour studies in theorising the working lives (or lack of remunerated work) of many persons who are not considered to be disabled. Moreover, personal constraints extend beyond a situation of severe impairment that denies access to the market.

Third, Article 27 lies within an international instrument that posits ideas of equality and of dignity.[8] These two notions also serve as a central moral compass for other international human rights documents referring to the general right to work, and apply to all persons – those within the market and those situated outside it. Additionally, equality and dignity are central to labour theory and thought,[9] and thus can be used to guide the reading of the general right to work as well. This notion is related to the idea of universalism. Currently, universalism is a concept that is viewed via the lens through which Zola presents it and as entrenched in the idea of 'universal design'. The CRPD defines 'universal design' as 'the design of products, environments, programmes and services to be usable by all people, to

[7] T Shakespeare and N Watson, 'The Social Model of Disability: An Outdated Ideology?' (2002) 2 *Research in Social Science and Disability* 9; T Shakespeare, *Disability Rights and Wrongs* (Abingdon, Routledge, 2006) ch 3.

[8] The Preamble of the CRPD begins with the following words: 'State Parties to the Present Convention *Recalling* the principles proclaimed in the Charter of the United Nations which recognize the inherent dignity and worth and the equal and inalienable rights of all members of the human family as the foundation of freedom, justice and peace in the world'.

[9] There have been several referrals to the idea of equality in labour studies. Some address it in the sense of dealing with inequality of bargaining power; some in respect of equality regarding disadvantaged groups; and it has also been discussed in relation to the right to work. See Bob Hepple's work discussed at p 69 below. The idea of dignity is also fundamental in labour studies and numerous pieces of scholarly work have addressed it. One of the latest discussions is found in MR Freedland and N Kountouris, *The Legal Construction of Personal Work Relations* (Oxford, Oxford University Press, 2011) 371.

the greatest extent possible, without the need for adaptation or specialized design' (Article 2). Accordingly, authors who put forward the idea of universality from within disability studies claim that the approach adopted for persons with disabilities can significantly affect others because there is a high probability that most people will be disabled at some point during the course of their lives, and also because developing regulations for persons with disabilities can positively affect others.

However, and as I claim in this chapter, a justification exists for universalising Article 27 to all society by leaning on labour insights on the reasons for inequality and lack of dignity regarding other groups that experience disadvantage. These theories point out that many others are also bound by the social, economic and physical environment, and that they, too, have personal constraints. Additionally, and crucially, those 'others' have become the majority in today's labour market. Therefore, universalising the right to work as established in Article 27 should not be justified only on the grounds of disability theory, which sees it as something that will *residually* benefit other members of society, but rather because Article 27 has *primary* shared theoretical grounds with labour studies on disadvantage. Hence, not only does a high probability exist that we will all be disabled at some point or another, but also the claim is that most of society is socially, economically and physically disabled, and therefore the attainment of dignity and equality for all should be based on the same basis as that demonstrated in Article 27. Notably, this should lead to the adoption of a similar approach towards other groups in society, without denying, however, the provision of special attention and consideration in the operation of the right to work to persons with disabilities.

I apply in this chapter two theories for the reading of equality and dignity as entrenched in the right to work in Article 27 and the CRPD. The first is critical disability studies and the second is Nussbaum's capabilities approach. On the basis of these two theories, I point out four principles that are particularly important for understanding the right to work of persons with disabilities: the structural–institutional equality principle; the individual freedom principle; the inclusion principle; and the state responsibility principle. I claim that a similar theoretical apparatus is found in labour literature on the disadvantage of many other groups, thus justifying the universalising of the approach adopted in Article 27 to other groups in the population.

Accordingly, the chapter is structured as follows: section I introduces the situation of persons with disabilities at work and the theoretical discussion on the right to work generally and on the right to work of persons with disabilities more particularly. Section II offers a reading of Article 27 along the lines of critical disability studies and Nussbaum's capabilities approach, while presenting the four principles outlined above. Section III puts forward a justification for the universal implications of the right of persons with disabilities to work from the field of labour studies, and section IV concludes.

I Persons with Disabilities and the Right to Work

The situation of persons with disabilities in the workforce is very disturbing.[10] No wonder, then, that the right to work as established in Article 27 is one of the cornerstones of the Convention.[11] Even though a high percentage of persons experiencing disability are able to work,[12] their labour force participation is low in many countries. Moreover, disabled persons who *do* work earn low wages and have poor working conditions. Article 27 was designed to address this situation, and it offers a structural–institutional equality approach to the right to work, while respecting one's dignity and by placing meaningful obligations on states. This part of the chapter begins with reviewing the data regarding the situation of persons with disabilities in the workplace, and then turns to discuss the general literature on the right to work.

A Persons with Disabilities at Work

In comparison to the general population, the labour force participation of persons with disabilities is very low. A study conducted by the Organisation for Economic Co-operation and Development (OECD) has shown that the employment rate of persons with disabilities in OECD countries stands at 44 per cent, in comparison to 75 per cent of persons without disabilities.[13] Among OECD member states, the rate of employment varies from country to country: in Poland, around 20 per cent of persons with disabilities are employed and 80 per cent are unemployed or inactive; in Austria, approximately 45 per cent of disabled persons are employed and 55 per cent are unemployed or inactive;[14] in the United Kingdom, 38.9 per cent of persons with disabilities are employed in comparison to 68.6 per cent of persons employed in the overall population; in the United States, 38.1 per cent are employed whereas 73.2 per cent of the general population work; while in Japan only 22.7 per cent of disabled persons are employed as opposed to 59.4 per cent of the general population.[15] Critically, some persons with disabilities do not search for jobs and thus the figures may not provide the full picture of their status in the market.

Moreover, when persons with disabilities *are* employed, they usually find themselves in low paid jobs, at inferior occupational levels, with very limited

[10] On the definition of persons with disabilities see discussion below at p 77.

[11] UN Human Rights Council (2012) 'Thematic Study on the Work and Employment of Persons with Disabilities' (A/HCR/22/25) 3.

[12] World Health Organization, *World Report on Disability* (WHO, 2011) 235.

[13] OECD, *Sickness, Disability and Work: Breaking the Barriers* (OECD, 2010), 23.

[14] I Shima, E Zólyomi and A Zaidi, *The Labour Market Situation of People with Disabilities in EU25* (European Centre, Policy Brief, 2008) 4.

[15] *World Report on Disability*, above n 12, 238.

promotional prospects and poor working conditions.[16] Persons with disabilities might need more flexibility in work, as they may require additional time to prepare for work, to commute and to deal with health concerns.[17] The barriers they face stem both from environmental causes (resulting from lack of physical, communicative and emotional access to employment requisites such as job interviews, the physical infrastructure, social events with colleagues, etc) and from their own impairment. Additional barriers are social and economic. Social barriers, for example, are commonly related to negative attitudes or opinions, stigma and stereotypes.[18] Persons with disabilities are often seen as unfit for the requirements of the labour market and incapable of carrying out the necessary tasks. For that matter, the market does not value other contributions that the employment of persons with disabilities entails (in addition to productivity), such as the maximisation of human resources; the promotion of human dignity and social cohesion; and the accommodation of the increasing numbers of persons with disabilities found in the working-age population.[19]

Limited access to education and relevant training is a key reason for the problematic employment data presented above, as is the isolation of persons with disabilities in distinctive workplaces like sheltered workshops and dependence on social security benefits. The education and training of persons with disabilities is poorer than that of persons without disabilities; the same OECD study shows that in 2007 on average, the share of persons with disabilities with less than upper secondary education was almost twice the share of those without disabilities.[20] Their possibilities of procuring employment in the open market have been even more challenged in recent years, due to changes in economic activities, especially skill-based technological changes, the emergence of new major trade partners in the global economy and the shifts in low-scaled activities away from OECD countries. These transformations have disadvantaged persons with disabilities disproportionally.[21] Simultaneously, technological advancements created potential opportunities for persons with disabilities to enter occupations to which they were previously denied access. This progress, however, did not necessarily bring about changes in their employment participation, due to other causes of exclusion.

An in-depth study conducted by the World Health Organization (WHO) in 2011 pointed to four main barriers that persons with disabilities face in entering the labour market: lack of access; misconceptions about disabilities; discrimination; and the over-protection of some labour laws.[22] Regulation is thus perceived not only as a way to promote the right to work of persons with disabilities, but also as a possible obstacle for fulfilling that right. This outcome can materialise not only when countries fail to adopt anti-discriminatory measures, but also

[16] UN Human Rights Council report, above n 11, 4.
[17] *World Report on Disability*, above n 12, 239.
[18] ibid, 237.
[19] ibid, 236.
[20] OECD, *Sickness, Disability and Work*, above n 13, 27.
[21] ibid.
[22] *World Report on Disability*, above n 12, 239–40.

following adoption of a protective approach towards disabled persons. Such a protective approach might include shorter working days, more rest periods, longer paid leave, adjusted minimum wage and supported or sheltered employment – only for this group of workers. While these regulations were set to increase the involvement of persons with disabilities in the market, they might bring employers to view them as less productive, more costly and therefore undesirable.

Closely related to their poor situation in the labour market, persons with disabilities are poorer than others. The WHO study states that households with a person with a disability have higher rates of poverty than those without a disabled member. The study also showed that persons with disabilities have worse living conditions and fewer assets. Such data highlight the connection between poverty and disability. Poverty may lead to disability, through malnutrition, poor health care and dangerous working or living conditions, and at the same time, disability may lead to poverty as a consequence of lost earnings resulting from lack of employment or underemployment, and the additional costs persons with disabilities must bear for medical care, transportation and housing.[23]

It is on the basis of this reality, and through an acknowledgment of the need to promote the equality of persons with disabilities and to fulfil their potential to enter the labour market and strive to advance that the right to work was established in Article 27 of the CRPD. The right to work of persons with disabilities is especially important. Work remains the main source of income that society offers, but beyond financial considerations, it brings about intangible benefits as well. Work is an important element of self-esteem, of one's identity and self-perception. Employment can affect social status and socialisation, and is also psychologically beneficial because it makes people feel valued.[24] Placing these important aspects of work against the disturbing factors presented above makes the right to work of persons with disabilities an ever-pressing human right to fulfil and promote.

Adopted on 13 December 2006, the CRPD has been declared a landmark in the struggle to reframe the situation of persons with disabilities in terms of human rights.[25] As Article 1 of the CRPD states: 'The purpose of the present Convention is to promote, protect and ensure the full and equal enjoyment of all human rights and fundamental freedoms by all persons with disabilities, and to promote respect for their inherent dignity'. The CRPD entails a paradigmatic shift from viewing disability as a social welfare issue based on charity and pity, towards a rights-based

[23] ibid, 263.

[24] V Schultz, 'Life's Work' (2000) 100 *Columbia Law Review* 1881. See also G Mundlak, 'The Right to Work – The Value of Work' in D Barak-Erez and A Gross (eds), *Exploring Social Rights: Between Theory and Practice* (Oxford, Hart Publishing, 2007) 341 and further references there; G Davidov, 'The Right to Work as a Community and Individual Right and its Constitutional Potential' in Y Rabin and Y Shani (eds), *Economic Social and Cultural Rights in Israel* (Tel Aviv, Ramot Publishing, 2004) 533 (Hebrew).

[25] The Preamble of the CRPD uses the terms 'human rights of persons with disabilities' several times; see also Kayess and French, above n 4, 1; AS Kanter, 'The Promise and Challenge of the United Nations Convention on the Rights of Persons with Disabilities' (2007) 34 *Syracuse Journal of International Law & Commerce* 287.

approach. It does not adopt any new human right, but rather applies existing human rights to the particular circumstances of persons with disabilities.[26] However, because historically human rights instruments have failed to promote equality and dignity among persons with disabilities, the direction put forward in the CRPD aims at achieving substantive equality for this group in the form of structural–institutional equality, meaning a duty to restructure the social institutions, resulting in proactive structural change, while acknowledging the social contextual causes of inequality. As Oddny Arnardóttir notes: 'the CRPD represents a deeper and more profound understanding of equality as the principle of equality reflected in the Convention clearly requires the express adaptation of what is perceived as universal rights to the unique situation of persons with disabilities'.[27]

The highly important Article 27 of the Convention states that:

> States Parties recognize the right of persons with disabilities to work, on an equal basis with others; this includes the right to the opportunity to gain a living by work freely chosen or accepted in a labour market and work environment that is open, inclusive and accessible to persons with disabilities.

The Article also notes that 'States Parties shall safeguard and promote the realization of the right to work, including for those who acquire a disability during the course of employment, by taking appropriate steps, including through legislation, to inter alia': (a) prohibit discrimination on the basis of disability; (b) protect the rights of persons with disabilities, on an equal basis with others, to just and favourable conditions of work; (c) ensure their labour and trade union rights; (d) provide effective access to general technical and vocational guidance programs, placement services and training; (e) promote employment opportunities and career advancement; (f) promote opportunities for self-employment and entrepreneurship; (g) employ persons with disabilities in the public sector; (h) promote the employment of people with disabilities in the private sector through appropriate policies and measures; (i) ensure reasonable accommodations in the workplace; (j) promote the acquisition of work experience in the open market; and (k) promote vocational and professional rehabilitation, job retention and return-to-work programmes.

The first step of my argument in this chapter offers a reading of Article 27 as proposed further below. On the basis of that reading I claim that the approach of Article 27 is innovative and that it addresses some of the main concerns raised in the literature regarding the right to work. The next section in this part of the chapter presents these main concerns.

[26] UN Press Release, 15 August 2005, available at: www.un.org/News/Press/docs/2005/soc4680.doc.htm.

[27] OM Arnardóttir, 'A Future of Multidimensional Disadvantage Equality?' in OM Arnardóttir and G Quinn (eds), *The UN Convention on the Rights of Persons with Disabilities: European and Scandinavian Perspectives* (Leiden, Martinus Nijhoff 2009) 41, 46.

B The Right to Work

The right to work has been established in a number of human rights documents, including Article 23 of the Universal Declaration of Human Rights; Articles 6, 7 and 8 of the Covenant on Economic, Social and Cultural Rights; Article 15 of the Charter of Fundamental Rights of the European Union; Article 1 of the European Social Charter; and a number of ILO Conventions.[28] In analysing these international human rights documents and their application in practice, scholars have voiced pessimism regarding the right to work. In his seminal article on this right, Bob Hepple states that it is meaningless to talk about a right to work that is enforceable against a state, arguing that what the law can help to guarantee is the fundamental right of individuals to equal treatment and equal respect.[29] The ensuing literature on the right to work remains pessimistic, especially regarding state obligations. Guy Mundlak, writing a few years ago, noted that 'the implementation of the right to work is weak, almost non-existent'.[30]

While pessimism dominates scholarly attitudes towards the general right to work, more optimistic voices are heard regarding the right to work of persons with disabilities. Indeed, the CRPD has been celebrated, as has Article 27, especially regarding the obligation it places on states to promote the right to work of persons with disabilities.[31] In this section, I wish to unpack the reasons for pessimism regarding the general right to work discourse and the main concerns raised in that line of literature, so as to later address these in light of the reading proposed here for Article 27.

A first step, though, is to discuss the meaning of the right to work. Hepple defined the right to work as including three kinds of obligations: the first against the state, the second against the employer and the third against unions. Regarding the first, he noted that the essence of this right, as it is found in the European Social Charter, is one that requires the state 'to maintain a full employment policy, to protect the opportunity of every worker to earn his living in an occupation freely entered upon, to establish and maintain free employment services for all workers, and to provide and promote vocational training'.[32] In his writing in

[28] Convention 159 of the ILO addresses particularly persons with disabilities. This Convention and further ILO instruments addressing persons with disabilities are discussed in A O'Reilly, *The Right to Decent Work of Persons with Disabilities* (Geneva, ILO, 2007) 4–13. See also C O'Cinneide in this volume, ch 6.

[29] B Hepple, 'A Right to Work?' (1981) 10 *Industrial Law Journal* 65, 81–82.

[30] G Mundlak, 'The Right to Work: Linking Human Rights and Employment Policy' (2007) 146 *International Labour Review* 189.

[31] UN Human Rights Council report, above n 11, 7–11; and S Bruyère and B Murray, 'The Human Rights of Workers with Disabilities' in J Gross and L Compa (eds), *Human Rights in Labor and Employment Relations: International and Domestic Perspectives* (Ithaca NY, Cornell University Press, 2009) 213, 216–19.

[32] Hepple, above n 29, 69.

recent years, Mundlak pointed to three components of the right to work.[33] The first is the liberty component, which includes references to the right to work as a liberty or as the freedom from government intrusion in one's occupation. The second is the right to have work and the corresponding duty of the state or of employers to provide work to individuals. The third and final component is the right to dignified work. The first component is the least controversial and the other two are not necessarily promoted or enforced.

Mundlak also notes a few critiques regarding the right to work. The main critiques are based on claims that the right to work differs from other social rights, and thus its essence should be questioned. The first is that the right to work, and particularly the right to be employed, is not a good to strive for because of the exploitative nature of work relations. The second is that the right to work is said to aim towards integrating people into the paid labour market, thus focusing mainly on paying jobs while excluding other sorts of work. The third and last is that it is questionable whether we should consider work to be a *right*, when often it is actually a *duty*.[34]

These concerns are relevant to persons with disabilities. Exploitation in the open labour market is very common, as it is in work environments and programmes that combine labour and rehabilitation objectives – like sheltered workshops, supported employment and regulations enabling the provision of lower minimum wage.[35] Moreover, many persons with disabilities find difficulty engaging in the remunerated market, thus relying on social security benefits. Lastly, policies aimed at assisting persons with disabilities to transition from welfare to work raise questions regarding whether such a shift, in effect, leads to a strengthening of the duty to work for this group. It is against this background that Article 27 adopts a different approach regarding the right to work. The Article poses obligations on states to promote and fulfil the right, requires them to be fully aware of the various obstacles that deny persons with disabilities to enter and be promoted in the market. It also emphasises the requirement for just and favourable conditions of work on an equal basis. Like other international human rights instruments, it refrains from mandating a duty to work; neither does it state, however, that such a duty – if imposed – is problematic. Yet as I will show further below, a duty to work infringes the fundamental principles of Article 27.

I suggest that the direction offered by Article 27 helps overcome the limitations of the general right to work as discussed in theory, because the CRPD and Article 27 are based on the ideas of equality and dignity – goals Hepple has noted that the right to work can achieve. More crucially, the deeper and more profound equality approach – the structural–institutional equality approach – reflected in the

[33] Mundlak, 'The Right to Work: Linking Human Rights and Employment Policy', above n 30, 192–93.

[34] ibid, 196 and Mundlak, 'The Right to Work – The Value of Work', above n 24 and also A Paz-Fuchs in this volume, ch 10.

[35] UN Human Rights Council report, above n 11, 6 and also see conclusion; *World Report on Disability*, above n 12, 239–40.

Convention, together with full respect of one's dignity – entrenched in the principles of personal freedom and inclusion – and the meaningful obligations of states, have made it possible to pose an alternative and welcome approach to this right.

II Reading Article 27 in Light of Critical Disability Studies and Nussbaum's Capabilities Theory

Alongside other rules in the CRPD, Article 27 arests on the ideas of dignity and equality. But what precisely do these concepts imply regarding the right to work? This present part of the chapter provides an account of Article 27 along the lines of two theories: critical disability studies and Martha Nussbaum's capabilities approach.

Critical disability studies started from what has been labelled the 'social model of disability'. The social model, which various movements of persons with disabilities in varying national contexts have adopted into differing versions,[36] was developed in contrast to the medical or the individual model of disability.[37] The latter focused on the impairment and individual condition, seeing it as the main cause for limitations in functioning and participation in society. While the medical (or the individual) model viewed impairment as an unwanted deficit, placing the individual in the sick role, where he or she is excused from social obligations,[38] the social model highlights the social, economic and physical environment as the main reason for limitation of opportunities and inclusion.[39]

At the heart of the social model lies the distinction between 'impairment' and 'disability'.[40] Impairment is viewed as a physical condition and disability as the loss or limitations of opportunities to take part in community life on a level equal with that of others.[41] Disability is a social product based on the view of impairment as problematic and tragic. The social model emphasises that impairment is not a tragedy that necessarily implies a low quality of life. Persons with impairments can be productive, valuable and able. Various disability studies

[36] Pfeiffer notes nine versions of the social model; see D Pfeiffer, 'The Conceptualization of Disability' in SN Barnartt and BM Altman (eds), *Exploring Theories and Expanding Methodologies*: Research in Social Science and Disability, vol 2 (Amsterdam, JAI, 2001) 29.

[37] Oliver, the academic most associated with the social model, has never used the term 'medical model' in his writings. Instead he preferred to use the notion 'individual model' or 'personal tragedy theory'. Oliver, *Understanding Disability*, above n 2, 31–32; M Oliver, *The Politics of Disablement* (London, Macmillan, 1990) 1. However, the medical–social dichotomy has become to be a defining characteristic of disability studies, Shakespeare, above n 7, 15.

[38] Pfeiffer, above n 36, 30.

[39] Oliver, *Understanding Disability*, above n 2, ch 3.

[40] ibid, 35–36.

[41] T Burchardt, 'Capabilities and Disability: The Capabilities Framework and the Social Model of Disability' (2004) 19 *Disability & Society* 735, 736.

scholars have claimed that the CRPD adopts the social model of disability.[42] I offer here a reading of Article 27 that builds on these studies, but claims that while the social model is important for understanding Article 27, I believe the Article embraces alongside that model an individualistic approach that offers a fuller account of one's dignity. I will explain this approach beginning with a discussion of the criticism regarding the social model.

Another central dichotomy offered by the social model is that between the social and the medical, seeing the former as 'right' and the later as 'wrong'. This dichotomy has been criticised by scholars from within disability studies. Shakespeare, for example, has posed the problems of viewing disability as resulting solely from social barriers and as having nothing to do with impairment, personal character, motivation and other issues. Accordingly, he says that the good idea that there are social factors in a disabled person's experience has 'become ossified and exaggerated into a set of crude dichotomies which were ultimately misleading'.[43] Thus, while accepting the social-contextual approach that the social model has offered, Shakespeare claims that theory should also be attuned to the impairment. Shakespeare accepts the distinction between impairment and disability. He does not see impairment as a tragedy that necessarily implies a low quality of life, although he stresses that the impairment should not be ignored for sometimes it does create a hurdle for full participation. There is a danger in ignoring pain, disregarding difficulties and overlooking the role of doctors and of medical needs in the lives of persons with disabilities.

Emerging from his theory are two insights that I believe are of particular importance for the analysis of Article 27. The first is the social-contextual character of disability, which has been emphasised by the social model.[44] The second is the importance of considering individual parameters, such as impairments, while accepting that these may impact the ability of *all* persons to enter fully the remunerated sphere of work. Recognition of both these insights requires that a just society should not necessarily adopt a conception of full engagement within the labour market. In other words, justice requires that society will envelop persons who stay fully or partially outside the world of paid work (while critically considering the reasons why they remain outside the labour market and the full social context). A person may thus not be fully 'productive' as the term is conceptualised today, but nonetheless be conceived of as a valuable member of society. This viewpoint corresponds with Nussbaum's capabilities approach, according to which value is not dependent on productivity. Her theory that developed in reaction to the social contract theory, sees the 'human being' in nature political, meaning that humans find deep fulfilment in political relations.[45] Nussbaum

[42] Kanter, above n 25; Kayess and French, above n 4; Bruyère and Murray, above n 31; S Ferraina, 'Analysis of the Legal Meaning of Article 27 of the UN CRPD: Key Challenges for Adapted Work Settings' (14 March 2012) *Gladnet Collection* 1, 9–12.

[43] Shakespeare, above n 7, 13.

[44] ibid, 42.

[45] Nussbaum, above n 5, 86.

notes that '[i]t would be odd to imagine the human being flourishing outside a network of such relations'.[46] Justice should promote such inclusion, which is particularly challenging for persons with disabilities, especially those with severe disabilities, as she says:

> The problem of extending education, health care, political rights and liberties, and equal citizenship more generally to such people seems to be a problem of justice, and an urgent one. Because solving this problem requires a new way of thinking about who the citizen is and a new analysis of the purpose of social cooperation (one not focused on mutual advantage), and because it also requires emphasizing the importance of care as a social primary good, it seems likely that facing it well will require not simply a new application of the old theories, but a reshaping of theoretical structures themselves.[47]

Accordingly, Nussbaum's theory acknowledges that not every person can be productive in the economic sense. Even those who are not fully productive or not productive at all are a part of society, because society is held together by a wide range of attachments – only some of which relate to productivity.[48] Therefore, claims made regarding persons with severe disabilities – that they are not unproductive and therefore society should include them within its social contract – are doomed to fail. Some persons with disabilities will need expensive and difficult arrangements in order to enjoy the list of capabilities. Nussbaum mentions several capabilities as the core that every person is entitled to. These are life, bodily health, bodily integrity, senses imagination and thought, emotions, practical reason, affiliation, other species, play and control over one's environment.[49] All are required. There is not one entitlement within this list that can substitute another. Fulfilling these capabilities depends on the individual, but the theory of capabilities requires governments to take steps towards that end, even if that means expensive redesigning. These steps will not necessarily bring about mutual advantages to all, but they will achieve social justice, upon which communal life relies.

Capabilities differ from resources. Resources cannot necessarily bring about capabilities. A person with disability might have resources, but lacks some of the capabilities on Nussbaum's list of capabilities. For example, resources do not necessarily bring about affiliation or control over one's environment. Therefore, by means of societal recognition of these capabilities as the source of dignity, the capabilities in question can be pursued for each and every person as an end, regardless of the quest for resource allocation and for productivity.[50] Moreover, capabilities differ from functioning, in the sense that capabilities provide individuals with the ability to function, but it remains up to them to decide whether they choose to function.[51]

[46] ibid.
[47] Nussbaum, above n 5, 2.
[48] ibid, 160.
[49] The list and her discussion of it are found in Nussbaum, above n 5, 76–78.
[50] Nussbaum, above n 5, 70.
[51] See her discussion and example on health in Nussbaum, above n 5, 79–80.

Nussbaum's theory of capabilities is attuned to the polity, and thus to the environment that creates disability. In this way, it corresponds with the view of disability as a matter of social context – a point raised by critical disability studies. In conjunction, it enables a focus on the individual, the steps that need to be taken to realise his or her capabilities and the person's own wishes and decisions; these are the components of dignity, which I believe Shakespeare's theory is also attuned to.[52] By shifting attention from resources or functioning to capabilities, the theory accepts variations among persons generally, including among those with disabilities, and seeks out each person's freedom. True, Nussbaum accepts that some persons with disabilities will not be able to make choices about their health care or sexual relations and thus for them, functioning rather than capabilities might be the appropriate goal.[53] But this is the case only in very rare instances.

Hence, at the basis of the theory lies a perception of justice as distinct from productivity. Pursuing capabilities is the way to achieve social justice, be it through paid work based on notions of economic productivity, or any other way. Nussbaum's capabilities theory claims that if persons are to have full human lives, they must have access to and the capability of attaining non-alienating, non-discriminatory and non-humiliating work; however, they are not necessarily required to work to be considered 'fully human'.

In this respect I see Nussbaum's theory and critical disability studies, especially Shakespeare's approach, as supplementing and strengthening one another. Additionally, both theories imply obligations on states to work towards inclusion of persons with disabilities in the market. Critical disability studies base such obligations on the right to equality, dignity, adding to it the state's responsibility to amend the wrongs it has created in the social formation of disability.[54] Nussbaum's quest for justice and human dignity calls on governments to respect and promote a list of core human entitlements, which comprise the bare minimum of human dignity.[55] Capabilities are political principles and provide a goal for governments to strive towards an idea of dignity for all. Hence, the state has a duty to make every effort for the realisation of the capabilities. All states should strive towards that end as a matter of justice.[56]

[52] On the similarities and variations among the idea of the social context as found in the social model and critical disability studies, and capabilities theory, see Burchardt, above n 41; S Mitra, 'The Capability Approach and Disability' (2006) 16 *Journal of Disability Policy Studies* 236; C Baylies, 'Disability and the Notion of Human Development: Questions of Rights and Capabilities' (2002) 17 *Disability and Society* 725.

[53] Nussbaum, above n 5, 172.

[54] S Mor, 'Equal Rights to People with Disabilities at Work: From Fixing the Person to Fixing Society' (2012) 35 *Iyuney Mishpat* 97 (Hebrew) 113–15.

[55] Nussbaum, above n 5, 70.

[56] Nussbaum's theory has been criticised in its relation to persons with disabilities. It has been said that her theory does not fully recognise the humanity and equality of those who function below the ten central capabilities on the list; that it does not sufficiently ensure participatory justice at a level that guarantees disabled persons' meaningful contact with the population at large; that it is directed towards achieving average capability levels rather than maximising individual talents; and that it does not consider the framework to impose culturally generated, external moral imperatives on others. See M Stein and PJS Stein, 'Beyond Disability Civil Rights' (2007) 58 *Hastings Law Journal* 1203, 1218–20.

A Four Principles Underlying the Right to Work of Persons with Disabilities

On the basis of the discussion above, I draw four principles that I believe underlie the right to work as it is established in Article 27: the structural–institutional equality principle; individual freedom; inclusion; and state responsibility. These four principles offer a way to fully realise both equality and dignity in respect to the right to work.

The *structural–institutional equality principle* draws on the social context of disability, which stems from both critical disability studies and Nussbaum's approach, paying particular attention to the social, economic and physical environment and their impact on the ability of persons to fulfil their right to work. This principle requires acknowledging social structures and cultures as creating and shaping people's ability to participate meaningfully in the work domain and on their possibilities of achieving adequate labour conditions. Emphasis is placed on asymmetrical structures of powers, privileges and disadvantages. The structural–institutional equality principle also acknowledges the particular attention that should be given to job requirements, merits and the perception of productivity. Such factors, as Sandra Fredman has noted in regard to merit, can incorporate 'the very discrimination they purport to eliminate'.[57] As such, this principle points to the causes that increase or maintain disadvantage, placing a duty to make reasonable adjustments in order to address them.[58] In other words, it requires the relevant actors to take measures to restructure the social institutions, resulting in proactive structural change, while acknowledging the social contextual causes of inequality.

Alongside the structural–institutional equality principle lies the principle of *individual freedom*. Amartya Sen saw the promotion of capabilities as furthering one's freedom.[59] Achieving this freedom requires an individualistic outlook on persons. According to this approach, persons are entitled to the set of capabilities regardless of any criteria, such as productivity or participation in the workforce, in order to provide them with basic freedom. As both critical disability studies and Nussbaum stress, this understanding is not based on withdrawing to the medical model. Its aim is to provide a basis of capabilities that will enable a person to fully participate in society, without denying, at the same time, the provision of care and other forms of social support in order to achieve capabilities. In very rare

Notwithstanding this criticism, several disability rights scholars have adopted concepts from her theory, as well as that of Sen, to promote a more holistic theory of the human rights of persons with disability (see references in n 52 above). And indeed, the contribution of the capabilities theory to the claims made above is considerable, and offers a meaningful way to address the right to work.

[57] Fredman, 'Disability Equality', above n 3, 204.

[58] The literature refers to this approach towards equality as 'substantial equality' (Fredman, 'Disability Equality', above n 3) or 'multidimensional disadvantage' (Arnardóttir, above n 27, 54–64).

[59] A Sen, 'Introduction' in A Sen, *Development as Freedom* (Oxford, Oxford University Press, 1999).

cases, as Nussbaum suggests, such an understanding will merely enable functioning. This idea furthers one's dignity.

Another principle stemming from the two theories is that of *inclusion.* While the better known theories on social inclusion are concerned with the outcome of inclusion as the aim or principle of justice,[60] Nussbaum's theory offers another perspective on inclusion. Inclusion exists due to one's humanity and is completed with the realisation of capabilities. Inclusion is not based on ideas of shared responsibilities, contributions, productivity and functioning; rather, it exists despite them. Hence, regarding the right to work, inclusion within society does not necessarily require that ultimately a person will be part of the labour market; it only requires that the state invests in enabling the development of capabilities so that a person can, if he or she desires, be fully engaged in work. Nussbaum does not necessitate an outcome of engagement in the labour market for a person to be seen as included. When read together with the structural–institutional equality principle and the principle of state responsibility, it seems that the principle of inclusion offered here is a hybrid of these two approaches. On the one hand, it does place emphasis on changing the structural–institutional framework, and sees the state as responsible for promoting the equality of persons with disabilities. On the other hand, however, it acknowledges that a person should be considered included in society even if he or she is not fully productive or even decides to remain outside the paying labour market.

State responsibility is the fourth and final principle, which stems from the two theories. Nussbaum's capabilities theory denotes a responsibility for the state to promote at the very minimum each and every citizen's capabilities. These capabilities, as noted above, are political principles and comprise a goal for governments to strive towards to achieve the ideal of providing human dignity for all. Viewing the right to work through this lens places a responsibility on states not only to refrain from interfering in subjects' freedom of occupation, but mainly to provide the necessary capabilities to all so that they can enter the work domain, develop and be fulfilled within it. On this basis, the state is thus obliged to provide employment, opportunities for employment and training. It is also obliged to secure equal prospects for dignified work. Basing state responsibility on capabilities ultimately means limited responsibility. This is because what the capabilities theory offers is the threshold of human dignity, not a full theory of social justice above that threshold.[61] However, in the reading proposed, the theory is supplemented by critical disability studies that see the state as responsible for enhancing the equality of persons with disabilities on the basis of the right to equality and the state's responsibility to amend historical disadvantages that it had taken part in creating. This notion poses a broader duty on the state with the aim of achieving equality.

[60] See H Collins, 'Discrimination, Equality and Social Inclusion' (2003) 66 *Modern Law Review* 16, 23.

[61] Nussbaum, above n 5, 75.

B Reading Article 27 in Light of the Four Principle Framework

The ideas of equality and dignity as set in the CRPD and in Article 27 are better understood along the lines of the four principles posed above. Meaningfully, the moral compass of the CRPD as set in Article 3 lies at the heart of this regulatory tool, including respect for the inherent dignity of persons with disabilities, non-discrimination, the full and effective participation of persons with disabilities in society and respect for difference and acceptance of persons with disabilities as part of human diversity and humanity. Moreover, the Preamble of the CRPD offers guidance in that it entails, among other issues, recognition of diversity (section i of the Preamble); the need to promote and protect all persons with disabilities, including those who require more intensive support (section j); full participation and provision of an enhanced sense of belonging (section m); and individual autonomy and independence, including the freedom to make their own choices (section n).

Additionally, the way in which the CRPD addresses persons with disabilities merits attention. Although it does not adopt a definition of 'persons with disabilities' as a result of controversies surrounding the issue,[62] Article 1 refers to persons with disabilities as *including* 'those who have long-term physical, mental, intellectual or sensory impairments which in interaction with various barriers may hinder their full and effective participation in society on an equal basis with others'. This definition, despite its several shortcomings,[63] embraces the view of disability as created not only by impairment, but necessarily by the interaction of persons with impairment and an environment that creates – in the wording of the Convention – 'various barriers', reflecting the social context of disability. The social context approach is strengthened in the Preamble, which states that disability results from the interaction between persons with impairments and attitudinal and environmental barriers that hinder their full and effective participation in society on an equal basis with others.

A careful analysis of Article 27 with the CRPD as its backdrop reveals the intrinsic inclusion of the four principles noted above. Two main requirements set in Article 27 – accessibility and reasonable accommodation – particularly demonstrate acceptance of the structural–institutional equality principle. Both view the social context as a cause for disability, and accordingly of the disadvantage experienced by persons with disabilities, leading to a duty, placed on employers, trade unions and the state, to restructure the social institutions of the labour market, with the aim of achieving a proactive structural change.

[62] Kayess and French, above n 4, 23.

[63] On these shortcomings, see Kayess and French, above n 4, 23–24.

Accessibility is justified as necessary to enable persons with disabilities to live independently and participate fully in all aspects of life. Its importance is mentioned in the Preamble (section v), with Article 9 elaborating on the rationale behind such accessibility and the requirements to achieve it. Article 27(1) requires an accessible work environment. The description focuses on social causes and the need to adjust them to enable access. It includes much more than physical accessibility. Article 9 states that access should be ensured to the physical environment, to transportation, to information and communications and to other facilities and services that are available or provided to the public, in both urban and rural areas. Such obligations involve furthering access of persons with disabilities *to* the workplace, as well as better enabling access *within* it.

The requirement for reasonable accommodation, as noted in Article 27(1)(i), also comprises an acceptance of the social context as creating disability, while requiring accommodating that context to persons with disabilities.[64] It is a precondition for accessing and achieving an outcome of inclusion in the open market when individual adaptations are needed. Although the obligation is individually based – it applies to a particular person who needs accommodation – this requirement has the potential of resulting in fundamental structural transformations of the norm.[65] Denial of reasonable accommodations is seen as an act of discrimination according to Article 2 of the CRPD. Like the requirement of accessibility, reasonable accommodation touches on more than the physical environment. For example, persons with intellectual disabilities may regard the following as fulfilling the obligation: working arrangements (ie, adjusting working time and leave, flexible work organisation including splitting one task into several); reorganisation of workstations by adapting existing equipment or acquiring new tools; installation and/or provision of ad hoc communication material like pictograms, readers, etc; and provision of tailored supervisory control and management and specialised training.[66]

The requirement for the accommodation to be *reasonable* is problematic, as it is limited to instances that do not impose a disproportionate or undue burden. Thus, what is actually required of employers remains unclear. However, theorists have claimed such limitation as imposing obligations on states to take upon themselves burdens that cannot be upheld by employers themselves.[67] While accommodations are viewed as costly and unusual, it is important to refer to them in light of accommodations given to the general public. As David Pfeiffer explains, all people in society receive subsidies and services, such as snow ploughing, fire, police, ambulance, tax supported sports arenas, mass transit, enterprise zones, tax

[64] The notion 'reasonable accommodation' is defined in the CRPD (Art 2) to mean 'necessary and appropriate modification and adjustments not imposing a disproportionate or undue burden, where needed in a particular case, to ensure to persons with disabilities the enjoyment or exercise on an equal basis with others of all human rights and fundamental freedoms'.

[65] Kayess and French, above n 4, 9.

[66] ibid, 16.

[67] UN Human Rights Council report, above n 11, 9–10; Bruyère and Murray, above n 31.

breaks to developers and others.[68] These governmental undertakings are very expensive but are rarely seen as a burden. Accommodation given to persons with disabilities should be thought of in similar ways.

The ideas of accessibility and reasonable accommodation are non-existent in other international human rights tools establishing the right to work. These notions are unique to Article 27 and the CRPD, illustrating the Article's innovation. This leads to obligations being placed on employers, unions and the state to fulfil the right to work.

Individual freedom is also prominent in Article 27 and the CRPD, which opens with a statement regarding the full enjoyment of fundamental freedoms by all persons with disabilities (Article 1). The idea of freedom lies at the heart of the Convention. In respect of the right to work, the individual component as recognised by the Convention is found in the requirement of reasonable accommodations and in the obligation to respect personal choice. Reasonable accommodation refers, as described above, to the fulfilment of substantial equality, dignity and freedom for persons with disabilities; its achievement requires individual reference. Adjustments are needed in reference to one's impairment, physical and social condition. This does not merit a retreat to the medical (or individual) model, but rather the opposite. It warrants recognition of the personal state of the individual, so as to enable the fulfilment of the right to work, with the social context as the backdrop. The obligation to respect personal choice is also a way to strive towards individual freedom. Article 3 states the 'respect for inherent dignity, individual autonomy including the freedom to make one's own choices, and independence of persons'. This requirement bestows acknowledgment of the entitlement of persons with disabilities, even severe disabilities, to make decisions regarding their lives, including, as can be understood from Article 27, the decision on whether to engage in remunerated employment and the venue of such engagement. Hence, the Article begins with establishing '*the right to the opportunity* to gain a living by work freely chosen or accepted in a labour market'[69] and also notes that opportunities should be given 'for self-employment, entrepreneurship, the development of cooperatives and starting one's own business'. The word choice of *the right to the opportunity* highlights the ideas of personal freedom and choice,[70] and when read together with the principles of Article 3 as stated above the fundamentality of these ideas becomes clear. They coincide with state responsibilities to offer an opportunity for choice, as discussed further below.

Inclusion is a general principle of the CRPD (Article 3). However, I claim that its meaning differs from the one entrenched in theories on social inclusion. It is a hybrid between those theories and the notion of inclusion stemming from Nussbaum's capabilities theory. Such understanding of the term 'inclusion' can

[68] Pfeiffer, above n 36, 43.

[69] Emphasis added.

[70] It is important noting that Art 6 of the Covenant on Economic, Social and Cultural Rights also uses the wording 'the right of everyone to the opportunity to gain his living by work which he freely chooses or accepts'.

be gleaned initially from the general approach of the Convention to view each person with disability – including those who cannot enter the free labour market – as rights bearers and as worthy of dignity and recognition in society. Not only those who are 'worthy' according to ideals of productivity, contribution or promotion of the common good viewed as deserving inclusion into society; rather, all persons are worthy of inclusion, regardless of such ideals. Such a principle of inclusion leads to fully respecting one's dignity. All the while, this does not imply a neglect to expose the causes for exclusion from the market and the structural–institutional change needed to address them, as well as the state's responsibility to amend previous arrangements to enable disabled people's market inclusion. This hybrid approach offers carrots and not sticks regarding the inclusion of persons with disabilities at work, while accepting their status as equal members of society regardless of their participation (or lack thereof) in the market.

Article 27 poses a duty on states to intervene in order to further the goals of equality and dignity, thus accepting the principle of *state responsibility*. It notes that:

> States Parties recognize the rights of persons with disabilities to work, on an equal basis with others . . . States Parties shall safeguard and promote the realization of the right to work . . . including through legislation, to inter alia: prohibit discrimination . . . promote employment opportunities and career advancement for persons with disabilities in the labour market, as well as assistance in finding, obtaining, maintaining and returning to employment . . . employ persons with disabilities in the public sector; promote the employment of persons with disabilities in the private sector through appropriate policies and measures, which may include affirmative action programmes, incentives and other measures.

State obligation in Article 27 is broader than the one set in other international human rights documents.[71] Such obligation can be explained by Nussbaum's capabilities theory, but it takes that responsibility further than capabilities. The various obligations it places demonstrate that it sees states as responsible for acting to fulfil the goal of equality and dignity at work along the lines described thus far by the other three principles. Such an approach coincides with the obligations imposed by critical disability theory.

When read according to the four principles presented, the innovation of Article 27 of the CRPD regarding the right to work of persons with disabilities becomes clearer. While promoting the right to work of persons with disabilities, the four principles and the Article itself meaningfully address some of the main concerns highlighted by the literature on the right to work. Returning to Mundlak's main critiques, the Article declares state obligation to take significant steps to promote

[71] The obligation in Art 6 of the Covenant on Economic, Social and Cultural Rights, eg, only poses a duty on states to: 'technical and vocational guidance and training programmes, policies and techniques to achieve steady economic, social and cultural development and full and productive employment under conditions safeguarding fundamental political and economic freedoms to the individual'. A similar limited obligation is found in the European Social Charter. On these other instruments, see C O'Cinneide in this volume, ch 6.

the right to work – not only to refrain from interfering in it. It emphasises the terms and conditions at work, so as to diminish as far as possible the exploitation of persons with disabilities in the labour market. Crucially, it does not adopt any particular measures for sheltered or other protective forms of employment and thus applies the same set of requirements to these forms of work that it does elsewhere.[72] As discussed above, it particularly notes other venues of work that should be promoted for persons with disabilities, and crucially, refrains from denying social inclusion or any rights of a person who is engaged in other activities that are not remunerated. Finally, one can read the CRPD and Article 27 as denying a possibility to place on persons with disabilities a duty to work, even though it strives for equal participation. According to the four principles, equal participation will be achieved by transforming the labour market to accommodate persons with disabilities, through the posing of state obligations, and by providing incentives to work (such as training, just and favourable conditions and others). Placing a duty comprises an infringement of the moral compass of this document as discussed above. Specifically the principles of individual freedom and inclusion as offered here contradict the creation of such a duty.

The Convention calls for the universal design of its measures, and the literature in the field of disability studies emphasises the importance of the universalisation of the rights of persons with disabilities to aid society at large. Is the universalisation of the right to work as set out in Article 27 justified not only by the field of disability studies, but also from the perspective of labour studies? This is the question I now turn to explore.

III Universalising the Right to Work of Persons with Disabilities?

Coming from the field of disability studies, Zola argues that an exclusively special needs approach to disability is suitable for the short term. The disability movement should strive for a universal approach, he claims, for two main reasons. The first reason is factually based – the entire population is at risk of becoming disabled, and most people will experience disability at some point or another during the course of their lives. The second reason is strategic – absent such universality, segregation will emerge, and a separate (even if equal) society of persons with disabilities will be created and perpetuated.[73] Other writers have offered further justifications for the universal approach. Rosemary Kayess and Phillip French justified such an approach on the grounds of diversity in society, saying that equality focuses on ensuring that legislation, social policies and environments reflect the

[72] This is a point that has been well thought of through the drafting process of the Art. Ferraina, above n 42, 26–27.

[73] Zola, above n 1.

full range of 'repertoires' that exist in society.[74] Jerome Bickenbach and others noted that universality acknowledges that every person in society has some form of disability, in the sense that no one human being has complete abilities. Therefore, disability is fluid and continuous.[75] In all these respects, universality opposes a minority group analysis that views disability as a group defining characteristic.[76] This is the theoretical underpinning of the notion universal design in the CRPD. It is based on the principle that there is only one group that contains individuals with diverse characteristics and abilities,[77] hence, the incorporation of features for buildings, products, environments and services that can be used by all.

In this part of the chapter I wish to argue that the universalisation of the right to work stems not only from the stream of disability studies, but also from labour theories. The starting point is that the abovementioned argument – that there is not one human being who is fully 'able' – is particularly relevant to other disadvantaged groups. In particular, this outlook is relevant to those who due to various reasons do not (cannot, or do not want to – perhaps because of the social structures and cultures in which they were raised and educated) follow the traditional model of a full-time, highly productive, available and fully 'abled' worker, and consequently experience inequality. In other words, similar environmental and personal factors limit various groups in society, bringing about inequality in the work domain.

A good illustration of such embeddedness in the social is found in Jill Rubery's work on equal pay. In a study conducted for the ILO in 2003, Rubery presents causes of pay inequality that are shared by various groups of gender, race and ethnicity, class, illegal migrants, rural migrants, youth and the elderly. She points to six such universal causes: perceptions regarding dependence on income sources other than own wages for subsistence; powerful employers; weak representation; job segregation; social valuation of skills; and social hierarchies.[78] Rubery shows how different life circumstances are reduced to these six causes, bringing about inequality and posing hurdles for achieving equal pay. These causes can explain not only state policies and decisions made by employers or trade unions, but also those of workers in the disadvantaged groups themselves. Moreover, they can describe inequality regarding not only low pay, but also market entrance and promotions. This framework can be very useful for understanding the inequality experienced by persons with disabilities. Persons with disabilities are viewed as depending on the state (and not on paid work) for their income. Powerful

[74] Kayess and French, above n 4, 11.

[75] JE Bickenbach, S Chatterji, EM Badley and TB Ustun, 'Models of Disablement, Universalism and the International Classification of Impairments, Disabilities and Handicaps' (1999) 48 *Journal of Social Science and Medicine* 1173, 1180.

[76] Fredman, 'Disability Equality', above n 3, 206–08.

[77] S Iwarsson and A Stahl, 'Accessibility, Usability and Universal Design – Positioning and Definition of Concepts Describing Person–Environment Relationships' (2003) 25 *Disability and Rehabilitation* 57, 61.

[78] J Rubery, 'Pay-Equity, Minimum Wage and Equality at Work: Theoretical Framework and Empirical Evidence' (ILO Declaration/WP/19/2003).

employers cite problems of workplace accessibility and medical needs to minimise their wages or to avoid hiring them. They are weakly represented by trade unions. They comprise of the main groups experiencing job segregation – especially in light of sheltered workshops or other exclusionary work practices. Social valuation of their skills is low: many people with disabilities are perceived as non-productive and as unable to perform the job similarly to able-bodied persons, while the market does not value other skills (ie, social skills) and further advantages, such as those of diversity.[79] Finally, their position in the labour market is related to social hierarchies that exist outside it. Some persons with disabilities hold these perceptions regarding themselves as well and act accordingly.[80]

Although the workplace situation of persons with disabilities is much worse than that of the groups Rubery discusses, it seems that the same theoretical framework applies to understanding their disadvantage, lack of dignity and lack of equality. All the abovementioned groups experience inequality for similar reasons. When considering them jointly, we can conclude that these disadvantaged groups – those whose life experiences differ from the traditional model and consequently experience inequality – have actually come to comprise the majority of the market. Importantly, stemming from this is the understanding that only a few in society are 'fully able'. The majority of persons are bound by social, economic and environmental factors. Scholars prescribing to such notions should thus justify universalising the norms set for persons with disabilities to all persons.

This understanding makes the two theories presented above for analysing Article 27 – critical disability studies and the capabilities approach – highly relevant for all or most persons in society. Capabilities in the sense that Nussbaum proposes relate to every person. In this respect, consensus exists that each person in society is worthy of dignity. Accordingly, the state is responsible for promoting these capabilities, accepting diversities and variations, and adopting a point of view that stresses individual freedom as a goal while considering environmental barriers and limitations. This is very true of the right to work, especially when recognising that work plays a central role in human society. The relevance of capabilities theories to the world of work is evident from the growing line of literature in the field of labour law that addresses these theories, using them as justifications for the regulation of work,[81] for applying rules regarding personal work contracts beyond employment contracts[82] and for the idea of social rights, including the move from welfare to work.[83] Capabilities that are recognised to be of particular importance to those who lack them seems to become a central ground for justifying universal rules in the field of labour.

[79] See discussion at p 66 above.
[80] *World Report on Disability*, above n 12, 238.
[81] V Mantouvalou, 'Labour Rights in the European Convention on Human Right: An Intellectual Justification for an Integrated Approach to Interpretation' (2013) 13 *Human Rights Law Review* 529, 549–51.
[82] Freedland and Kountouris, above n 9, 371–82.
[83] S Deakin and F Wilkinson, *The Law of the Labour Market: Industrialization, Employment and Legal Evolution* (Oxford, Oxford University Press, 2005) ch 5.

More controversial, perhaps, is the universalisation of the ideas stressed by critical disability studies. Critical disability studies have developed with a vision targeted towards persons with disabilities. This model has yielded a major contribution in recognising the particular barriers placed by the environment, experts and legal instruments to maintain and enhance the disadvantage of persons with disabilities in various spheres of life, including the labour market. However, as noted above, studies from the field of labour have raised similar types of arguments, showing that the environmental principle is relevant to explaining the situation of various other disadvantaged groups. These theories led to a call for the adoption of particular measures that will bring structural–institutional equality to the market.[84] Therefore, the theoretical basis upon which the obligations in Article 27 that go beyond the threshold of capabilities were set – ie, those explained by critical disability studies – shares similarities with theories regarding other disadvantaged groups. Furthermore, the idea of equality is not only found in the CRPD, but also in various other legal documents targeted towards those others.[85] Equality and dignity should be shared by all and, as Hepple noted, can be promoted regarding the right to work. As I argue here, there is good reason for applying the four principles of structural–institutional equality, individual freedom, inclusion and state responsibility to all persons, recognising that many are bound by the social and face constraints.

IV Conclusion

This chapter has highlighted the new and innovative approach that Article 27 of the CRPD has adopted regarding the right to work of persons with disabilities. My aims here were twofold: to offer an account of the right to work by drawing on critical disability studies and Nussbaum's capabilities theory and to lean on that analysis to assess whether a universal application of this norm in the field of labour can be justified. I have herein presented the claim that a reading of Article 27 (the latest human rights instrument adopted regarding the right to work) according to the two theories mentioned above addresses some of the main concerns raised in the general literature regarding the right to work. I have shown how it adopts a structural–institutional equality approach towards this right, while respecting one's dignity and placing meaningful obligations on states. To demonstrate this accomplishment of the Article, I noted in particular four princi-

[84] Some measures have been adopted for other disadvantaged groups, ie, gender-mainstreaming programmes and family-friendly policies.

[85] See, eg, the Preamble of the Universal Declaration of Human Rights which begins with the following statement: 'Whereas recognition of the inherent dignity and of the equal and inalienable rights of all members of the human family is the foundation of freedom, justice and peace in the world'. This is repeated in the International Covenant on Economic, Social and Cultural Rights. These values are also mentioned in Conventions on particular disadvantaged groups; see, eg, Arts 1 and 2 of the Convention on the Elimination of All Forms of Discrimination against Women.

ples that lie at its heart: the principles of structural–institutional equality, personal freedom, inclusion and state responsibility.

Others have claimed that a universal application of such an approach can be highly valuable to society at large. But does justification exist to adopt the universal approach of Article 27 to others not only from within the field of disability studies, but also from a broader labour perspective? I claim that it does. The justification stemming from labour studies brings us to the same conclusion – albeit with a different meaning – as Zola reached in the sentence opening this chapter: 'what is done in the name of disability today will have meaning for all of society's tomorrows'.

5

Aristotle, Arendt and the Gentleman: How the Conception of Remuneration Figures in our Understanding of a Right to Work and Be Paid

JE PENNER*

Introduction

This chapter is part of a larger work concerning what I call 'property fetishism', which is, briefly and roughly, a particular phenomenon or outlook in moral and political philosophy under which the 'social thesis' is denied, or obscured, or diminished. The 'social thesis' is the thesis that the 'default' characterisation of human existence for the purposes of exploring interpersonal (including political) morality is not that of a hermit in some state of nature who shares no interests with others, but one in which interpersonal relations of real significance are native or natural to human existence. As such, those normative means, like the power to consent or to make agreements so as to be able to act cooperatively with others, are not some cultural achievement which we could plausibly be without, but are part and parcel of our natural endowments, in the same way as our basic responsiveness to reasons[1] makes us (in part) the kind of creature that we are. Property fetishism works to deny, obscure, or diminish the significance of this human sociability principally by characterising acting in the social and political sphere as the interaction of 'self-owners', as individuals principally constituted by the way in which they interact as possessors of property.[2] As a rough picture that will do for the nonce; we shall return to the idea below.

* I am grateful to Lisa Austin, Larissa Katz, Dennis Klimchuk, Robert Lamb, Virginia Mantouvalou, Chris Pierson, John Salter and Katrina Wyman for comments. All errors and infelicities remain with the author.

[1] See J Gardner, 'Nearly Natural Law' (2007) 52 *American Journal of Jurisprudence* 1.

[2] See JE Penner, 'Property, Community, and the Problem of Distributive Justice' (2009) 10 *Theoretical Inquiries in Law* 121.

What I am concerned to look at here is how we conceive of the way in which valuable human social activity, which may, in a sense, be broader than the conventional notion of 'work', is remunerated. My claim will be that how we conceive of remuneration has a reflex action in characterising the way we think of work itself. As will become clear below, what we think we are contributing to another when we pay them for a service reflects the way we characterise that service itself, in particular whether we regard that other's service as merely 'labour power' or as something more like their participation in a valuable enterprise the benefits of which both of us share. In getting at this idea I shall draw principally upon Arendt's[3] distinction between labour, work and action, who draws these distinctions from Aristotle.[4]

I Labourers, Makers and Actors

Arendt, in *The Human Condition*, distinguishes human activity by distinguishing between labour, work and action. Arendt's account is subtle and nuanced and I cannot do full justice to it here, but even in outline it poses interesting questions for our understanding of work and the way we conceive of remuneration.

Labour, according to Arendt, is the toil which consists in those activities which sustain biological life. It is the toil that is necessary for the very existence of people. According to Arendt, the ancient Greeks regarded this sort of activity as the lowest form of human activity, so much so that it really didn't count as genuinely *human* activity at all, for acting merely to survive did not distinguish a man from a beast. A life devoted to attending to human necessity in this way was not regarded as a human life at all, for a life devoted to such labours prevented one from that activity that truly made one human, the life of *action*, life lived as a citizen of the polis.

This perspective on labour, the toil of biological necessity, the production of food, clothing, shelter and so on, was clearly directly related to the classical defence of the institution of slavery, ie, that some men must be slaves, must attend to necessity, not only for themselves but for their masters, for only then could their masters be free from necessity so as to participate in the genuinely human life of the polis. In short, some must need be slaves so that a genuinely human existence (albeit only for some) could occur at all.

As Arendt makes clear, it is not the status of a slave that makes his activity labour, his activity slavish; it is his activity of tending to necessity which makes him a slave:[5]

[3] H Arendt, *The Human Condition* (Chicago, University of Chicago Press, 1958).

[4] Principally from Books 1 and 7 of *The Politics*: Aristotle, *The Politics* (trans B Jowitt, S Everson (ed)) (Cambridge, Cambridge University Press, 1988).

[5] Arendt, above n 3, 84.

> The institution of slavery in antiquity, though not in later times, was not a device for cheap labour or an instrument of exploitation for profit, but rather to exclude labour from the conditions of a man's life. What men share with other forms of animal life was not considered human. (This, incidentally, was also the reason for the much misunderstood Greek theory of the non-human nature of the slave. Aristotle, who argued this theory so explicitly, and then, on his deathbed, freed his slaves, may not have been so inconsistent as moderns are inclined to think. He denied not the slave's capacity to be human, but only the use of the word 'men' for members of the species man-kind as long as they are totally subject to necessity.)

'Labour', so described, is to be contrasted with 'work', which is not similarly tied to necessity. Work is distinguished by its products – artefacts – which are creations having an existence, once created, which outlives their production. By contrast, all labour is merely transitory, the toil that goes into tilling and herding and cooking and cleaning; in a sense labour is just the exploitation (and ensuing strain and exhaustion) of human bodily power, whereas by contrast, work is the planned and instrumental production of the human environment, the bringing into being of all those artefacts, from clothing to buildings to works of art which provide for a more commodious living. *Homo faber*, the craftsman, is distinguished from the labourer in the different instrumentality of his activity. Artefacts are first conceived, then their production executed. Whilst their production, the effort that brings them about, may be as irksome as labour in a psychological or physical sense, there is a fundamental difference from labour in so far as they do not respond to urgent physical necessity. Indeed, in the case of the craftsman who produces tools, they dominate labour, for by producing new tools for the labourer the essence of the labour required to meet needs can be transformed.[6]

Furthermore, work, unlike labour, creates a public realm, that of the marketplace. Work is visible in the production of artefacts, and being artefacts rather than the mere exertion of bodily power in labour, once created they have an existence independent of the individual, a life of their own, as it were, such that they naturally are subject to alienation from one owner to another in a way that labour (at least in so far as labour is not commodified as a 'transfer' of bodily power from one to another) is not. Arendt's characterisation of the modern attitude to social life is, very roughly, that it confuses labour with work in an attempt to assert the equality of all human economic contribution, with the result that it models the public realm as a marketplace.[7] The public realm becomes imbued with the instrumentalism of *homo faber*, the producer of objects, the existence of which is sought in order to provide for the ease or comfort of individuals in the private realm. The public realm's very existence is to provide for the private realm of individuals.

What is missing in the modern world is a proper understanding of 'action'. Action, for the ancient Greeks, encompasses the idea that a man's life, *qua* human life, concerns his acting and speaking with others, so as to give his life significance.

[6] ibid, 121–22.
[7] ibid, 160–67, 295–325.

It is only in the light of being with others, and being remembered by them, that each person is made real and individual, rather than just existing as a biological organism amongst a plurality of others of the same species. This is what life in the *polis* promised: a place of discourse and deed, in which an individual could reveal the distinct identity of his own character; every individual would have his own story, in respect of which he was, to a large extent at least, an author. For the purposes of our concern here, the main point of this conception of action, whatever the specifics of the activity involved, is that human life on this understanding is the point of existence, the reason for which both labour *and* work are carried out. The ease and comfort that these provide would literally be senseless unless understood as the creation of the conditions for action.

The public realm of action could not be more different from the public realm of *homo faber*, the marketplace, the whirl of commerce and trade. Rather than serving the private realm, the private realm is *its* servant, for the public realm of action is the realm of life itself.[8] Perhaps, as conceived by the ancients, for whom oratory, politics and war seemed chiefly to demarcate the public world of action, this picture is not particularly attractive.[9] And perhaps it can be 'domesticated' in the sense that action need not be conceived to be public in a kind of personally visible, political sense. Indeed, I suggest something along those lines in a moment when we get to the gentleman. At this point I merely want to claim that one aspect of the world of action depicted here surely is undeniably attractive, that is, that there may be values to be realised in a well-lived life beyond the private satisfactions of ease, comfort and diversion.

II The Gentleman

In terms of the *quid pro quo* received by the labourer and the worker for their activity, there are obvious differences. The labourer is either a slave, or a wage-earner. A worker, or maker, by contrast, is of course a trader, who sells his activity through the sale of the objects he produces. Of course the difference between these two has blurred in the modern world – all sorts of 'remuneration' for one's economic activity can be lumped under the concept of 'employment income', however it is legally constituted, via an hourly wage, through an annual salary, as payment for services, as year-end bonuses, whatever. But there is still here a contrast between work and labour, on the one hand, and action on the other. The person of action, the actor in the polis, is not, of course, paid anything for what he does. Rather, unless he has property – some sort of right to income through the

[8] There is an obvious sense in which, however the public realm is conceived, as a marketplace or a polis, the prioritising of the public over the private may be thoroughgoingly sexist, to the extent that fitness for participation in one realm rather than the other is 'gendered'.

[9] Arendt points out that the ancient public realm of the polis was essentially agonistic, in which one, at least, of the chief purposes of action was to attain distinction. Arendt, above n 3, 41, 175–76.

labour or work of others so to be sufficiently independent of labour or work himself – he cannot act in this realm at all.

And this thought takes us to an idea of property which Arendt claims is rather different from our own. Arendt clearly points out that property, in its ancient and early modern sense, diverges from our modern idea of property as economic wealth. Property, so understood, is rather the basis upon which one is free from the requirement to work, or labour, that is, to participate in the active life.[10] However, as I read her, Arendt seems to miss the following thread in the transformation of property to our modern understanding of it, that is, property conceived of as wealth, as a substantial 'share' in the national economic output.

Burke's defence of the right to property and his antagonism to commerce and the 'monied interest' is evocative of this thread.[11] Property, including the property of the Church, is, for Burke, a foundation for the nobility and the clergy, and the importance of this is that it affords, and *entitles*, those persons with property to more or less create the society, the manners and character, of their country. It is not, in spirit, a million miles away from the ancient claim that some must be free of work so as to live the life of the human.

But despite the apparent commitment to inequality, there is something promising in this Burkean line of thought. In the first place, for Burke the public realm of politics is not truly the realm of action, as it was conceived to be by the ancients. True, somewhat like the freemen of the ancient polis, the sovereign, peers and elected representatives in the Commons have the right to rule because their education and connection to society make them fit to govern. But government *per se* is not the end of their education and connection to society; rather, the reverse. Government institutions are through and through practical, and their practical orientation is towards the preservation and improvement of the society in which men find their true satisfactions in life. It is this very practical, not to say mundane, function of the state that so violently stirs Burke against the theoretical, abstract mode of thinking which he sees in the revolutionaries in France. The revolutionaries have squandered their very society in order to place above it and glorify what should be a mere instrument fitted to serve it.

But what of this nobility, these men of society? What is their *action*, which justifies their freedom from want and toil? It is, I think, interesting that in defending the rights of property Burke does not justify the existence of the nobility as a historically entitled military caste, despite that fact about their origin. Rather, they, like the clergy and the classes from whom the members of the Commons are drawn, are justified in their positions by the various ways they are intended to contribute to the society of the country. Burke, as a gentleman and philosopher, benefited from the institution of property by way of patronage and not from his own property, but it can be reckoned that this sort of patronage, which allowed

[10] Arendt, above n 3, chs 7 and 8.

[11] E Burke, *Reflections on the Revolution in France* (edited and with an 'Introduction' by CC O'Brien) (London, Penguin, 1968) (1790) 138, 142, 174, 180, 209–14, 264, 274.

him to pass into society and become one of the governing classes, was for Burke one of the very strengths of that institution.

And this, finally, brings us to the gentleman. What I am concerned with is the way in which payment for the time of a gentleman was originally conceived when the renaissance and enlightenment began to give rise to the 'professional', the member of a society of learning, whether scientific or legal, whose learning might sometimes be applied for the benefit of a requesting individual. Of course, if a gentleman were 'retained' by a magnate for an extended period, as Burke was, we have the well-known relationship of patronage. But what is interesting and less well known is that even in the case of one person seeking the occasional assistance of a gentleman, such as that of a client seeking the advice or advocacy of a barrister, the understanding of the nature of the payment was essentially the same.

III Remuneration as a 'Contribution to One's Living'

As in the case of patronage, the purpose of payment was not payment to 'compensate' for the gentleman professional's labour, nor to meet the 'price' of his services as if, like *homo faber*, he were offering goods in the marketplace, but rather as a contribution to 'his living'.[12] Such financial contributions were conceived as contributions to the very freedom from labour and work which permitted the gentleman professional to acquire and pursue the learning which made him the gentleman professional he was. Furthermore, it counted as an acknowledgement that the science or learning possessed by the gentleman professional was of some value in its own right, of some value beyond any instrumental or transactional value it might have when employed to solve any particular problem, or factor in some individual transaction.

Now, this conception of remuneration is interesting to me because it is anti-property fetishistic. The very relationship of remuneration is one which emphasises the life itself of the recipient; he is not being remunerated for a slice of his labour power, or his work product, but for his willing participation in an enterprise which both he and his patron consider worthy of his time. Rather than conceiving of the gentleman professional as someone who *has* something of value, which he can exchange, he is rather a *doer*, someone who can participate in some action with another or others to the advantage of them both.[13] For the gentleman

[12] I must indicate that I have not made up the following account of the way payments to gentlemen were conceived, but that for the life of me I cannot find, despite serious endeavour, where I read it described in detail. All pointers to sources will be most gratefully received. The fact that the remuneration of a parish priest (vicar or rector) was called a 'living' is the most suggestive usage reflecting the underlying idea. However, even if this conception of remuneration of the profession was not universal, or even widespread, it is worth pursuing as one way in which remuneration *can* be conceived.

[13] In making her critique of the 'distributive paradigm', which has many affinities with 'property fetishism', Iris Young says that this paradigm emphasises 'having' over 'doing'; Iris Marion Young, *Justice and the Politics of Difference* (Princeton NJ, Princeton University Press, 1990) ch 2, 25, 26. The

professional, the activity is valuable in its own right as an expression of his learning, and an application of it which will itself enhance his own learning – it is an opportunity to learn more; for the patron or client, it is the bringing to bear on his own life a world of science or learning, to participate in an enterprise which is determined not by his immediate wants or necessities,[14] but by a larger picture of human understanding and value.

As I said, I find this picture of remuneration attractive because it seems to offer a 'non-property fetishistic' way of thinking about the employment relationship and the way in which employees are remunerated. In the employment context, property fetishism is the social condition that arises when, by virtue of common 'theoretical' or 'ideological' orientation, people regard themselves not as participants in the organisation of collective activity to provide for the needs and wants of themselves as participants, but as individual recipients of such shares as they can, by hook or by crook, extract from an alien and more or less imposed social and economic structure. This has nothing to do with the size of the share any individual manages to extract. An abused worker who takes what little his employer meanly insists is the most he can offer is no different from a hedge fund manager who regards with malice any regulation of his market conduct. What binds them together is their treating the entirety of their employment or broader economic relations with others as a series of transactions, at best transactions akin to contractual exchanges of property rights, at worst transactions akin to extortion or theft. Words are often revealing, and it is interesting to note the fairly recent rise of the word 'compensation' to mean payment or remuneration. 'Executive compensation' arguably reflects a property fetishised view of economic activity, in which the executive employee receives money damages for the injury of having to work, for the 'loss' caused by having to contribute to an enterprise. Nothing could be further from this conception of remuneration than the 'contribution to one's living' model that I have just sketched.

Moreover, I find the 'contribution to one's living' model attractive because it coheres much better with Collins's claim that a right to work can only ultimately be founded on a right to self-realisation[15] than do other conceptions of remuneration. If we regard work as more than merely offering a piece of one's time and learning for money received in exchange, but also as an endeavour which is importantly social and public, that is as an expression of one's 'sociable humanity', or to put this another way, as taking action with others in response to reasons for action in genuinely value-generating ways, then on this account, work is intimately involved with life and self-realisation itself, and so remuneration, if it should still be conceived in that way, naturally involves a distribution of economic wherewithal that is intended to preserve that 'living', that *doing*.

main difference between Young and myself is that Young reserves a substantial role for the concept of distributive justice, whereas I think, properly understood, her arguments and others establish that the very concept is ill-conceived.

[14] Which may not even be thoughtful or well-formed; think of the patron consulting an architect.

[15] See H Collins in this volume, ch 2.

But is this conception of remuneration, as patronage or a contribution to one's living, a living in which one's very self is in part realised and determined by how one acts with others, just fanciful, even romantic? Is it even possible to suggest that in the modern world this understanding of a contribution to one's living could be generalised across the economy? Can we escape the twin concepts of remuneration – wages for labour or the sale of one's services – which so predominate in the modern era?

It seems to me that, if we rooted out property fetishism, we might. But there is an obvious initial objection. Whilst modern societies have through technological advance freed many if not most individuals from the sort of 'necessitous labour' that perhaps few would, just for the sake of doing it, voluntarily undertake, there will, one suspects, always be a need for some to labour, that is, to undertake work which in itself cannot, or rarely could, serve as a robust means of self-realisation; and since someone's got to do it, doesn't this entail that some will always have the status (partial, to be sure) of slaves to necessity, who must be compensated in keeping with the nature of their efforts, with wages? I can think of two replies, but I must first pause to say, as Collins does, that it is true that participating in any collective enterprise can, at least in principle, serve as an opportunity for self-realisation simply in virtue of the fact that one forms relationships of value with one's co-workers, and indeed, in so far as the workplace allows any worker some measure of self-direction, initiative, decision-making with others, no one should deny that these features alone importantly serve self-realisation. So that's all to the good. But to my mind the problem remains, which is that, as everyone understands, some jobs are better than others, or if this is not absolutely so, that some jobs will always be seen in a social context as more interesting, public, vital, significant for how the society goes, than others.

The first reply is that it is incorrect to regard the modern day labourer or worker as the whole of the person we remunerate. A person is not to be perceived only as the job he has. Surely we think this is true. As a social actor, partly in his work but also much more importantly outside it in these cases, such a person is just as much in need of the freedom from toil to participate in the genuine, non-instrumentally valuable, life of the community, perhaps its politics in particular. As such, the cleaner of my office just as much as I do needs and deserves a remuneration which frees him, for most of his time (a 40-hour work week is, one hopes, not so exhausting in itself that there could be no life in the 'leisure' hours that remain) to pursue a life of action with others.

Second, Arendt's division between labour, work, and action, whilst analytically fruitful, is clearly too pure as a practical matter, in economically advanced Western societies at least. Most modern occupations involve some of all three. As any academic or artist or politician will tell you, the life of an academic or artist or politician, though surely action in Arendt's or Burke's sense in many respects, also includes the exhaustive, life-spending aspects of labour (even if not directly related to meeting biological necessity) and the instrumental concerns that go with making. I do not think that anyone would nowadays so sharply distinguish the work of the hands from the work of the mind so as to suggest that the former is inherently more irksome than the latter. (There are many occasions when I would gladly do a hundred press-ups rather than mark *another* script.) Despite what the ancients thought of sculptors, neither is it any longer true (if it ever was) that working with one's hands is less 'meaning generating' than the work of the mind. Without disparaging the importance for the modern world of double-entry bookkeeping, surely it would be foolhardy to claim that the profession of accountancy is, for the individuals who practise it, more self-realising than is the work of the jeweller or painter or acrobat, just on the basis that the former was not the 'work of the hands'.

There is, furthermore, a positive argument for the 'contribution to one's living' conception of justified remuneration that can be made on egalitarian grounds. After all, how much does one need to be free to act socially in one's community? Remuneration on this basis suggests not an inegalitarian distribution, but rather a fairly radical departure from current practice in the direction of equality: on this view the idea of the 'living wage', which has received so much press of late and deservedly so, is a much more extensive notion than that of merely being able to afford reasonable shelter, nutrition and clothing without relying upon charity or government support. It would suggest a 'minimum contribution to the living' of any employed individual so as to enable them to participate fully in the public and social life of their communities, cultural, artistic and educational life included.

It seems to me that once this way of looking at remuneration is envisaged, we understand the nature of the resentment every right-thinking person feels towards bankers' bonuses and similar outrageous payments, whereas nothing like the same disquiet is felt over the Wilt Chamberlain example,[16] or over footballers' salaries, or over the piles of money Madonna has got. Whatever one's egalitarian intuitions, at least it can be said of Madonna and the athletes that their lavish remuneration really is based upon willing 'buyers' and willing 'sellers' of an identifiable product or contribution. It would, however, seem entirely implausible to say the same for the finance 'industry', since the bankers and traders could only claim their right to bonuses and so on by way of a claim to legitimacy based upon their talent suitably honed by education, ie, their professional expertise, to which they can still lay claim irrespective of the outcome of its employment:[17]

> it is not our fault that our various manipulations caused the world economy to tank; that is just the way the modern world of finance *is*; and *you* couldn't have done any better; we, after all, are the best and brightest; we have the Nobel Prize winners on our side.

But if this is so, then their spectacularly lavish compensation is not justified on the same basis as Madonna's is, who can conceivably fall under the *homo faber*,

[16] R Nozick, *Anarchy, State and Utopia* (Oxford, Basil Blackwell, 1974) 161–64.

[17] Which is not to say that bodies of professionals cannot be judged by the outcomes of their performances. Doctors, lawyers and politicians, for example, are regularly so judged.

Arendtian 'work' category of human activity.[18] They can only claim to be regarded as *actors*, whose basis of payment is the gentleman's claim to a contribution to his living. And on what possible basis could anyone claim a contribution to a living so stratospherically lavish? There is, of course, no such basis, for no one needs even a fraction of that 'compensation' to live, and live well, so as to be meaningfully free from the toil which takes one away from one's learning and the practice thereof.

There is a final objection to taking seriously the model of remuneration I am advocating, which is that modelling the justice of remuneration upon patronage simply offends human dignity. A free market allows one to enter into a consensual contract on terms one chooses oneself. To be the object of patronage, by the opposite token, is equivalent to being 'kept', like a mistress, or worse, a slave; recall that one of the defences of slavery was that a slave owner had an interest in 'keeping his slaves well' not only to ensure their capital value, but also to keep them reasonably content so that they would contribute dutifully to his enterprises – whereas the wage-giver had no such interest. Indeed, on this account 'wage-slavery'[19] was worse than true slavery, because it was in the interest of the wage-payer to pay the absolute minimum, to pay just as little as he could so as to extract the labour-power he required, with no regard for the welfare of the worker whatsoever; when this one was 'used up', another could always be found to replace him. But surely such considerations don't mean that slavery is actually preferable to wage-slavery; the former offends human dignity in a way that even the most exploitative forms of employment contract, even indentured servitude, cannot. The upshot, then, of this argument, is that only where remuneration of employment is conceived of in terms of 'exchange', whereby what is given in exchange by the employee is simply the value he can give to the enterprise, deracinated from any larger, self-realising aspect of his interest in participation in that enterprise, is the employee's dignity preserved. The patronage relationship, like that of slavery, is one in which the employer becomes akin to an owner of the employee.

There is, however, I should argue, a confusion here. Remuneration conceived as a contribution to one's living or patronage has nothing to do with any negation of consent or dignity. Rather, it establishes differently than do wage contracts the nature of the terms consented to. I get to decide whether I enter a contract of employment in any case, but on the 'being kept' model, I understand the offer of remuneration as a contribution to my living, one which is intended to 'keep' me in the standard of life that is supposed to facilitate my participation in the enterprise, ie, to give it the benefit of my expertise and to pursue my learning further,[20]

[18] Although through the manipulation of language, eg, by framing the provision of 'financial *services*' as the selling of '*financial products*' a stab is made at equating their position in the same sort of terms, as makers and traders of goods.

[19] The term has various shades of meaning, but the basic idea is that a true slave is 'bought', whereas a wage-slave is only 'rented'; the employer of wage-slaves, it follows, is only interested in the wage-slave so long as they are profitably employable, and so long as no cheaper wage-slave comes along. In particular, not 'owning' wage-slaves, the employer can discard them (terminate their employment) when they are no longer fit for work, and no obligation is owed to them as regards their continuing survival.

[20] There are few jobs today in which there is no element of 'continuing professional development'.

as well as to ensure that I have sufficient leisure and opportunity to become a full actor in the life of my community. Where my employment with one business or institution is full-time according to the sense of 'full-time' which operates in our society, then my employer, my patron, must conceive of my remuneration as completely providing me with the economic wherewithal I require to live a self-realising life. And to put the boot on the other foot – the 'wage/exchange' model of employment implicitly accepts the possibility, which has been widely actualised, of remuneration which falls very short of providing a genuine living for many economic participants. I have already mentioned the struggle for a living wage. So what claim to dignity is being advanced here? In the context of modern, Western economies, where there is a widespread belief that all citizens should have genuine opportunities to lead worthwhile lives, this claim about the dignity of the wage/exchange model goes hand in hand, usually implicitly to be sure, with the view that businesses which pay less that the living wage have the right to 'externalise' the cost of living of their employees. That is, someone other than they are to provide what is necessary to bring their employees up to a reasonable standard of living, either private charity or public assistance of one kind or another. How does an employee's being put in that position reflect their dignity?

And, in my experience anyway, the conceptual terms of the 'being kept' model of employment contract could hardly be worse than the other models,[21] which have more and more come to be embraced explicitly by university administrators (to consider the case closest to my own experience). Perhaps academics, including libertarians and Rawlsians working in academic political theory departments, should ask themselves the question: in comparison to the alternative modes of economic remuneration, *is it really so bad to be 'kept'*?

[21] I should say here at once that I am not in the least sceptical of the 'nobility of contract', which allows strangers to enter cooperative relationships. See JE Penner, 'Voluntary Obligations and the Scope of the Law of Contract' (1996) 2 *Legal Theory* 325; JE Penner, 'Promises, Agreements and Contracts' in G Klass, G Letsas and P Saprai (eds), *Philosophical Foundations of the Law of Contract* (Oxford, Oxford University Press, 2014). But employees and their employers, while not 'intimates', like friends and family members, are not strangers either. A relationship of 'patronage' or 'contributing to one's living' is not one that can hold of strangers.

6

The Right to Work in International Human Rights Law

COLM O'CINNEIDE

Introduction

Article 23(1) of the Universal Declaration of Human Rights (UDHR) recognises that the right to work is a fundamental right: 'Everyone has the right to work, to free choice of employment, to just and favourable conditions of work and to protection against unemployment'. The universal and fundamental character of the right to work is also affirmed in the provisions of a range of international human rights treaty instruments, such as Article 6 of the International Covenant on Economic, Social and Cultural Rights (ICESCR); Article 11(1)(a) of the Convention on the Elimination of All Forms of Discrimination against Women (CEDAW); Article 1 of the European Social Charter (ESC); Article 15 of the EU Charter of Fundamental Rights (hereafter the EU Charter); Article 15 of the African Charter on Human and People's Rights (the African Charter); and Article 6 of the Additional Protocol to the American Convention on Human Rights in the Area of Economic, Social and Cultural Rights (the San Salvador Protocol).[1] The Preambles of a number of International Labour Organization (ILO) conventions, including in particular the Employment Policy Convention of 1964, also state explicitly that their provisions are intended to give effect to the right to work.[2] State parties to these treaty instruments, which include most of the Member States of the UN, are thus subject to legally binding obligations under international law to respect this right: however, what giving effect to this obligation entails is often a matter of debate.

[1] See also Art 5(e)(i) of the International Convention on the Elimination of All Forms of Racial Discrimination (CERD); Art 32 of the Convention on the Rights of the Child (CRC); Arts 11, 25, 26, 40, 52 and 54 of the International Convention on the Protection of the Rights of All Migrant Workers and Members of Their Families (the 'Migrant Workers Convention'); Art 27 of the International Convention on the Rights of Persons with Disabilities (CRPD).

[2] The fundamental nature of the right to work has also been affirmed by the United Nations General Assembly in Art 6 of the Declaration on Social Progress and Development, GA Resolution 2542 (XXIV) of 11 December 1969, UN Doc A/7630 (1969).

The conceptual core of the right to work as defined and set out in these international human rights treaty instruments is easy to delineate. It protects and gives expression to the human interest in engaging in productive labour. This can be viewed as an instrumentalist good, in the sense that combining together with others in work enables individuals to participate as autonomous members of society in the social, economic and political life of their community. It also can be viewed as an intrinsic good, in the sense that humans express themselves and derive dignity from how they interact with their environment through their work. Both of these aspects of the right are acknowledged in General Comment No 18 on the right work issued in 2005 by the UN Committee on Economic, Social and Cultural Rights (CESCR), which sets out the Committee's interpretation of Article 6 ICESCR:

> The right to work is essential for realizing other human rights and forms an inseparable and inherent part of human dignity. Every individual has the right to be able to work, allowing him/her to live in dignity. The right to work contributes at the same time to the survival of the individual and to that of his/her family, and insofar as work is freely chosen or accepted, to his/her development and recognition within the community.[3]

However, different views exist as to what constitutes the scope and normative content of the right to work and the exact nature of the moral and legal obligations that it imposes on national authorities. Like other socio-economic rights, its contours have not yet been systematically mapped out through the incremental development of national and international human rights jurisprudence, unlike the case with civil and political rights such as freedom of association.

For example, some element of choice in how one disposes of labour is generally assumed to be included within the scope of the right – Article 6 ICESCR states that the right to work 'includes the right of everyone to the opportunity to gain his living by work which he freely chooses or accepts', while Article 1 ESC provides that states in giving effect to the right to work must 'protect effectively the right of the worker to earn his living in an occupation freely entered upon'.[4] However, how far this freedom should extend is an open question. Are the

[3] CESCR, General Comment No 18: The Right to Work, Article 6 of the International Covenant on Economic, Social and Cultural Rights, UN Doc E/C.12/GC/18 (2005) (hereafter General Comment No 18). Note also the Preamble to ILO Convention No 168 concerning Employment Promotion and Protection against Unemployment 1988: 'the importance of work and productive employment in any society not only because of the resources which they create for the community, but also because of the income which they bring to workers, the social role which they confer and the feeling of self-esteem which workers derive from them'. For a more critical view of the status of the right to work which draws upon the writings of Paul Lafargue, see J Sparrow, 'A Right to be Lazy?' available on the *Right Now: Human Rights in Australia* blog, 14 April 2014, at: rightnow.org.au/featured/a-right-to-be-lazy/.

[4] Similarly Art 15 of the EU Charter provides that 'Everyone has the right to engage in work and to pursue a freely chosen or accepted occupation', while Art 6 of the San Salvador Protocol provides that 'Everyone has the right to work, which includes the opportunity to secure the means for living a dignified and decent existence by performing a freely elected or accepted lawful activity'. Note however that the provisions of Art 15 of the African Charter do not refer to freedom of occupational choice: it states that 'every individual shall have the right to work under equitable and satisfactory conditions, and shall receive equal pay for equal work'.

requirements of the right satisfied if individuals have access to 'decent' work and are not compelled to engage in forms of labour that are incompatible with human dignity? Or does it encompass a substantive entitlement to enter into and freely engage in one's chosen occupation or profession, as recognised in German constitutional law?[5] In the United States, various state legislatures have enacted 'right to work' legislation which prohibit 'union security agreements' and other forms of compact between employers and trade unions that make the payment of financial contributions to union funds a condition of employment. Is this a legitimate interpretation of the right to work, or a distortion of its principled basis?[6]

The scope and extent of the positive obligations that this right imposes on national authorities are also controversial.[7] The classic typology of human rights obligations refers to the need for states to 'respect, protect and fulfil' fundamental rights[8] – how then should states go about respecting, protecting and fulfilling the right to work, given the wide range of possible legal and policy measures that could have an impact on the enjoyment of this right? Is the state under an obligation to take steps to maximise employment opportunities? If so, how far does this obligation extend? Is it sufficient if national authorities refrain from discriminating against certain groups and put certain legal guarantees in place which provide some protection against exploitation in the workplace, or is more expected?

The relationship between the right to work and other human rights is also uncertain. To what extent can its scope and content be distinguished from that of other labour rights, such as the right to just and favourable conditions of work (protected by Article 7 ICESCR and Article 3 ESC among other treaty provisions), or from well-established civil and political rights such as freedom of association, freedom from discrimination and freedom from slavery and forced labour?[9] Does it add anything of substance to the normative content of these other rights, or is it best conceived of as an amorphous concept that can inform the interpretation of other human rights but remains essentially indeterminate?

This chapter does not attempt to answer all these questions. Instead, it examines how the right to work has been defined, interpreted and applied in

[5] See Art 12 of the German Basic Law 1949; see also BVerfG 7, 377, 11 June 1958 (the '*Apotheken-Urteil*' case).

[6] See K Stone in this volume, ch 15. See also B Collins, *Right to Work Laws: Legislative Background and Empirical Research*, Congressional Research Service Report 7-5700 (6 December 2012), available at: www.fas.org/sgp/crs/misc/R42575.pdf.

[7] See further H Collins, in this volume ch 2.

[8] See H Shue, *Basic Rights: Subsistence, Affluence and US Foreign Policy*, 2nd edn (Princeton NJ, Princeton University Press, 1996); A Eide, UN Special Rapporteur for the Right to Food, 'The Right to Adequate Food as a Human Right: Final Report' UN Doc E/CN.4/Sub.2/1987/23 (1987) [67]–[69].

[9] Freedom of association is protected, inter alia, by Art 22 of the International Covenant on Civil and Political Rights (ICCPR) and Art 11 of the European Convention on Human Rights (ECHR). Freedom from discrimination is guaranteed by Art 21 ICCPR and Art 14 and Protocol 12 of the ECHR, while prohibition on forced labour is set out, inter alia, in Art, 8 ICCPR and in Art 4 ECHR. Certain forms of forced labour can be understood as a form of slavery, in line with the approach of the European Court of Human Rights in *Siliadin v France* (2006) 43 EHRR 16 and *Rantsev v Cyprus and Russia* App no 25965/04 (ECtHR, 7 January 2010): see V Mantouvalou 'Servitude and Forced Labour in the 21st Century: The Human Rights of Domestic Workers' (2006) 35 *Industrial Law Journal* 395.

international human rights law, and in particular within the framework of perhaps the two most prominent treaty instruments concerned with socio-economic rights, namely the ICESCR and the ESC. As set out in what follows, the expert bodies charged with interpreting the provisions of both these treaties, the CESCR and the European Committee on Social Rights (ECSR) respectively, have adopted a similar reading of the scope and normative content of the right to work which draws upon the provisions of relevant ILO instruments and other international standards and reflects a shared understanding of the general substantive parameters of the right.

This common interpretative approach is not without its flaws, as discussed further below. However, the interpretation given by the CESCR and the ECSR to the provisions of the ICESCR and the ESC respectively is generally acknowledged to be highly authoritative.[10] As a result, the manner in which both bodies have interpreted the right of work serves as a highly significant point of reference for national governments, courts, civil society and other international bodies. Consequently, examining how the right to work has been interpreted and applied by the CESCR and the ESC helps to shed some light on its scope and content, not least by providing a starting point for wider critical exegesis.

I The Right to Work Within the Framework of the International Covenant on Economic, Social and Cultural Rights (ICESCR)

The ICESCR is an international human rights instrument which commits States Parties to work towards securing the 'full realisation' of a comprehensive list of fundamental socio-economic rights. Adopted by the UN General Assembly in 1966, it came into force in 1976: as of March 2014, it has been ratified by 161 states. The Covenant is perhaps the best known and most prominent socio-economic rights instrument in the world: its provisions have been central to the development of social rights discourse over the last few decades.[11]

Article 2(1) ICESCR requires each State Party to

> take steps, individually and through international assistance and cooperation . . . to the maximum of [their] available resources, with a view to achieving progressively the full

[10] In *RMT v UK* App no 31045/10 (ECtHR, 8 April 2014) the European Court of Human Rights commented that the 'interpretative value' of the ECSR's jurisprudence was 'generally accepted by states and the Committee of Ministers [of the Council of Europe]': see [92]–[94].

[11] For an overview of the origins and textual provisions of the ICESCR, see M Craven, *The International Covenant on Economic, Social and Cultural Rights: A Perspective on its Development* (Oxford, Clarendon Press, 1995); B Saul, D Kinley and J Mowbray, *The International Covenant on Economic, Social and Cultural Rights: Cases, Materials, and Commentary* (Oxford, Oxford University Press, 2014).

> realization of the rights recognized in the present Covenant by all appropriate means, including particularly the adoption of legislative measures.

Article 2(2) builds on this general requirement by requiring States Parties to guarantee that the rights set out in the Covenant 'will be exercised without discrimination', while Article 4 provides that any limitations on the enjoyment of these rights must be 'compatible with the nature of these rights and solely for the purpose of promoting the general welfare in a democratic society'.[12]

By virtue of Article 16, States Parties are required to report to the UN Economic and Social Council (ECOSOC) on how they are giving effect to their obligations under the Covenant. Since 1985, ECOSOC's functions in this respect have been performed by CESCR.[13] The Committee is a body of independent experts which monitors implementation of the Covenant and addresses concerns and recommendations to States Parties as appropriate by issuing 'concluding observations' in respect of the state reports which are submitted to it on a five-yearly basis. The CESCR also issues 'General Comments' which set out its authoritative interpretation of specific provisions of the Covenant.[14]

A Overview of the Scope and Content of the Right to Work as Protected by Article 6 ICESCR

The right to work is protected by Article 6 ICESCR in the following terms:

> Article 6 – The Right to Work
>
> 1. The States Parties to the present Covenant recognize the right to work, which includes the right of everyone to the opportunity to gain his living by work which he freely chooses or accepts, and will take appropriate steps to safeguard this right.
>
> 2. The steps to be taken by a State Party to the present Covenant to achieve the full realization of this right shall include technical and vocational guidance and training programmes, policies and techniques to achieve steady economic, social and cultural development and full and productive employment under conditions safeguarding fundamental political and economic freedoms to the individual.

[12] For an overview of the nature of state obligations under ICESCR, see CESCR, General Comment No 3: The Nature of States Parties' Obligations, UN Doc E/1991/23. See also P Alston and G Quinn, 'The Nature and Scope of States Parties' Obligations under the International Covenant on Economic, Social and Cultural Rights' (1987) 9 *Human Rights Quarterly* 156; M Sepúlveda Carmona, *The Nature of the Obligations under the International Covenant on Economic, Social and Cultural Rights* (Antwerp, Intersentia, 2003); 'The Limburg Principles on the Implementation of the International Covenant on Economic, Social and Cultural Rights', UN Doc E/CN.4/1987/17, annex (1987).

[13] The CESCR was established on 28 May 1985 by Resolution 1985/17 of the Economic and Social Council.

[14] By virtue of the Optional Protocol to ICESCR which came into force in 2013, the Committee can also receive and consider communications from individuals claiming that their rights under the Covenant have been violated, undertake enquiries into grave or systematic violations of its provisions and consider interstate complaints: however, as yet, only 12 states have ratified this Protocol and no such communications, enquiries or complaints have been received or initiated by the Committee.

This is the first substantive individual right set out in the text of the Covenant.[15] The right to work is thus implicitly acknowledged to be fundamental in nature: the enjoyment of certain of the other socio-economic rights set out in subsequent provisions of the ICESCR, including in particular the right to just and favourable conditions of work set out in Article 7 of the Covenant, can be viewed as linked to and dependent upon this right.

The wording of Article 6 also makes clear that all persons ('everyone') subject to the authority of a State Party are protected by its provisions. It is also apparent that individuals should be free to choose which forms of labour they engage in ('work which he freely chooses or accepts'), and that States Parties are subject to wide-ranging positive obligations to take 'appropriate steps to safeguard this right' which should be directed towards the achievement of 'steady economic, social and cultural development and full and productive employment' under 'conditions safeguarding fundamental political and economic freedoms'.

In other words, non-discrimination in access to employment, free choice in how individuals dispose of their labour and the orientation of national policy towards securing full employment and dignified working conditions for all workers are all integral elements of the normative content of the right to work as set out in Article 6 ICESCR. In contrast, 'just and favourable conditions of work' as protected by Article 7 of the Covenant, which encompasses the entitlement to fair and decent remuneration, safe and healthy working conditions, equal opportunity and rest and leisure time (including 'reasonable limitation of working time and periodic holidays with pay'), fall outside the scope of Article 6 and thus the right to work as defined within the framework of the ICESCR.

However, the rights guaranteed in Article 7, along with the right to form a trade union and to engage in strike action as provided for in Article 8 of the Covenant, are logically interlinked with the right to work.[16] As a result, Article 6 needs to be interpreted with reference to the requirements of Articles 7 and 8 along with the other provisions of the Covenant. The content of the right to work within the framework of the ICESCR is primarily focused on guaranteeing access to employment, but its provisions must to be applied in a manner that harmonises with the guarantees of dignity at work and the other fundamental socio-economic rights set out in the Covenant.

[15] Art 6 is the first provision in Part III of the Covenant, which is concerned with setting out the substantive economic, social and cultural rights that come within its scope.

[16] This is implicitly recognised in the reference contained in Art 6(2) ICESCR to states achieving full employment under conditions which safeguard 'fundamental political and economic freedoms', which presumably include the fundamental rights guaranteed in other provisions of the Covenant such as Arts 7 and 8.

B General Comment No 18 – How the CESCR has Interpreted the Right to Work

Further guidance on the scope and content of Article 6 can be found in the jurisprudence of the CESCR. Of particular importance in this context is General Comment No 18 on Article 6, adopted by the Committee on 24 November 2005, which sets out the Committee's authoritative interpretation of the right to work. This General Comment is perhaps the most comprehensive overview of the right to work that exists within the framework of international human rights law, and deserves close attention.

In the General Comment, the CESCR notes that the right to work as set out in Article 6 imposes specific legal obligations on State parties to the ICESCR rather than simply outlining a 'philosophical principle'.[17] The Committee goes on to emphasise that 'respect for the individual and his dignity is expressed through the freedom of the individual regarding the choice to work'.[18] It also makes the obvious point that Article 6 should not be understood as establishing an absolute and unconditional right to obtain employment, but instead 'affirms the obligation of States parties to assure individuals their right to freely chosen or accepted work'. This entitlement encompasses the right 'not to be deprived of work unfairly' or to be 'forced in any way whatsoever to exercise or engage in employment'. It also includes a 'right of access to a system of protection guaranteeing each worker access to employment' and 'not to be unfairly deprived of employment'.[19]

The Committee goes on to discuss the relationship between the right to work as set out in Article 6 and other provisions of the Covenant. It notes that the right to work is an 'individual right that belongs to each person and is at the same time a collective right', which 'encompasses all forms of work, whether independent work or dependent wage-paid work'.[20] Article 6 'proclaims the right to work in a general sense': subsequently, the individual dimension of the right is developed 'through the recognition in Article 7 of the right of everyone to the enjoyment of just and favourable conditions of work', while its collective dimension is 'addressed in Article 8, which enunciates the right of everyone to form trade unions and join the trade union of his/her choice as well as the right of trade unions to function freely'.[21] In line with the harmonious approach to interpreting the Covenant outlined above, the Committee emphasises that these rights are 'interdependent'.[22]

This means that '[w]ork as specified in Article 6 of the Covenant must be *decent work*', which 'respects the fundamental rights of the human person as well as the rights of workers in terms of conditions of work safety and remuneration',

[17] General Comment No 18, [2].
[18] ibid, [4].
[19] ibid.
[20] General Comment No 18, [6].
[21] ibid, [2].
[22] ibid, [8].

'provides an income allowing workers to support themselves and their families' and is not incompatible with the 'physical and mental integrity' of the worker in the exercise of his/her employment'.[23] The Committee also refers to other international instruments in this context, in particular the provisions of ILO Convention No 158 Concerning Termination of Employment (1982) which requires states to establish adequate redress mechanisms to cover cases of unjustified dismissal.[24]

The right to work in Article 6 is thus best viewed as obliging states to take action to secure access to 'decent work' as defined by both the provisions of the ICESCR and other relevant international instruments. This is an important dimension of the right to work as set out in the ICESCR framework: states are required to ensure access to decent employment, not just 'bare' employment.

Having set out its interpretation of the general scope of Article 6 and its relationship with other provisions of the Charter in the opening paragraphs of the General Comment, the Committee attempts to flesh out the normative content of this right in greater detail. It takes the view that states must take steps to give full effect to the 'following interdependent and essential elements' of the right to work:[25]

> (a) *Availability*. States parties must establish specialised services to assist and support individuals in order to enable them to identify and find available employment. The Committee makes clear that this element of the right imposes an obligation on the state to give effect to policy measures directed towards achieving 'full employment'.[26]
>
> (b) *Accessibility*. This element of the right has three distinct dimensions, all linked to opening up access to the labour market. First of all, states must prohibit discrimination in access to and maintenance of employment across the range of grounds set out in Articles 2(2) and 3 of the Covenant, namely race, colour, sex, language, religion, political or other opinion, national or social origin, property, birth, physical or mental disability, health status (including HIV/AIDS), sexual orientation, or civil, political, social or other status. States parties must also design and implement national policies to promote equality of opportunity and eliminate discrimination, with a view to protecting disadvantaged and marginalised individuals and groups in particular.[27] Secondly, states must take measures to ensure that workplaces are physically accessible, as an aspect of their obligations to persons with disabilities. Thirdly, the concept of accessibility includes the 'right to seek, obtain and impart information on the means of gaining access to employment', meaning that states are obliged to establish data networks and other information-sharing facilities in relation to access to the employment market 'at the local, regional, national and international levels'.[28]

[23] ibid, [7].
[24] ibid, [11].
[25] ibid, [12].
[26] ibid, [19].
[27] In this respect, the Committee cross-refers to the provisions of ILO Convention No 111 Concerning Discrimination in Respect of Employment and Occupation, again invoking other international instruments in support of its interpretative approach.
[28] General Comment No 18, [12].

(c) *Acceptability and quality*. This element relates to the requirement that work must be 'decent'. States must take steps to protect the rights of workers to enjoy just and favourable conditions of work, to form trade unions and freely to choose and accept work, ie, to enjoy their rights under Articles 7 and 8 ICESCR. The Committee also reaffirms the need for states parties to 'abolish, forbid and counter all forms of forced labour', as required by Article 10 ICESCR. States are also required to adopt measures to protect vulnerable categories of workers against exploitation.

Turning to the specific nature of the obligations imposed upon States parties by virtue of these interconnected normative elements of the right, the Committee invokes the standard 'respect, protect and fulfil' typology of human tights obligations (already referred to) and sets out to provide a detailed overview of what states must do to conform to the requirements of Article 6.

In this regard, the Committee makes clear that states are under the obligation to *respect* the right to work by, inter alia, 'prohibiting forced or compulsory labour and refraining from denying or limiting equal access to decent work for all persons, especially disadvantaged and marginalized individuals and groups', which include prisoners or detainees, members of minorities, migrant workers, women and young persons.[29] In particular, states must take effective measures to prohibit labour of children under the age of 16 and 'all forms of economic exploitation and forced labour of children'.[30]

The obligation to *protect* the right to work requires States parties to take measures that 'prevent third parties from interfering with the enjoyment of the right to work', by prohibiting non-state actors from engaging in discrimination and/or exploitative practices. States must take measures 'to reduce to the fullest extent possible the number of workers outside the formal economy' who have little or no protection of their employment rights. Moreover, 'domestic and agricultural work must be properly regulated by national legislation so that domestic and agricultural workers enjoy the same level of protection as other workers'. Significantly, the Committee also considers that states are under an obligation to ensure that 'privatisation measures do not undermine workers' rights' and that measures that increase labour market flexibility do not 'render work less stable or reduce . . . social protection'.[31] In addition, effective legal remedies, including 'adequate reparation' should be provided for cases of unfair dismissal and discriminatory treatment.[32]

The obligation to *fulfil* the right to work requires states to adopt and implement a detailed and sufficiently well-resourced national employment strategy directed towards stimulating economic growth, raising standards of living and overcoming 'unemployment and underemployment'. Appropriate benchmarks should be established to monitor progress as part of this policy framework, which should be based on established ILO labour market indicators such as the rate of unemployment and

[29] ibid, [23].
[30] ibid, [24].
[31] ibid, [25].
[32] ibid, [48].

the ratio of formal to informal work.[33] Furthermore, this policy should be drawn up 'on the basis of a participatory and transparent process' of consultation with civil society, experts on labour issues, trade unions, the private sector, international organisations (including the ILO) and marginalised social groups.[34] Special measures should also be taken to reduce the unemployment rate among disadvantaged groups, including women, younger and older persons, migrant workers and persons with disabilities. The Committee also considers that states should also establish vocational education and employment services at national and local levels, along with a 'compensation mechanism' in the event of loss of employment.[35]

In general, the Committee concludes that States parties to the ICESCR are subject to a duty 'to take whatever steps are necessary to ensure that everyone is protected from unemployment and insecurity in employment and can enjoy the right to work as soon as possible'.[36] States are therefore under a specific and continuing obligation 'to move as expeditiously and effectively as possible' towards the full realisation of Article 6, which, inter alia, requires them to 'adopt, as quickly as possible, measures aiming at achieving full employment',[37] and to avoid taking retrogressive measures that have a negative impact on the enjoyment of the right to work.[38]

In addition, they are required to take immediate steps to give effect to certain 'core' obligations, namely to guarantee the right of individuals to access employment 'without discrimination of any kind', regulate the activities of third parties to prevent them engaging in exploitative activities, avoid measures which weaken protection for employment rights and to adopt and implement the type of comprehensive national employment strategy outlined above.[39] States will be in breach of their obligations under Article 6 if they fail to give effect to these obligations in their national law and/or practice.[40]

Significantly, the Committee suggests that states will also be in violation of their obligations if they enter into bilateral or multilateral agreements with other states, international organisations or private actors 'which are manifestly incompatible with international obligations in relation to the right to work'.[41] States

[33] ibid, [46].

[34] ibid, [38]–[44].

[35] ibid, [26].

[36] ibid.

[37] General Comment No 18, [19].

[38] In respect of any 'deliberately retrogressive steps', states 'have the burden of proving that they have been introduced after consideration of all alternatives and that they are duly justified by reference to the totality of the rights provided for in the Covenant in the context of the full use of the States parties' maximum available resources'; General Comment No 18, [34].

[39] General Comment No 18, [31].

[40] The Committee also considers that states should establish 'educational and informational programmes to instil public awareness on the right to work' and 'recognise the right to work in national legal systems': the General Comment provides little detail as to what these specific obligations should entail in practice. The Committee also suggests that the right to work should be made legally enforceable in national law, through incorporation of ICESCR and ILO conventions into domestic law, in order to strengthen effective enjoyment of the right. See General Comment No 18, [49].

[41] General Comment No 18, [32].

should also cooperate and take 'joint and separate action' to realise the right to work, while giving adequate weight to the importance of the right to work in their interaction with international financial institutions. In particular, the Committee emphasises that

> strategies, programmes and policies adopted by States parties under structural adjustment programmes should not interfere with their core obligations in relation to the right to work and impact negatively on the right to work of women, young persons and the disadvantaged and marginalized individuals and groups.[42]

C Analysis – The Strengths and Limits of the Right to Work as Protected by Article 6 ICESCR

The CESCR's interpretative approach to Article 6 has much to commend it. Through General Comment No 18, it has given the right to work a wide-ranging and well-developed interpretation. In essence, the Committee has recognised that the right to work has different normative dimensions: it requires states to take active measures to make work *available* through combating unemployment and underemployment, to make work *accessible* by legislating against discrimination and protecting workers against unfair dismissal and to make work *acceptable* by combating exploitation and protecting workers' rights with a view to ensuring that they enjoy decent working conditions.

The Committee has also recognised that the requirements of Article 6 need to be reflected both at national and transnational level, if full and substantive effect is to be given to the right to work in current conditions of global competition and open markets: the General Comment makes it clear that 'outward-facing' national trade and development policy should reflect the obligation to ensure that workers enjoy access to decent work, just as should 'inward-facing' national employment law and policy. In the General Comment, the CESCR also recognises the reality that 'all members of society have responsibilities regarding the realization of the right to work', especially private employers,[43] and that trade unions and human rights commissions play an important role in defending the right to work, with trade unions described as playing a 'fundamental' role in this regard.[44] The CESCR's approach is also noteworthy for the extent to which it sets out in quite specific detail the types of measures that states must implement in order to give effect to the right: for example, the General Comment makes it clear that states must introduce legislation providing for adequate redress in cases of unfair dismissal, and also draws attention to the need to provide special protection for domestic and agricultural workers.

The CESCR's interpretation of Article 6 is therefore very developed when it comes to delineating the normative scope and content of the right of work.

[42] ibid, [30].
[43] ibid, [52].
[44] ibid, [54].

Furthermore, the CESCR has applied its interpretation of Article 6 in framing its concluding observations in respect of national reports, which provide further guidance as to what forms of state (in)action will constitute a violation of the right to work taken in tandem with other ICESCR rights such as the Article 2 right to non-discrimination.

For example, the Committee has thus 'noted with concern' the failure of certain states to enact comprehensive cross-ground anti-discrimination legislation, to impose a general reasonable accommodation requirement upon employers,[45] or to address the vulnerability of workers on fixed-term contracts.[46] It has also 'recommended' that states take more active steps to combat youth unemployment,[47] to close the gender pay gap and to improve employment opportunities for ethnic minorities.[48] The Committee has also commented negatively on prison inmates being assigned labour duties as part of their sentence,[49] on cuts to unemployment benefit[50] and on the negative impact of austerity measures on vulnerable socio-economic groups.[51]

However, the CESCR's concluding observations can at times be lacking in detailed analysis as to what precisely will constitute a failure to give effect to the requirements of Article 6.[52] This reflects the inherent limits of national reporting mechanisms under international human rights treaty mechanisms: states often provide expert committees such as the CESCR with inadequate information on which to base more detailed and comprehensive conclusions, while the committees themselves usually lack the resources to conduct in-depth analysis of national law and policy. Furthermore, the CESCR in its concluding observations is at times slow to identify what exactly constitutes a violation of the ICESCR, choosing instead to frame its conclusions in terms of recommendations and expressions of concern.[53]

[45] See, eg, CESCR, 'Concluding observations on the 5th periodic report of Denmark' (6 June 2013) E/C.12/DNK/CO/5, para 11.

[46] See, eg, CESCR, 'Concluding observations on the 3rd periodic report of Japan' (10 June 2013) E/C.12/JPN/CO/3, para 16.

[47] See, eg, CESCR, 'Concluding observations on the 3rd periodic report of New Zealand' (31 May 2012) E/C.12/NZL/CO/3, para 15.

[48] See, eg, CESCR, 'Concluding Observations concerning the 4th periodic report of Belgium' (23 December 2013) E/C.12/BEL/CO/4, para 12.

[49] See, eg, CESCR, 'Concluding observations on the 3rd periodic report of Japan' (10 June 2013) E/C.12/JPN/CO/3, para 14.

[50] See, eg, CESCR, 'Concluding observations on the 5th periodic report of Denmark' (6 June 2013) E/C.12/DNK/CO/5, para 10.

[51] See, eg, CESCR, 'Concluding observations on the 5th periodic report of Spain' (6 June 2012) E/C.12/ESP/CO/5, paras 8–12.

[52] See, eg, the thin contents of the Committee's most recent observations in respect of the UK: CESCR, 'Concluding observations on the combined 4th and 5th periodic reports of the UK' (12 June 2009) E/C.12/GBR/CO/5, paras 18–20.

[53] This reluctance to focus on what counts as a violation of Covenant rights partially reflects the uncertain scope of the obligation set out in Art 2 ICESCR on states to give 'progressive realisation' to the rights set out in the Covenant: see A Chapman, 'A "Violations Approach" for Monitoring the International Covenant on Economic, Social and Cultural Rights' (1996) 18 *Human Rights Quarterly* 23.

This means that the 'baseline' of state obligations under Article 6, ie, what measures states should take *at a minimum* to give immediate effect to the core of the right to work while also moving in an expeditious and effective manner towards its full realisation, is not always clear. For example, the CESCR's concluding observations do not provide much detail as to the measures states should adopt to further the goal of achieving full employment as part of their national employment strategy. They also do not delineate the concrete steps that states should take to respect the right to work in their external trade and development policies. In these areas, the Committee's approach to the interpretation of Article 6 remains underdeveloped.

However, in general, the Committee's interpretative approach to Article 6 has put flesh on the bone of the abstract language of the ICESCR. It has clarified the scope and normative content of the right to work, outlined the nature of state obligations that arise in respect of this right and established that states are required to make work available, accessible and acceptable (ie, 'decent'). States must do more than just legislate against discrimination, even though that is an important element of the right: they must actively devise and implement job creation policies which are directed towards securing access to decent employment. This approach echoes ILO standards:[54] furthermore, as discussed in what follows, a similar interpretative approach has been applied by the ECSR in respect of the European Social Charter.

II The Right to Work Within the Framework of the European Social Charter (ESC)

Adopted in 1961,[55] the European Social Charter was a ground-breaking instrument. It predated the ICESCR by five years, and was the first international human rights treaty to set out binding legal obligations to respect socio-economic rights. It was intended to complement the provisions of the European Convention on Human Rights (ECHR): just as the ECHR was designed to ensure respect for fundamental civil and political rights, the Charter was intended to ensure that the Member States of Europe also respected core economic and social rights.

The ESC contains an extensive set of labour rights, including Article 2 (the right to just conditions of work), Article 3 (the right to healthy and safe working conditions) and Article 4 (the right to fair remuneration). These rights are equivalent to the right to just and favourable conditions of work set out in Article 7 ICESCR, and are concerned with ensuring that workers are treated with dignity in

[54] ILO Convention No 168 concerning Employment Promotion and Protection against Unemployment 1988 contains similar requirements.

[55] The European Social Charter was signed by 13 Member States of the Council of Europe in Turin on 18 October 1961 (CETS no 35; 529 UNTS 89). It entered into force on 26 February 1965.

the workplace. However, the right to work itself is protected through the provisions of Article 1 of the Charter.

A Overview of the Scope and Content of the Right to Work as Protected by Article 1 ESC

i Article 1 – The Right to Work

With a view to ensuring the effective exercise of the right to work, the Parties undertake:

1. To accept as one of their primary aims and responsibilities the achievement and maintenance of as high and stable a level of employment as possible, with a view to the attainment of full employment.
2. To protect effectively the right of the worker to earn his living in an occupation freely entered upon.
3. To establish or maintain free employment services for all workers.
4. To provide or promote appropriate vocational guidance, training and rehabilitation.

As with the ICESCR, the placing of work at the beginning of the list of substantive rights is no accident, but rather reflects its fundamental importance in the overall scheme of social rights. Furthermore, it is a 'core' provision of the Charter: states are only obliged to commit themselves to adhering to a certain minimum number of the rights set out in the Charter, but Article 20(1)(b) requires all states to consider themselves to be bound by at least five of the seven core provisions, which include Article 1. (By way of contrast, the 'just conditions of work' provisions of Articles 2–4 are not listed as being among the 'core'.)

The right to work can thus be seen as a cornerstone of the Charter, as it is with respect to the ICESCR: the other social rights set out in its text, including the other core provisions such the Article 12 right to social security and the Article 13 right to social assistance, follow and built upon the foundational right to work. This reflects the values and historical experience of post-war Europe, where the post-1945 welfare states were constructed upon the economic foundations laid down by high levels of employment. It also could be viewed as reflecting the reality that the right to work is the most 'universal' of social rights, in the sense that it is the right which touches most directly upon the daily lives of all people living in Europe. Rights to social protection, housing and so on will primarily benefit the disadvantaged minority who are in greatest need, but ensuring that the vast majority of a national population enjoy the right to work is a *sine qua non* for social rights to have any tangible reality at all.

Compliance with the Charter is monitored by the ECSR primarily through a process whereby States Parties submit periodic reports to the Committee, setting out the steps that they are taking to give effect to their obligations under the Charter. When it receives the reports, the ECSR adopts reasoned conclusions on the reports submitted by the states, on an Article by Article basis.[56] The ECSR does not adopt General Comments setting out its general interpretative approach to particular Charter rights, unlike the CESCR. However, the conclusions of the ECSR formulated in response to national reports have over the years generated an authoritative case law, which as with the interpretative approach of the CESCR have given concrete shape and definition to the abstract provisions of the Charter. In addition, the ECSR's decisions in collective complaints, which reach the Committee from States Parties which have ratified the Additional Collective Complaints Protocol of 1995, also help to clarify the scope and content of the Charter rights.[57]

As with many Charter rights, Article 1 is a complex provision, which is broken down into separate different subsections, discussed in sequential order in what follows.

a Article 1(1) – Full Employment

> With a view to ensuring the effective exercise of the right to work, the Parties undertake to accept as one of their primary aims and responsibilities the achievement and maintenance of as high and stable a level of employment as possible.

The language of Article 1(1) reflects very clearly the time period when the Charter was drafted. It reflects the Keynesian faith in the ability of states to regulate their domestic employment levels which thrived in the post-war Bretton Woods era. In contrast, it eschews nineteenth-century Malthusian theories that viewed unemployment as natural, inevitable and even desirable in certain respects, which later were to be echoed in some of the 'Chicago School' theories developed by Milton Friedman and others.[58] Furthermore, it places the positive obligations of the state front and central to the definition of the right to work: active action by State Parties to maintain high and stable levels of employment is viewed as 'one of their primary aims and responsibilities'.

[56] R Brillat, 'The Supervisory Machinery of the European Social Charter: Recent Developments and their Impact' in G de Búrca and B de Witte (eds), *Social Rights in Europe* (Oxford, Oxford University Press, 2005).

[57] CETS no 158, opened for signature in Strasbourg on 9 November 1995. This procedure allows international NGOs with consultative status with the Council of Europe (and national NGOs, if the State party consents to this), as well as national employer and employee associations, to bring complaints to the Committee alleging the existence of a situation of non-conformity that has a 'collective' dimension, ie, which is not confined to individual cases. See R Churchill and U Khaliq, 'The Collective Complaints System of the European Social Charter: An Effective Mechanism for Ensuring Compliance with Economic and Social Rights?' (2004) 15 *European Journal of International Law* 417; Holly Cullen has noted that the collective complaints procedure is the first 'quasi-judicial' process in international human rights law which has been designed specifically for socio-economic rights: H Cullen, 'The Collective Complaints System of the European Social Charter: Interpretative Methods of the European Committee on Social Rights' (2009) 9 *Human Rights Law Review* 61.

[58] See, eg, M Friedman, 'Comments' in GP Shultz and RZ Aliber (eds), *Guidelines, Informal Controls and the Market Place: Policy Choices in a Full Employment Economy* (Chicago, Chicago University Press, 1966): M Friedman, 'The Role of Monetary Policy' (1968) 58 *American Economic Review* 1.

The ECSR has interpreted the wording of Article 1(1) as requiring State Parties to pursue a policy of full employment. This means on the one hand that states must adopt and follow an economic policy which is conducive to creating and preserving jobs, and on the other must take adequate measures to assist those who become unemployed in finding and/or qualifying for a job. Article 1(1) is an obligation as to means rather than as to result: as with Article 6 ICESCR, failure to achieve full employment does not lead to a conclusion of nonconformity. However, the efforts made by states must be adequate in the light of the existing economic situation and the level of unemployment.[59]

This interpretative approach is in line with that adopted by the CESCR in General Comment No 18. However, unlike the CESCR, the ECSR has attempted to define in some detail what will constitute adequate steps to achieve and maintain a high level of employment. The Committee's assessment of the adequacy of state measures makes use of a number of economic and social indicators. First, the Committee examines a wide range of indicators relating to the national economic situation (for example, GDP growth, inflation, job growth) and patterns of employment (for example, the employment rate, part-time and fixed-term employment). In respect of the latter, it pays special attention to the employment position of vulnerable groups such as youth, the long-term unemployed, ethnic minorities and the disabled.[60] In the light of this information, it then proceeds to examine state employment policy. It examines statistics related to the scope of the employment measures implemented by the state under examination (for example, the number of participants in job creation schemes as a proportion of all unemployed, and the average duration of unemployment that is required before an individual can participate in such a scheme). It will also take into account the amount of resources devoted to national job creation schemes (for example, total expenditure on such schemes as a share of GDP) and the balance struck by the state in question between active and passive policy measures. The Committee also examines the output side of employment policy, notably the effects of different active measures (training, guidance, subsidised jobs, etc) in terms of creating lasting employment.

The Committee thus uses a large number of indicators in an attempt to build up a clear picture of how states are giving effect to their commitment to maximise employment under Article 1(1). It has in certain cases found national situations to be in breach of the Charter:

a. where there was an absence both of a declaratory commitment to full employment and of any concerted employment policy;[61]

[59] ECSR, 'Conclusions I, Statement of Interpretation on Article 1(1)' 13. All conclusions of the ECSR in respect of national reports and the Committee's decisions in collective complaints can be found online at: www.coe.int/t/dghl/monitoring/socialcharter/ecsr/ecsrdefault_en.asp.

[60] ECSR, 'Conclusions XVI-1, Statement of Interpretation on Article 1(1)' 9.

[61] ECSR, 'Conclusions XVI-1, Netherlands (Netherlands Antilles and Aruba)' 464. In contrast, a declared state policy of maintaining an 'optimum' level of unemployment would in all probability constitute an automatic violation of Art 1(1), even if governments rarely make such policies explicit.

b. where unemployment, and especially youth unemployment and long-term unemployment, was extremely high and in the light of which the measures taken were insufficient (as indicated, inter alia, by a very low number of participants involved in active job-creation measures);[62]
c. when there were negative developments in the employment policy, both in terms of activation of unemployed persons and a decline in overall expenditure, at a time when unemployment was increasing sharply while economic growth remained positive.[63]

In other words, the Committee will find a situation to be in nonconformity with Article 1(1) where there is clear evidence of state failure to take its obligations seriously. However, if a state has a reasonably well-formulated employment policy in place and allocates a reasonable level of resources to ensure its implementation, the situation will be in conformity with the requirements of the Social Charter. Given the difficulties of formulating and implementing an effective employment policy in contemporary conditions of economic globalisation, the ECSR affords states a wide margin of appreciation in this sphere: only a clear failure to implement an employment policy will qualify for a conclusion of nonconformity.

b Article 1(2) – Free Choice of Employment

> 2. With a view to ensuring the effective exercise of the right to work, the Parties undertake to protect effectively the right of the worker to earn his living in an occupation freely entered upon.

Article 1(2) is in many ways the 'core' of the right to work as set out in the ESC, at least from the point of view of the Committee's interpretative approach to Article 1, taken as a whole. It requires states to provide effective protection to the entitlement of workers to earn their living in an occupation that they wish to pursue. In its case law, which is very similar in this regard to the approach adopted by the CESCR, the Committee has identified three different types of protection that states may apply:

1. The prohibition of all forms of discrimination in employment.
2. The prohibition of forced or compulsory labour.
3. The prohibition of any practice that might interfere with workers' right to earn their living in an occupation freely entered upon.[64]

ii Prohibition of all Forms of Discrimination in Employment

The Committee has interpreted Article 1(2) as requiring that states should prohibit any discrimination in employment on grounds of sex, race, ethnic origin,

[62] ECSR, 'Conclusions 2004-1, Bulgaria' 21.
[63] ECSR, 'Conclusions XVI-1, Poland' 521–24.
[64] ECSR, 'Conclusions II, Statement of Interpretation on Article 1§2' 4.

religion, disability, age and sexual orientation, ie, on the 'suspect grounds' that are recognised in EU law and the case law of the European Court of Human Rights as constituting forms of discrimination of an especially problematic character.[65] It is not enough that states do not discriminate themselves; they must also introduce legislation to prohibit third parties discriminating, and ensure that such legislation is effective.

As a result, national legislation should prohibit both direct and indirect discrimination on the suspect grounds.[66] In addition, states must provide for: (i) the setting aside or amendment of any provision contrary to the principle of equal treatment which appears in collective labour agreements, in employment contracts or in firms' own regulations;[67] (ii) protection against dismissal or other retaliatory action by the employer;[68] (iii) appropriate and effective remedies in the event of an allegation of discrimination; and (iv) a shift in the burden of proof.[69]

States must also supplement the rights of victims of discrimination to take legal action by providing for some form of third-party action. States should adopt a combination of the following measures: recognise the right of trade unions to take action in cases of employment discrimination, including action on behalf of individuals;[70] grant groups with an interest in obtaining a ruling that the prohibition of discrimination has been violated the right to take collective action; or set up a special, independent body to promote equal treatment, particularly by providing discrimination victims with the support they need to take proceedings. These measures are important in ensuring that the prohibition on discrimination is effective: in general, the Committee stresses the importance in its case law of ensuring that labour rights are effectively protected.

Part-time work must also be accompanied by adequate legal safeguards against discrimination. In particular, there must be rules to prevent non-declared work through overtime, and equal pay, in all its aspects, between part-time and full-time employees.[71]

[65] ECSR, 'Conclusions XVI-1, Statement of Interpretation on Article 1§2' 9. This provision is inherently linked with other provisions of the Charter, in particular Art 20 (equal opportunities and equal treatment in matters of employment and occupation without discrimination on grounds of sex) and Art 15(2) (right of persons with disabilities to employment). Where a State party has accepted these provisions, non-discrimination in employment in relation to women and persons with disabilities is examined under these more specific provisions.

[66] In defining what constitutes discrimination, the Committee has drawn on Art G of the Charter and the standard approach adopted by the Court of Justice of the EU and the European Court of Human Rights. See in particular the Committee's decisions in Collective Complaint no 6/1999 *Syndicat national des Professions du Tourisme v France* (Decision on the merits, 5 December 2000) and Complaint no 13/2002 *Autisme-Europe v France* (Decision on the merits, 4 November 2003) [52].

[67] ECSR, 'Conclusions XVI-1, Iceland' 313.

[68] ibid.

[69] Collective Complaint no 24/2004 *Sud Travail et Affaires Sociales v France* (Decision on the merits, 16 November 2005) [33]; Collective Complaint no 7/2000 *International Federation of Human Rights Leagues v Greece* (Decision on the merits, 5 December 2000) [22].

[70] ECSR, 'Conclusions XVI-1, Iceland' 313.

[71] ECSR, 'Conclusions XVI-1, Austria' 28.

As it regards discrimination on grounds of nationality, the Committee gives Article 1(2) a similar interpretation as that given to the provisions of Article 19 and other provisions of the Charter, which explicitly require equal access to employment and associated benefits for citizens of other State Parties to the Charter who have a legal right of residence in the state concerned. This means that states can only ban nationals of State Parties to the Charter from occupying jobs for the reasons set out in Article G of the Charter, ie, for reasons associated with the protection of the public interest or national security and involving the exercise of public authority. The Charter does not provide for freedom of movement, but does recognise the existence of a solidarity bond between its signatory states, which is manifested in this specific and unique nondiscrimination principle.[72]

iii Prohibition of Forced or Compulsory Labour

The Committee has also interpreted Article 1(2) as requiring states to prohibit all forms of forced or compulsory labour, on the clear textual basis that this is incompatible with the notion of an occupation 'freely entered into'. The definition of forced or compulsory labour used by the Committee reflects its adherence to an integrated approach to other human rights standards, whereby it tries to ensure that ICESCR, ILO and ECHR standards are reflected in its interpretative approach to Charter rights: the Committee's definition is based on the provisions of Article 4 of the ECHR and ILO Convention No 29 on forced labour, and covers 'all work or service which is exacted from any person under the menace of any penalty and for which the said person has not offered himself voluntarily'.

In its Conclusions in respect of national reports, the Committee has tended to focus on legal provisions which are incompatible with this prohibition of forced or compulsory labour. In particular, the Committee has found the existence of a violation when legislative or administrative requirements impose the following constraints on freedom of occupation:

a. the imposition of criminal sanctions in the event of disciplinary offences on the part of seamen, or sanctions for seamen who abandon their post, when the safety of a ship or the lives or health of the people on board are not at stake;[73]
b. requirements that career army officers who have received several periods of training complete a term of compulsory service that may last up to twenty-five years, or rules that refuse them the right to seek early termination of their commission unless they repay to the state at least part of the cost of their education and training;[74]

[72] There is potential here for the Committee to develop its case law further, given that socio-economic background and other factors can also play an important role in excluding individuals from employment in their profession of choice.
[73] Collective Complaint no 7/2000 *International Federation of Human Rights Leagues v Greece*, [22].
[74] ECSR, 'Conclusions 2004, Ireland' 260.

c. powers to requisition labour in exceptional circumstances, when they are too broadly defined.[75] Any such powers must be defined with sufficient clarity and fall within the scope of Article G of the Charter.

Furthermore, the Committee also requires that prison work must be strictly regulated, in terms of pay, working hours and social security, particularly if prisoners are working for private firms. Prisoners may only be employed by private enterprises with their consent, and in conditions as similar as possible to those normally associated with a private employment relationship.[76]

The Committee's case law used to lack a well-developed set of standards as to the scope of state positive obligations in respect of the need to prevent forced labour in the private sphere, especially when it comes to domestic workers and other vulnerable groups. This absence reflected the historic focus of the Committee's work on orthodox forms of employment, which has begun to shift. Now, the Committee is developing standards relating to the treatment of domestic workers and other vulnerable groups working in non-orthodox or precarious forms of employment, which draw upon other international standards such as the ECtHR judgments in *Siliadin v France* and *Rantsev v Cyprus and Russia* and the new ILO Convention No 189 on Domestic Workers.[77] In particular, states are expected to ensure that their domestic legislation provides adequate protection against exploitation and abuse for domestic workers and workers employed in family enterprises.[78]

iv Prohibition of Other Practices that might Interfere with Workers' Rights to Earn their Living

The Committee has taken the view that several other practices may give rise to issues under Article 1(2), by analogy to the prohibition on discrimination and compelled labour. In particular, the Committee has interpreted the Charter text as requiring that the length of civilian service (ie, non-military service in those countries which retain a form of conscription) must be reasonable, on the basis that it represents an interference with the right to work in one's own freely chosen occupation. Where the length of alternative service exceeds one and a half times the length of military service, it will generally be contrary to Article 1(2).[79]

The right of workers to privacy, and to maintain 'the frontier between professional and private life' must also be protected by national law: in this context, the Committee has expressed concern about the potential for emerging technologies

[75] ECSR, 'Conclusions XVI-1, Greece' 283.

[76] ECSR, 'Conclusions 2012, General Introduction' 5–6.

[77] V Mantouvalou, 'Human Rights for Precarious Workers: The Legislative Precariousness of Domestic Labor' (2012) 34 *Comparative Labor Law & Policy Journal* 133.

[78] ECSR, 'Conclusions 2012, General Introduction' 11.

[79] Collective Complaint no 8/2000 *Quaker Council for European Affairs v Greece* (Decision on the merits, 25 April 2001) [23]–[25]; see also 'Conclusions 2012, General Introduction' 7.

and new 'always on' work practices to encroach upon the private life of employees outside working hours.[80]

Significantly, the Committee has recently developed a new dimension to its case law in this context, relating to situations where access to social welfare benefits is made conditional on unemployed persons accepting certain types of job offer. The Committee has taken the view that such requirements may constitute an unjustified restriction on freedom to work where the person concerned is compelled, on pain of losing benefit, to accept jobs which involve qualifications or skills far below those of the individual concerned; or which require a particular level of physical or mental health or ability which the person does not possess at the relevant time; or which are unsafe or incompatible with the dignity and integrity of workers; or for which the pay offered is lower than the relevant national or regional minimum wage; or which would place an unreasonable burden on the individual concerned as regards travelling time, periods away from home or family obligations.[81]

Making access to benefits conditional on unemployed individuals taking up job offers has thus been conceptualised as a form of compelled labour, which is only justifiable if the job is compatible with the dignity of the individual concerned and her family responsibilities. It remains to be seen how this new dimension to the jurisprudence of the ECSR will be applied in concrete national contexts. However, given that European states are increasingly making access to unemployment benefit conditional on acceptance of job offers, it represents a significant development in the ECSR's interpretation of the substantive content of Article 1(2).

a Article 1(3) – Employment Services

> 3. With a view to ensuring the effective exercise of the right to work, the Parties undertake to establish or maintain free employment services for all workers.

This paragraph of Article 1 is narrowly focused and precise: it guarantees the right to free employment services which operate effectively throughout the national territory and in all sectors of the economy. The Committee has interpreted the clear and specific provisions of this paragraph as requiring basic placement services (such as registration of jobseekers and notification of vacancies) to be provided free of charge for both employees and employers wishing to take advantage of them. Quantitative indicators are used to assess the effectiveness in practice of free employment services, including the placement rate (ie, the placements made by the employment services as a share of notified vacancies) and the respective market shares of public and private (ie, fee-charging) services.[82] Once again, the emphasis is on ensuring that states put a basic system into place. Finally, the Committee has taken the view that trade union and employers' organisations must participate in organising and running employment services, again on

[80] ECSR, 'Conclusions 2013, General Introduction' 6.
[81] ECSR, 'Conclusions 2012, General Introduction' 6–7.
[82] ECSR, 'Conclusions XIV-1, Statement of Interpretation on Article 1§3' 39.

the basis that their participation is essential to ensure the effectiveness of the system.[83]

b Article 1(4) – Vocational Guidance and Training

> 4. With a view to ensuring the effective exercise of the right to work, the Parties undertake to provide or promote appropriate vocational guidance, training and rehabilitation.

Article 1(4) guarantees the right to vocational guidance, continuing vocational training for employed and unemployed persons and specialised guidance and training for persons with disabilities. The Committee has interpreted this provision as requiring that states must at least provide these services, grant access to them and ensure equality of treatment for nationals of other State Parties to the Charter and for persons with disabilities.[84] Article 1(4) is complemented by Articles 9 (right to vocational guidance), Article 10(3) (right to continuing vocational training of adult workers) and Article 15(1) (the right of persons with disabilities to guidance, education and vocational training), which contain more specific rights to vocational guidance and vocational training.

B Analysis – The Strengths and Weakness of the Right to Work as Protected by Article 1 ESC

The right to work is fundamental within the ESC framework of social rights protection, as recognised in how this right has been placed first within the textual scheme of the Charter. The text of Article 1, which is couched in more precise terms than Article 6 ICESCR, makes it clear that the normative content of this right within the ESC framework is focused on securing the *availability* and *accessibility* of work. The ECSR has confirmed this in its interpretative approach to Article 1 ESC, which has read the right to work as requiring states to (i) take positive steps to achieve and maintain high levels of employment through the implementation of adequately resourced national employment and job creation policies, and (ii) to protect individuals against discrimination, forced labour and other forms of exploitation.

In contrast, issues related to the *acceptability* of work (ie, 'decent work') tend to be considered by the ECSR under the rubric of other ESC rights, including in particular Article 2 (the right to just conditions of work), Article 3 (the right to healthy and safe working conditions) and Article 4 (the right to fair remuneration). This makes for an interesting contrast with the approach of the CESCR, which recognises the existence of a more explicit and direct link between the availability and accessibility aspects of the right to work and issues relating to the acceptability of work. However, the Committee's reading of the other labour

[83] ECSR, 'Conclusions XV-1, Addendum, Poland' 143.
[84] ECSR, 'Conclusions XII-1, Statement of Interpretation on Article 1§4' 67.

rights contained in the Social Charter, which set out strong standards relating to decent work conditions, forms part of the general interpretative backdrop that it takes into account when interpreting and applying the provisions of Article 1. The same is true for other ESC rights relating to vocational education, social protection and the treatment of vulnerable groups. As a result, the difference between the approaches of the CESCR and ECSR in this respect may be more apparent than real.[85]

The ECSR's jurisprudence in respect of the right to work remains a work in progress. Article 1 has been interpreted by the ECSR as giving rise to a wide range of commitments, which however for the most part, tend to be couched at a relatively high level of abstraction. This usually means that states can readily demonstrate formal compliance with the Charter provisions, which can lack much in the way of real substance aside from the non-discrimination requirements (and the developing issue of forced labour). Under the Social Charter, as under the ICESCR, it is not always very clear what a *failure* to respect the right in its wide sense would look like. This demonstrates the need for greater normative clarity as to what are the scope and parameters of the right to work.

III Overview and Conclusion

When one compares the interpretative approach to the right to work adopted by the CESCR and ECSR, there are clear similarities and overlaps. Both bodies can be said to adopt a common or integrated approach, which reflects ILO and other international human rights standards. The right to work is understood to impose obligations on states to secure the availability and access of 'acceptable' employment (ie, 'decent work') for the individuals coming within their jurisdiction.

This common interpretative approach is based in turn on a shared understanding of the conceptual basis of the right to work, which views this right as concerned with protecting the freedom of workers to seek and obtain decent work. This shared vision of the right recognises the intrinsic value of work to the individual, and the expressive dimension of labour. It also sees these elements of the right to work as closely linked to rights that relate to fair treatment and dignity in work, as embodied by provisions relating to the enjoyment of these rights follow sequentially on from Article 6 ICESR and Article 1 ESC respectively.

This common vision of the right to work that is shared by the ECSR, CESCR and other international human rights bodies such as the ILO is perhaps the closest thing that exists to an authoritative interpretation of its scope and content. The

[85] It is notable in this respect that the Appendix to the ESC provides that Art 1(2) 'shall not be interpreted as prohibiting or authorising any union security clause or practice', thus precluding the interpretation of the right adopted by anti-union 'right to work' statutes in the United States. For further discussion of the relationship between the right to work and the right to decent work, see V Mantouvalou in this volume, ch 3.

interpretation these bodies have given to the right demonstrates that it is possible to delineate its scope and normative content with some precision, and that it is not as open-ended and indeterminate as some socio-economic rights sceptics would suggest.

However, it is noteworthy that the right to work in the context of the ICESCR and the ESC can at times still lack clear definition. It is clear that discrimination, forced labour and other forms of exploitation, and a refusal on the part of a state to formulate and implement a national employment policy will constitute clear violations of this right. However, beyond that, both Article 6 ICESCR and Article 1 ESC can at times lack tangible content. More needs to be done to flesh out the substance of the right to work, if it is to become something more than a background entitlement of general application whose vagueness makes it easy to assimilate to existing state practice.

7

The Right to (Decent) Work in a European Comparative Perspective

MARK FREEDLAND AND NICOLA KOUNTOURIS

Introduction – Declaratory Framings and Practical Interventions

At the beginning of the 1980s, Bob Hepple presented in a published lecture what was immediately recognisable, and has retained its standing, as a masterly comparative analysis of the idea of 'the right to work' and its potential place in the development of the labour law of the United Kingdom.[1] He took as his starting point a proposal which had recently been advanced in a survey of poverty in the United Kingdom for a 'legally enforceable right to work' for everyone over the age of compulsory education.[2] Although decidedly sceptical of the viability and utility of a 'right to work' as a legally enforceable right, he justly regarded the proposal as a good starting point for a critical discussion of some of the key issues and deep tensions in UK labour law and relations. In this chapter, we revisit – more than 30 years later – some of the issues raised by Bob Hepple; we seek to do so in a way which brings into play some further elements of EU law and somewhat further develops a European comparative perspective upon this set of issues.

Our methodology for so doing will be to compare and contrast some theoretical/ideal or declaratory framings of the 'right to work' with some actual legal interventions or areas of regulation in the European region which invoke or depend upon ideas in the nature of the 'right to work'. Of the various declaratory framings of the 'right to work' which are to be found in instruments of international law and in national constitutions, we shall argue that it is most useful to concentrate on those formulations which enjoin nation states first to confer freedom to work upon their own citizens (and sometimes citizens of other states) and second to take measures to ensure that their own citizens (and perhaps sometimes

[1] B Hepple, 'A Right to Work?' (1981) 10 *Industrial Law Journal* 65.

[2] See ibid, 65 and fn 1, citing P Townsend, *Poverty in the United Kingdom: A Survey of Household Resources and Standards of Living* (California, University of California Press, 1979) 926.

citizens of other states) have the opportunity of earning their living within their national labour economy. We shall find that such declarations generally do not explicitly distinguish between citizens and non-citizens: we suggest that such a distinction will normally be assumed in those declarations so far as they are intended for implementation by nation states; but we will argue that such assumptions turn out to be all too controversial when tested out in 'real world' national contexts. We shall point out the way in which those declaratory framings are typically associated with declaratory framings of a right to fair or decent terms of employment, and we shall argue that although these two kinds of declaratory framings are often regarded as complementing each other in an uncontroversial way, there is in fact an inherent tension between them – a tension which is at the heart of the regulatory dilemmas which confront labour law.

We shall go on to argue that this tension – between the 'right to work' pure and simple and the right to fair and decent terms of work – becomes very clearly visible when we turn from declaratory framings of the 'right to work' to areas of practical regulatory intervention in which a 'right to work' is engaged or could be regarded as engaged. Our principal aim in so doing will be to challenge a tacit but widespread assumption that there is little if any connection between declaratory framings of the 'right to work' and the day to day life of labour law, the former being no more than aspirational, and the latter embodying no significant recognition of a 'right to work' in any meaningful sense. We argue that there are some real points of contact between these two discourses – some real world embodiments of 'right to work' thinking. However, at these points of contact between the two discourses, there is little harmony between them; on the contrary, identifying real world approaches to 'right to work' thinking serves primarily to illustrate how inherently fraught a process it is to try to give effect to a 'right to work' within the framework of labour law's regulation, at least in the labour economies of the European region if not more generally throughout the world.

In developing this argument, we shall be taking a very broad view of what is meant by 'labour law's regulation', one in which 'labour law' is inseparably intertwined with social security law and with the law of labour migration. Thus, having considered some relevant declaratory framings of the 'right to work', we shall use them as a backdrop to an examination of three aspects or domains of labour law's regulation, in that extended sense, in the European region. The first such aspect or domain consists of labour law's regulation of terms and conditions of work taken in conjunction with the 'workfare' regimes which are imposed and sustained by the social security systems of EU Member States. The second such aspect or domain consists of labour law's regulation of discrimination in the employment sphere. The third such aspect or domain consists of labour law's regulation of terms and conditions of work taken in conjunction with the 'freedom of movement of workers' regime which is imposed by the EU itself and sustained, actually in rather varying ways, in the Member States.

I Declaratory Framings – International and National–Constitutional Framings of the Right to (Decent) Work

The character of the 'right to work' as an essentially complex and fraught one starts to reveal itself, even before we start to explore its real world manifestations, in the various framings of it in international declarations of human and fundamental rights and in national constitutions. We can see this character in the highest of all such formulations, that of Article 23(1) of the Universal Declaration of Human Rights of 1948: '(1) Everyone has the right to work, to free choice of employment, to just and favourable conditions of work and to protection against unemployment'. We immediately have the problem of whether and how far the latter three rights form part of the 'right to work' and if so how far they are an exhaustive enumeration of that general right.

When, on the other hand, the declaratory framing of the 'right to work' is an absolutely cryptic one, as is often the case in national constitutions, the formulation may simply conceal unresolved problems. Thus it is with the French constitutional proposition that: 'Chacun a le devoir de travailler et le droit d'obtenir un emploi'.[3]

This opens up the question of how, if at all, the notion of 'le droit d'obtenir un emploi' differs from the notion of 'le droit au travail'. Is this a 'right to a job' as distinct from a more generalised 'right to work'? How does this definition relate to the formulation of the 'right to work' in Article 15 of the EU Charter of Fundamental Rights as: '1. Everyone has the right to engage in work and to pursue a freely chosen or accepted occupation'?

Moreover, how intimately is this 'right to work' bound up with the *duty* to work, which is proclaimed, equally delphically, in that same proposition of the French Constitution?

On the other hand again, even if we turn to relatively full and detailed declaratory framings of the 'right to work', such as that which is contained in Article 1 of the European Social Charter, we still find that some key definitional questions remained unanswered. Thus, Article 1 articulates that:

> With a view to ensuring the effective exercise of the right to work, the Parties undertake:
>
> to accept as one of their primary aims and responsibilities the achievement and maintenance of as high and stable a level of employment as possible, with a view to the attainment of full employment;
>
> to protect effectively the right of the worker to earn his living in an occupation freely entered upon;

[3] Preamble to the Constitution of 1958, referring to the fifth paragraph of the Preamble to the Constitution of 1946; see further S Robin-Olivier in this volume, ch 11.

to establish or maintain free employment services for all workers;

to provide or promote appropriate vocational guidance, training and rehabilitation.[4]

This makes it clear enough that, in this framing, the 'right to work' is conceived of as imposing upon participating states an obligation not just to maintain a liberal freedom of opportunity to work, but also actively to intervene to maximise the availability of such opportunities. However, even with that clarification, two large questions still present themselves, upon which we shall especially concentrate in the remainder of this chapter.

The first of those two questions, which started to emerge when we considered Article 23(1) of the Universal Declaration of Human Rights, is how far and in what way the right or claim to just, fair and decent conditions of work is integrated into the 'right to work'. In some of the declaratory framings which we have been examining, that further right is expressly integrated, as in the case of Article 23(1); but even then the nature and degree of that integration may remain obscure, as in Article 23(1) itself. In other such framings, as for example that of European Social Charter, the right to just, fair, or decent conditions of work is not folded into the 'right to work', but is juxtaposed to it as a separate but adjacent proposition or set of propositions[5] – in which case the relationship between the two rights is an even more debatable question.

There is then a second, and equally important, question the answer to which seems to be concealed in the universalist language of all these declaratory framings of the 'right to work': it is the question of who enjoys the 'right to work'. These international and national–constitutional articulations of the 'right to work', if they define the subjects of the 'right to work' at all, do so by means of formulae such as 'all workers' or 'each person' or 'everyone'. Such universalism seems obviously appropriate in these declaratory contexts; but these words or phrases gloss over questions which are inescapable when one considers how a 'right to work' might and should be implemented in detail within an actual system of legal regulation in a region or nation state.[6] We turn to explaining the way in which we seek to pin down and tackle such problems in the course of this chapter.

II From Theoretical to Comparative-Empirical Analysis of 'Right to Work' Regulation

There are various ways in which we could attack the questions which we have opened up, operating in a theoretical mode. Some of these possible lines of attack

[4] European Social Charter (revised, 1996); see, generally, C O'Cinneide in this volume, ch 6.

[5] European Social Charter Art 2 deals with 'The right to just conditions of work'; Art 3 with 'the right to safe and healthy working conditions'; and Art 4 with 'the right to a fair remuneration sufficient for a decent standard of living for [the workers] themselves and their families'.

[6] cf, in this respect, E Albin in this volume, ch 4 and V Mantouvalou in this volume, ch 3.

are pursued to very good effect in the first section of this volume, in which the discussion focused primarily on philosophical, moral and policy-based approaches to the expounding of the 'right to work'. Another possible approach of that kind could consist of exploring the currently widely discussed notion of 'pre-distribution' as a way of evaluating the utility of developing the 'right to work'. This is a notion apparently originally advanced by Jacob Hacker in 2011;[7] it represented the virtue of 'market reforms which encourage a more equal distribution of economic power and rewards even before government collects taxes or pays out benefits' – the point being that such market reforms, being 'pre-distributive' or *ex ante* in character, would be more acceptable and sustainable than taxes or benefits which can be viewed as merely 'redistributive' or *ex post* in their nature. Thus, we might wish to argue that some conceptions of the 'right to work' were more genuinely or deeply pre-distributive than others, and as such more likely to give rise to progressive and effective regulatory interventions.

Alternatively, we might wish to attack the problems which we have opened up concerning the nature and functioning of the 'right to work' by focusing, more empirically, upon the actual or possible content of the 'right to work' in particular legal systems, as several chapters in the present volume also very valuably do. However, this chapter has the particular ambition or project of instituting a process of reflection, upon 'right to work' interventions which would be not only empirical, but also comparative in character as between European national legal systems, and moreover based upon or influenced by EU regulation. We need to explain somewhat more fully our reasons for having that ambition and pursuing that project.

First, we need to explain the notion of 'right to work interventions', which defines our project. We use that terminology as shorthand to refer to regulatory interventions which could be regarded as implementing or furthering any of the possible conceptions of the 'right to work' which we identified in the previous section, but more particularly the conception of it which sees it as imposing upon nation states an obligation not just to maintain a liberal freedom of opportunity to work, but also actively to intervene to maximise the availability of such opportunities. Our use of this shorthand notion of 'right to work' interventions includes the idea that it is useful to think about certain regulatory interventions in the general sphere of labour law as implicating the 'right to work' even if they do not explicitly proclaim that character. In this way, we entitle ourselves to consider that various bodies of regulation which do not openly wear the livery of the 'right to work' may nevertheless demonstrate and play out the real problems and quandaries associated with the 'right to work' more fully and meaningfully than do the declaratory framings of the right to work which we looked at in the previous section.

[7] JS Hacker, 'The institutional foundations of middle-class democracy' *Policy Network* (6 May 2011), available at: www.policy-network.net/pno_detail.aspx?ID=3998&title=The+institutional+foundations+of+middle+class+democracy.

We then need to explain why our project of comparative enquiry into 'right to work' interventions, as so defined, should concentrate upon European national legal systems, and why moreover it should focus on those interventions which are based upon or influenced by EU regulation. All such selections of a zone of comparison are of course in some sense arbitrary, but this particular one has the advantage that there is a considerable breadth and depth of relevant regulatory material to work on, an *acquis*, as it were, from the experience of the Member States of the European Union. Moreover, the EU itself has engaged in a number of relevant regulatory or coordinatory interventions, such that a reflection upon the impact of those interventions in the Member States provides a reasonably coherent framework for better understanding the functioning of 'right to work' thinking in the real world of labour law. That is the rationale for the European comparative enquiry which we shall pursue in the next and most crucial section of this chapter.

III Comparing EU-Based or EU-Influenced Right to Work Interventions in European National Legal Systems

In the previous section of this chapter, we advanced a notion of 'right to work' interventions which was a deliberately inclusive one, enabling us to bring into our zone of comparative analysis various types of regulatory intervention in the wider sphere of labour law which can be regarded as in some sense vindicating a 'right to work' even though they do not openly claim or profess to do so. Furthermore, we made a case for singling out some EU regulatory or coordinatory interventions as providing a framework for grouping and analysing the relevant regulatory interventions in the Member States. We thus arrive at the three following kinds of EU-based or EU coordinated 'right to work' interventions which we think can usefully be subjected to comparative analysis:

1. National employment policy and/or workfare regimes, as co-ordinated by the European Employment Strategy;
2. EU-based controls on discrimination in the sphere of employment and occupation; and
3. EU freedom of movement of workers as implemented in the Member States.

Each of these is briefly considered in the course of this section, drawing chiefly on the annual monitoring of the operation of each of these interventions in the Member States which is provided by the European Commission, either directly, as in the case of the European Employment Strategy (detailed below) or through the work of the networks of experts or rapporteurs which have been set up for this purpose.[8]

[8] As in the cases of EU-based controls on discrimination in the sphere of employment and occupation, and EU free movement of workers, as detailed under those respective headings.

It follows from what has been said in earlier sections of this chapter that our approach to this comparative reflection consists of regarding each of these three streams of regulatory intervention as in some measure vindicating a notion of the 'right to work', but as doing so in a real world context in which the ideals and the idealism which are embodied in the notion of the 'right to work' find themselves in tension with practical economic exigencies and become diluted, sometimes to vanishing point. This is even more especially the case if and to the extent that the ideal of the 'right to work' is, in the ways that we have discussed, combined with the ideal of the right to fair or just or decent conditions of work. Examination of the playing out of these essential tensions in the Member States of the EU reveals a great variety of outcomes in detail, but also enables us to discern some general trends emerging through those variations.

A The European Employment Strategy National Employment Policy and/or Workfare Regimes and the Right to Work

It might be felt that, despite the foregoing attempts at justification, our enterprise of considering the European Employment Strategy and its national counterparts in the Member States of the EU as 'right to work' interventions is a far fetched one. The European Employment Strategy consists of a series of initiatives taken by the EU from 1994 onwards by which it has been sought to coordinate the policies and actions of the Member States in pursuit of a goal of maximising employment and moving towards full employment.[9] Thus, it might be thought that, from the outset, the role of 'full employment' in the European Employment Strategy was that of a pious ideal rather than a practical goal, and moreover that even this ideal faded as the notion of 'flexicurity' – the policy or policies of combining and reconciling the goals of flexibility and security in the functioning of the labour market – became progressively more prevalent as the embodiment of a more and more accommodating compromise with economic exigencies which were making the creation of 'more and better jobs' seem little more than a pipe dream.[10] That rhetoric of 'more and better jobs' of course seeks to disguise the tension between 'more jobs' and 'better jobs' which, as we argued in the initial sections of this

[9] The classic study of the European Employment Strategy and its impact in the Member States in its earlier years is D Ashiagbor, *The European Employment Strategy: Labour Market Regulation and New Governance* (Oxford, Oxford University Press, 2005). Annual monitoring of the EES is provided directly by the European Commission, which annually produces, jointly with the EU Council, a Joint Employment Report detailing the compliance of the Member States with the EU Employment Guidelines, as is mandated by TFEU Art148. The latest such report, for 2012, put forward in draft as COM (2012) 750 final, was adopted by the Council in February 2013 (CEU 6799/13) and is cited here as JER 2012.

[10] Ashiagbor, above n 9, 243 presciently foresees how the rhetoric and practice of 'flexicurity', then developing in the Netherlands and the United Kingdom, might become pervasive. A tipping point can perhaps be discerned in the Joint Employment Report for 2008–09 (EU Council 7435/09) which is infused with the idea of 'flexicurity' as a guiding ideal for the European Employment Strategy. cf generally S Fredman, 'Women at Work: The Broken Promise of Flexicurity' (2004) 33 *Industrial Law Journal* 299.

chapter, is at the heart of attempts at practical realisation of the very idea of the 'right to work'; and this essential evasion might be thought to cast doubt on any claim to regard the European Employment Strategy as embodying a right to work in any meaningful sense.

However, we still maintain, despite such possible doubts, that the European Employment Strategy and its counterparts in the Member States should not be dismissed out of hand as embodying notions of a 'right to work' even if those are rather thin ones. The European Commission's Employment Guidelines do embody, at an aspirational level at least, something of the spirit of the 'right to work' as expounded in the European Social Charter.[11] When, in 2007, a group of us published a three-year study of the law and functioning of public employment services in some of the Member States,[12] we thought it appropriate to depict the Active Labour Market Policies of those states – that is to say, in effect, the national counterparts of the European Employment Strategy – as expressive of 'right to work' thinking, albeit by then somewhat qualified by a growing tendency towards tighter and tighter workfare arrangements, that is to say arrangements which make the availability of welfare benefits, particularly unemployment benefits, dependent upon more and more strict conditions of willingness to seek work and to accept work when it is offered.[13]

Moreover, the fact that in real world regulatory interventions we encounter the 'right to work' in thin versions and in embattled contest with policies which undermine or oppose it, is not, in our view, a reason to dismiss those interventions as irrelevant to the 'right to work'. On the contrary, we contend that this is the 'real deal'; that in the European region at least, when we encounter the 'right to work' as playing a part in regulatory interventions, we can expect that it will be in these etiolated and contested forms. All that said, we need to consider the recent and current evolutions of the national counterparts of the European Employment Strategy to see whether and how far that theoretical position remains a tenable one.

If we look for that purpose at the Joint Employment Report for 2012 (JER 2012), it must be confessed that what we find does not make very encouraging reading. It is admitted from the outset that 'the Employment situation across the EU is worsening with divergences between Member States across a range of employment and social indicators widening' and that 'the impact has been more severe on certain groups, with those already at risk suffering the worst effects'.[14]

[11] The current Employment Guidelines are those which were formulated in 2010 and published as a Council Decision of 21 October 2010 on guidelines for the employment policies of the Member States (2010/707/EU) ; they are due to remain in force until 2014; see: epp.eurostat.ec.europa.eu/portal/page/portal/employment_social_policy_equality/employment_guidelines .

[12] M Freedland, P Craig, C Jacqueson and N Kountouris, *Public Employment Services and European Law* (Oxford, Oxford University Press, 2007).

[13] See ibid, ch 6, 'Active Labour Market Policies: Between "Right to Work" and "Workfare"', and more especially section 4 of that chapter, 'The Problematic Face of Modern ALMPs: Compulsion and the "Right to Work"'.

[14] JER 2012, 2.

The Report boldly and optimistically asserts that: 'This is the situation for which the European Employment Strategy was created and with which it can deal effectively, especially with the strengthened governance being embedded in 2013'[15]; but it is hard to escape the conclusion that any claim that the European Employment Strategy is in the course of vindicating the 'right to work' has receded into the far distance.

This impression that the European Employment Strategy has somewhat ground to a halt as a 'right to work' intervention is mirrored in what the Report has to say about developments in the Member States. There are a number of general indications that even that degree of maintenance of levels of employment which is being achieved is being purchased at the cost of increasing precarisation of work arrangements, especially for already vulnerable sections of the workforce. Thus, it is reported that 'labour market segmentation has continued to rise with temporary contracts and part-time work expanding'; that 'young people are strongly over-represented in temporary work on the EU labour markets'; that 'part-time employment has accounted for a significant share of the job growth experienced during the crisis'; and that, in most Member States, 'there are recent signs of deterioration in the job matching process on European labour markets'.[16]

Moreover, the Report goes on to describe some particular developments in some Member States which, behind the partly upbeat and partly opaque reportage, can be regarded as – if anything – retrogressive in 'right to work' terms, in particular because they imply that normative balances are tipping away from 'right to work' towards duty to work. Thus, if we may quote from the Report *in extenso*:

> Some Member States have taken measures adapting unemployment benefits to facilitate the return to work (BE, ES, IE, IT, SE).[17] In BE, the adopted reform of the unemployment benefit system implies that allowances are decreasing earlier and faster than previously. In ES, the unemployment benefit has been reduced for several groups. In [Portugal] a new law reduces the maximum duration and amounts of unemployment benefits with the view to reduce the risk of benefit dependency and long-term unemployment. In SE, more strict eligibility rules, lower income replacement rates and maximum durations for unemployment benefits have been introduced.[18]

This seems to describe various evolutions towards ever tighter workfare regimes. Then it is further reported that:

> Member States are taking measures to reduce early exit from the labour market (AT, BE, ES, DK, IE, NL, HU, UK).[19] In AT, reforms have been introduced to reduce the number of invalidity pensions. In BE, the age limit for older employees to access the time-credit system has been increased and the system of part-time early-retirement has

[15] ibid.

[16] ibid, 10–14. (The pagination in this footnote and the immediately suceeding ones follows that of the Draft Report which is annexed to the Final Report.)

[17] Belgium, Spain, Ireland, Italy, Sweden.

[18] See JER 2012, 16.

[19] Austria, Belgium, Spain, Denmark, Ireland, the Netherlands, Hungary and the United Kingdom.

> been discontinued. In DK, disability pension reform plans require that activation possibilities are depleted before early retirement can be considered. In ES, the schedule for increasing the statutory retirement age will be accelerated, the early retirement age will increase from 61 to 63 with increased penalties for early retirement, and a suspension of access to partial retirement for two years. In IE new initiatives will allow people receiving an Illness or Invalidity payment to both work and receive income support and the legal retirement age will increase to 68 by 2028. In NL, steps are being taken to gradually raise the pension age to 67 by 2023 and hereafter it may be linked to life expectancy. In HU early retirement has been abandoned as a general rule. The UK government has recently announced plans to link pension age with life expectancy. Measures also focus on the promotion of longer working lives (AT, BE, BG, DE, EE, FI, LU, PL, UK).[20] [21]

This in our view testifies to various ways in which the promotion of work into old age, arguably a form of 'right to work' intervention, is in fact figuring in the real world of the Active Labour Market Policies (ALMPs) of many Member States as something far more resembling a duty or compulsion to work into old age.

However, if our characterisations and criticisms of these various ALMP measures are accepted, it may nevertheless be felt that we are allowing our discussion to stray rather far from the heartlands of labour law in which our discussion of 'right to work' interventions should properly be located. We return to that more central territory in the next subsection.

B National Implementations of EU-Based Controls on Discrimination in the Sphere of Employment and Occupation as 'Right to Work Interventions'

In this subsection we consider EU-based controls on discrimination in the sphere of employment and occupation, and seek to evaluate their implementation in the Member States as a species of 'right to work' intervention. Apart from a certain amount of debate with regard to 'occupation' as distinct from employment,[22] it does not, as we have indicated, require much argument to locate this body of legal regulation within the fold, indeed within the modern heartland, of labour law; but we do need to explain in what sense we regard it as a set of 'right to work' interventions. We take that view because and insofar as this kind of intervention is essentially concerned with making access to employment universal as between groups of workers or work seekers distinguished by characteristics reliance upon which as the basis of exclusion is deemed to be discriminatory, and with securing

[20] Austria, Belgium, Germany, Estonia, Ireland, Finland, Luxembourg, Poland and the United Kingdom.

[21] See JER, 17.

[22] There is a vigorous contention that EU-based controls on discrimination in the sphere of occupation, as opposed to employment, should *not* be regarded as properly within the sphere of labour law; see C McCrudden, 'Two Views of Subordination: The Personal Scope of Employment Discrimination Law in *Jivraj v Hashwani*' (2012) 41 *Industrial Law Journal* 30 – with which view, however, the present authors presume to disagree; see M Freedland and N Kountouris, 'Employment Equality and Personal Work Relations – A Critique of *Jivraj v Hashwani*' (2012) 41 *Industrial Law Journal* 56.

equal treatment between workers regardless of those differences and appropriate adaptations to those differences; we regard this as a central part of the business of 'right to work' intervention.

Acting on this conviction, we proceed to engage in a brief reflection on the state of development of the national implementations or counterparts of some of the main EU anti-discrimination measures in the fields or on the grounds of gender, race, disability, religion or belief, sexual orientation and age; we concentrate particularly upon gender and age.[23] This is an enquiry which in our view could usefully be pursued in breadth and depth; we confine ourselves on this occasion to highlighting a few main points which serve to identify a continuity of concerns and problems as between this kind of 'right to work' intervention and those which we have considered in the previous subsection and shall consider in the next subsection. Our central and underlying concern, as outlined in the initial sections of the chapter, is with the tension between notions of a 'right to work' which concentrate simply upon access to work of any description and those which insist that the access must be to decent work if the whole idea is to be a meaningful one.

Thus, it will be recalled that in the previous subsection and in the context of Active Labour Market Policies and other employment policy interventions, we identified the way in which such 'right to work' interventions can come into tension or conflict with the concern for fair, just and decent working conditions, in particular with regard to the precarisation of arrangements for employment. Reporting on actual evolutions with regard to gender equality in the Member States points out a heightened propensity for negative equalisation in times of economic crisis – a convergence towards precarisation for men at least as much as for women. Thus GER 2012 described:

> There has been a levelling downwards of gender gaps in employment and unemployment over the downturn, as male employment fell more and male unemployment rose faster. The EU-wide gender gap in the employment rate has gone down some 3.2 percentage points from a 14.1 percentage points at (pre-crisis) peak level to 10.9 points in the first quarter of 2012. The gender unemployment gap reversed again in 2012, with women displaying marginally lower unemployment than men (-0.2 percentage points). Reversal had already occurred in the first recessionary dip.[24]

The same Report went on to record that:

[23] In so doing, we draw upon the following sources of comparative reporting and comparative assessments: (1) for gender equality, 'The impact of the economic crisis on the situation of women and of gender equality policies' (European Commission, Luxembourg, 2013), available at ec.europa.eu/justice/gender-equality/files/documents/130410_crisis_report_en.pdf (GER 2012) and 'Progress on equality between women and men in 2012' (European Commission Staff Working Document, Brussels, 8 May 2013) SWD (2013) 171 final, available at: ec.europa.eu/justice/gender-equality/files/swd_2013_171_en.pdf (GER 2013)); for other kinds of equality, the European Commission Annual Report for 2011, 'Developing Anti-Discrimination Law in Europe, The 27 EU Member States, Croatia, Former Yugoslav Republic of Macedonia, Iceland, Liechtenstein, Norway and Turkey compared' October 2012, prepared by experts from the European Anti-Discrimination Legal Network (DADL 2012).

[24] GER 2012, 14.

> The worsening of working conditions has spared neither men nor women, but has affected them differently. In 2010, the worst year of the crisis within our reference period, the involuntary share of total part-time work had risen to 38.1%, up 5.8 points from 2007. Among women the corresponding value was 24%, up 3.8 percentage points. Absolute figures tell a different story. In 2010 female involuntary part-time workers numbered 7.3 million as against 3.2 million for men. The growth from 2007 totalled 1.3 million for women against 773 thousand for men. One year later – 2011, the latest on record – involuntary part-time work had decreased for both sexes, but remained considerably higher than pre-recession levels. [25]

GER 2013 confirmed that:

> Gender gaps decreased in several domains in the last five years. A closer insight shows that this decrease is not the consequence of an improvement of the situation of women but to a faster deterioration of the situation of men as compared to women, in particular in the first period of the crisis. Therefore, the EU has experienced a levelling down of gender gaps in employment, unemployment, wages and poverty in recent years.[26]

We do not argue that these negative outcomes are themselves *consequences* of 'right to work' interventions in pursuit of gender equality, but we point out how such interventions do at least permit or leave space for such levelling down even if they do not themselves cause or encourage it.

Rather differently, but again picking up on issues identified in the previous subsection, we might usefully reflect upon the possibly mixed effects in the Member States of 'right to work' intervention against age discrimination in the rather complex area of retirement age. DADL 2012 reports upon the variety of outcomes as between Member States:

> The Employment Equality Directive permits national law to include a range of exceptions in relation to both direct and indirect age discrimination [. . .] As a consequence, there remains very substantial uncertainty across the states as to which forms of age discrimination will be treated as justified by national courts [. . .] A key issue relating to the age provisions of the Employment Equality Directive is retirement. In principle, compelling employees to leave work because they have reached a certain age is direct age discrimination which will require objective justification. Meanwhile, Recital 14 indicates that retirement ages may be regarded as justified age discrimination. It states that 'this Directive shall be without prejudice to national provisions laying down retirement ages'. National law varies greatly in this area, ranging from states with no national compulsory retirement age (eg, the Czech Republic) to states which permit compulsory retirement by public and private employers at a specific age (eg, Italy).[27]

It does seem worth pointing out, as we did in the previous subsection, the risk that this kind of intervention in favour of workers' *rights* to longer working life may also operate to create pressures and incentives amounting to the imposition of *duties* to remain in work until progressively greater ages; and this in turn brings out the underlying tension between rights to continuing access to work of any

[25] ibid, 16.
[26] GER 2013, 4.
[27] DADL 2012, 32.

quality and to work of decent quality. We suggest that these various very evidently agonising national debates, which we suggest are to a significant extent concerned with the universalising of access to employment within the European Union, have to be understood against the backdrop of the EU free movement of workers regime. This is arguably the most significant and complex of all the EU 'right to work' interventions whose national implementations we are concerned with in this section, and it is to that crucial area that we turn our attention.

C The EU Free Movement of Workers Regime and its National Implementations as 'Right to Work Interventions'

In the previous subsection, we concentrated on the EU employment equality regime and its national counterparts as a species of 'right to work' intervention in the sense, particularly, that they are concerned with the universalising of access to employment; this brought into focus a set of issues concerning the 'right to work' regardless of gender and age: and this in turn begins to touch upon questions concerning nationality and the 'right to work' and the claim to freedom of labour migration. In that context and in that sense, the EU free movement of workers regime represents one of the most significant of those bodies of regulation which we have chosen to consider as 'right to work' interventions, for it momentously institutes and maintains the right of EU citizens to move freely between Member States in search of or in order to engage in work. There is not the opportunity within the confines of this chapter to engage in depth with the ramifications of the EU free movement of workers regime and its national implementations, but a couple of points will be made to suggest the kind of tensions and conflicts which seem to be increasingly attendant upon this most high profile of real world 'right to work' interventions.[28]

As in relation to the two areas of regulation considered in the two preceding subsections, we have the advantage of being able to draw upon a system of frequent or annual reportage on the implementation and working of this regime in the Member States, and it is useful to set out the key summary of the latest such report:

> During the period under consideration, free movement of workers has become a subject of less consensus among the political and media circles of the Member States. While in most Member States there has been little discussion of the right and its use, including some of the largest Member States such as Germany, Poland and Romania, in some other Member States the right has been subject to substantial attention, such as France, the Netherlands and the UK. There seem to be two types of attention paid to free movement of workers. First, in some Member States where there is little or no discussion, there is little concern about numbers of persons using their rights even when these are substantial (such as in Germany) or there is little inward movement of EU workers

[28] An excellent account of this body of EU law is provided in C Barnard, *EU Employment Law*, 4th edn (Oxford, Oxford University Press, 2012) ch 4 on 'Free Movement of Workers'.

(Finland, Slovenia, Greece etc). In some states there is concern about nationals of the state being required to leave to search for work in another Member State. While this may be the subject of criticism in the media against economic situations, it is not seen as a ground to limit the right to move in search of work. In other states where there is media and political attention, such as Denmark, the Netherlands, the UK or France, the concerns expressed are narrowly focused on two groups – third country family members of EU citizens who have exercised their free movement rights (for example Denmark, the Netherlands and the UK), or citizens of Member States which joined the EU in 2004 and 2007 (for example the Netherlands, France). There does not appear to be any sustained correlation between concerns about free movement of workers and unemployment rates among the Member States.[29]

There is, we suggest, a still larger field for European comparative investigation of the national implementation of this 'right to work' regime. This field is opened up by extending our perspective from the EU free movement of workers regime to the complementary regimes concerning freedom of establishment and posting of workers.[30] Hesitating to venture on this occasion into the whole territory of the *Viking* and *Laval* case law of the Court of Justice (CJEU), we content ourselves with making the suggestion that from this larger perspective we can observe most clearly the tensions which arise between 'right to work' interventions of this particular genre and claims of competing rights to fair or just conditions of work as defined by the normative institutions of each particular EU Member State.

A ground-breaking article by Catherine Barnard provides us with an admirably rich case study of a labour dispute in the United Kingdom in 2009 which invokes exactly this set of issues.[31] This section and this article conclude by calling for more such investigations in the future, and by suggesting that some at least of that work could take place on a European comparative basis and under the conceptual heading of 'the right to work in a practical context'. In that way, we could hope to replicate and build upon Bob Hepple's earlier deployment of the idea of the 'right to work' as one of a number of critical tools for the assessment of the social adequacy of a given system of labour law. We are conscious of putting forward these reflections at a time when European labour law is in crucial need of such assessments and action upon those assessments. This is a task in which we have recently engaged with a group of colleagues, many of whom are contributors to the present volume, under the banner of 'Resocialising Europe'.[32] We hope that this chapter may have made a case for regarding the 'right to work' as playing an important part in that discourse.

[29] 'European Report on the Free Movement of Workers in Europe in 2011–12' 1, available at: ec.europa.eu/social/keyDocuments.jsp?pager.offset=20&langId=en&mode=advancedSubmit&year=2013&country=0&type=3&advSearchKey=european%20report%20on%20the%20free%20movement%20of%20workers%20in%20europe%202011-2012 (Executive Summary).

[30] This is the extension which Barnard makes in ch 5, 'Labour Law and the Internal Market' of her EU Employment Law treatise, see above, n 28.

[31] C Barnard, '"British Jobs for British Workers": The Lindsey Oil Refinery Dispute and the Future of Local Labour Clauses in an Integrated EU Market' (2009) 38 *Industrial Law Journal* 245.

[32] See N Countouris and M Freedland (eds), *Resocialising Europe in a Time of Crisis* (Cambridge, Cambridge University Press, 2013).

8

Giving Up on the Human Right to Work

JAMES W NICKEL

Introduction

In 1980 I published an essay on the right to work that offered a qualified defence of an international human right in this area.[1] At that time the human rights movement was taking off, starting to have some significant influence in domestic politics and international relations. And in the 1990s, after the Cold War ended, human rights flew high and lots of institutional development occurred. Economic and social rights, however, have never been among the high flyers – with the exception, perhaps, of the rights to food and education.[2] And the 'right to work' (RTW), in particular, never really got off the ground. As an international legal human right, RTW seems not to get taken very seriously or to accomplish much. Even in the current crisis of unemployment in southern Europe it has not played much of a role. As an early defender of RTW I say this with sadness. Nonetheless, I do not think that RTW is destined for a brighter future.

This chapter diagnoses and explains RTW's failure. The first section discusses the nature of work. Section II argues that access to work and economic opportunities are very important goals or ideals and suggests that it is probably impossible to complete a justification for RTW as a fully-fledged legal human right. Section III looks at the formulation of RTW in the International Covenant on Economic, Social, and Cultural Rights (ICESCR, United Nations, 1966) and finds it weak in ways that suggest that even the authors of this formulation of RTW were not prepared to endorse associated duties requiring governments to provide employment to all the willing and qualified who were unable to find work elsewhere. The final section discusses the question of whether the importance of RTW diminishes further in countries that successfully guarantee an adequate minimum income. My worries about RTW are not based on a general rejection or downgrading of economic and social rights.

[1] J Nickel, 'Is there a Human Right to Employment?' (1980) X *Philosophical Forum* 149.

[2] See D Beetham, 'What Future for Economic and Social Rights?' (1995) 43 *Political Studies* 41.

I Work and Economic Opportunities

'Work' has broad and narrow senses. The broad sense is simply *productive activity requiring effort*. In this sense work is doing something that is thought to be useful or good for someone – self or others. A couple who spend an arduous day planting a vegetable garden can correctly say that they worked all day on the garden even if their motivations for having a garden are not at all commercial or income-oriented. Everyone engages in work in the broad sense. As living beings whose bodies require hydration, nutrition and maintenance, as householders, as managers of personal finances, as family members and social beings and as citizens there is much useful but arduous activity to be engaged in daily.

The narrow sense is work that is in some organized form of production (as in farms, factories and offices) and oriented towards generating income and making a living. Here we can say that Jones works at Microsoft or that Smith works in her own insurance company.

RTW is about work in the narrow sense. It is about being able to engage in organized and sustained production of goods and services that is likely to yield an adequate income for oneself and one's dependants, if any. 'Organized' does not mean that one cannot work alone as a solo producer of such things as food, clothing or health services; it rather means that the activities and methods of work are regular and institutionalized – and often occurring in a special workplace.

Not all work in the narrow sense involves having a job (in the sense of working for a person, company or government) and not all unemployment is joblessness. Self-employment must be included. Because the historical origins of RTW were in the labour movement it often seems to be about being employed by someone else, but orienting RTW entirely towards employment by others is a big mistake in today's economies. It neglects creating one's own productive enterprise – and this is important in both developing and developed economies.

As an international legal human right, RTW needs to apply in all countries, including those that are least developed. Furthermore, it needs to apply to indigenous peoples as well. Consequently, work needs to cover subsistence farming, making food or handicrafts and selling them on the street, animal husbandry, fishing, hunting, weaving by hand and many other forms of economic activities. The section on rural women in the Convention on the Elimination of All Forms of Discrimination against Women (CEDAW, United Nations 1979) provides a good illustration of how to move the focus away from employment by others. Article 14 on 'the particular problems faced by rural women' says that they shall enjoy rights

> (e) to organize self-help groups and co-operatives in order to obtain equal access to economic opportunities through employment or self employment;
>
> (f) to participate in all community activities;

(g) to have access to agricultural credit and loans, marketing facilities, appropriate technology and equal treatment in land and agrarian reform as well as in land resettlement schemes.

The big change in this formulation is that the worker – in this case a female worker – is now conceived as an agent active in arranging and managing production. Self-employment, cooperatives, financing for businesses and farms, technology and access to land are part of the picture. To overstate the contrast a little, instead of work being seen as getting a job that someone else has organized, it is seen as taking active steps to make use of opportunities for productive activity within a supportive social, political, economic and regulatory environment.

II The Importance of Access to Work and Economic Opportunities

The trouble with RTW has never been that people's access to work and economic opportunities is unimportant. In many parts of the world unemployment and underemployment remain high – and this makes many other social and personal problems worse. The serious recession that began in 2008 in much of the world has resulted in disastrously high levels of unemployment in southern Europe and elsewhere.

Further, the trouble with RTW as a legal human right has never been that it is a cry in the wilderness, trying to promote a political goal that no one wants. In most countries both citizens and politicians recognize the great value of access to work and economic opportunities and make it a prominent political goal. Motivation to develop the economy and create jobs is not something that governments lack until they attend to RTW.[3] They already have this motivation in most cases because development and job creation are popular with their citizens (including their political elites) and because success in this area improves tax revenues and the country's reputation. Economic development, growth and opportunities are important political goals nearly everywhere. This popularity seems to be good news for RTW, but in fact it is two-edged. Because the main political goal that RTW promotes is already popular, the value added by a legal RTW is small: it just sings to the choir.

One can counter the worry that a legal RTW adds little motivational value by emphasizing the ways in which a right is more demanding than a goal.[4] A fully-fledged legal human right usually applies to each and every individual person

[3] Governments are likely, however, to want a less demanding goal that allows them to use monetary policy to control inflation even if that increases unemployment.

[4] See J Nickel, 'Goals and Rights – Working Together?' in M Langford et al (eds), *The Millennium Development Goals and Human Rights: Past, Present and Future* (Cambridge, Cambridge University Press, 2013).

without discrimination. Viewed in this way, RTW would require that each and every adult individual who wants work and is able and qualified to work productively should have an effectively claimable right to a job on an equal basis with others. This move, however, greatly increases the difficulty of getting governments to accept RTW, makes it much harder and more expensive to realize and is contrary to its actual formulation in the ICESCR – which does not include a requirement that governments are employers of last resort.

Joel Feinberg proposed dividing the case for a claim right into two parts.[5] The first part explains why it is so important – morally, politically and/or practically – for the right-holders to have access to the object of the right (the freedom or benefit that the right is to). He called this justifying the *claim-to* the object. In the present context, this would involve showing why having access to work and economic opportunities is so important normatively. The second part of the case for a right shows that it would be justifiable and feasible for some parties to be obligated to act in ways that make the object of the right available to all the right-holders. Feinberg called this justifying the *claim-against.*

One argument for the importance of the *claim-to* work draws on the idea that one important role of legal human rights is to ensure each person the conditions of a minimally good life. Remunerative work provides the most generally available, reliable and acceptable means of providing for one's survival and basic well-being, and this is one reason why people have a claim to it. For most adults, their own productive activity provides the main means of providing for their survival, social and family life, security and happiness. If remunerative work is unavailable, the ordinary adult's life prospects will be poor. (I discuss below the objection that government income grants can sever the link between remunerative work and having a minimally good life.)

A second argument uses as a premise the idea that an important role of legal human rights is to enable people to *lead* their lives, to at least make some key choices about what to do with one's months and years and ultimately one's life. Access to remunerative work gives a person an important area of choice and generates income that allows access to other choices. Of course, many features of a person's life are already determined or constrained by nature and culture. One does not get to choose who one's parents are, whether one is male or female, in which country one is born, what one's native language and culture are and what innate talents and disabilities one has. And fairness to others often requires us to accommodate their lives, needs, desires and choices. But, in spite of these limits, there is still much choosing to be done – and life often takes surprising turns. The same is true in the economic arena. Most people have to work and do not choose whether they are born into a family, region or country that is rich or poor. Further, occupational choices may be limited. But even apart from deciding whether to migrate to richer areas, one can choose among the occupations available and fill in the details within those occupations in various ways. The scope for choice may

[5] J Feinberg, 'The Nature and Value of Rights' (1970) 4 *Journal of Value Inquiry* 245.

be limited, yet workers typically have thousands of days to put their own stamps on their work and to find their own particular niches. And those who are inventive and enjoy basic economic liberties are sometimes able to create new occupational paths to better suit themselves. The fact that work (in both the broad and narrow senses) is necessary to most people's survival and flourishing means that most humans engage in it and take access to it to be important.[6] This argument also shows the close relation between the claim-to access to work and the right to free choice of employment.

A third argument, closely related to the second, suggests that work provides extremely important opportunities for self-development, for becoming a person of skill and accomplishment. Hugh Collins's chapter (two) in this volume offers a nice version of this argument:

> Jobs can be exhausting and fairly monotonous, but people can feel a sense of achievement at a job well done, fulfilment from the opportunity to use their skills in partnership with others to achieve something, and can identify themselves with the outcome of their labours. It is the opportunity for self-realisation through work that explains why the right to work requires a positive aspect, so that having a job matters for its own sake and not simply because it affords material benefits or avoids welfare dependency . . . The need to co-operate with others within the division of labour of organisations further improves the extent to which work offers opportunities for self-realisation.[7]

A fourth argument suggests that excluding some persons or groups from access to remunerative work and economic opportunities is a severe form of unfairness. The severity of unfairness in access to work and economic opportunities depends on the degree and pervasiveness of the bias, whether malicious intent is present, and the number, duration and severity of the harms the unfairness causes. If access to work and economic opportunities is heavily biased against people without much education, those without political connections, and women and minorities, most of these conditions for severe unfairness will be met.[8]

These four arguments provide a case for a *claim-to* work. But the case for a claim *against* governments to ensure the availability of work and economic opportunities to all right-holders still needs to be provided. The case for a universal legal human right is not complete when one has shown the great importance of its object. This only gets the case started. The harder parts are justifying the duties the right will impose and showing that they are feasible in most countries.[9] Knowing that something is very important normatively does not ensure knowing

[6] This paragraph is adapted from J Nickel, *Making Sense of Human Rights*, 2nd edn (Oxford, Blackwell, 2006) 128.

[7] See H Collins in this volume, ch 2.

[8] A similar set of arguments is found in K Karst, 'The Coming Crisis of Work in Constitutional Perspective' (1997) 53 *Cornell Law Review* 523.

[9] Doubts about duties to provide work are found in C Coope, 'Justice and Jobs: Three Skeptical Thoughts about Rights in Employment' (1994) 11 *Journal of Applied Philosophy* 71, and B Cullen, 'The Right to Work' in J Evans (ed), *Moral Philosophy and Contemporary Problems* (Cambridge, Cambridge University Press, 1988) 165.

how to make it available to all – or even that doing so is possible, or possible without incurring costs that greatly outweigh the benefit.

This said, we should note that even when a justified *claim-to* something is not accompanied by a justified *claim-against* someone, the claim-to is still a significant norm. It does not impose duties, but is well suited to serve as an ideal or goal and may even constitute, as Feinberg suggested, a right in a weak or 'manifesto' sense. Human rights activists frequently emphasize the important practical role of human rights as inspirational ideals for the disadvantaged. But if you think that international legal human rights should be more than ideals or manifesto rights, as I do, then justifying a *claim-to* work is just the beginning.

The next step, justifying a claim-against governments to promote the availability of employment and serve as employers of last resort, needs to show, I believe (1) that the burdens this imposes are justifiable; and (2) feasible in a majority of the world's countries.[10] It is when we focus on these requirements that we start to understand why RTW seems problematic as a serious right.

III Formulating RTW as an International Legal Human Right – Right or Goal?

Work is too important in human life to be ignored by human rights declarations and treaties, particularly since in human history the workplace has often been a place of slavery, servitude, violence, exploitation, dangerous and harsh working conditions, discrimination and exclusion. We find, consequently, that RTW arrives together with a large family of other human rights dealing with work opportunities, workers, health and education. Other members of the entourage include: (1) no slavery or forced labour; (2) freedom from discrimination in the areas of education, work and economic opportunities; (3) economic liberties including freedom of movement and right to acquire, hold and use property; (4) 'social security' and unemployment insurance to provide income when one cannot work; (5) fair remuneration for the value of work done including equal pay for equally valuable work; (6) safe and decent working conditions including rest and leisure; (7) protection against dismissal from employment without a lawful reason; (8) trade union rights that allow workers to balance the power of employers; (9) the right to development – so that the context in which one pursues a living is not so impoverished that there is little chance of success; (10) the right to education – so that one has some productive skills to offer or use; (11) rights to food and health – so that one is healthy and energetic enough to learn, work and pursue opportunities; and (12) protections for migrant workers and their children.

[10] These two tests are defended in Nickel, *Making Sense of Human Rights*, above n 6, 78–86. In the chapter on economic and social rights it is argued that both the right to subsistence and the right to education can pass these tests.

The Universal Declaration of Human Rights (UDHR, 1948) puts RTW in this family context when it says that 'Everyone has the right to work, to free choice of employment, to just and favourable conditions of work and to protection against unemployment'. The European Social Charter (Council of Europe, 1961) obligates the contracting parties 'to accept as one of the primary aims and responsibilities the achievement and maintenance of as high and stable a level of employment as possible, with a view to the attainment of full employment'. The ICESCR requires countries joining the treaty to

> recognize the right to work, which includes the right of everyone to gain his living by work [and] take appropriate steps to safeguard this right [including] technical and vocational guidance programs [and] policies and techniques to achieve steady economic, social and cultural development and full and productive employment.

Most of the world's countries have ratified this Treaty.

Based on the UDHR, drafted between 1948 and 1954, finally approved by the General Assembly in 1966 and entering into force in 1976, the ICESCR comes to us from a different economic and political world. When its drafting began the Cold War was in its early stages and the Korean War had begun. Communism and socialism were still strong and optimistic political forces. Entrenched racism and sexism were only beginning to be combated. Decolonization was incomplete. Europe, the Soviet Union and Japan were under post-war reconstruction. Most of Asia was poor. 'Industrialization' was the word for what we now call development – and 'deindustrialization' was not yet in use. Labour unions were strong. The movement of women into the workplace was in its early stages. Farming was less technological and usually on a smaller scale but provided work for many more people. The world population was less than three billion. The environmental movement had not yet flowered. And carbon-forced climate change was present but undiscovered.

The heart of the ICESCR lies in the nine Articles (6 to 15) that provide its list of rights. This list begins with work-oriented rights: the right to work (Article 6); free choice of work (Article 6); just and favourable conditions of work (Article 7); and labour union rights (Article 8). The following Articles set out rights to public services such as social security (Article 9); family assistance (Article 10); adequate standard of living (Article 11); freedom from hunger (Article 11); adequate housing (Article 11); health care (Article 12); and education (Articles 13, 14). This ordering differs from the UDHR's, which started with the right to social security and then moved to work.

We can speculate that putting RTW first was meant to recognize the fact that most people gain their livelihood through work in the narrow sense (and that families were mostly supported by their working members). Before we get to education in Article 13, the right to work in Article 6 already calls for 'technical and vocational guidance and training programs'.

Inability to comply with a moral or legal duty is generally a good excuse if one is genuinely unable to do what the duty requires while continuing to meet one's other obligations of higher priority. Consequently, the ICESCR's commitment clause could have been just like the one in the Civil and Political Covenant: 'Each State Party to the present Covenant undertakes to respect and to ensure to all individuals within its territory and subject to its jurisdiction the rights recognized in the present Covenant'. The authors of the ICESCR recognized, however, how far many countries were from development and full employment and consequently opted for a weaker clause that requires a ratifying country to 'take steps . . . to the maximum of its available resources, with a view to achieving progressively the full realization of the rights recognized in the present Covenant by all appropriate means'. This seems like agreeing to make a good faith effort to realize a goal, and this 'goalish' flavour seeps into all the ICESCR rights except for the right to basic education (which in Article 14 requires a stronger commitment).[11]

Although the ICESCR's right to work is listed first, it is accompanied by other rights that cover conditions of work, wages and developing people's capacity to work through nutrition, education and health services. These are important parts of the Treaty's formulation, but not our present concern. The ICESCR clauses that directly pertain to access to work and economic opportunities are:

- 'The right to work'.
- 'Appropriate steps to safeguard this right'.
- 'Policies and techniques to achieve steady economic, social and cultural development and full and productive employment'.
- 'Technical and vocational guidance'.
- 'Training programmes'.
- 'Social insurance' – which presumably includes unemployment benefits as well as care and compensation for injuries at work.
- 'Safeguarding fundamental political and economic freedoms to the individual'.

All these measures are to be available to everyone (or at least to all adult residents) without discrimination.

This list of required steps includes plausible and feasible steps to assist people in finding suitable employment and dealing with work injuries and temporary employment. And we could expand it to include lots of other things that can be done to promote the fair distribution of work and the benefits it brings. So the problem is not that RTW lacks associated duties; the trouble is that it lacks duties that will actually make its object (work and economic opportunities) available to all. The most striking thing about this list is what is missing from it, namely a requirement that a ratifying government itself provides jobs and serves as the employer of last resort. Vocational guidance programmes, work training programmes and unemployment insurance are good things that help a little in

[11] The 2000 Constitution of Finland, s 18.2, also offers a 'goalish' formulation, saying that 'The public authorities shall promote employment and work towards guaranteeing for everyone the right to work'.

making access to work available. And economic liberties have great importance.[12] But these are the frosting without the cake.

It is easy to understand the political reasons for leaving out a requirement that government serves as employer of last resort.[13] This does not, however, change the fact that the duties under RTW are not fully analogous to those found in the rights to food and education. Under those rights governments have direct responsibilities for providing food assistance when necessary. But under RTW a country can fulfil the duties listed without directly providing jobs or coming close to making work available to everyone willing and able to engage in it.

At this point one might ask about the duties of businesses to hire more workers and retain the ones they have. With big qualifications added, this might be part of the right to work as an *ethical* norm. But as an international treaty the ICESCR imposes legal duties on states, not on corporations and other employers, and it does not require ratifying countries to enact legislation requiring that employers hire frequently and dismiss rarely. Further, it will not help to model RTW on the right to marry in Article 23 of the International Covenant on Civil and Political Rights. That right must be understood as a right to marry someone *if* he or she is willing to marry you. Formulated in this way, the right to work would just be the right to work for a company *if* it was willing to hire you. When companies were not doing much hiring that sort of right would not be of much help to the unemployed.

The ICESCR General Comment No 18 on RTW, which balloons the content of RTW in lots of other ways, also refrains from requiring governments to be employers of last resort. When the ICESCR Committee gives examples in paragraph 36 of 'Violations of the obligation to fulfil' it only mentions 'failure to adopt or implement a national employment policy designed to ensure the right to work for everyone', 'the failure to monitor the realization of the right to work at the national level' and 'the failure to implement technical and vocational training programmes'.

Government as the employer of last resort is an unpopular idea in many countries because its implementation is expensive; it inflates the ranks of government agencies and bureaucracies, and often results in 'make work' jobs whose productive value is very low or absent.[14] This unpopularity led to a formulation of RTW that puts the emphasis instead on choosing and implementing economic policies that promote full employment. Even if we were sure which policies these are, they would neither promise nor deliver a job to every person who is willing and able to work.

When we put together the progressive implementation clause and the absence of a duty of governments to be the employer of last resort, the result is to make the ICESCR's RTW unavailable for individual claiming. In regard to RTW's core concern with making employment available to all who are willing and qualified to

[12] See the defence of economic liberties in Nickel, *Making Sense of Human Rights*, above n 6, 123–36.

[13] On these reasons see K Stone in this volume, ch 15.

[14] See J Elster 'Is There (or Should There Be) a Right to Work?' in A Gutmann (ed), *Democracy and the Welfare State* (Princeton, Princeton University Press, 1988).

work, governments do not commit to doing anything that will ensure such availability: they just agree to do progressively some things that will *promote* such availability (if they work).

If this is all that the ICESCR's RTW does, statements about a *right* to employment will be viewed either as involving a very weak sense of 'right' which does not generate individual claims to jobs or as simply a misleading and rhetorical way of talking about the *goal* of full employment. The result, I fear, is to destroy most of the point of asserting that access to work and economic opportunities is a human *right*. Once we substitute Keynesian macroeconomic policies for socialism the key part of RTW turns into a goal. There's nothing wrong, of course, with being a political goal that is established by legislation or treaty. Goals can have high priority and be very useful guides to political action by individuals and governments, but they are significantly different from rights.

Interestingly, discourse within the United Nations about access to work and economic opportunities has returned to the language of goals (a vocabulary that economists and development experts have always found more comfortable). The first Millenium Development Goal (MDG), 'Eradicate extreme poverty and hunger', includes the goal of achieving 'full and productive employment and decent work for all, including women and young people'. Unfortunately, this MDG has not received much attention.

IV Does a Guaranteed Minimum Income Undermine the Weight of RTW?

Developed countries often have programmes to ensure people a minimum income even if they do not find a job or other productive activities. Giving out money is a lot easier than giving out work and productive opportunities. An income guarantee just involves depositing money in someone's account while a job guarantee involves (1) giving out money; (2) a workplace and equipment; and (3) supervision. For people whose productivity is unlikely to be high, governments may find it cheaper and easier to forget (2) and (3) and just give out money and services.

Reduced opportunities for work (in the narrow sense) may well be the way of the future. Suppose that computerization, automation and robots substantially reduce the need for workers and nothing else emerges to recharge that need. The result will be that a smaller portion of the population has jobs or is fully self-employed. Suppose further that governments ensure a minimum income to all their residents that make it possible to have a decent life without working. The question that I want to pose is whether under this scenario RTW loses a substantial part of its normative weight.[15]

[15] For an interesting discussion of this scenario in relation to *ethical* human rights, see J Griffin in *On Human Rights* (Oxford, Oxford University Press, 2008) 207. He thinks that 'there is no right to

If this scenario were realized many people would still consider work a very important good for themselves and others. Working (in the narrow sense) would usually provide higher incomes than the basic income grants do. It would also give people something to do with their time and provide opportunities for social interaction and self-development. But, on the other side, it seems likely that many people would be happy to live on their income grants rather than seek work – and under our supposition there won't be that many jobs available anyway. Some would pursue volunteer work or home-based productive activities (say as musicians, writers, artists, bakers, home gardeners, or furniture builders) that generate some income but not enough to live on. Perhaps governments would encourage and facilitate these hobby businesses along with volunteer work. Add to this picture that some people would work for a while and then stop and that others would find that their hobby businesses had turned into fully-fledged self-employment.

My question is whether the people and governments of such countries should still assign substantial weight to RTW or whether it would be reasonable for them to view access to work as much less important when having a decent life does not require working. My guess is that it would be the latter. Living on one's income grant allows one to survive and be healthy, to have lots of leisure to pursue one's interests and social relationships and to choose the course of one's life (with fewer options than high-income workers would have but more time for activities other than work). Further, such a system does not seem severely unfair or cruel. Some people would surely be frustrated by not being able to find a job, but since very large numbers of people would be jobless (or jobless but pursuing a hobby business or volunteer work), the stigma of joblessness would disappear or decrease. Beyond this, the bad consequences of widespread joblessness (and surely there would be some) would be balanced by the absence of many of the bad consequences of the previous system in which many had to survive by working in low-paid jobs that they hated. Commuting costs would also be reduced. My hunch is that in such a society RTW would lose even more of its steam. If the scenario envisioned here is the future of developed countries, RTW will be even more of a failure as a human right in the future than it has been so far.

V Conclusion

By 'giving up on RTW' as an international legal human right I do not mean deleting it from the ICESCR. That will not happen, and the reporting system under the ICESCR will continue to require governments to report on their policies, successes and failures in this area. There is no harm in that. I rather mean giving up hope that RTW will be taken seriously as a human right and will be a significant

work. There is certainly a right to the resources needed to live as an agent, but those resources do not have to come from work'.

part of a solution to unemployment worldwide. Equal access to work and access to economic opportunities is a very important ethical and political goal, but calling it an international legal right has not been a winning proposition – and that is unlikely to change. We might as well get used to thinking of access to employment as a very important goal or ideal but not as a serious legal human right.

9

Only Fools and Horses: Some Sceptical Reflections on the Right to Work

ALAN L BOGG

> Cause where it all comes from is a mystery,
> It's like the changing of the seasons
> And the tides of the sea
> But here's the one that's driving me berserk:
> Why do only fools and horses work?

Introduction – Only Fools and Horses

Like all fine comedies, the much-loved BBC television series 'Only Fools and Horses' offers a deep reflection on some enduring themes. One of those themes is the value of work. As the lyrics to the title song to the television programme suggest, the protagonists in 'Only Fools and Horses' regard work as a human activity with little intrinsic value, something for fools and horses. The main characters, brothers Del and Rodney Trotter, spend their lives in Peckham working the markets and selling goods of dubious provenance from their base in 'Nelson Mandela House'. Their aim is to get rich quick as a way of escaping from the grind of work and to live a life of leisure. Work is instrumental, a means to an end, which is to acquire sufficient resources to cease the need to engage in it. It is also subordinate to other forms of value such as leisure, friendship and family. This is often centred on the working class community in the Nag's Head pub. Their work is self-employment, and it often occurs at the edges of illegality and in illicit contexts. In many ways, in their relentless quest for wealth the Trotters were representatives of their age, as the television comedy reached its height of popularity during the deregulatory era of the 1980s. Eventually, the brothers become millionaires and so can escape the hard drudgery of their lives on the edge, but it would be to give too much away to let the reader know whether the brothers find happiness and fulfilment in their escape; or whether the escape from work is a final one.

As a meditation on the *value* of work, 'Only Fools and Horses' provides a way into thinking about the *right* to work. For if Del Trotter is correct in the claim that work is an activity fit only for fools and horses, it is difficult to see how it could be configured as a fundamental human right. This chapter will proceed in the following way. In section I, I offer the view that Del Trotter is only half right about the value of work. For many of us, work *is* valuable. It is not only instrumentally valuable as a source of income to enable us to live a life; it can itself be part of what makes life valuable. Work can be an activity where we find meaning and self-esteem, form social connections and express our creativity. Nevertheless, in liberal societies characterised by value pluralism, there should also be recognition of the fact that there will be those who regard work as Del Trotter regards it. This is simply a reflection of the reasonable pluralism that obtains in liberal communities: work is a valuable activity, but it is not the only activity that is valuable, and it is reasonable for individuals not to recognise its value but to realise well-being in other ways such as through friendship, surfing or religious contemplation.

Section I offers no argument as such against the idea of a moral right to work. Furthermore, it does not deny (how could it?) that the right to work is a human right as a matter of positive international law, for the right to work is specified expressly in a range of international human rights conventions.[1] In fact, given its status as a widely recognised human right, I am quite comfortable with the idea that there is a moral right to work. What I want to suggest in section I, however, is that one can take the value of work very seriously indeed as a political matter, but without constitutionalising a legal right to work in a national legal system. Following Joseph Raz and Ronald Dworkin, I will suggest that governments (and private actors) are under duties to protect and promote human well-being, and as an element of this duty there are duties to promote decent work. These duties are not correlative to rights, but exist as freestanding duties. It is therefore possible to take work very seriously as a matter of public political concern through this duty-based analysis. In fact, I argue in section I that the duties to promote decent work generated by these overarching duties to promote well-being are likely to be much more significant and extensive than the correlative duties associated with a moral or human right to work.

In section II, I draw a distinction between moral rights and legal rights. The case for recognising an abstract legal right to work in the English legal system is assessed, and I identify three important concerns that incline against the recognition of an abstract legal right to work: the right to work as corrosive of worker solidarity; the right to work from the perspective of distributive justice; and the institutional context of the right to work, especially the role of the English courts. It is important to emphasise the relatively limited scope of this argument. It does

[1] See, eg, the Universal Declaration of Human Rights 1948, Art 23(1); International Covenant on Economic, Social and Cultural Rights 1966, Art 6(1); European Union Charter of Fundamental Rights 2000, Art 15.

not purport to be a general argument against constitutionalisation of the right to work in all legal systems: the concerns are mostly animated by a localised scepticism about the role of English judges, deploying common law understandings of the right to work and its political significance. An abstract legal right to work would leave too much interpretive discretion to judges in a legal system that is still, at base, erected upon a common law foundation. While these arguments fall short of a conclusive argument against a legal right to work, they should certainly give us pause for thought before proceeding to juridify the moral right to work in the English legal system. While Del Trotter may be wrong in the claim that only fools and horses can find value in the activity of work, it is suggested that only a fool would entrust the interpretation and enforcement of a right to work to the English judiciary at the current time.

Finally, a word on what I take to be the right to work for the purposes of this argument. I am concerned with the right to work as a distinct right rooted in the right to a job that gives opportunities for self-realisation.[2] Sometimes the right to work is regarded as the most fundamental of all labour rights, providing a justificatory basis for other supporting labour rights such as the right to non-discrimination, the right not to be unjustifiably dismissed, or the right to fair and just working conditions.[3] I have no quarrel with the claim that these different labour rights can be viewed as elements in a coherent set, yoked together by the common objective of promoting decent or non-exploitative work.[4] However, I know of no argument suggesting that these other labour rights are tied to the right to work in some stronger sense, such that these rights derive their normative force from their connection with the right to work. These various labour rights are regarded as distinct in international human rights treaties. Their foundations seem to be pluralistic,[5] with distinct labour rights reflecting their own distinct locus of values and concerns. Furthermore, it is not clear at the level of political strategy what is to be gained by emphasising the indivisibility of labour rights, with the right to work as the foundation. Rights such as the right to non-discrimination or the right not to be unjustifiably dismissed have now acquired their own autonomous bodies of doctrine and critical scholarly reflection, and are more highly developed than the right to work. For this reason, critical reflection on the right to work should not be viewed as extending to other fundamental labour rights: there is no assumption of guilt by association.

[2] See H Collins in this volume, ch 2.

[3] For a particularly expansive conception of the right to work and its connections with other labour rights, see G Mundlak, 'The Right to Work: Linking Human Rights and Employment Policy' (2007) 146 *International Labour Review* 189, 193–94.

[4] See V Mantouvalou in this volume, ch 3.

[5] J Tasioulas, 'Towards a Philosophy of Human Rights' (2012) 65 *Current Legal Problems* 1.

I The Value of Work and Duties to Protect and Promote Well-Being

A The Value of Work

There is good reason to resist Del Trotter's characterisation of work as an activity only for fools and horses. On the contrary, work seems to *matter*, and matter appropriately, to many human beings. It is regarded by many as a valuable activity in the structure of their lives, and one that contributes in significant ways to human flourishing. There are many different philosophical accounts of how and why work matters. Indeed, the activity of work is often regarded as so fundamental that it figures explicitly in ethical theories. For example, in Finnis' account of the 'basic goods', work itself is marked out as one of the basic human goods, one of the bedrock components of human flourishing, characterised as '*skilful performance*, in work and play, for its own sake'.[6] In Martha Nussbaum's account of the 'capability approach', work is located within the central human capability of 'control over one's environment' in its material aspect, encompassing 'the right to seek employment on an equal basis with others . . . [and] being able to work as a human being, exercising practical reason and entering into mutual relationships of mutual recognition with other workers'.[7] Work might also be regarded as an activity for the development and realisation of other central human capabilities, such as 'senses, imagination, thought' (the ability 'to imagine, think, and reason . . . in a "truly human" way') and 'affiliation' ('being able to live for and towards others, to recognize and show concern for other human beings, to engage in various forms of social interaction').[8] Examples of the significance of work to the good life and human flourishing in ethical theory can doubtless be multiplied.[9]

Having identified work as a *human good* of fundamental significance, perhaps it is natural enough (for lawyers, at least) to want to regard it as a *human right* of fundamental significance too. And perhaps, all things considered, the right to work is such a human right. However, drawing upon the work of Raz and Dworkin, I want to suggest another way of thinking about the political significance of work that is more powerful in its promise than can be delivered by a rights-based understanding. This is captured in the basic idea that 'the promotion

[6] J Finnis, *Natural Law and Natural Rights*, 2nd edn (Oxford, Oxford University Press, 2011) 448.

[7] M Nussbaum, *Women and Human Development: The Capabilities Approach* (Cambridge, Cambridge University Press, 2001) 78–80.

[8] ibid. For an interesting discussion of these capabilities within the context of workplace freedom of association, see T Novitz, 'Information and Communication Technology and Voice: Constraint or Capability?' in A Bogg and T Novitz (eds), *Voices at Work: Continuity and Change in the Common Law World* (Oxford, Oxford University Press, 2014) 436.

[9] For a full discussion of work and its value, see G Mundlak, 'The Right to Work – The Value of Work' in D Barak-Erez and A Gross (eds), *Exploring Social Rights: Between Theory and Practice* (Oxford, Hart Publishing, 2007) 341.

of well-being is the pivotal ethical precept of public action'.[10] There are of course many ways in which governments might promote the well-being of their citizens other than through rights. One important mode of protection is through the existence of freestanding *duties* to promote well-being, duties that are not correlative to anyone's rights.[11] As Raz explains, such duties characteristically arise in respect of common goods such as a tolerant public sphere, civility in public spaces, a pleasant physical environment, or a well-functioning democratic system, where it is difficult to justify individual rights to those common goods.[12] To this list we might add the common good of an inclusive structure of employment opportunities, underpinned by a deeply entrenched culture of respect for fundamental labour rights providing a broad and diverse range of different job-types and career opportunities for all citizens under conditions of equal opportunity. It is difficult to see how any individual could assert a *right* to such a common good, for each individual's interest would seem to fall some way short of justifying 'holding so many people to a duty to behave in the way which is required for its production or preservation'.[13] Nevertheless,

> the non-existence of individual rights to common goods is, of course, compatible with the existence of duties to provide and preserve them. Typically governments and other public authorities have duties to protect the common goods of a community, because such duties derive from the basic function of governments to serve their subjects. Their duties are to the community as a whole rather than to any individual right-holder. Similarly, individuals may well have a duty to bear their share in providing and protecting common goods, a duty which is also based on the interest of members of the community generally in their existence.[14]

The idea that governments are under duties to protect and promote the well-being of citizens finds support across the full spectrum of liberal thought. We see different versions of this idea in the perfectionist liberalism of Raz and the anti-perfectionist liberalism of Dworkin.[15] Each of these theories offers an account of human well-being, and the duties of the state in relation to the well-being of its citizens. As one would expect, there are significant differences between Raz's and Dworkin's accounts of liberalism. There are nevertheless two important features that each of these liberal approaches have in common. First, an *active* conception of well-being underlies both theories. For Raz, well-being consists 'in the whole-hearted and successful pursuit of valuable activities'.[16] Dworkin's account of

[10] J Raz, *Ethics in the Public Domain* (Oxford, Oxford University Press, rev edn 1996) vi.

[11] For another (albeit distinct) duty-based approach to politics based on 'imperfect obligations', see O O'Neill, 'The Dark Side of Human Rights' (2005) 81 *International Affairs* 427.

[12] Raz, *Ethics in the Public Domain*, above n 10, 34.

[13] ibid.

[14] ibid, 34–35.

[15] On Raz's political philosophy as it relates to this issue, see particularly Raz, *Ethics in the Public Domain*, above n 10, and J Raz, *The Morality of Freedom* (Oxford, Oxford University Press, 1986). On Dworkin's political philosophy as it relates to this issue, see particularly R Dworkin, *Sovereign Virtue: The Theory and Practice of Equality* (Cambridge MA, Harvard University Press, 2002).

[16] Raz, *Ethics in the Public Domain*, above n 10, 3.

well-being is captured in his 'challenge model' of ethics, which stands for the view that,

> living a life is *itself* a performance that demands skill, that it is the most comprehensive and important challenge we face, and that our critical interests consist in the achievements, events and experiences that mean that we have met the challenge well.[17]

It is unsurprising, therefore, that work should figure as an *activity* of significance in the realisation of human well-being in both forms of liberalism, and a feature of the well-lived life. Second, both theories emphasise the importance of the state's duty to support the social, cultural and economic *structures* that provide the necessary contexts for citizens to participate in valuable activities. Once we adopt this structural perspective on the political salience of work, we are less concerned with the individual citizen's interest in a particular job; we are, however, acutely concerned with the existence of a set of social, cultural and economic structures that provide a rich mosaic of decent job-types and careers that provide the contexts for citizens' participation in the activity of work. We shall first set out the main elements of each theoretical approach. Then, we will consider whether this duty-based approach might have particular advantages over the rights-based approach to the regulation of work.

B Work, Well-Being and Duties in Liberal Theory

Raz is not specifically concerned with the value of work, though work is an important element in his account of human well-being. Well-being is achieved through the successful participation in valuable activities. Consistent with Raz's commitment to value pluralism, the range of valuable activities is pluralistic: 'activity is to be understood to include the pursuit of a career in medicine, the pursuit of a hobby like chess, attending to one's relations with friends, institutions, or communities, living as befits one's station in life'.[18] In this way, 'conscientious performance of a job' is an activity of value amongst others such as participation in hobbies, being a friend, acting as a good neighbour.[19] In his discussion of the ways in which well-being can be impeded or destroyed, rendering a person 'unemployed' is listed as a mode of harming along with killing, maiming, disabling, terrorising, and intimidating.[20] That rendering unemployed is regarded as such a grave form of harming emphasises the importance of occupations and careers to his account of well-being. Nevertheless, states are subject to more extensive duties than the mere duty to refrain from harming well-being. The protection and promotion of well-being may encompass assisting citizens to 'acquire the skills they need . . . but also by providing them with the material resources, and with the

[17] Dworkin, *Sovereign Virtue*, above n 15, 253.
[18] Raz, *Ethics in the Public Domain*, above n 10, 4.
[19] ibid, 5.
[20] ibid, 9.

natural, social, cultural and economic environments, which facilitate a good life'.[21] For Raz, this duty (and its limits) is captured in two guiding principles. The principle of 'basic-capacities' requires that states support citizens to acquire and develop the basic capacities necessary to choose from and participate in an adequate range of options.[22] This might encompass appropriate forms of lifelong education, social insurance provision in the event of accidents or illness, and support for occupational mobility through welfare support or reskilling and vocational training. The state is also required to ensure that there is an adequate range of options, including occupational options, that provide contexts where citizens can apply and develop their technical expertise and social skills, imagination, physical stamina and so forth. Consistent with Raz's commitment to liberal perfectionism, it will sometimes be necessary for the state to support occupations as valuable social forms – it is only possible to be a teacher or a doctor in a society where the role is socially and politically recognised; subject to its occupational norms, role-responsibilities and standards of excellence; and with schools and hospitals supported by schemes of professional accreditation and training.[23] Yet, given their character as collective goods, it is difficult to conceive of the existence of stable and adequate structures of employment opportunities as being the subject of any individual's *right*. In addition to the principle of basic-capacities, Raz also recognises the independent role of the principle of 'adequate access'. This requires that states ensure that all citizens have access to an adequate range of options to enable them to lead successful lives. This would require public action, such as the legal techniques of anti-discrimination law, to remedy the exclusion of certain groups –'foreigners, the poor, people of colour, people with a disapproved-of sexual orientation' – so that they enjoy adequate access to valuable occupations.[24] So on Raz's account of well-being, work is of vital importance in framing the citizen's opportunities to live a successful and flourishing life. Furthermore, the state has an extensive range of duties in relation to the provision of work that are mediated by the principles of basic-capacities and adequate access.

Dworkin's account of well-being is more abstract than that of Raz, and it is less specific on the particular significance of different activities, such as work, in the successful life.[25] Dworkin draws a distinction between two conceptions of the metric of a successful life. On the one hand, the 'impact' model of value focuses upon the consequences of a life on the world as the measure of its goodness. For those heroic souls who produce great poetry, or discover a cure for a horrible disease, their life is correspondingly a better life than the mundane souls whose

[21] ibid, 10.

[22] ibid, 17.

[23] See Raz, *The Morality of Freedom*, above n 15, 307–13.

[24] Raz, *Ethics in the Public Domain*, above n 10, 24.

[25] This abstractness is based in Dworkin's philosophical aspiration to develop an ethical theory of liberalism, while allowing space for different substantive conceptions of the good to be pursued in a liberal community in a way that is consistent with liberal neutrality: for discussion, see S Mulhall and A Swift, *Liberals and Communitarians*, 2nd edn (Oxford, Blackwell, 1996) 282–83.

imprint on the world is lighter.[26] On the other hand, the 'challenge' model of value focuses upon the skill that an individual brings to the art of living, within the particular circumstances and context in which she finds herself. Even if one's imprint on the world is invisible, a life has been successful if it has been lived skilfully, performed in the right spirit and responding appropriately to the challenges that life sets.[27] So in his illustrative discussion of an inventor's contribution to the world, Dworkin considers that the metric of value

> might be thought to depend, for example, on the degree of difficulty involved in its making, or in its originality, or in the degree to which the author made full use of or stretched his abilities, or in the intensity of his dedication, or in the way in which his work flowed from his sense of his role in or his dedication to a particular community or tradition.[28]

This discussion points to the ways in which work, as one important form of valuable activity, provides one of the important contexts within which citizens can live skilfully.[29] Like Raz, Dworkin's account of well-being is pluralistic: there are many valuable activities that go to make up the well-lived life, and the particular configuration in a life will depend upon taste, abilities and capacities and social context. Furthermore, Dworkin is also sensitive to the importance of cultural structures in framing the opportunities for citizens to realise well-being.

In his famous discussion of whether a neutral liberal state can support art, Dworkin argues that the liberal state can support a rich cultural structure, a trustee of 'the diversity and innovative quality of the culture as a whole rather than (what public officials take to be) excellence in particular occasions of that culture'.[30] In this way, the gap between Dworkin's liberal neutrality and Raz's liberal perfectionism is closer than one might think in respect of cultural, economic and social structures.[31] And while Dworkin does not engage explicitly with this point, a parallel argument in respect of structures of employment opportunities might also be made using the 'challenge' model of ethical value: that, just like the cultural structure, the neutral liberal state is a trustee of 'the diversity and innovative quality' of employment opportunities in a political community, while at the same time avoiding the protection of particular occupations or job-types on the ground that they embody a particularly worthy form of activity.

These liberal conceptions of well-being, and the relationship between work and well-being, offer an appealing view of the ethical value and significance of work. Certainly, these pluralistic conceptions of value keep the activity of work in proper perspective. Work may be regarded as an activity of great value in both the Razian

[26] Dworkin, *Sovereign Virtue*, above n 15, 251–53.

[27] ibid, 253–54.

[28] ibid, 256.

[29] There are likewise interesting points of contact with Finnis' formulation of the good of 'skilful performance' in work and play: see Finnis, above n 6.

[30] R Dworkin, 'Can a Liberal State Support Art?' in R Dworkin, *A Matter of Principle* (Oxford, Oxford University Press, 1985) 221, 233. See also Dworkin, *Sovereign Virtue*, above n 15, 274.

[31] For discussion, see Mulhall and Swift, above n 25, 300–08.

and Dworkinian accounts, but it is not the only activity of value. Nor is it obviously of any greater value or significance than activities such as leisure and hobbies, family and friendship, civic and political activism, or meditative contemplation. And nor is a life without work *necessarily* a stunted or defective form of life. This certainly leads to a deflation of the value of work when compared with some Aristotelian or Marxist accounts of its role in the good life.

From an Aristotelian perspective, David Wiggins suggests that work is something 'momentous' such that

> the power and possibility to do proper work is something that is central to the life and being of a human person. To have no work to do . . . is among the very worst things that can befall someone, even if he or she can escape starvation.[32]

On this view, a government that promotes the dispensing of human labour in the interests of efficient automation perpetrates a 'mortal injury' on its people.[33] Marxist theory also elevates work as a human good which identifies 'our distinctive excellence' as the development and exercise of the 'capacity for freely cooperative production. To produce in a way that stunts this capacity is to be "alienated" from our true "species-nature"'.[34] Was it a moral catastrophe for Del Trotter to abjure work and live a well-travelled life of leisure beyond the environs of Peckham once he became a millionaire? That kind of ethical perfectionism seems overstated. While some of us might disagree reasonably with Del Trotter that work is *just* for fools and horses, reflecting the fact of reasonable pluralism in respect of the good, it would be difficult to argue that a life without work, but filled with leisure, human relationships and cultural exploration, is a stunted or defective form of life. Nor is it clear that a technologically advanced and prosperous society where much of the work to be done had disappeared, but where there were adequate resources for citizens to engage in other activities of value, would necessarily be a worse society in respect of human well-being.[35] The state's duty to protect and promote well-being would require it to support social forms that enabled valuable activities other than work to be pursued by citizens. There seems to be more than a bit of truth in Will Kymlicka's claim that 'there are many values that may compete with unalienated production, such as "bodily and mental health, the development of cognitive facilities, of certain character traits and emotional responses, play, sex, friendship, love, art, religion" '.[36]

This account of well-being also seems to get the relationship between work and self-respect right. Hugh Collins is sceptical of attempts to ground the right to

[32] D Wiggins in this volume, ch 1.

[33] ibid.

[34] See W Kymlicka, *Contemporary Political Philosophy: An Introduction*, 2nd edn (Oxford, Oxford University Press, 2001) 190.

[35] On the intersections between work and technological development, see E Brynjolfsson and A McAfee, *The Second Machine Age* (New York, WW Norton and Co, 2014). The prospect of a future with the disappearance of work is discussed in J Nickel in this volume, ch 8.

[36] Kymlicka, above n 34, 193.

work in the value of self-respect, and rightly so.[37] As an example of this self-respect argument, take James Nickel's original and highly influential argument in defence of a human right to employment. According to Nickel, one of the reasons that might be adduced in favour of such a right is that 'the ability to support oneself through work provides grounds for respect; inability to support oneself is apt to be considered a serious weakness and may place one in a class with the sick and retarded.'[38] We might raise serious questions over the very controversial assumption that an inability to work through illness or diminished capacity is a position that leads to a loss of self-respect for the citizen. To regard persons in that position as having lost self-respect might have some purchase in political communities whose social conventions prize rugged and self-reliant individualism, but it seems less acceptable in political communities with well-established schemes of solidaristic welfare provision for vulnerable citizens.[39] Collins also draws attention to those engaged in unpaid care work, often in the family home, or unpaid interns acquiring valuable work experience while being supported financially by parents.[40] Furthermore, if strategies based upon an 'unconditional basic income' were to gain political traction,[41] it is again difficult to see what would be demeaning or self-disrespecting in choosing a life of surfing and the contemplation of sunsets with friends from the vantage point of a camper van, living frugally on one's basic income. Both Raz's and Dworkin's accounts of self-respect leave space for these intuitions about work and self-respect. For Raz, self-respect

> implies a belief that one's capacity for rational action, and one's endeavours to conduct one's life through the responsible exercise of that capacity, give value to one's life . . . A person's well-being is the successful pursuit of worthwhile goals. Self-respect is earned by the endeavour to live a life of such pursuits.[42]

As we have seen, work is one valuable pursuit amongst many, and there are ways other than through work that one can engage in the responsible exercise of rational capacity. There would therefore seem to be no simple linkage between work, welfare and self-respect. This would be true of Dworkin's 'challenge model' of ethics too. For Dworkin, living well is 'responding in the right way to one's situation', where that situation includes one's health, talents and capacities, social position and so forth.[43] There is absolutely no reason to suppose that someone who is disabled and unable to work, but otherwise lives well and skilfully in other domains of activity, has somehow forfeited her self-respect on this 'challenge model' approach.

[37] H Collins in this volume, ch 2.

[38] J Nickel, 'Is there a Human Right to Employment?' (1978–79) X *Philosophical Forum* 149, 159.

[39] On the US approach to welfare, see M Weir, 'The Collapse of Bill Clinton's Third Way' in S White (ed), *New Labour: The Progressive Future* (Basingstoke, Palgrave, 2001) 137.

[40] H Collins in this volume, ch 2.

[41] The terminology of 'unconditional basic income' is taken from S White, *The Civic Minimum* (Oxford, Oxford University Press, 2003) 16. See, further, P Van Parijs, *Real Freedom for All: What (if anything) Can Justify Capitalism?* (Oxford, Oxford University Press, 1995).

[42] Raz, *Ethics in the Public Domain*, above n 10, 38–39.

[43] Dworkin, *Sovereign Virtue*, above n 15, 260.

Finally, these general theories of well-being provide some additional support for Collins' identification of the particular value of work as consisting in the endeavour of self-realisation. Collins suggests that the particular value of work lies in the scope that it provides for people to 'feel a sense of achievement at a job well done, fulfilment from the opportunity to use their skills in partnership with others to achieve something, and . . . identify themselves with the outcome of their labours'.[44] This is facilitated where workers are given some latitude to use their skills and imagination to devise and execute tasks, rather than being utilised as unthinking cogs in an organisational machine. We might also include forms of work where the satisfaction is derived from the sheer physical stamina and exertion required for the task.[45] Raz's 'active' account of well-being and Dworkin's 'challenge' model both highlight the importance of wholehearted engagement in activities of value, working (and living) skilfully and successfully, and one can readily identify self-realising work as an important way in which persons can achieve well-being through activity. The fact that Collins' particular account of the value of work as self-realisation finds support in more general philosophical theories of well-being lends his conception of the right to work extra plausibility.

C The Appeal of a Duty-Based Analysis

So far, we have defended the view that it is possible to take the value of work very seriously indeed through an appreciation of the state's duty to protect and promote the well-being of its citizens. This recognition is not inconsistent with there being a human right to work, and I can readily accept that there is such a human right. However, if we are concerned with the promotion of opportunities for decent work, I want to suggest three reasons that might lead us to concentrate our political energies on the development of these well-being duties rather than on the constitutionalisation of a right to work: (i) the duties associated with a rights-based approach are unlikely to generate significant political change in the legal regulation of work, when compared with freestanding duties associated with the duty-based approach; (ii) the duty-based approach leads to clearer thinking on the relationship between the right to work and the duty to work; (iii) finally, the duty-based approach avoids a slide into judicialisation that would seem inevitable if the right to work was constitutionalised.

i Rights-based duties and freestanding duties compared

The first reason is reflected in the contrast between the nature and extent of the duties envisaged on a duty-based well-being approach, as compared with the

[44] H Collins in this volume, ch 2.

[45] In this respect, I have happy memories of my time spent as a plasterer's mate in a former life, and the satisfaction of a physically demanding job well done.

duties envisaged as correlative to a right to work. In his carefully crafted defence of a 'right to work' in this volume, Collins argues the following:

> If the right to work exists, therefore, it must contain the positive right to a job at its centre . . . In the case of the right to work, the duty of governments may be limited to the progressive realisation of the positive right to a job by taking measures that support full employment, whereas for employers the duty may be confined to prohibitions against unjustified discrimination in hiring practices.[46]

Against this, it is worth considering the full range and extent of the duties that might arise out of the general duties to protect and promote well-being on both states and private actors such as employers. In this respect, it is worth considering the guidelines articulated in the European 2005 Integrated Guidelines for Growth and Jobs 2005–08 as an illustrative example.[47] The following employment guidelines are set out:

> [I]implement employment policies aimed at achieving full employment, improving quality and productivity at work, and strengthening social and territorial cohesion; promote a lifecycle approach at work; ensure inclusive labour markets, enhance work attractiveness, and make work pay for job seekers, including disadvantaged people and the inactive; improving matching of labour market needs; promote flexibility combined with employment security and reduce labour market segmentation, having due regard to the role of the social partners; ensure employment-friendly labour costs development and wage-setting mechanisms; expand and improve investment in human capital; adapt education and training systems in response to new skill requirements.[48]

Each of these guidelines might figure as an element in duties to protect and promote well-being that relate to the provision of employment. Furthermore, it is possible to conceive of many of the guidelines as giving rise to duties placed on both governments and private actors such as employers or trade unions. For example, the guideline of expanding and improving investment in human capital might give rise to duties on the state to distribute resources to appropriate training providers or to provide training schemes directly to workers; it might give rise to duties on employers to provide training or to provide paid time off for workers to undertake skills training; and it might give rise to duties on employers and trade unions to negotiate about training provision in particular sectors of labour market activity. The examples can be multiplied as we move through each of the guidelines.

There are three main contrasts between the duties that are potentially encompassed by the well-being approach explored in this section, and the duties that are encompassed by the rights-based approach defended by Collins. Each of these contrasts supports a preference for the duty-based approach over the rights-based approach. First, the duties encompassed by the duty-based approach, in respect of

[46] H Collins in this volume, ch 2.

[47] European Commission, 'Integrated Guidelines for Growth and Jobs 2005–08' COM (2005) 141.

[48] These are set out and discussed in C Barnard, *EU Employment Law*, 4th edn (Oxford, Oxford University Press, 2012) 103.

both states and private actors, are far more extensive than the duties encompassed by the rights-based approach. This is particularly striking in respect of duties on private actors. For Collins, this is likely to extend no further than a negative duty to refrain from illegitimate discrimination in hiring practices. This is very modest indeed, and would in any event be covered by the existing norms of discrimination law. By contrast, the duties arising out of an employer's duty to protect and promote well-being might extend to all manner of positive duties: duties to provide training; duties of reasonable accommodation in respect of groups excluded from the labour market; duties to facilitate flexible and part-time working; and duties to negotiate policies to promote the expansion of opportunities for decent work with representative trade unions. The relative modesty of the rights-based correlative duties reflects the fact that the individual's interests figure in justifying the imposition of duties on others. As we have seen, individual interests are insufficient to justify the wide-ranging duties associated with the maintenance of collective goods. As such, this interest-based constraint does not stifle the development of free-standing duties to protect and promote well-being.

Second, the duties encompassed by the duty-based approach are targeted predominantly at the social and economic structures that frame employment opportunities, whereas the duties on the rights-based approach seem to be more narrowly targeted and more tightly constrained. This flows from Collins' claim that a right to work 'must contain the positive right to a job at its centre'.[49] The subject matter of the individual right – the job itself – will inevitably shape the nature and content of the correlative duties. By contrast, well-being duties tend to be more concerned with the collective goods that give shape to the range of valuable activities in a society. It is only by attending to those structural elements that significant and enduring social change is likely to occur.

Finally, the duties encompassed by the duty-based approach are more 'dynamic' when compared with the duties arising under a rights-based approach.[50] The dynamism of duties means that their scope and content evolves and changes over time, and is sensitive to social, economic and institutional circumstances. So in respect of the kinds of duties that might potentially be associated with employment policy interventions, it is worth considering Barnard's discussion of the different 'flexicurity' pathways delineated by the European Commission.[51] These pathways, which set out distinct prescriptions and policy priorities, are sensitive to the particular labour market situations of different Member States. For example, pathway 4 focusing on 'improving opportunities for benefit recipients and informally employed workers' would contain a mix of policy objectives and techniques that were suited to countries that had undergone significant industrial restructuring that had led to significant numbers of long-term unemployed.[52] Moreover, the configuration of duties might change markedly within a particular

[49] H Collins in this volume, ch 2.
[50] Raz, *The Morality of Freedom*, above n 15, 171.
[51] Barnard, above n 48, 106–11.
[52] ibid, 110.

country where it is faced with a new set of labour market challenges, such as persistently high levels of youth unemployment or skills deficits in particular areas of labour market activity. By contrast, while rights-based duties are certainly dynamic, the institutional need to resolve the legal rights and duties at issue between the litigants, consistent with the value of legality, means that the scope for dynamism is reduced significantly.[53] Courts are not institutionally well positioned to reformulate duties rapidly and flexibly in response to changes in a labour market context when compared with the legislature or the executive.

ii The right to work and the duty to work

The second reason in favour of the duty-based approach is that, in its explicit engagement with the issue of well-being, it enables us to see more clearly what is at stake in debates around the 'duty to work'. Bob Hepple has drawn attention to the fact that the duty to work was often conceptually bound up with the right to work in socialist countries, whereas in market economies such as the United Kingdom,

> the duty to work forms a part only of social security law since it is a condition for the receipt of various social benefits that a person is not voluntarily unemployed, is not dismissed for misconduct and is available for employment. In other words, with us the duty to work corresponds only to a right to social security, and not to a right to work.[54]

The elision of the duty to work and the right to work is both conceptually and normatively problematic, while also being very common in political discourse around work; and it is an elision that often occurs under the mistaken guise of the correlativity of rights and duties.[55] In its explicit focus on the nature of well-being, and without the clutter of rights discourse, the duty-based approach rules out one important argument that might be made in defence of a duty to work. Such an argument would focus on the special value of work in the good life, with the function of a duty to work to ensure that citizens engage in a virtuous life of valuable activity. In this way, the duty to work is a form of paternalistic intervention to steer citizens in the direction of activities (such as work) that contribute to their own best interests. Thus, Raz observes that

> people's well-being is – ultimately – up to them and to them alone. Nobody can take over their life and make it prosper for them. No one but I can make me a good teacher, a good parent or friend . . .While it is logically impossible to make other people's lives go well, it is possible to try to do so, and such attempts are often disastrous.[56]

For this reason, support for the well-being of others should be confined to creating the conditions and structures within which individuals can realise well-being

[53] B Langille and B Oliphant, 'The Legal Structure of Freedom of Association' (2013), available at: papers.ssrn.com/sol3/papers.cfm?abstract_id=2355976.
[54] B Hepple, 'A Right to Work?' (1981) 10 *Industrial Law Journal* 65, 70.
[55] For discussion, see A Paz-Fuchs in this volume, ch 10.
[56] Raz, *Ethics in the Public Domain*, above n 10, 9.

through their own endeavours. In a similar vein, Dworkin defends a 'constitutive' view of the good life under the 'challenge' model:

> [M]y life cannot be better for me in virtue of some feature or component I think has no value . . . it is the performance that counts, not mere external result, and the right motive or sense is necessary to the right performance.[57]

This need for the agent herself to endorse the value of activities in which she is engaged places strict limits on the scope for paternalistic enforcement of self-regarding duties. Of course, there may be other good arguments in favour of a duty to work, and forms of conditionality in respect of welfare entitlements.[58] What this does establish, however, is that the well-being or virtue of the duty-bearer is not a good reason in favour of a duty to work. The duty-based approach enables clearer thinking about what is at stake in respect of the duty to work.

iii The institutional context of the rights-based and the duty-based approach

Finally, the duty-based approach leaves open a set of important institutional questions as to how these duties are to be formulated and enforced. It may be that some of the duties will be enacted democratically through legislation enforced ultimately through litigation in the courts. Some of the duties may be implemented through softer processes such as those characteristic of the European 'Open Method of Coordination'. Others still may be devolved to social actors such as employers and trade unions to be developed and reshaped incrementally in deliberative processes in civil society. These more deliberative techniques have advantages in allowing for duties to be developed in a spirit of democratic experimentalism,[59] responsive to the shifting needs of different groups in the labour market in the light of changing economic and social conditions. These deliberative techniques are particularly well developed in the sphere of employment policy interventions, and it is surely no coincidence that this is so.[60] These regulatory techniques enable expansive duties to be developed dynamically and flexibly in response to labour market challenges that are often a set of rapidly moving targets. By contrast, the strategy of *constitutionalisation* of social rights seems to lead inexorably to a *judicialisation* of social rights as an institutional centrepiece of social rights protection.

There is now a rich literature on social rights that engages in a sophisticated and sensitive way with the institutional dimension of social rights protection. As

[57] Dworkin, *Sovereign Virtue*, above n 15, 268–69.

[58] See White, *The Civic Minimum*, above n 41; A Paz-Fuchs, *Welfare to Work: Conditional Rights in Social Policy* (Oxford, Oxford University Press, 2008).

[59] For a theoretical basis to this approach, see M Dorf and C Sabel, 'A Constitution of Democratic Experimentalism' (1998) 98 *Columbia Law Review* 267.

[60] See, eg, M Freedland, 'Employment Policy' in P Davies, A Lyon-Caen, S Sciarra and S Simitis (eds), *European Community Labour Law: Principles and Perspectives Liber Amicorum Lord Wedderburn* (Oxford, Oxford University Press 1997) 275.

an example, Jeff King defends a highly sophisticated 'multi-institutional' account of social rights protection, such that legislatures, executive branches of government, specialist tribunals, ordinary courts and constitutional courts each participate collaboratively in the task of furthering a social rights agenda.[61] King is cautious about the role of courts, and this leads him to develop a set of principles of judicial incrementalism that embody appropriate deference by courts in the sphere of social rights adjudication. He is, nevertheless, emphatic that courts and judicialisation have an indispensable role to play in the enforcement of social rights. There is no doubt that social rights adjudication, particularly in the European Court of Human Rights, has been politically progressive. In areas as diverse as 'modern slavery' and freedom of association, human rights jurisprudence has remedied egregious wrongs perpetrated on vulnerable workers.[62] There is a need for particular caution, however, as far as the right to work is concerned. As section II will elaborate, the abstract right to work is not unknown to the English legal system. Indeed, it was once regarded as a fundamental *common law* right. It was a right that was used most prominently by common law judges to challenge trade union rather than employer practices, and in this respect it emerged historically as a fundamental right that was arguably antithetical to workers' interests. Given these common law antecedents, there is a need for particular caution before we subject this open-textured social right to the interpretive jurisdiction of the English courts. It is therefore a particular attraction of the duty-based approach that it leaves this institutional enquiry much more open.

It is important to stress that none of these arguments is incompatible with duties to promote well-being existing *alongside* a right to work. That is perfectly possible. Yet these arguments do suggest that once we appreciate the advantages of the duty-based approach, particularly the extensive reach and richness of those well-being duties, the right to work is rather eclipsed as a matter of political strategy. Paradoxically, perhaps, the concerns that motivate those who advocate a legal right to work most passionately are likely to be addressed more effectively through a focus on duties to promote well-being.

II A Legal Right to Work?

There are many international human rights instruments that give explicit recognition of the right to work as a fundamental human right. So as a matter of posi-

[61] J King, *Judging Social Rights* (Cambridge, Cambridge University Press, 2012) 41–57. See also the powerful arguments set out in V Mantouvalou, 'In Support of Legalisation' in C Gearty and V Mantouvalou, *Debating Social Rights* (Oxford, Hart Publishing, 2010).

[62] K Ewing and J Hendy, 'The Dramatic Implications of *Demir and Baykara*' (2010) 39 *Industrial Law Journal* 2; V Mantouvalou, 'Labour Rights in the European Convention on Human Rights: An Intellectual Justification for an Integrated Approach to Interpretation' (2013) 13 *Human Rights Law Review* 529.

tive international law, there is a human right to work. Does it not then follow that we should enact a legal right to work in domestic law in recognition of its status as a human right in international law? According to Amartya Sen's work, it does not so follow. Sen's analysis of a theory of human rights argues that such a theory

> cannot be sensibly confined within the juridical model in which it is frequently incarcerated. For example, public recognition and agitation (including the monitoring of violations) can be part of the obligations – often imperfect – generated by the acknowledgment of human rights. Also, some recognized human rights are not ideally legislated, but are better promoted through other means, including public discussion, appraisal and advocacy.[63]

This is an interesting position, though it runs up against the following important objection. If a state is bound by a treaty obligation under international human rights law to guarantee a human right, is it not bound to enact that very right in its national legal order? Not necessarily. It may discharge its obligations under international law by enacting a range of more specific legal rights the effect of which is to ensure that the abstract human right is respected in practice. For example, the international guarantee of freedom of association may be protected in national legal orders through a structure of discrete legal rights, such as the right not to be denied access to employment on trade union grounds, the right to participate in trade union activities at an appropriate time, rights of property access to the employer's property for trade union representatives and so forth. The cumulative effect of these legal rights might be to ensure respect for freedom of association consistent with international standards. Likewise, a legal system that had effective protection against discrimination in employment, a right not to be unjustifiably dismissed, effective unemployment insurance and so forth, but no legal right to work as such, might likewise meet the standard of a right to work as an international human right.

That there is a moral or human right to work is only one step in the argument towards its recognition as an abstract legal right in a national legal system. I want to suggest that there are three arguments against the enactment of an abstract legal right to work that deserve to be taken seriously, especially in the context of the English common law based system of labour law: concern about the effects of a legal right to work on worker solidarity; the distributive context to a decision to juridify the right to work; and the institutional context of a right to work. These arguments are by no means conclusive. They may carry less weight in different legal systems with different institutional arrangements from the English system. It might also be the case that by decomposing an abstract 'right to work' into more discrete and precisely defined legal rights, many of the democratic concerns with the judicial role in labour law adjudication that underlie the scepticism here can be palliated.

[63] A Sen, 'Elements of a Theory of Human Rights' (2004) 32 *Philosophy & Public Affairs* 315, 319–20.

A Rights, Conflict and Worker Solidarity

In recent years there has been increasing interest in the significance of conflicts between groups of workers and the objectives of labour law. In this vein, Guy Mundlak has invoked the idea of a 'third function' for labour law such that it 'seeks not only to influence the distribution of rents, power, rights, resources, and economic risks among labour and capital, *but also between workers* (broadly defined to include all people of employment age, hence those who can work)'.[64] Anne Davies has developed this analytical focus, looking at the specific ways in which UK labour law regulates conflicts between the diverse worker constituencies who may have different preferences, values, interests and needs: 'the employed, the unemployed, people with different types of contract and different levels of participation in the labour market, men and women, people with children and people with no children, people of many races and religions, and so on'.[65]

This fragmentation of labour as a cohesive class with unitary needs and a coherent identity is undoubtedly a very real phenomenon, warranting public policy recognition and regulatory attention. What is particularly interesting is how the right to work marks out a space within which these conflicts of labour are played out in the form of competing rights-claims. For example, Davies suggests that 'the most basic manifestation of the "winners" and "losers" problem is the argument that there is a conflict between those who have jobs and those who are unemployed'.[66] Often, this is presented as a conflict between the need for job creation through the reduction of costs associated with employment rights, as against the employment conditions of those in work. This might be configured as a conflict between the right to work of the unemployed on the one hand, and the right to fair and just working conditions of the employed on the other. Sometimes, the conflict might involve a direct confrontation between different workers' rights to work. In this context, Davies discusses the intergenerational conflict between younger and older workers in respect of mandatory retirement ages.[67] The removal of mandatory retirement ages might be regarded as a just vindication of older workers' rights to work, and one that has broad appeal in the context of fiscal concerns about the sustainability of pension provision. Nevertheless, as Davies points out, 'younger workers may feel that their prospects of entering the labour market and obtaining access to the profession of their choice are likely to be reduced or eliminated if older workers are no longer forced to retire'.[68] Another

[64] G Mundlak, 'The Third Function of Labour Law: Distributing Labour Market Opportunities among Workers' in G Davidov and B Langille (eds), *The Idea of Labour Law* (Oxford, Oxford University Press, 2011) 315, 317.

[65] ACL Davies, 'Identifying "Exploitative Compromises": The Role of Labour Law in Resolving Disputes Between Workers' (2012) *Current Legal Problems* 269, 270.

[66] ibid 273–74.

[67] ibid 281–82.

[68] ibid, 281.

context in which multiple confrontations of the right to work occur is economic restructuring, where difficult questions of whether restructuring should lead to job losses might arise, and if so how to allocate job losses between workers.

This exposes a tension of some significance for labour law. As Mundlak has observed, 'labour's side is therefore swayed by multiple interests and forces that can either pull workers together or break them apart'.[69] The right to work is deeply implicated in this tension, for its key regulatory site is precisely these conflicts between 'multiple interests' within 'labour's side'. In this way, the right to work is often a labour right at war with itself, situated predominantly at the frictional borders between worker constituencies in conflict with each other over the allocation of work (and unemployment). In this respect, it is unlike most other labour rights that predominantly mediate the frictional boundaries between capital and labour. It is not the only social right that has this quality. As an example, the right not to be discriminated against because of age seems similar in nature. Moreover, the expansion of protected characteristics in equality law, particularly in respect of religion and sexual orientation, has also opened up new sources of conflict in the workplace.[70] Nevertheless, the right to work seems to display this characteristic of *internal* conflict more strongly than most other labour rights, and in this way it raises very special concerns from the perspective of worker solidarity.

This conflictual feature of the right to work provides a reason against its characterisation as a legal right. In this respect, Mary Ann Glendon's work on the corrosive effects of an inflationary 'rights discourse' on public dialogue in the US context is especially apt:

> Our rights talk, in its absoluteness, promotes unrealistic expectations, heightens social conflict, and inhibits dialogue that might lead toward consensus, accommodation, or at least the discovery of common ground. In its silence concerning responsibilities, it seems to condone acceptance of the benefits of living in a democratic social welfare state, without accepting the corresponding personal and civic obligations. In its relentless individualism, it fosters a climate that is inhospitable to society's losers, and that systematically disadvantages caretakers and dependents, young and old. In its neglect of civil society, it undermines the principal seedbeds of civic and personal virtue. In its insularity, it shuts out potentially important aids to the process of self-correcting learning. All of these traits promote mere assertion over reason-giving.[71]

Given the confrontational individualism of rights discourse, and given that the right to work often pits worker against worker, it may be that the *legal right* to work generates centrifugal forces that erode the potential for worker solidarity. Of course, the idea that rights might have this 'confrontational' edge can be a real virtue, particularly where those rights regulate the conflictual interface between capital and labour. When considering the impact of rights within the sphere of conflicts between workers, however, the fragmentary tendencies engendered by

[69] Mundlak, 'The Third Function of Labour Law', above n 64, 323.

[70] Davies, above n 65, 284.

[71] M Glendon, *Rights Talk: The Impoverishment of Political Discourse* (New York, Free Press, 1998) 14.

rights-claims might leave workers worse off overall where it militates against workers reaching (in Glendon's terms) 'toward consensus, accommodation, or at least the discovery of common ground' with each other.

This might lead us to explore alternative techniques for regulating conflicts between workers in respect of the allocation of work that avoid the right to work's potential for corrosive effects on worker solidarity. One such technique might be based on conceptions of deliberative democracy. Thus, Davies discusses the role of the European Works Councils Directive which she characterises as a procedural response to

> the well-documented problem of pan-European firms pitting the workforces of different Member States against each other in a competition for jobs . . . The EWC Directive cannot be expected to stop this from happening . . . but EWCs could also provide workers' representatives from different Member States with an opportunity to discuss and even resolve some of the conflicts between them.[72]

The design of procedures for conflict resolution between different groups of workers requires careful thought. This is particularly the case with traditional forms of collective bargaining which might be thought to have reinforced 'the myth of a unitary voice' and so 'reluctant to give access to multiple voices'.[73] The challenge is to create deliberative spaces where different identities of worker voice may find recognition and expression, so that

> employers and workers (of very divergent kinds and with different interests) would not merely engage in a bargain between vested interests . . . but a genuine exchange of views which challenges existing assumptions and in so doing comes to a conclusion that is in the interests of all, which each participant can understand, and to which each participant can commit themselves.[74]

An important aspect of this deliberative strategy would be the implementation of human rights guarantees to empower different groups of workers to give voice to their own needs and perspectives.[75] And Davies has drawn attention to the powerful role of equality norms, such as sex discrimination law, in ensuring that vulnerable groups of workers are not simply sold down the river in 'exploitative compromises' negotiated by trade unions and employers.[76] Yet the right to work as a human right cannot make a constructive contribution to the resolution of these difficult problems of deliberative compromise, for it merely restates in the

[72] Davies, above n 65, 290–91.

[73] Mundlak, 'The Third Function of Labour Law', above n 64, 326.

[74] A Bogg and T Novitz, 'Investigating "Voice" at Work' (2012) 33 *Comparative Labor Law and Policy Journal* 323, 336.

[75] ibid 334. For an interesting exploration of workers' voices, collective bargaining and equal pay norms, see LJB Hayes, 'Women's Voice and Equal Pay: Judicial Regard for the Gendering of Collective Bargaining' in A Bogg and T Novitz (eds), *Voices at Work: Continuity and Change in the Common Law World* (Oxford, Oxford University Press, 2014) 35.

[76] Davies, above n 65, 281. This notion of 'exploitative compromise' was first developed in S Leader, 'Review of *Labour Law and Freedom: Further Essays in Labour Law* by Lord Wedderburn' (1996) 25 *Industrial Law Journal* 83.

language of clashing rights that there is a deep distributive conflict over work. In so doing, it may undermine the solidaristic resources needed for a deliberative solution to that conflict, based on dialogue and consensus.

B From Moral Rights to Legal Rights – The Role of Distributive Justice

In John Gardner's analysis of the role of distributive justice in the law of torts, he rightly emphasises the distinction between rights in morality and rights in law. In morality, no distributive question arises since 'raw moral rights and duties are not allocated by anyone . . . They come and go with the reasons for and against their existence'.[77] The same is not true for legal rights and duties, when legislators and courts are deciding on which of the many 'raw' moral rights and duties should be enforced through legal machinery. These decisions inevitably engage issues of distributive justice. As Gardner points out, there are many distributive dimensions to the allocation of legal rights and duties. Determining that a moral right should be enforced as a legal right gives the right-holder a legal power to seek redress from the court, which effectively means that 'public authority (the authority of the court) is put at the disposal of the wronged person'.[78] Given the scarcity of public resources, this means that some rights (and hence some claimants) will be given privileged public support in the pursuit of their claims of corrective justice against wrongdoers. Nor are the distributive dimensions to the allocation of legal rights driven solely by the financial costs associated with the administration of justice, such as court costs or publicly supported legal aid. There is also the point that the 'Rule of Law' 'favours the existence of non-juridified space in which people can readily steer clear of the law',[79] necessitating decisions as to which moral rights should be institutionalised through law and which should be entrusted to other forms of protection such as social pressure or voluntary collective action. Obviously, these concerns extend beyond the law of torts. They have the same character and urgency in determining which moral rights should be recognised and enforced as legal rights in employment law.

There are many ways in which distributive concerns are engaged in the right to work. One important distributive issue is the extent to which it is legitimate to adjust the configuration of the right to work relative to other labour rights such as the right to fair and just working conditions. Should we encourage more flexible forms of employment with fewer legal rights in order to incentivise job creation? Or should we expand the scope of self-employment (and so contract the scope of dependent employment) as a way of using entrepreneurship as a pathway into the

[77] J Gardner, 'What is Tort Law for? Part 2. The Place of Distributive Justice' (2013) Oxford Legal Studies Research Paper no 62/2013, 7, available at: papers.ssrn.com/sol3/papers.cfm?abstract_id=2269615.

[78] ibid, 9.

[79] ibid, 11.

activity of work?[80] This raises very important political questions (and ones that are not legitimately amenable to judicial resolution). I want to address another distributive question, and one that is prior to these other enquiries. To what extent should the legal system recognise and enforce an abstract legal right to work, understood in Collins' sense as a right to a job that gives the job-holder scope to participate in self-realising activity, at all? Since juridification is an exercise governed by distributive norms, how should we go about prioritising which moral rights should become legal rights? I can do more than sketch four possible approaches to this distributive enquiry. I would suggest, tentatively, that we might be more concerned to use the legal system to ensure that work is safe and healthy, equitably remunerated, free from bullying and harassment, protected from unfair dismissal, with proper access to trade union representation, before we use the legal system to ensure that work is self-realising through the enactment of a specific legal right. In short, there are many more pressing regulatory problems to be addressed first before we reach the point where we might give serious consideration to juridifying the moral right to a job that provides opportunities for self-realisation.

The first approach might simply be to ask what workers actually want in terms of juridification priorities. There are some excellent examples of studies that have surveyed workers' preferences in the field of work,[81] and it would be an interesting exercise to ascertain whether workers are more concerned with opportunities for self-realisation, or a safe working environment, or time off for family emergencies, or protection from unfair dismissal. Nevertheless, this approach also has limitations. Workers might not value a right if it relates to a state of affairs that they have not been fortunate enough to experience. It might be that if a worker was exposed to the opportunity of self-realising work, she would value it more highly than she might have originally anticipated.[82] Furthermore, there might be some rights that we think are very important but might not be recognised as such by most workers. Take the example of a duty of reasonable accommodation in respect of disability. Many workers who have never experienced disability, and who regard it as remote from their own concerns, might regard such a right as a low priority for the legal system. In normative terms, however, such a right might be regarded as a priority candidate for juridification.

The second approach would pose a different question, which would be to ask what workers might want hypothetically if they were to decide upon a scheme of fundamental rights behind a 'veil of ignorance'. In an important analysis of labour law based upon a theory of fundamental rights, Collins applies the methodology of John Rawls' work on justice to the determination of fundamental rights in

[80] For a discussion of the growth in involuntary 'self-employment' in the UK see, 'Self-employment surge across UK hides real story behind upbeat job figures' *The Guardian* (6 May 2014), available at: www.theguardian.com/society/2014/may/06/self-employment-uk-job-figures-analysis.

[81] RB Freeman and J Rogers, *What Workers Want* (Ithaca, Cornell University Press, 1999).

[82] For the classic work on 'adaptive' preferences, see C Sunstein, 'Legal Interference with Private Preferences' (1986) 53 *University of Chicago Law Review* 1129.

labour law.[83] This requires the agent to reason about the distribution of rights and resources from behind a 'veil of ignorance' – she does not know her own conception of the good, her skills and talents, her socio-economic position, what kind of work (if any) she is engaged in – in order to arrive at a stable scheme of fair cooperation amongst worker-citizens. According to Collins, a right to work is likely to emerge from reasoning in the 'original position', because 'even behind this veil of ignorance, it seems plausible that an individual would be concerned about enjoying a right to work, given how important work can be for income, meaning, and a sense of self-worth'.[84] It is not clear to me why an individual in the 'original position' would not simply choose a political structure based upon well-being duties, including duties to promote structures of decent work opportunities; or a political arrangement based on an 'unconditional basic income'. Furthermore, we should remember that once entering the 'original position' we do not know whether, like Del Trotter, we will regard work as only for fools and horses or, like Collins, we will regard it as essential for meaning, self-realisation and a sense of self-worth. This follows from the fact that we do not know our own conception of the good behind the 'veil of ignorance'. Given this ignorance of the good, it is difficult to see why an agent would be acutely concerned with enacting a 'right to work' if she then came to discover that, like Del, she regarded work as a pitiful activity for fools and horses. Despite these reservations about Collins' particular argument, the use of a philosophical method is in general terms much more interesting as a strategy for identifying fundamental labour rights, hence strong candidates for juridification, than simply tracking workers' preferences.[85]

The third approach draws upon recent work in capabilities theory. Nussbaum has done valuable work in elaborating a list of central human capabilities that mark out especially valuable forms of human well-being.[86] This has been further developed in recent work by Jonathan Wolff and Avner De-Shalit, who introduce the idea of 'fertile functioning' and 'corrosive disadvantage' as a way of identifying which particular central capabilities are likely to underpin and support the acquisition and development of a wide capability set, and conversely which forms of capability deprivation are likely to be especially corrosive of the wider set of capabilities.[87] A similar distinction might be applied to labour rights. For example, Brian Langille has identified freedom of association as a labour right of particular

[83] H Collins, 'Theories of Rights as Justifications for Labour Law' in G Davidov and B Langille (eds), *The Idea of Labour Law* (Oxford, Oxford University Press, 2011) 137.

[84] ibid, 150.

[85] Of course, there are other philosophical methods that may be used to identify fundamental labour rights. For a different approach that draws upon philosophical theories of non-domination, see A Bogg and C Estlund, 'Freedom of Association and the Right to Contest: Getting Back to Basics' in A Bogg and T Novitz (eds), *Voices at Work: Continuity and Change in the Common Law World* (Oxford, Oxford University Press, 2014) 141.

[86] Nussbaum, *Women and Human Development*, above n 7.

[87] J Wolff and A De-Shalit, *Disadvantage* (Oxford, Oxford University Press, 2007), discussed in M Nussbaum, *Creating Capabilities: The Human Development Approach* (Cambridge MA, Harvard University Press, 2011) 44.

importance. According to Langille, freedom of association should be regarded as a fundamental right in labour law given its role in harnessing the self-governing capacities of workers in the labour market: substantive matters such as wages, working time and health and safety are more likely to be respected and even ratcheted up through workers exercising their associational freedoms, in a kind of virtuous circle effect.[88] By contrast, where freedom of association is under-protected, this is likely to lead to a wider corrosion of procedural and substantive standards in the workplace. This strategy would seem to elevate *collective* labour rights rather than individual labour rights such as the right to work as priorities for effective juridification.

The fourth approach might be to identify moral rights that have a particular symbolic significance in the scheme of employment protection, and to give those rights priority in respect of legal protection. In this respect, the right not to be unfairly dismissed is often regarded as a talismanic labour right. For example, Collins described the right not to be unfairly dismissed as the tail wagging 'the whole dog of the employment relation'.[89] In Jeremias Prassl's recent critique of the new concept of 'employee shareholder', a form of employment status that excludes protection from unfair dismissal, there is a strong sense that the dismantling of this particular right might have more seismic consequences for the wider edifice of employment protection.[90] The right to unfair dismissal was a citadel that even Margaret Thatcher dared not breach during the deregulatory agenda of her government. Once the right to unfair dismissal falls, perhaps a symbolic boundary has been transgressed, and other employment rights will fall more easily. There seems to be some plausibility in this symbolic account of normative significance, and other rights such as health and safety at work seem also to be compelling candidates for inclusion in the relevant set. The general fate of the protective whole is bound up very closely with the particular fate of these key talismanic rights. It is not clear, however, that the right to work is imbued with the same symbolic significance not least because the right to work has never been explicitly enacted in English law.

None of this is to deny that the possession of a job giving opportunities for self-realising work is a good thing. It certainly is. In time, perhaps, it may be a strong candidate for juridification. At the present time, however, with freedom of association under political attack,[91] unfair dismissal either excluded entirely or strangulated through procedural reforms[92] and the shameful under-enforcement of

[88] B Langille, 'Core Labour Rights – The True Story (Reply to Alston)' (2005) 16 *European Journal of International Law* 409, 434–35.

[89] H Collins, *Justice in Dismissal* (Oxford, Oxford University Press, 1992) 270; cited in J Prassl, 'Employee Shareholder "Status"? Dismantling the Contract of Employment' (2013) 42 *Industrial Law Journal* 307, 331.

[90] Prassl, ibid, 330.

[91] A Bogg and KD Ewing, *The Political Attack on Workplace Representation: A Legal Response* (London, Institute of Employment Rights, 2013).

[92] D Mangan, 'Employment Tribunal Reforms to Boost the Economy' (2013) 42 *Industrial Law Journal* 409.

health and safety laws,[93] the enactment of a legal right to work would be a political distraction and a misallocation of the scarce resource of juridification and enforcement.

C The Right to Work and the English Courts

In recent years, the debate about social rights has moved beyond rather sterile disputes centred on the conceptual pedigree of social rights – are they *really* human rights? Are they too vague in constitutional formulations? Are the positive duties associated with social rights inherently non-justiciable? [94]– towards more fruitful terrain. Scholars are now engaging in a highly sophisticated way with the institutional dimensions of social rights protection and enforcement. For example, Virginia Mantouvalou rejects a social rights strategy that is exclusively court-centred. While constitutional courts have an important role to play, she acknowledges that 'the legislature has the primary obligation to promote social rights. Legislatures and courts ought to work in partnership for the legal protection of social rights'.[95] She then explores the arguments *against* judicial enforcement, such as expertise, judicial hostility and democratic legitimacy, reframing these as arguments *in favour* of an appropriately defined judicial role in respect of social rights.[96] In a similar vein, King also favours a 'multi-institutional' approach to social rights enforcement.[97] Constitutional courts have an appropriate role to play in this 'multi-institutional' strategy, and it is a role that must be sensitive to considerations of polycentricity, democratic legitimacy, expertise and flexibility. These considerations underpin a sophisticated theory of judicial incrementalism in respect of social rights adjudication. These scholars are keenly aware of the limitations of the judicial role and court institutions, but nevertheless make a strong case in favour of a legitimate adjudicative role in respect of social rights violations. In my view, the scholarly debate about social rights adjudication has now moved to exactly where it needs to be. In the light of this, it might seem like a foolish move to suggest the English courts should have no role whatsoever in adjudicating disputes over a constitutionalised abstract 'right to work'.

All labour lawyers are familiar with *Lochner v New York* where a majority of the United States Supreme Court declared unconstitutional legislation that limited the working hours of bakers in the interests of their health and safety.[98] The constitutional basis for invalidating the legislation was the Fourteenth Amendment, which protected freedom of contract as a constitutional right. According to King, conventional accounts of the *Lochner* case suggested that it 'opened a period of

[93] S Tombs and D Whyte, *Regulatory Surrender: Death, Injury and the Non-Enforcement of Law (London, Institute of Employment Rights, 2010).*

[94] King, above n 61, sets out a list of 'bad' arguments against social rights: 4–5.

[95] Mantouvalou, 'In Support of Legalisation', above n 61, 89.

[96] ibid, 116–30.

[97] King, above n 61, 41.

[98] *Lochner v New York* 198 US 45 (1905).

aggressive judicial interventionism, from 1905 to 1937, that led, on one estimate, to the nullification of approximately 170 labour statutes alone'.[99] There is nothing revelatory about this to labour lawyers. 'Freedom of contract' has been the perennial enemy of social progress in the regulation of work since labour law began.

But King poses the following absolutely fascinating question:

> One might argue that the failure to include social rights in a constitution is more likely to lead to the outcome found in *Lochner* . . . That may well be so. But one may equally ask whether *Lochner* might have been decided similarly on the grounds of the employee's right to work.[100]

Indeed one might. Scholars such as Mantouvalou and King might well suggest that the risks of this are minimised where judges observe appropriate norms of institutional deference. I want to suggest otherwise. This is not based upon any general argument against social rights adjudication, for the work of scholars such as King and Mantouvalou demonstrates that such general arguments are often crude and dogmatic. My most acute concerns are with the right to work as such, and the historical track record of the English courts in adjudicating claims based on the right to work under the English common law.

One might be forgiven for thinking that the English common law was way ahead of the game in the sphere of social rights, for the right to work was recognised by Lord Denning in *Lee v Showmen's Guild of Great Britain* in 1952.[101] Patrick Elias and Keith Ewing have described the common law right to work as 'a nebulous and ill-defined right which has developed largely under the impetus of Lord Denning'.[102] According to Lord Wedderburn, 'when British judges – especially Lord Denning MR – spoke of a "right to work" they meant the right not to be a member of a trade union whilst taking such work as was going'.[103] This common law right came into its own in *Nagle v Fielden* which involved a challenge to the practice of sex discrimination in the issuing of trainer licences by the Jockey Club.[104] The discretionary reach of the common law right to work was confirmed in the trade union case of *Edwards v SOGAT*,[105] which involved a challenge to a union rule that permitted expulsion of temporary members in certain circumstances without a hearing. In a statement of principle of staggering breadth, Lord Denning observed that

> I do not think this trade union, or any other trade union, can give itself by its rules an unfettered discretion to expel a man or to withdraw his membership. The reason lies in the man's right to work. This is now fully recognised by law. It is a right which is of especial importance when a trade union operates a 'closed shop' or '100 per cent.

[99] King, above n 61, 109.
[100] ibid, 110.
[101] *Lee v Showmen's Guild of Great Britain* [1952] 2 QB 329.
[102] P Elias and KD Ewing, *Trade Union Democracy, Members' Rights and the Law* (London, Mansell, 1987) 38.
[103] Lord Wedderburn, *The Worker and the Law*, 3rd edn (Harmondsworth, Penguin, 1986) 234.
[104] *Nagle v Fielden* [1966] 2 QB 633.
[105] *Edwards v SOGAT* [1971] Ch 354.

> Membership': for that means that no man can become employed or remain in employment with a firm unless he is a member of the union. If his union card is withdrawn, he has to leave the employment. He is deprived of his livelihood. The courts of this country will not allow so great a power to be exercised arbitrarily or capriciously or with unfair discrimination, neither in the making of rules, nor in the enforcement of them. The law has means at its disposal . . . If the union should assume to make a rule which destroys that right or puts it in jeopardy – or is a gratuitous and oppressive interference with it – then the union exceeds its powers. The rule is ultra vires and invalid.[106]

The right to work, if it were to be enacted as a constitutionalised social right in the United Kingdom, has a (common law) history. It is not that the individuals in both *Nagle* and *Edwards* lacked a legitimate moral grievance. The conduct of the Jockey Club and SOGAT was, in different ways, capricious and harmful. What is interesting, however, is that the common law right to work came into its own as a legal technique to attack trade unions, in a way that flagrantly outflanked the statutory exclusions of restraint of trade doctrine from trade union rules and purposes hence undermining the democratic legitimacy of the court's role. The appropriate way to address the wrongs in *Nagle* and *Edwards* was through democratic legislation. But again social rights advocates might ask: now that deference and judicial minimalism is more firmly established in these more enlightened times, could we not trust the modern judiciary with a right to work?

I am very sceptical. The common law remains a deeply regressive force in the regulation of employment,[107] and the common law right to work may lurk in the judicial unconscious in adjudicating a constitutionalised social right to work. This caustic suspicion of the English judiciary was the leitmotif of Lord Wedderburn's conception of *collective laissez-faire*, and we dispense with that caution at our peril. In this respect, we would do well to remember Raz's reflections on the case for constitutional judicial review.[108] According to Raz, the adjudication of constitutional rights is political, but it is political in a distinctive way:

> The politics of the common good, questions regarding what is and what is not in the public interest, are as controversial as other political issues. But they are relatively free from conflict. By and large they concern the question of what is in the interest of all.[109]

This can be contrasted with the politics of conflicting interests, where constitutional courts are less institutionally apt as forums for resolving disputes. The problem with the right to work is that it is riven with conflicting interests, and so it does not seem easily characterised as part of the 'politics of the common good' unlike many other familiar constitutional rights. To invite the English courts to interpret a general right to work, against the backdrop of its common law history,

[106] ibid, 376.

[107] M Freedland and N Kountouris, 'Common Law and Voice' in A Bogg and T Novitz (eds), *Voices at Work: Continuity and Change in the Common Law World* (Oxford, Oxford University Press, 2014) 352.

[108] Raz, *Ethics in the Public Domain*, above n 10, 55–58.

[109] ibid, 56–57.

is asking for trouble. There is a great risk that an abstract right to work, with the detail to be filled in by English judges using their interpretive discretion, would be a false friend for British workers.

III Conclusion

It may be that this chapter is swimming against the tide. There are signs that the right to work may now have come of age. Indeed, the Conservative Chancellor George Osborne surprised many in his recent announcement that the Coalition Government is now committed to 'full employment'.[110] Perhaps the right to work might be a fundamental social right that could form the basis of a new political consensus, rather like the right to a minimum wage in UK employment law. Then again, the more cynical observer might wonder whether the right to work and 'full employment' are so open-textured that they provide cover for a wide range of political projects, not all of which are progressive. Where full employment consists of involuntary 'self-employment' and proliferating forms of 'casualised' and 'zero hours' contractual arrangements, it is not obvious that full employment is an attractive political goal at all. Perhaps there is still much to be said for a legal strategy that focuses on rights *at* work rather than the right *to* work, while pursuing the goal of promoting decent employment opportunities using the levers of employment policy.[111]

The arguments in this chapter are far from definitive. Its spirit is exploratory rather than conclusive. Certainly, work is a very important activity that contributes in a variety of ways to human well-being. As a valuable activity, governments and private actors have duties to promote *decent* work that are derived from more general duties to protect and promote the well-being of citizens in a political community. In my view, faithful discharge of these well-being duties will create a structure of opportunities for decent work that proponents of a social right to work would recognise as part of their own political agenda. Whether there should be a legal right to work, understood as an abstract constitutional standard, is an altogether more difficult question. For the English labour lawyer, much will depend upon one's view of the common law and the common law judges, and the extent to which they can be trusted with something as important as the regulation of work.

[110] 'George Osborne commits to "fight for full employment"' BBC News (1 April 2014): www.bbc.co.uk/news/uk-26814423.

[111] For an excellent analysis of the linkages between employment policy and labour law from the perspective of governance theory, see C Kilpatrick, 'New EU Employment Governance and Constitutionalism' in G de Búrca and J Scott (eds), *Law and New Governance in the EU and the US* (Oxford, Hart Publishing, 2006) 121.

10

The Right to Work and the Duty to Work

AMIR PAZ-FUCHS

The right to work and the duty to work are inseparable.
East German Constitution, Article 24

For a long time we have been seeking the philosopher's stone. It is found, it is work.[1]

Introduction

Social and economic rights present a unique and fascinating case study for the observer of theory and practice. Perhaps more than anywhere else, a vast rift exists between the pronounced consensus that asserts the inability to seriously distinguish them from civil and political rights,[2] and the frustrating failures, time after time, to grant them true legal force in courts in Western countries.[3] This is true of the right to education as it is true of the right to health; of the right to decent housing as it is of the right to welfare entitlements. But even within this group of de facto second class rights, the right to work is often deemed less than worthy.

I would like to suggest here that part of the reason for this demoted status of the right to work lies with the burden it carries, a spectre that looms above: the fact that the right to work is understood as intimately connected to the duty to work, or perhaps even *is* 'a duty to work in disguise'.[4] In the course of enquiring why this

[1] Cited in P Rosanvallon, *The New Social Question* (Princeton NJ, Princeton University Press, 2000) 70.

[2] J Waldron, 'Introduction' in J Waldron (ed), *Theories of Rights* (Oxford, Oxford University Press, 1984) 1, 11; R Gavison 'On the Relationship Between Civil and Political Rights and Social and Economic Rights' in JM Coicaud, MW Doyle and AM Gardner (eds), *The Globalization of Human Rights* (Tokyo, United Nations University Press, 2003) 24; V Mantouvalou 'In Support of Legislation' in C Gearty and V Mantouvalou, *Debating Social Rights* (Oxford, Hart Publishing, 2010) 85; D Barak-Erez and A Gross (eds), *Exploring Social Rights: Between Theory and Practice* (Oxford, Hart Publishing, 2007).

[3] See, eg, P O'Connell, 'The Death of Socio-Economic Rights' (2011) 72 *Modern Law Review* 532.

[4] G Mundlak, 'The Right to Work – The Value of Work' in D Barak-Erez and A Gross (eds), *Exploring Social Rights: Between Theory and Practice* (Oxford, Hart Publishing, 2007) 341, 342.

is so, it is possible that we may find, in effect, that all rights carry with them at least the possibility, the potential, of being perceived as duties. If so, a discussion of the somewhat peculiar 'right is duty' corollary with respect to the right to work may offer some insight as to the nature and understanding of human rights, in general. A less ambitious (or, perhaps, frightening) conclusion could be that the traits that distinguish the right to work in such a manner characterize 'only' social and economic rights and not just rights in general. This tack may offer insights that are relevant to the ongoing discussion regarding the uniqueness of social and economic rights.

A third avenue would narrow the perspective even further, suggesting that, after all, perhaps the right to work *is* unique, at least in this respect. According to this line of enquiry, there is good reason why the extreme flanks of the political Left and Right, along with mainstream, third-way ideologies converge almost exclusively on the right to work when conflating the right and the duty. The reason for this focus may, perhaps, be related to the character of the right to work. It is impossible to ignore the fact that debate over the duty to work is taking place within a capitalist society, where preserving a duty to work serves the interests of those who enjoy an oversupply of cheap labour.[5] Taking this position to the extreme, some have forcefully argued that slavery and servitude were only *formally* abolished in the late nineteenth century. In reality, they were replaced with industrial bondage, which was similar in important respects to the odious historical institution.[6]

Finally, when looking closely at the duty to work as imposed by contemporary welfare states, one must be cautious so as not to confuse, as some have, the right to work with the right to public assistance. Contemporary 'welfare-to-work' programmes, which figure prominently in discussions regarding the duty to work, offer public assistance 'in exchange' for one's obligation to work. They do not offer (as some would like) a government commitment to provide work, as an employer of last resort. Instead, governments provide public assistance, thus viewing the monetary benefit that derives from work and enables subsistence, as the only relevant aspect of the right. One may even suggests that, as such, the substitution of a right with a monetary value is part of a wider trend that can only be noted here, one that relates to the ability to 'buy out' human rights.

The chapter will first suggest how a theoretical analysis of rights may support, or perhaps even lead to, a conflation of rights and duties. Then, focusing on the right and duty to work, the second and third sections will expand on the two central categories of justifications in favour of a right to work, each entailing a variety

[5] See Mundlak, above n 4, 345.

[6] JG Pope, 'Contract, Race and Freedom of Labor in the Constitutional Law of "Involuntary Servitude"' (2010) 119 *Yale Law Journal* 1474, 1507; and see Lord Wilberforce, 'Introduction' in R Sawyer, *Slavery in the Twentieth Century* (London, Routledge & Kegan Paul, 1986) vii: 'It is hard for us to appreciate that in spite of great efforts made by the emancipators and their successors, in spite of the revolution in public opinion as regards all forms of slavery, in spite of the plethora of international agreements for the suppression of slavery (some 300 of them), the problem of slavery in the twentieth century is as great, indeed greater than it was in the 1830s'.

of subsets. The first category concerns the relation between the individual and society. Justifications in this 'type' suggest that individuals need work as an avenue towards social inclusion, towards true participation and standing in society. Such justifications will be discussed under the heading of 'Citizenship'. The second category focuses on the moral and material well-being of the individual.

I How Can Rights Become Duties?

The cause for theoretical embarrassment from the above question arises, it would seem, from the legal and intuitive notion that a right to X includes also the right not to X. Thus, the right to freedom of speech includes the right not to speak.[7] It seems obvious, therefore, that one's right to speak (or pray, or marry, or join a union) does not carry with it one's *duty* to speak (or pray, or marry or join a union).[8] An individual's right to autonomy justifies allowing her to decide whether or not to make use of her given rights.[9] They provide a strong reason to place a duty on the state, and not on the individual herself. And yet, as explained below, the governing theory of rights, known as the 'Interest (or Benefit) Theory', carries with it the seeds of correlation and conflation, the danger that, if one is not careful, a right to X would seem inseparable from a duty to do X. It is therefore important to briefly outline the Interest Theory of rights.

A simple account of the Interest Theory holds that Jack has a right that Jill performs A, and hence Jill has a duty towards Jack to do A, if and only if Jill has a duty to do A *and* performance of A by Jill would benefit Jack.[10] We find, therefore, that the Interest Theory identifies rights by reference to the duty that society holds, and only if it is understood that the duty is grounded in the putative right-holder's interest. As simple as this account is, two matters must be highlighted before moving forward: first, the duty discussed here is *not* the duty held by the putative right-holder, but rather by another individual or by society at large. This is, if you will, the 'classic' understanding of rights and duties: my right corresponds to your duty; rather than the peculiar relationship discussed here, between my right and my duty. Despite the clear difference between the two – classified as

[7] *Speiser v Randall* (1958) 357 US 513 (conditioning veterans' benefits on oaths not to overthrow the government held unconstitutional because it violates one's right not to 'speak').

[8] In the United States and Britain, this right is set by law: the Taft–Hartley Act, Pub L. 80-101, 61 Stat 136 (1947), and the Trade Union and Labour Relations (Consolidation) Act 1992 (c 52), respectively. In Israel, it was the National Labour Court that eliminated closed shops – *Tzim v the Histadrut*. Of course, the right *not* to join a union is one of the (mainly American) interpretations of the 'right to work'.

[9] This does not mean, of course, that rights are absolute. They are subject to limitations, set by the rights of others or by collective interests.

[10] J Raz, 'Promises and Obligations' in PMS Hacker and J Raz (eds), *Law, Morality and Society* (Oxford, Clarendon Press, 1977) 210, 213.

'correlative' and 'converse' duties, respectively, it is surprising to note how often the fundamental distinction is overlooked.[11]

Second, the fact that the duty must be beneficial to the putative right-holder is meant to distinguish duties that do not correspond to rights ('relative' duties, in the jargon of early legal positivists)[12] from duties that emanate from rights. So we may know that people have a duty not to hurt animals or to litter beaches, but does this mean that dogs have a right not to be harshly treated or that beaches have a right to be clean? To answer this question, according to the Interest Theory, we must resolve whether the duty is grounded in the interests of dogs or beaches, or whether the duty is grounded in the interests of others. This would mean, in turn, that even when we are confident that a duty exists, we are not always certain that there is a right that corresponds from it. To establish the latter, crucial element, we need to assess the justification, or justifications, for the duty.

Against this background, it should be clear that HLA Hart was correct in criticizing the Interest Theory for bringing rights and duties uncomfortably close:

> [I]f to say that an individual has such a right means no more than that he is the intended beneficiary of a duty, then 'a right' in this sense may be an unnecessary, and perhaps confusing, term in the description of the law; *since all that can be said in a terminology of such rights can be and indeed is, best said in the indispensable terminology of duty* (emphasis added).[13]

Hart's critique is directly relevant to the case at hand, which concerns the right (and the duty) to work. To put matters quite simply, Hart points out that, in the course of establishing whether a particular interest should be granted the status of a legal right, we turn to the collective wisdom, which will help us assess whether an individual's interest justifies placing a duty on another. In the case of the right to work, we will ask whether such a right justifies placing a duty on the state, or on an employer, and if so – what that duty entails. *This* correlation between rights and duties brings forth the threat of a conflation of rights and duties. Though this threat may seem novel, one may be reminded that Jean-Jacques Rousseau insisted that justice could be achieved only by uniting rights and duties.[14] Similarly, John Finnis notes that in certain African tribal regimes, 'right' and 'duty' are terms covered by a single word, normally translated as 'ought' or 'due'. Finnis explains that this phenomenon has its cultural source in the approach that emphasizes 'duty and obligation, rather than the nuance of modern Western society, with a stress on rights'.[15] So, instead of claiming that the ideas themselves are in any way

[11] J Knox, 'Horizontal Human Rights Law' (2008) 102 *American Journal of International Law* 1, 39.

[12] J Austin, *Lectures on Jurisprudence* (London, Murray, 1880) 161–62 (Lect XII); H Kelsen, *General Theory of Law and State*, A Wedberg trans (Cambridge MA, Harvard University Press, 1949) 85–86; J Bentham, *An Introduction to the Principles of Morals and Legislation* (Oxford, Clarendon Press, 1996) 265.

[13] HLA Hart, 'Bentham on Legal Rights' in *Oxford Essays in Jurisprudence*, 2nd Series (Oxford, Clarendon Press, 1973) 171, 190.

[14] JJ Rousseau, *The Social Contract* (Hertfordshire, Wordsworth Ware, 1998) II.vi.

[15] M Gluckman, cited in J Finnis, *Natural Law and Natural Rights* (Oxford, Oxford University Press, 1982) 209.

novel, it would be more accurate to state that it is their prominence in modern, Western legal and political thought that deserves investigation. But here we have one additional move. To recap: Hart was concerned, in the passage quoted above, with the way rights and their 'correlative' duties (that should be taken up by someone other than the right-holder) have come closely together (to form an 'ought' or a 'due'). Now we move to the centre of our investigation, with the claim that the right-holder is said to be holding a duty as well, as an integral part of her right.

Where, then, lies the explanation for the rise of this legal ideology that posits rights as dependent on duties? Obviously, the conflation of rights and duties has very little to do with legal theory. Instead, it stems from a concern, to put it mildly, common to the political Left and Right, that Western society has become over-inflated by rights-talk, individualistic focus and legal methods of solving disputes.[16] The driving force of this sorry state of affairs is, per these critiques, the 'imbalance of rights and responsibilities'.[17] Both sides of the political spectrum, and a sizeable portion of its mainstream, bemoan the manner in which human rights discourse has disintegrated society, thus leading to 'the triumph of the individual over society, or rather, the breaking of the threads which in the past had woven human beings into social textures'.[18] The fact that individuals can act irresponsibly, neglecting their health, education and immediate living environment, and afterwards lay claims to the government, demanding that their rights be acknowledged, seems to reflect for many an unnatural and unfair state of affairs. How did this new ideology gain such prominence?

Instead of answering this question in the abstract, it would be useful to return to our case study – of the right to work. Here, we find two main justifications in favour of a right to work, each entailing a variety of subsets. The first category concerns the relation between the individual and society. Justifications in this 'type' suggest that individuals need work as an avenue towards social inclusion, towards true participation and standing in society. Such justifications will be discussed below under the heading of 'Citizenship'. The second category focuses on the material and moral well-being of the individual. According to this justification, the unemployed are 'dutiful but defeated', and forcing them to work is likened to awakening them from sleep. This array of (self-conscious) paternalistic justifications will be discussed under the heading of 'Individual Well-Being'.

Both are serious justifications for the right to work. However, bearing in mind the theoretical overview offered above, a real concern lurks in the shadow of the right to work – the danger that these justifications will be *too* convincing, and be taken one step further. If work is intimately tied to citizenship, thus justifying an

[16] B Saul, 'In the Shadow of Human Rights' (2001) 32 *Columbia Human Rights Law Review* 565, 569.

[17] A Chapman, 'Reintegrating Rights and Responsibilities: Toward a New Human Rights Paradigm' in K Hunter and T Mack (eds), *International Rights and Responsibilities for the Future* (Westport CT, Praeger, 1996) 3.

[18] E Hobsbawm, *The Age of Extreme: A Short History of the Twentieth Century 1914-1991* (New York, Vintage, 1994) 15.

individual's demand for work, can 'true' citizenship, or rights associated with citizenship, be enforced? Can it be conditioned on work, and denied from those who refuse to work? And if work is so crucial to an individual's welfare, is it not the case that an individual who refuses to work is behaving irrationally, thus paving the way for paternalistic coercion, for her own benefit? The following two sections discuss these justifications for the duty to work.

II The Duty to Work as a Condition of Citizenship

The rich consensus that supports a conflation of the right to work and the duty to work includes an impressive array of governments, of very different political climates, cultural heritage and general ideology.[19] In 1997, this consensus led to the introduction of a draft Declaration of Human Responsibilities which states, in its Preamble, that 'exclusive insistence on rights can result in conflict, division, and endless dispute, and the neglect of human responsibilities can lead to lawlessness and chaos'. Based on the Declaration, the UN Human Rights Commission proposed, in 1999, a resolution to consider preparing a 'declaration on human rights and responsibilities'.[20]

The draft Declaration is a convenient juncture for a discussion of the relation between rights and duties in general and of the right to work, in particular, for several reasons: first, because it is a declaration of duties and obligations proposed and discussed in forums that are generally associated with the advancement of human rights. Second, because of the way this vision is shared by 'liberal' and 'conservative' leaning countries, traditional and modern, religious and secular. And, finally, and most specifically, because the list therein enables a more concrete discussion of the relevant duties and obligations, and perhaps suggests a distinction between those that may readily be acknowledged and those that are far more contentious.[21]

Among the less contentious obligations one finds duties that, in effect, stem from the rights of others, including the responsibility to respect life and to refrain from injuring (including torturing or killing) others (Article 5), not to steal (Article 8), to help the needy (Article 10), to respect others (Article 16). The second category of duties, however, may be viewed as 'duties of citizenship'. Their beneficiaries are unspecified, and the goods that derive from them arguably add to the general welfare of the public as a whole. Common examples include the duty to obey the law, to pay taxes and to participate in military service. To this list two duties are often added: the duty to vote and the duty to work. It is notable that political theorist Judith Shklar chose precisely two acts – voting and earning – as

19 Saul, above n 16, 575–80.
20 UN ESCOR, 55th Sess, UN Doc E/CN.4J1999/L.85 (1999).
21 For a similar analysis see Knox, above n 11, 38.

the pillars forming the centrepiece of (American) citizenship.[22] The peculiarity stems from two character traits that the two have in common: first, they are frequently discussed both as rights and as duties;[23] and, second, these are precisely the two 'duties of participation' that served as touchstones for Communist regimes.[24]

Since the most enthusiastic support for a strict, unabashed duty to work as a condition for citizenship in contemporary political circles is often among the extreme Right, it is fascinating to note how similar language was common in socialist nations. Thus, the Soviet constitution included a surprising citation of a biblical aphorism: 'He who does not work, neither shall he eat'.[25] And as Louis Henkin highlights, it is in socialist countries that we found that 'socially useful work determine[s] . . . a person's status in society'.[26] This paradigm bred a series of 'anti-parasite laws', passed in the various republics of the Soviet Union between 1957 and 1961. The most notable of them was the Russian Republic Law of 1961, the 'Law on Strengthening the Struggle against Persons Who Avoid Socially Useful Work and Lead an Anti-Social Parasitic Way of Life'.[27] The law included sanctions such as two to five years of enforced resettlement with confiscation of goods gained by non-labour means, and *the obligation* to work. In addition, anti-parasitism was incorporated into the Criminal Code of the Russian Republic in 1970, and included a penalty of one-year deprivation of liberty or correctional tasks, or two years for repeat offenders.[28]

The following year, Cuba enacted 'The Law on Loafing', which branded the unproductive worker or the non-worker as a traitor, not bearing her fair share, while prepared to 'free ride' the labour of others.[29] And the law explicitly posits the duty to work as a reciprocal obligation to the right to work:

> Work is a right guaranteed by the Revolution. The Revolutionary Government will see to it that all able-bodied citizens are able to obtain a job in keeping with their

[22] J Shklar, *American Citizenship: The Quest for Inclusion* (Cambridge MA, Harvard University Press, 1991) 84. Needless to say, Shklar chose her terminology carefully in opting for 'earning' and not for 'work'. Work outside the market, often performed by women and the elderly, does not live up to the demand – see Mundlak, above n 4, 351.

[23] See, eg, Saul, above n 16, 583.

[24] L Henkin, 'Rights: Here and There' (1981) 82 *Columbia Law Rev* 1582, 1598; Inga Markovits points out that *all* East European constitutions contain statements on the obligation of able bodied citizens to work: I Markovits, 'Law or Order – Constitutionalism and Legality in Eastern Europe' (1982) 34 *Stanford Law Review* 513, 517, fn 21.

[25] USSR Constitution of 1936, Art 12, cited in Henkin, above n 24.

[26] USSR Constitution, Art 14, cited in Henkin, above n 24, 1601.

[27] [1961] 26 Ved RSFSR Item 371, cited in I McColl Kennedy, 'Cuba's Ley Contra La Vagancia – The Law on Loafing' (1973) 20 *University of California at Los Angeles Law Review* 1177, 1178, fn 6.

[28] ibid.

[29] See above n 27, 1182. The Preamble to the Law reads: 'Whereas: In the new society, besides being a right guaranteed by the state, work is an unavoidable social duty for all able-bodied men and women . . . In contrast to the upright attitude of the vast majority of our workers, there are still those who, intent on living as parasites, without working, exhibit an anti-social behavior which constitutes a bad example for the new generations . . . The working class condemns all forms of loafing as crimes similar to robbery' cited ibid, 1185.

> abilities. *In turn*, all citizens who are physically and mentally fit have the social duty of contributing to the community with their work.[30]

In East Germany, the 'unity of right and duty' was made manifest in the constitutional provision stating that 'The right to work and the duty to work are inseparable'.[31] While the Marxist aphorism is often known as 'from each according to his capabilities, to each according to his needs', this was actually an evolution from the original pronouncement set in the *Critique of the Gotha Programme.* There Marx introduced the 'performance principle', which stated: 'from each according to his capabilities, to each according to his *labor*',[32] thus aligning an individual's status against her performance as a labourer. This version of the performance principle was incorporated *verbatim* in the Constitutions of East Germany, Hungary, Poland and the USSR,[33] and did not remain a dead letter, either. Inga Markovits argues that 'to each according to his labor' has 'significantly influenced the East German way of thinking about law' including, but not limited to, 'effective work incentives'.[34]

This attitude, conflating the right and duty to work, characterizes not only socialist nations. Gosta Esping-Andersen explains that Bismark contemplated 'legislating the right (or obligation, if you wish) to employment as part and parcel of his larger vision of *Soldaten der Arbeit*: workers as soldiers in an economy functioning like an army'.[35]

It may be useful, at this stage, to make explicit the link between these political developments and the theoretical background developed in the previous section. This link is not obvious because the Interest Theory of rights focuses on A's right as dependent on the justification that exists to place a duty *on B*. In contrast, we find here that A's right to X is seen as inseparable from, or even dependent on, *A's* duty to do X. Upon closer inspection, however, the relationship between the two scenarios becomes clearer. In some cases, and perhaps – especially when the right is not self-evident (such as the right to bodily integrity, for example), the Interest Theory suggests that making the case in favour of the right to X involves showing why X is of fundamental importance. Thus, if we accept that work (or voting) is of such central importance, that society should be obliged to guarantee it as a right to individuals, it is a short step towards the conclusion that the very same significance justifies *forcing* the individual to act upon that right (to work, or to vote). The same line of thought that suggests that a right to X is justified by the value *society* places on X, may (though by no means, must) lead to the conclusion that 'the right to X and the duty to do X are inseparable'.

[30] Preamble to Art 1, Law 1231, cited ibid, 1189.

[31] Art 24, para 2 of the East German Constitution, cited in I Markovits, 'Socialist vs Burgeouis Rights – An East–West German Perspective' (1978) 45 *University of Chicago Law Review* 612, 621.

[32] See the discussion in Markovits, 'Socialist vs Burgeouis Rights', above n 31, 632.

[33] East German Constitution, Art 2, para 3; Hungarian Constitution, Art 14; Polish Constitution, Art 19; USSR Constitution, Art 14.

[34] Markovits, 'Socialist vs Burgeouis Rights', above n 31, 633.

[35] G Esping-Andersen, *The Three Worlds of Welfare Capitalism* (Cambridge, Polity, 1990) 40.

Moving closer to the present day, Article 29(6) of the 1981 African Charter of Human and People's Rights states that 'The individual shall also have the duty . . . to work to the best of his abilities and competence, and to pay taxes imposed by law'.[36] And the Preamble to the 1946 French Constitution made explicit mention of the right and duty to work.[37]

Discussing the attitude towards citizenship in the United States, Shklar notes that

> [t]o be a recognized and active citizen at all he must be an equal member of the polity, a voter, but he must also be independent, which has all along meant that he must be an 'earner', a free remunerated worker, . . . neither more nor less.[38]

In America, at least, one cannot ignore the fact that this position has a chequered history, strongly related to slavery. Nothing in American law states explicitly that there was a legal duty to work, and yet, in every jurisdiction it was a crime, punishable by imprisonment, not to work or to be seeking work, if one was able-bodied without other means of support. This crime, known as vagrancy, was one of the few acknowledged crimes of status in American law.[39] As James Pope explains: 'an individual excluded from productive labor would become a noncontributing, dependent idler unfit for citizenship in a democracy - in effect an involuntary vagrant'.[40]

Needless to say, race played a central role in the construction of (mainly American)[41] slavery.[42] Though a discussion of the racial facets of the obligation to work would take us too far astray,[43] it is worth noting that, not only are these facets of importance, they are the result of a conscious effort. Shklar describes the attempt, most notable in Thorstein Veblen's celebrated book, *The Theory of the Leisure Class*, to shame not the poor and the non-whites, but rather idle rich, who shunned work and engaged in 'damaging activities, such as religious observance, government and war'.[44] As Shklar notes, 'No contemporary advocate of workfare has expressed this uneasiness [about idleness] with greater anxiety'.[45] And yet, the racial elements that governed Western slavery saw to it that the obligation to work was never seriously directed at the idle rich, but only towards the (mainly

[36] For an analysis of the African Charter see Knox, above n 11, 16–22.

[37] See discussion in Henkin, above n 24, 1594.

[38] Shklar, above n 22, 64.

[39] K Orren, *Belated Feudalism* (Cambridge, Cambridge University Press, 1991) 72.

[40] Pope, above n 6, 1533.

[41] Phillips suggests that while racial elements were always present within slavery, their importance was different in different places and times, but nowhere as central as in the American manifestation. WD Phillips, 'Continuity and Change in Western Slavery: Ancient to Modern Times' in ML Bush (ed), *Slavery and Serfdom: Studies in Legal Bondage* (London, Longman, 1996) 87.

[42] O Patterson, *Slavery and Social Death* (Cambridge MA, Harvard University Press, 1982) 7–8.

[43] On this see W Bell, *Aid to Dependent Children* (New York, Columbia University Press, 1965) 29–41; FF Piven and R Cloward, *Regulating the Poor*, updated edn (New York, Vintage, 1993) 139–43; J Handler, *The Poverty of Welfare Reform* (New Haven CT, Yale University Press, 1995) 25; J De Parle, *American Dream: Three Women, Ten Kids, and a Nation's Drive to End Welfare* (New York, Viking, 2004) 86–87.

[44] Shklar, above n 22, 88.

[45] ibid, 91.

non-white) poor.[46] The latter, but not the former, risk social exclusion and equal citizenship as a result of their failure to participate in the workforce. Such an ideology was a driving force behind welfare-to-work programmes in the late 1990s, a force that is still apparent today.

While there are important differences in the details of welfare-to-work programmes and, of course, in the background context of the employment relationship against which they are set, they have some characteristics in common. They all view work as a central tool in dealing with many social and economic ills, from poverty through drug abuse to homelessness and social exclusion. They focus on the lowest social and economic tiers (as noted – the idle rich are not a concern). But the central common element is the ideology behind conditioning rights on the fulfilment of obligation. In introducing yet harsher measures on jobseekers in Britain in 2013, the Secretary of State for Work and Pensions, Iain Duncan Smith, explained that they will mark an end to Britain's 'something for nothing culture'.[47] In this he was not original, even within his own party. Exactly 20 years earlier, the Secretary for Social Security at the time, Peter Lilley, stated unequivocally that 'those who think that this is a "something for nothing" society can forget it'.[48]

Across party lines, Labour continued very similar policies, for slightly different reasons: focusing on the benefit to the individual who is forced to work, and on the need to enforce reciprocity to ensure that the public will continue to support the system. Frank Field, who took charge of welfare reform under the Blair government, identified the main problem for welfare policies not by reference to cost or morality (supporting single mothers, immigrants or minorities), but in a 'legitimacy crisis'.[49] Saving the system, it is argued, can be done only if the taxpaying public can identify with the people whom they are supporting. And this objective entails enhancing reciprocity and strict work requirements. This argument, it should be noted, seems to rely more on intuition than on empirical data. In fact, it has been argued that such requirements encourage a perception of 'us and them' and undermine 'a principle of citizenship, which is that everybody should be treated on an inclusive, equal basis'.[50]

Blair himself expressed this sentiment when he wrote that 'the best defence against social exclusion is finding a job'.[51] And even more ardently, it has been

[46] The mention of slavery begs the question: how does the duty to work not violate the numerous provisions, international and domestic, that forbid indentured servitude? The answer to this question is that the two are different forms of obligation to work. As James Pope clarifies: 'Slavery was considered evil not because it entailed labor (all able-bodied adults were expected to work for a living), but because the labor of slaves was coerced, degraded, and uncompensated' – Pope, above n 6, 1533.

[47] R Mason, 'Benefit reform will end "something for nothing" culture says Duncan Smith' *The Guardian* (1 October 2013).

[48] Department of Social Security, Press Release (6 October, 1993), cited in C Jones and T Novak, *Poverty, Welfare and the Disciplinary State* (London, Routledge, 1999) 97.

[49] G Standing, *Global Labour Flexibility* (Basingstoke, Macmillan, 1999) 229; also Rosanvallon, above n 1, 43.

[50] Standing, above n 49, 326.

[51] T Blair, 'Foreword by the Prime Minister' in Social Exclusion Unit, *Bridging the Gap: New Opportunities for 16–18 Year Olds Not in Education, Employment or Training* (Cm 4405, 1999) 6.

suggested that 'inclusion through labor should remain the cornerstone of every struggle against exclusion'.[52] This position, of course, serves as one of the prominent rationales for welfare-to-work programmes, that 'having a job is a necessary condition of what has been called social dignity'.[53] Shklar sums it up when she states: 'What is really astonishing is the degree of agreement between these critics and defenders of welfare . . . All want to make good citizens out of the "underclass" by getting them a job and making them, too, earning members of society'.[54]

While the ideology behind current programmes identifies an 'underclass' that is created as a result of labour market exclusion, the attention of critics is increasingly turned to an 'underclass created by the increasing demands for the unemployed to accept lower benefits and demeaning, low-paid work'.[55] Against the reality of an economy that may not have enough jobs to offer everyone, policies of enforced integration into the workforce may, in fact, be demanding the impossible.[56] As such, they exhibit not only the opportunity for inclusion, but also the threat of increased exclusion.[57] First, there is the inevitable exclusion of those who cannot, for whatever reason, comply with the rules.[58] They are in danger of boarding an 'exclusion trajectory' and suffering even more stigmatization due to their failure to comply with rules that target them. As Ian Kennedy concludes, in his analysis of the Cuban Law on Loafing:

> The 'parasite', the man who lives by the toil of others, is an easily identified target. To represent him as the enemy of progress, the one who holds Cuba back, is immediately to tap a well of pent-up emotion in the masses which they can then direct not only at isolating and vanquishing the enemy but also, more important, at demonstrating what good patriots they are by renewing their commitment, bearing greater sacrifice, and redoubling their work effort.[59]

In addition, such programmes have, at times, *reduced* the chances of *meaningful* integration into the labour market. Nowhere is this more apparent than in one scheme, common to many welfare-to-work programmes: 'workfare'. Workfare schemes require that claimants 'work for their benefits' with designated corporations, or at least spend their day at the jobcentre, supposedly gaining career skills by infusion.[60] The most recent version of the British scheme was successfully

[52] Rosanvallon, above n 1, 65.

[53] A Gutmann and D Thompson, *Democracy and Disagreement* (Cambridge MA, Harvard University Press, 1996) 293; Mundlak, above n 4, 358.

[54] Shklar, above n 22, 96.

[55] J Clasen, A Gould and J Vincent, *Long Term Unemployment and the Threat of Social Exclusion* (Bristol, Policy, 1997) 14; also A Atkinson, 'Social Exclusion, Poverty and Unemployment' in A Atkinson and J Hills (eds), *Exclusion, Employment and Opportunity* CASEpaper 4 (London, 1998) v, 15.

[56] U Beck, *The Brave New World of Work* (Cambridge, Polity, 2000).

[57] L Boltanski and E Chiapello (trans G Elliott), *The New Spirit of Capitalism* (London, Verso, 2005) 233.

[58] R Plant, 'Citizenship and Social Security' (2003) 24 *Fiscal Studies* 153, 164.

[59] McColl Kennedy, above n 27, 1240.

[60] For further details see A Paz-Fuchs, *Welfare to Work: Conditional Rights in Social Policy* (Oxford, Oxford University Press, 2008) 47.

challenged by a geology graduate whose ambition was to work in the museum sector and who wished to volunteer at the museum, but was sent to stock shelves in a multi-million pound retail company.[61] The Court of Appeal accepted the submission on the administrative ground, namely – that the 2011 Jobseeker's Allowance Regulations,[62] as drafted, reach beyond the powers prescribed by section 17A of the Jobseeker's Act. Sections 17A and 17B were added to the Jobseeker's Act 1995 in 2009, empowering the Secretary of State to impose on claimants, through regulations, to participate in 'work for your benefits' schemes in place. Section 17A states that these regulations must designate schemes of a 'prescribed description', for a 'prescribed period', indicating 'prescribed circumstances' that will be taken into account in determining whether a participant had good cause for failure to comply and, in case of failure, the period of sanction must also be 'prescribed' in the regulations. The Court of Appeal found that the regulations did not meet the requirement set in the Act to prescribe in sufficient detail the description, period and conditions of sanctions that may be placed within a designated scheme.

However, it should be noted that, insofar as the rationale governing section 17A ('work for your benefits') is concerned, the Court noted that, as such schemes are 'designed to assist the unemployed to obtain employment . . . it is not easy to see what objection there could be to them'.[63]

On the very day the Court of Appeal handed down its decision, the 2011 Regulations were replaced with new regulations, which were drafted with a view to addressing the conclusion that was in fact reached by the Court of Appeal.[64]

The Supreme Court rejected the government's appeal, and accepted the Court of Appeal's reasoning.[65] Interestingly for present purposes, it chose to expand more on an issue that the Court of Appeal dealt with brevity, namely – whether workfare falls foul of the provision against forced labour, in Article 4 of the European Convention on Human Rights. Relying on *Van Der Mussele*,[66] the Supreme Court explained that the right *not* to be forced to work (ie, the negative aspect of the right to work) may be limited by the 'idea of the general interest'.[67]

This 'idea of the general interest' brings us back to the role of work in promoting citizenship. Guy Standing argues that while having a job may integrate a person into society in some cases, in other cases – epitomised as 'McJobs' – the focus on inclusion is potentially *dis*-integrating. Moreover, he suggests, 'if people are

[61] *Reilly and Wilson v Secretary of State for Work and Pensions* [2013] EWCA Civ 66, 1 WLR 2239.

[62] Jobseeker's Allowance (Employment, Skills and Enterprise Scheme) Regulations 2011/917.

[63] *Reilly and Wilson*, above n 61, [72] (Stanley Burnton LJ).

[64] Jobseeker's Allowance (Schemes for Assisting Persons to Obtain Employment) Regulations 2013 (SI 2013/276).

[65] *R (Reilly and another) v Secretary of State for Work and Pensions* [2013] UKSC 68 [*Reilly SC*]

[66] *Van Der Muessle v Belgium* (1983) 6 EHRR 163.

[67] *Reilly SC*, above n 65, [82]. The SC also noted that the argument equating workfare programmes with forced labour failed on at least three different occasions in Strasbourg: *X v Netherlands* (1976) 7 DR 161; *Talmon v Netherlands* (1997) EHRLR 448; *Shuitemaker v Netherlands*, App no 15906/08 (unreported, 4 May 2010).

driven through fear, insecurity and coercion, they will respond like cattle'.[68] This assessment is somewhat similar to the conclusion that the Poor Law was exacerbating the problem it was set to deal with by 'reinforcing, and not averting, destitution'.[69]

Therefore, the process may be described in the following manner: moral and cultural norms supposedly identify who is included and who is excluded. It is submitted that the excluded should be brought within society's bounds. Before moving to do so, however, the perception of individuals as rejecting society's shared appreciation for work, family and the like (though, as numerous authors have pointed out, this is often a fallacious assumption)[70] diverts the attention to the personal traits of the excluded, rather than to the structures that lead to that exclusion. This process leads to a lack of empathy that makes it easier to stigmatize and dehumanize excluded groups such as the unemployed.[71]

The steps as described assure that the unemployed arrive at the negotiating table in a precarious position. Their exclusion is not only a descriptive assessment, but an evaluative one as well. They are not perceived as having legitimate claims on society's resources, but rather it is the generosity of society that allows for the offer of benefits and job opportunities.[72] If the claimants now refuse the conditions offered to them, they are re-categorised as not only excluded, but as also *undeserving* of society's assistance towards inclusion. By making 'exclusion and inclusion entirely a matter of law',[73] this process, as mentioned, leads to the danger of *further* exclusion.

III The Duty to Work and Individual Well-Being

As mentioned, the 'citizenship' justification focuses on the relationship between the individual and society. An additional, secondary justification views work itself as a moral endeavour, as a 'normalcy' or normative attitude, even endowing it with reverent religious attributes.[74] Often explicitly paternalistic in nature, policymakers and theorists suggest that work has 'the power to save the soul', and thus can justifiably be enforced.[75] This approach is unabashedly paternalistic, as society

[68] Standing, above n 49, 345.

[69] S Deakin and F Wilkinson, *The Law of the Labour Market: Industrialization, Employment and Legal Evolution* (Oxford, Oxford University Press, 2005) 111.

[70] See, eg, R Walker, 'The Dynamics of Poverty and Social Exclusion' in G Room (ed), *Beyond the Threshold* (Bristol, Policy Press, 1995) 102, 116.

[71] B Barry 'Social exclusion, Social Isolation and the Distribution of Income' in J Hills, J Le Grand and D Piachaud (eds), *Understanding Social Exclusion* (Oxford, Oxford University Press, 2001) 13, 25–26; B Lund, *Understanding State Welfare* (London, Sage, 2002) 206.

[72] N Fraser and L Gordon, 'Civil Citizenship Against Social Citizenship? On the Ideology of Contract Versus Charity' in B van Steenbergen (ed), *The Condition of Citizenship* (London, Sage, 1994) 90.

[73] Shklar, above n 22, 92.

[74] Handler, above n 43, 22.

[75] De Parle, above n 43, 162; D Macarov, *Work and Welfare – The Unholy Alliance* (London, Sage, 1980).

employs an existing mechanism to reach out to groups that suffer from social exclusion, from immoral lifestyles and from poor material conditions.

A The Moral(istic) Justification

This perception views a productive life as one of the important common traits of a decent citizen in a decent society. The claimant is said to possess a different set of moral and cultural values, and his immorality explains his reluctance to accept an offer of work.[76] Contemporary supporters of conditioning benefits on participation in the labour force argue that 'the distribution of welfare is one of the great teaching forces open to advanced societies'.[77] This approach is on a par with the view advocated by Lawrence Mead, the contemporary proponent of a paternalistic approach to welfare. Mead views the poor as 'dutiful but defeated'.[78] Though they are naturally inclined to work, they are exposed to a system that leads to 'the degradation of the character of the labouring class'.[79] For this reason, the system should create incentives to work through conditioning of benefits. Like children, the poor are to be shown the right path. Devoid of the ability to assess their options rationally, they almost demand authority to be imparted upon them.

And yet, since this position has become less fashionable in the twentieth century, we do not find explicit pronouncements as we did in the past. There, we find that the English New Poor Law sought to modify the behaviour of the poor and unemployed by holding them to a strict disciplinary regime within the workhouse, justified on the basis that 'it has been found that the pauperism of the greater number of [able-bodied individuals] *originated in* indolence, improvidence or vice, and might have been averted by ordinary care and industry' (emphasis added).[80] The Poor Law Commissioner's report of 1832–34, which provided the basis for the New Poor Law, described the impact the workhouse has on the pauper. The workhouse is seen as infusing

> new life, new energy into the constitution of the pauper; he is aroused like one from sleep, his relation with all his neighbours, high and low, is changed; he surveys his former employers with new eyes. He begs a job – he will not take a denial.[81]

For those who were previously employed, it seemed even clearer that 'their way of life had been anchored in the discipline of work, and so that discipline had to be restored'. The way to do so was to shift 'from direct relief to work relief'.[82] The

[76] Macarov, above n 75, 124; W Quigley, 'Backwards into the Future' (1998) 9 *Stanford Law & Society Review* 101, 105–06.

[77] F Field, 'A Rejoinder' in A Deacon (ed), *Stakeholder Welfare* (London, IEA, 1996) 107, 111.

[78] L Mead, 'Welfare Employment' in L Mead (ed), *The New Paternalism* (Washington DC, Brookings, 1997) 39; A Deacon, *Perspectives on Welfare* (Buckingham, Open University Press, 2002) 49–63.

[79] The 1824 Select Committee, cited in Deakin and Wilkinson, above n 69, 133.

[80] *Poor Law Report* (1834) 264 cited in D King, *In the Name of Liberalism* (Oxford, Oxford University Press, 1999) 228 (emphasis added).

[81] ibid, 227.

[82] Piven and Cloward, above n 43, 80–81.

idea that destitution may be attributed to personal irresponsibility, a central facet of modern welfare reforms,[83] was employed to justify poor law measures, including the workhouse.[84]

A different form of the paternalistic attitude reverses the chain of causation. Instead of viewing moral decrepitude as the cause of unemployment, it suggests that the socially excluded, the drug users and alcoholics, the disconnected youths and the homeless, all can be made to amend their ways if they are forced to work. A charitable approach would suggest that the motivation for this position lies in the bettering of the condition of those involved. Charles Murray's choice of words is characteristically colourful: 'young males are essentially barbarians for whom marriage – meaning not just the wedding vows – is an indispensable civilizing force. Young men who don't work don't make good marriage material'.[85] Socializing young men into their preordained roles in the workforce and in society has been characterized as the moral notion underlying the 'British New Deal for Young People'.[86]

A more cynical interpretation would view it as concerned more with 'social control and the moral improvement of the lower orders'.[87] Indeed, Frances Fox Piven and Richard Cloward advance an even more troubling thesis, arguing that though social control is a foundational explanation for the institution and expansion of public relief, it is social control driven by fear of revolt.[88]

B The Material Justification – A Right to Work or a Right to Income Support?

In a large part of the discussion above, the focus was on the philosophical and institutional coupling of the duty to work and the right to work.[89] Supplementing the moralistic justification for this coupling is the more intuitive appeal of work – the material benefits that derive from it. However, if that is indeed the case, then the right that corresponds to the duty need not necessarily be the right to work. In its stead, it could be displaced with the right to income support. It may be suggested that, as such, the transformation of a right to work with a right to income support represents a larger trend, whereby rights to particular social goods are replaced with their monetary equivalent. At the very least, it would seem that the right to work manifests a prime case study within this phenomenon.

[83] Mead argues that the 'social contract' entails viewing responsibilities as being on a par with entitlements: L Mead, *Beyond Entitlement* (New York, Free Press, 1986).

[84] S Deakin, 'The Capability Concept and the Evolution of European Social Policy' in M Dougan and E Spaventa (eds), *Social Welfare and EU Law* (Oxford, Hart Publishing, 2005) 3, 8.

[85] C Murray, *The Emerging British Underclass* (London, IEA, 1990) 23.

[86] C Grover and J Stewart, *The Work Connection* (Houndmills, Palgrave, 2002) 96–112.

[87] K Lawes, *Paternalism and Politics* (Basingstoke, Macmillan, 2000) 66.

[88] Piven and Cloward, above n 43, 20–21.

[89] The term 'institutional coupling', used in this context, is Mundlak's, above n 4, 358.

Guy Standing's succinct description of the twentieth century as 'the century of the labouring man' is instructive:

> It began with calls echoing around the world for the rights of labour – the right to improved social status, dignity and autonomy . . . By mid-century . . . reformers were demanding the right to labour, seeking to ennoble the drudgery of being in a job and hinging everything on 'Full Employment' . . . The century is ending with libertarians and many others advocating and introducing policies to strengthen the duty to labour, the state-enforced obligation to obtain entitlements and to be treated as citizens and receive state benefits.[90]

It is thus perhaps possible to expand on this description of the dynamic in the following way: if, in the past, the right to work was understood as correlative to the duty to work, it *is the former, but not the latter, that evaporated.* No right to full employment exists, and the right to be engaged in work (and not only to be paid wages), or to remain in a job against an employer's will, is narrowly upheld, in most countries. The duty to work thus remained as the axis, but against it we now find the right to public assistance.

Indeed, as Bob Hepple explains, 'with us the duty to work corresponds only to a right to social security, and not to a right to work'.[91] He describes how the French Constitution of 1849 replaced the *droit du travail* with *droit a l'assistance*; and how, following the defeat of the English 'Right to Work' Bill of 1907, which was to position the local authority as the employer of last resort, the emphasis shifted to a right to income maintenance.[92]

The shift from 'duty to work as a condition for a right to work' to 'duty to work as a condition for social assistance' became the paradigm for Anglo-American welfare-to-work programmes. Thus, when announcing the new Jobseeker's Allowance policy, the British government stressed the link between the right to benefits and claimants' responsibilities, and stated that the latter would take concrete form in the obligation to take up work.[93] Stuart White identifies the contractual paradigm as the dominant theme in both American and British welfare reform:

> [*A*]*ccess to welfare benefits* is one side of a contract between citizen and community which has its reverse side various responsibilities that the individual citizen is obliged to meet; as a condition of eligibility for welfare benefits, the state may legitimately enforce

[90] Standing, above n 49, 337.

[91] B Hepple, 'A Right to Work?' (1981) 10 *Industrial Law Journal* 65, 70.

[92] ibid, 72. An interesting example of the transformation of the right to (be engaged in) work to the right to its monetary equivalent is observed in cases where workers demand not only to be paid wages, but also to be engaged in work. Subject to certain exceptions, courts have generally ruled that it is the employer's prerogative to pay wages, without providing work. In Britain, the main exception is the case where the parties agreed otherwise: *Langitoa v AUEW* [1974] ICR 180 (CA) 190; in Israel – additional considerations are: proven damages to the worker's earnings (eg, when a significant part of her wages is dependent on bonuses), to her reputation or to her future career – Labor Appeal 51/4-21 *The Histadrut v Water Planning for Israel* (1991). See Hepple, above n 91, 75.

[93] DSS, *A New Contract for Welfare: The Gateway to Work* (Cm 4102, 1998); A Bryson, 'The Jobseeker's Allowance: Help or Hindrance to the Unemployed?' (1995) 24 *Industrial Law Journal* 204.

> these responsibilities, which *centrally include the responsibility to work* (emphasis added).[94]

To what extent can this trend, which correlates monetary benefits with civic duties, be generalized? It is becoming increasingly established that the new welfare-to-work regime represents a 'fundamental change in the balance between rights and obligations in the provision of assistance'.[95] Anthony Giddens is probably the most prominent intellectual who leads the charge for 'a redefinition of rights and responsibilities'. Giddens condemns 'old style democracy' for treating rights as 'unconditional claims' and asserts that 'unemployment benefits should carry the obligation to search for work, for example'.[96] Giddens is sensitive to the allegation that welfare rights have been singled out in this construction, and makes clear that as 'an ethical principle "no rights without responsibilities" must apply not only to welfare recipients, but to everyone . . . otherwise – the precept will be held to apply only to the poor or to the needy'.[97] And yet, it seems less than surprising that Giddens does not offer an example of a civil and political right (to privacy, to pray, to speak) that is also governed by the 'no rights without responsibilities' dictum.

IV Conclusion

This chapter sought to show how rights in general, and the right to work in particular, may collapse, or even be transformed, into a duty. It was suggested that the prevailing theory of rights harbours the seed for such a move, and that contemporary political fashions build on this potential. The main thrust of the combination of theory and politics is that the same justifications for the right to work can be taken to its logical conclusion: if work is indeed important for social inclusion, for moral standing and for economic subsistence, what prevents society from forcefully incentivizing reluctant individuals to participate in the labour market? And should an objection to current policies and ideology concerning the duty to work necessarily negate the importance of both justifications of 'citizenship' and 'individual well-being'? Is it completely untrue that work may be related to social citizenship? That it contributes to material welfare?

Obviously, this is not *necessarily* the case. As explained, labour inclusion can correlate with social exclusion, and some who work improve their material well-being, even dramatically. And yet, the swelling ranks of the working poor serve as evidence to the fact that employment and affluence do not always go hand in

[94] S White, 'Social Rights and the Social Contract' (2000) 30 *British Journal of Political Science* 507.

[95] Fafo Institute for Applied Social Science, *Workfare in Six European Nations* (Oslo, Norwegian Ministry of Health and Social Affairs, 2001) 46 in Handler, above n 43, 144; Also Jones and Novak, above n 48, 143; Mead, *Beyond Entitlement*, above n 83.

[96] A Giddens, *The Third Way* (Cambridge, Polity, 1998) 65.

[97] ibid, 65–66.

hand. Moreover, the empirical response does not stand alone. Social and cultural norms obviously play a role in policies concerning work, welfare and family. Acknowledging this fact, however, does not demand accepting the *prevailing* legal mandates that pertain to these (and other) institutions, as dictated by the state, as justified.[98] In fact, it is under socialist and fascist regimes that law was to ensure the conformity of individuals to state goals, granting social rights under the condition of loyalty and moral desert.[99]

And even if there are good moral reasons for people to work, this does not necessarily entail that a *legal duty* should exist. As Joseph Raz explains:

> Though several moral philosophers use 'ought' and 'duty' interchangeably, many moral views presuppose a distinction between what one ought to do and what it is one's duty to do. The common view is that one ought to do that which one has a duty to do but that one does not always have a duty to do that which one ought.[100]

And it is possible to suggest – at least in the present context – that between 'ought' and 'duty' lies the border of the legal realm. The question, therefore, is whether the moral imperative is so strong that it serves as grounds for a legal duty. And if so, how strong is that legal duty? In other words, apart from the general idea (whether true or not) that society would be better off if individuals participated in the labour market, we should ask if there are justifiable legal ramifications laid on those failing to uphold the duty. At least in this respect, the right to work, and not to work, should play a role in the deliberation.

[98] Deakin, above n 84, 13–15.
[99] Markovits, 'Law or Order', above n 24, 523; Esping-Andersen, above n 35, 40.
[100] J Raz, *The Morality of Freedom* (Oxford, Oxford University Press, 1986) 185.

11

The French Approach to the Right to Work: The Potential of a Constitutional Right in Ordinary Courts

SOPHIE ROBIN-OLIVIER

Introduction

In French law, the right to work as a right to employment, or right to obtain work (*droit d'obtenir un emploi*) is protected by the Constitution. The Preamble to the French Constitution of 1958 refers to the Constitution of 1946, which proclaims: 'everyone has a duty to work, and a right to employment'.[1] However, the legal force of this constitutional reference is not obvious at first glance. Certainly, it requires, and justifies, employment policies on the part of the government, but it will come as no surprise that French constitutional law does not give unemployed persons an individual right to obtain work, as opposed to the right to employment that was granted by decree in 1848, or more recently, to the subjective right to housing, introduced by an Act of 2007.[2] In line with French liberal tradition, the right to work is faced with resistance to the idea that the government, or private employers, could be bound by an enforceable duty to provide employment. This does not mean that the right to work cannot be invoked by individuals against the state or even in private relations: there is no absolute rejection in French law of the horizontal effect of constitutional rights,[3] as long as this does not imply setting aside a statute (judicial review is the monopoly of the *Conseil constitutionnel* (hereafter Constitutional Council)[4] to which statutes must be

[1] Fifth paragraph of the Preamble: 'Chacun a le devoir de travailler et le droit d'obtenir un emploi'.

[2] Law no 2007-290, 5 March 2007.

[3] For an illustration, see below, the developments on freedom to work.

[4] The Constitutional Council was established by the Constitution of the Fifth Republic adopted on 4 October 1958. It is a court vested with various powers, including in particular the review of the constitutionality of legislation. The Constitutional Council is not a supreme court that is hierarchically superior to the Conseil d'État or the Cour de cassation. For more information on this court, see: Conseil constitutionnel, 'General presentation', available at: www.conseil-constitutionnel.fr/conseil-constitutionnel/english/presentation/general-presentation/general-presentation.25739.html.

referred for review, under rather strict conditions). The obstacle concerns the content of the right, and not the legal force of the constitutional provision.

Having pointed out this limit, one must also note, from the outset, that the inclusion of the reference to a 'right to obtain work' in the Constitution of 1946, along with the constitutionalisation of other social rights considered essential to the development of the welfare state, has proved to be more than purely formal recognition. The French version of the right to work is not deprived of any influence on the legal system, although this influence is strictly circumscribed because it has to be reconciled with other constitutional objectives, rights or principles[5]. A sign of the living nature of the French constitutional right to work, that right is regularly invoked in courts. For instance, in a very recent case concerning prison work, in which the refusal to consider that prisoners were engaged in labour contracts was challenged as unconstitutional, claimants referred to the 'right to obtain employment', together with other constitutional provisions.[6] This does not mean, of course, that the right to obtain employment, mentioned in the French Constitution, is very powerful, as this decision and many others show. But it does not seem irrelevant to rely on that right and expect that it will have *some* impact.

By contrast, 'freedom to work' is more efficiently protected under French law, especially in employment relationships. As a fundamental freedom protecting individuals against government's power, or any other exercise of power that would encroach upon it, freedom to work has led to a series of important developments in labour and employment law. Negatively, freedom to work justifies, for instance, actions against workers occupying the employer's premises during a strike, when this occupation prevents access to non-strikers.[7] Positively, it implies that workers must be free to resign, or challenge clauses of their work contracts (non-competition or exclusivity clauses, in particular) for the reason that they restrict individual freedom.[8]

Indeed, freedom to work, just as the 'freedom to choose an occupation and right to engage in work' mentioned in Article 15 of the Charter of Fundamental Rights of the European Union, belongs to the category of classic civil rights, derived from individual freedom (*droits-libertés*, in French), and meant to protect individuals against restrictions that could stem from state power. In turn, the right to work fits in the group of 'social rights' (*droits-créances*), a 'second generation' of human rights.[9] But there is a substantial connection between the freedom and the right to work. The former is often considered a dimension of the latter: to

[5] On the notion of constitutional objective, as compared with constitutional rights or principles, see F Luchaire, 'Brèves remarques sur une création du Conseil constitutionnel: l'objectif de valeur constitutionnelle' (2005) 64 *Revue française de Droit Constitutionnel* 675.

[6] Conseil constitutionnel, DC 2013-320/321 QPC, 14 June 2013.

[7] See for instance, Cour de cassation, Chambre sociale, 21 June 1984, no 82-16596, deciding that expulsion of strikers is justified, when occupation of the company's premises violates freedom to work and the right to free enterprise.

[8] On this aspect of freedom to work, see below.

[9] In the French Constitution, civil and political rights are, for the largest part, contained in the Declaration of the Rights of Man and the Citizen of 1789, whereas social rights are mentioned in the Preamble of the Constitution of 1946 (which is also part of French constitutional law).

ensure free access to work can be considered a way to contribute to the individual right to work. As a matter of fact, the language used by French courts does not always distinguish clearly between the two.

Considering developments that took place in French courts, the aim of this contribution is to compare, and contrast, the limited impact of the right to work, as a social right, when invoked for the purpose of judicial review, to the role of this right in ordinary courts, where freedom to work is efficiently protected and where fundamental rights have been actively enforced in recent times.

I The Right to Work in Judicial Review – A Limited Impact

Circumscribing the legal nature and force of the right to work, mentioned in the Preamble of the Constitution of 1946 is not an easy enterprise. Only since 1971[10] has the Constitutional Council made it clear that the Preamble of the 1946 Constitution belonged to the set of constitutional references to be considered in judicial review proceedings. But this recognition did not solve all the issues concerning the legal status of the right to work under the French Constitution. Was it only an objective to be taken into account by the legislator, or a constitutional right deserving the same consideration as, for instance, freedom of expression or the principle of equality? The exact normative value of that 'reference' remained unclear. A few years ago, the Constitutional Council affirmed that the right to work, cited in the Preamble of the Constitution of 1946, belonged to the category of 'rights and liberties' that the French Constitution guarantees.[11] However, this elevation to the status of a constitutional right did not induce substantial changes in the law: deference to legislative choices remained unchanged and, confronted with the right to free enterprise, whose status as right is not contested, the right to work continued to lose much of its force.

A Judicial Deference to Legislative Choices

There is no doubt that the authors of the Constitution of 1946 had no intention of recognising a right to employment for the unemployed or, more generally, of giving the right to work a strong legal value. On the contrary, the whole catalogue of social and economic rights contained in the Preamble, presented as 'social principles particularly necessary for our time', was explicitly excluded from the field of binding constitutional rights. Since then, however, things have evolved: when the

[10] Conseil constitutionnel, DC 71-44, 16 July 1971 (freedom of association).

[11] Conseil constitutionnel, DC 2010-98 QPC, 4 February 2011 (compulsory retirement) and DC 2011-139 QPC, 24 June 2011 (conditions required for the exercise of a professional activity).

Preamble started to serve as a ground for judicial review in 1971, it became possible for the Constitutional Council to consider the right to work, when assessing the constitutionality of legislative acts. In 1983, in its first decision concerning that right, the Constitutional Council ruled that it was up to the legislator to adopt the rules ensuring, as much as possible, the individual right to employment.[12] In that case, it was decided that the right to employment could justify the introduction of a tax applied to those cumulating wages and old-age benefits.[13] This approach already indicated not only that the right to work could play an effective role as a justification for government actions, but also that implementing measures to achieve that right were to be left in the hands of the legislator.

Since that first decision, judicial deference to the legislator has characterised the case law of the Constitutional Council concerning the right to work. For the Constitutional Council, the legislator is competent to decide on the appropriate rules ensuring that the right to employment is guaranteed to everyone, while at the same time 'ensuring the exercise of that right for the largest number'.[14] Since 1983, that language has been reproduced in a number of cases concerning the right to work. In a decision of 2007, for instance, a statute meant to foster the use of supplementary hours through reduced taxes was challenged, for the reason that promoting overtime would restrict the number of new workers being hired.[15] The Constitutional Council repeated that 'the right to work only requires that the legislator adopts proper rules to ensure that everyone has a right to employment, taking into account that the exercise of this right should be possible for as many people as possible'.[16] Considering the history of the Act concerned, the Constitutional Council decided that the contested measure aimed at increasing growth and employment through greater flexibility of working time, and thus aimed at enforcing the right to work mentioned in the Preamble of the Constitution. As a result, no violation of that right could be found.

These decisions are focusing on the collective dimension of the right to employment: that right is not guaranteed to individuals, but the legislator must strive to ensure full employment globally, through policies aimed at increasing employment. Since the success or failure of these policies, and the economic theories supporting them, are not assessed by the Constitutional Council, the review can only consist of a limited control to ensure that the measures at stake are not manifestly inappropriate to reach the aim pursued. Indeed, in its decision of 2007,[17] the Constitutional Council pointed out that it did not have 'a general discretion and decision power of the same nature as that of Parliament' and, for that reason,

[12] 'Il lui appartient de poser les règles propres à assurer au mieux le droit pour chacun d'obtenir un emploi en vue de permettre l'exercice de ce droit au plus grand nombre possible d'intéressés'. (It is for the legislator to adopt rules ensuring, as best as possible, the right for everyone to obtain a job in order to allow the exercise of this right to the greatest possible number of persons)

[13] Conseil constitutionnel, DC 83-156, 28 May 1983 (pensions, 'solidarity' contribution).

[14] ibid.

[15] Conseil constitutionnel, DC 2007-555, 16 August 2007.

[16] ibid.

[17] ibid.

was not entitled to investigate alternative means of reaching the objective pursued by the legislator, as long as the measure chosen was not obviously inappropriate for reaching that objective.

In some cases, the superficial scrutiny applied by the Constitutional Council reaches a particularly high level. For instance, when the very controversial statute creating a specific work contract for younger workers was challenged in 2006,[18] the argument that allowing dismissal without cause during the first two years of employment was violating the right to work was simply brushed away. For the Constitutional Council, the law aimed precisely at enforcing the right to work (through increased flexibility), and it did so in a manner which was not obviously inappropriate. That was enough to save the statute from a finding of unconstitutionality.

More recently, in a decision concerning the automatic dismissal of employees reaching the statutory pensionable age,[19] the Constitutional Council decided that 'the measure was founded on objective and rational criteria, directly connected with the aim of the Act contested, and, thus, has not violated the right to work of the preamble of the Constitution of 1946'. Such reasoning is in line with the approach followed by the Court of Justice of the European Union. In a case in which compulsory retirement of civil servants at pensionable age was challenged, the Court pointed out that the prohibition of discrimination on grounds of age set out in Directive 2000/78 must be read in the light of the right to engage in work recognised in Article 15(1) of the Charter of Fundamental Rights of the European Union.[20] However, this only required, according to European judges, that 'particular attention . . . be paid to the participation of older workers in the labour force and thus in economic, cultural and social life': no strict scrutiny was applied, to say the least.

The reasoning was also particularly thin, leaving vast discretion to the government, in a decision of the Constitutional Council of 2011 concerning the conditions (professional title) required for the exercise of certain economic activities (crafts).[21] The Constitutional Council recalled that the legislator is in charge of working out both the fundamental principles of labour law and the appropriate rules to ensure 'the right for everyone to employment'. It continued with this brief statement: 'considering that the requirement of a professional title for the exercise of certain activities does not, as such, affect the right to employment'.

This rapid survey of the case law of the Constitutional Council shows that, notwithstanding slight variations from case to case, the margin of discretion left to the legislator is always extensive. In US terminology, the test would probably be called a 'rational basis' one and, in the European language, that approach could be described as a refusal of the Constitutional Council to engage in a 'strict proportionality' test. The deference to legislative power shown by the Constitutional

[18] Conseil constitutionnel, DC 2006-535, 30 March 2006.

[19] Conseil constitutionnel, DC 2010-98 QPC, above n 11.

[20] Joined Cases C-159/10 and 160/10 *Fuchs and Köhler v Land Hessen* [2011] ECR I-06919.

[21] Conseil constitutionnel, DC 2011-139 QPC, above n 11.

Council immunises, for better or for worse, social policies resulting from collective choices against claims based on the individual right to work that could force reconsideration. The social principle mentioned at the fifth paragraph of the Preamble to the Constitution of 1946 serves as a justification for public policies, which must strive to ensure full employment at a collective level, but are neither constitutionally required to succeed (there is no golden rule in that respect) nor strictly scrutinised in case of challenges based on the right to work.

B The Confrontation of the Right to Work with the Right to Free Enterprise

According to the Constitutional Council, the legislator must, when implementing the social and economic principles mentioned by the Preamble of the Constitution of 1946, combine them with freedoms guaranteed by the Constitution.[22] When the right to work is concerned, this means in most cases that it has to be reconciled with the right to free enterprise. On the one hand, the Constitutional Council has recognised that the legislator is entitled to introduce limitations to the right to free enterprise when taking measures to achieve, to the extent that this is possible, the right to employment (considered a 'constitutional requirement'), as long as the restriction is not disproportionate, in consideration of the objective pursued by the contested statute.[23] On the other hand, the right to work does not allow measures that would excessively encroach upon the right to free enterprise.

In the last decade, the balancing test, in which the right to free enterprise is weighed up against the right to work, was applied in a number of cases concerning workers' protection against dismissal. In a much debated case,[24] the Constitutional Council overturned a statute restricting the possibility of companies relying on economic reasons to justify collective redundancies. In that case, the Council decided that the Act did not achieve a proper balance between the right to employment and the right to free enterprise. According to the Constitutional Council, the right to free enterprise was excessively affected by the new Act. As compared with the many cases mentioned above, the Constitutional Council, for once, resisted the decision made by Parliament to limit collective redundancies. As a result, the decision reached by the legislator could not enter in force.

In a decision of 2005,[25] the right to work was invoked against a statute limiting the right to reassignment of workers, when the employer failed to elaborate a social plan in order to limit dismissals. The Constitutional Council considered that, by limiting cases of reinstatement, the legislator adequately reconciled the right to work and the right to free enterprise. In the absence of a manifest error of

[22] Conseil constitutionnel, DC 2001-455, 12 January 2002 (*loi de modernisation sociale*).
[23] ibid.
[24] ibid.
[25] Conseil constitutionnel, DC 2004-509, 13 January 2005.

appreciation, the balance achieved by the statute had to be respected. That decision failed to explain, let alone justify, the connection between employees' reinstatement and the right to free enterprise. However, the decision is important: for the first time, protections against dismissal granted to workers were linked with the constitutional right to work. In that particular case, the Constitutional Council considered that the right to be reassigned to another position in the company, in case such possibility exists, is directly derived from the right to work. Thus, the right to work seemed to have become more concrete than a vague constitutional objective, abandoned in the hands of the legislator. But neither in that particular case nor in the subsequent case law, has this concretisation of the right to work led to a much stronger protection of workers' rights, in cases of conflict with the right to free enterprise.

The most recent case in this field concerned, once again, collective redundancies.[26] The claimants challenged the provision of the law reserving to workers with a seniority of at least two years the possibility of having their dismissal annulled, and of being reinstated, once an annulment order had been granted. The Constitutional Council decided that this condition respected the need to reconcile the right to work and the right to free enterprise, and considered that the choice made by the legislator was not obviously unbalanced (*manifestement déséquilibré*). No violation of the Constitution was found. As this recent decision makes clear, the right to work, although mentioned in the Constitution and considered a basis for judicial review, has not proved very efficient in challenging legislative provisions. In all cases in which the Constitutional Council exercised judicial review based on the constitutional right to work, it always rejected the claim, considering that no violation of that right could be found.

II The Right to Work in Ordinary Courts – Beyond the Protection of Freedom to Work?

In French ordinary courts, the right to work has proved more powerful when construed as a freedom to work, than as a social right for workers allowing them, for instance, to request protection against dismissal or other measures leading, directly or indirectly, to the termination of work contracts. However, the recognition of direct effect for the right to housing in administrative courts, resulting from enforcement of international labour law, opens a new path for the protection of fundamental social rights in French courts. Whether it can lead to an evolution in the protection of the social right to work will be explored, in order to assess whether the right to work could reach beyond freedom to work.

[26] Conseil constitutionnel, DC 2012-231/234, 13 April 2012.

A The Effective Protection of Workers' Freedom to Work

Since the 1990s, the freedom to work has been successfully invoked against certain clauses contained in work contracts. In particular, judges decided that the effects of non-competition or exclusivity clauses had to be limited, in order to avoid excessive restriction on the freedom to work. As far as non-competition clauses are concerned, the landmark cases were decided in 1992 and 2002. In 1992, the French highest courts for civil matters (Cour de cassation) decided that non-competition clauses had to respect a series of conditions: they must be necessary to protect the interests of the company, limited in time and space and have to take into account the employee's specific skills, in order not to prevent access to employment.[27] In 2002, the Court referred, more broadly, to the 'fundamental principle of free exercise of a professional activity', and required, for a non-competition clause to be valid, that financial compensation be paid to the employee, in addition to the three conditions previously mentioned.[28] A similar approach was applied to exclusivity clauses, which compel workers to work exclusively for one employer. In cases concerning commercial agents, employed part-time but committed to exclusivity, judges, drawing inspiration from the case law regarding non-competition clauses, decided that such exclusivity clauses were only legal under three conditions: the clause must be necessary to protect the legitimate interests of the company; justified in consideration of the tasks accomplished by the employee; and proportionate to the aim pursued.[29] Freedom to work has also been successfully invoked in the case of a bonus that had to be repaid to the employer in case the worker resigned within a period of six months: this condition violated workers' freedom to work, according to French judges.[30]

In these circumstances, workers' individual liberty is protected, and market freedoms benefit employees rather than employers. Workers are protected as participants in the labour market, and employers are barred from restricting competition in such manner that they infringe the workers' freedom. Decisions are intended to achieve an acceptable balance between companies' interests in restricting competition and workers' market freedom.

The relative strength of freedom to work, when invoked in civil courts in the field of labour law may also explain why it was recently invoked against the prohibition of Sunday work.[31] The Cour de cassation was asked to refer to the Constitutional Council a question on the constitutionality of that prohibition. The Court refused to raise the question with the Constitutional Council, but

[27] Cour de cassation, Chambre sociale, 14 May 1992, Bull civ V, no 309.
[28] Cour de cassation, Chambre sociale, 10 July 2002, Bull civ V, no 239.
[29] Cour de cassation, Chambre sociale, 11 July 2000, no 98-43240.
[30] Cour de cassation, Chambre sociale, 18 April 2000, no 97-44235.
[31] Cour de cassation, Chambre sociale, 12 January 2011, no 10-40055.

mentioned that the law was not inconsistent with the right to work or the freedom to work, as it was pursuing legitimate objectives having the same constitutional value as the right to work (protection of health and safety of workers, and protection of family relations).[32] As opposed to non-competition clauses, freedom to work was balanced, in that case, not with the interests of private corporations (which were not threatened) but with general interests, including workers' collective interests, which are also secured by the Constitution. Therefore, to reject a claim based on the freedom to work, the Court refers to social principles protected in the Constitution. This already suggests that there can be an impact in ordinary courts of the 'social' right to work, a social principle that can be compared to the protection of the health and safety of workers or family relations: it may be used to shield a statute from judicial review.

B Towards Protection of the Social Right to Work in Ordinary Courts?

There is no decision of either of the two French superior courts (the Cour de cassation, for civil matters, and the Conseil d'Etat, for administrative matters) in which workers have successfully invoked the right to work in order to obtain protection against dismissal, or indeed against any other measure that may lead to termination of work contracts (deportation, for instance). The limits to the right to work as a right to employment were well illustrated in a case decided in 2010 by the Cour de cassation.[33] An employee claimed reinstatement after having been dismissed without cause. French law does not provide such a remedy, unless the employer agrees to reinstatement. In that particular case, the employee argued that such solutions violated his right to work, considering his seniority (27 years in the company) and the fact that he had not managed to find another job since he was dismissed five years earlier. The Court did not grant reinstatement, considering that the right to work needed to be reconciled with the right to free enterprise. In assessing whether a proper balance was struck between the two rights, the Court did not apply a high level of scrutiny. Undoubtedly, the sole existence of a balancing test is a slight opening towards giving some efficiency to the right to work. But the case law developed by the Constitutional Council, mentioned above, does not allow for excessive optimism in this respect.

Another aspect of the 2010 decision deserves attention. Indeed, that decision is not only based on the principle that a proper balance must be achieved between the right to work and the right to free enterprise, it is also grounded on the International Covenant on Economic, Social and Cultural Rights of 1966. To make its decision, the Court examined whether French law contained any

[32] ibid.

[33] Cour de cassation, Chambre sociale, 14 April 2010, no 08-45247.

restriction on the right to work, laid down by Article 6(1)f that Convention.[34] Such consideration given to international law, in the field of labour law, is one of the most important and interesting evolutions of recent French case law.[35] Even in a monist system such as French law, it is neither trivial nor easy for ordinary courts to rely on international law, especially in private relations. The issue of direct effect of the norms at stake, and the problems with the interpretation of international conventions, stand in the way, and judges are not always keen to set aside national law or overrule previous interpretations of that law to give force to international conventions. In recent years though, International Labour Organization (ILO) conventions, the European Convention for the Protection of Human Rights, the European Social Charter or the Charter of Fundamental Rights of the European Union have been used, and sometimes combined, in a number of important cases.[36] Indeed, more often than before, French labour law is contested for the reason that it violates international law. For instance, when a recent reform[37] limited the capacity of trade unions to represent workers in the organisation receiving at least 10 per cent of the votes cast (at company level), that condition was challenged on the ground that it was inconsistent with the fundamental right to form and join trade unions for the protection of workers' interests protected by international labour law.[38] As far as the right to work is concerned, French judges have made use of Article 6 of the International Covenant on Economic, Social and Cultural Rights in order to set aside a provision of the law denying the benefit of a financial compensation for workers submitted to a non-competition clause.[39]

In the case law of the Conseil d'Etat, reference to international law has a particular role: administrative judges consider that some constitutional references are too imprecise to be enforced, but can be granted direct effect if they are clarified by a statute or by the provisions of an international agreement that have been incorporated into French law. This applies to the right to work. In two of the rare

[34] According to that Article:

'1. The States Parties to the present Covenant recognise the right to work, which includes the right of everyone to the opportunity to gain his living by work which he freely chooses or accepts, and will take appropriate steps to safeguard this right.
2. The steps to be taken by a State Party to the present Covenant to achieve the full realisation of this right shall include technical and vocational guidance and training programmes, policies and techniques to achieve steady economic, social and cultural development and full and productive employment under conditions safeguarding fundamental political and economic freedoms to the individual'.

[35] On the impact of international labour law on French labour law cases, see S Robin-Olivier, 'European Legal Method from a French Perspective. The Magic of Combination: Uses and Abuses of the Globalization of Sources by European Courts' in U Neergaard, R Nielsen and L Roseberry (eds), *European Legal Method: Synthesis or Fragmentation* ? (Copenhagen, DJØF Publishing, 2011) 307.

[36] *cf* Cour de cassation, Chambre sociale, 1 July 2008, no 07-44124 (applying directly ILO Convention 158 to set aside a French statute establishing a '*contrat nouvelles embauches*', allowing dismissal at will during the first two years of employment).

[37] Law no 2008-789, 20 August 2008.

[38] Cour de cassation, Chambre sociale, 14 April 2010, no 09-60426.

[39] Cour de cassation, Chambre sociale, 16 December 2008, no 05-40876.

cases in which that right was invoked before the Conseil d'Etat, judges decided that the right to work was not sufficiently precise to be enforced, and needed to be made more concrete by legislative acts or international conventions. One of the decisions concerned the transfer of a member of the military to another position, which forced him to move his residence.[40] In the other, the right to work was used as an argument to challenge a deportation measure against an illegal immigrant.[41] Undoubtedly, as both claims failed, the first conclusion that can be drawn from the case law of the administrative court is that the efficiency of the right to work is limited, if not inexistent, for the moment. But the Conseil d'Etat has also made clear that, if precision could be found in international law, the right to work might become effective.[42]

Such an evolution, derived from international law, was achieved in a recent case concerning the right to housing. In April 2012, the Conseil d'Etat decided that a measure excluding some categories of migrants from the right to housing was illegal because it violated Convention 97 of the ILO concerning migrant workers, which requires equal treatment in matters of accommodation (Article 6).[43] Although referring to international law is not unusual for the administrative court, the case is important, not only because it calls into question choices made by the legislator in the field of social policy in order to enforce an international convention, but also, and mostly, because it determines the conditions of direct effect of these conventions. Direct effect is recognised when, in the light of the intentions expressed by the parties, the system of the treaty, and the language and content of the norms concerned, these norms do not aim exclusively at ruling relationships between states and do not require further Acts or measures to produce effects on individuals. Provisions of a treaty cannot, the administrative court adds, be deprived of such effects only because they mention that states are bound by the obligations they contain.[44]

Transposing this solution to the right to work, one could argue that, provided the conditions for direct effect are fulfilled, international law could support a more efficient interpretation of that right in French courts. The problem, as far as the right to work is concerned, is to find instruments of international law having direct effect, and allowing an evolutive interpretation of that right.

Article 6 of the International Covenant on Economic, Social and Cultural Rights of 1966 recognising 'the right of everyone to the opportunity to gain his living by work which he freely chooses or accepts', which was considered in the decision made by the Cour de cassation in 2010,[45] is not deprived of any direct effect. But whether this language allows an interpretation of the right to work, reaching beyond the protection of workers' freedom to work is uncertain. As

40 Conseil d'Etat, 13 March 2009, no 319916.
41 Conseil d'Etat, 28 December 2005, no 274204.
42 See for instance, Conseil d'Etat, 13 March 2009, above, n 40.
43 Conseil d'Etat, 11 April 2012, no 322326.
44 ibid.
45 Cour de cassation, 14 April 2010, above n 38.

compared, the European Social Charter recognises not only that 'everyone shall have the opportunity to earn his living in an occupation freely entered upon',[46] but also that the right to work requires the parties to the Charter

> to accept as one of their primary aims and responsibilities the achievement and maintenance of as high and stable a level of employment as possible, with a view to the attainment of full employment; to protect effectively the right of the worker to earn his living in an occupation freely entered upon; to establish or maintain free employment services for all workers; to provide or promote appropriate vocational guidance, training and rehabilitation.[47]

Of course, the text is not very different from Article 6 of the 1966 Covenant, but it includes the right to free employment services (also protected under Article 29 of the Charter of Fundamental Rights of the European Union), which could be a basis for actions in French courts, in case these services became too indigent, or if, for instance, equal treatment of all workers, notwithstanding their geographical situation, was not ensured.[48]

Less certain is the potential incidence of the obligation for states to 'protect effectively the right of the worker to earn his living in an occupation freely entered upon'. As compared to the International Covenant of 1966, the Social Charter protects a right for the worker to gain his living, and not only the right to an opportunity to do so. But it is doubtful whether this slightly more demanding language achieves the necessary 'clarification' that administrative case law requires, in order for the right to work to become enforceable. In addition, whether the different provisions of the Social Charter have direct effect remains an open question. In French administrative case law, direct effect of the Social Charter has been rejected in most cases,[49] and the criteria laid down in the decision of 2012[50] do not clearly impose another approach. In private law cases, some decisions have taken the Social Charter into account, when it was invoked together with other international conventions,[51] but doubt remains concerning its direct effect.[52] As a result, the potential of international labour law to transform the French conception of the right to work seems, for now, rather uncertain.

[46] Part I, point 1.

[47] European Social Charter, Part II.

[48] Such inequalities were documented, and denounced, in a recent study: J Baruch, J-B Chastand and A Léchenet, 'La grande inégalité des chômeurs face à Pôle emploi' *Le Monde* (21 September 2013) available at: www.lemonde.fr/emploi/article/2013/09/21/pole-emploi-des-moyens-tres-mal-repartis_3482198_1698637.html.

[49] See: Conseil d'Etat, 23 December 2010, no 335738 (Arts 11 and 13 do not have direct effect); Conseil d'Etat, 19 March 2010, no 31723; and Conseil d'Etat, 2 October 2009, no 301014 (same solution concerning Art 4); Conseil d'Etat, 7 June 2006, no 285576 (same solution concerning Arts 11, 12, 13 and 17); Conseil d'Etat, 15 May 1995, no 152417 (no direct effect of Arts 11 and 12). cp Conseil d'Etat, 25 July 2007, no 292730, recognising that some provisions of the Social Charter could have direct effect.

[50] Conseil d'Etat, 11 April 2012, above, n 43.

[51] See, eg, Cour de cassation, Chambre sociale, 15 May 2013, no 12-18860.

[52] To circumvent the issue of direct effect, judges prefer citing, as an authority, Art 151 of the Treaty on the Functioning of the EU, which refers to the Social Charter. For an illustration of this method see, eg, Cour de cassation, Chambre sociale, 24 April 2013, no 11-28398.

III Conclusion

Although the right to work is constitutionally protected in French law, its impact in courts remains limited. When invoked before the Constitutional Council for the purpose of judicial review, the right to work, as a social right, does not imply any strict scrutiny test, and deference to legislative choices is observed in most instances. In addition, the active protection of the right to free enterprise constitutes a major limitation. Indeed, if the Constitutional Council admits that the legislator is entitled to introduce limitations to the right to free enterprise in order to achieve, as best as it can, the right to employment, the balancing test also implies that protecting the right to work must not lead to excessive infringement of the right to free enterprise. As a result, the legislator has not been allowed, in particular, to introduce limits to collective redundancies that were considered too strict to be reconciled with the right to free enterprise.

In ordinary courts, the right to work is efficiently protected when construed as freedom to work. As such, it has been successfully invoked against clauses contained in work contracts limiting workers' individual liberty and economic freedoms. By contrast, no claim in which workers invoked the right to work in order to obtain protection against dismissal, or any other measure that may lead to termination of work contracts, such as deportation, has been successful. Considering the impact of international labour law in French courts, relying on international conventions to buttress the effects of the right to work protected under French law, is not totally unrealistic today. However, doubts concerning the direct effect of international norms protecting the right to work suggest that such evolution, if not impossible, is far from certain.

12

The Development of Right to Work Theories of Labour Law in Japan: A Comparative Perspective

KENJI ARITA

Introduction

Article 27, paragraph 1 of the Constitution of Japan states that, 'all people shall have the right to work and obligation to work'. Under this provision the government and the Parliament have enacted many statutes in order to secure 'the right to work' for people in Japan. When the drastic changes wrought by the legislation coincided with changes in the labour market, great debates on the right to work developed.[1]

As structural changes in the labour market caused by globalisation of the economy and changes in demographic structure continue, the government has developed labour market policies, which promote the function of the labour market as a 'market'. The government and the Parliament of Japan have also developed labour legislation, which supports the above labour market policies. How do we evaluate those policies and legislation? And how do we fix their future course? These questions constitute a very important theme in labour law today in Japan.

The development of 'right to work theories' of labour law seems to be a clue towards answering these questions. The aim of this chapter is to restructure the import of the right to work to labour law, through a comparative investigation of the theories of the right to work in labour law in Japan, some other countries and the United Nations.

[1] See A Nomura, 'Rodoken Ron' ('The Theories of the Right to Work') in T Momii (ed), *Rodoho Gakusetsu Shi* (*The Histories of the Theories of Labour Law*) (Tokyo, Rodo Junposha, 1996) 594.

I Development of Right to Work Theories of Labour Law in Japan

A The Theory of the Right to Work as a Constitutional Right

i The Theory of the Right to Work as a Programmatic Provision of the Constitution

Japanese academic labour lawyers have started to develop a theory of the right to work relating to its constitutional effects. Ishii has maintained that the right to work protected in Article 27, paragraph 1 of the Constitution of Japan is a declaration of the state's 'political obligation', and that it is a 'programmatic provision'.[2] This opinion, referring to German theories on the right to work, states that there are two concepts of the right to work. The first is the 'complete concept of the right to work', which means that a person who has an intent and capability to work, has a right to claim to be provided a chance to work in the society where he or she belongs. The second is the 'incomplete concept of the right to work', which means that a person who has an intent and capability to work, when he or she cannot get a chance to work in the private sector, has a right against the state to claim to be provided with a chance to work, and when he or she cannot do so, has a right to claim moderate living expenses from the state. According to this opinion, Article 27, paragraph 1 of the Constitution of Japan is composed of the second incomplete concept of the right to work, since it is difficult to see it as a concrete right to claim to be provided with a chance to work against the state, because of the lack of the provisions to realise it. So Article 27, paragraph 1 is a programmatic provision, which declares the right to work as a political responsibility of the state.

The theory of the right to work as a programmatic provision of the Constitution, which interprets the constitutional effect of the right to work as a political responsibility of the state, recognises that (1) if the state takes action which prevents anyone from realising the right to work in contravention of the responsibility to strive to realise the right to work, the legislation shall be void and the action taken by the state shall be illegal; (2) a contract between the individuals or action in an organisation that has the effect of causing an aggressive infringement of the right to work shall be interpreted to be void; and (3) as far as it recognises that an aggressive infringement of the right to work shall be interpreted to be void, the right to work establishes the new 'public policy'.[3] But the theory of the right to work as a programmatic provision of the Constitution insists that it is difficult to restrict employers' freedom of dismissal on the ground of the right to work, as a

[2] T Ishii, *Rodo Kihonken* (*Fundamental Rights of Labour*) (Tokyo, Yushindo, 1957, first published 1948) 45.

[3] T Ishii, *Rodoho Soron Zohoban* (*The General Remarks of Labour Law: An Enlarged Edition*) (Tokyo, Yuhikaku, 1957) 288–301.

matter of legal theory, since the right to work is secured between the people and the state.[4]

As far as the relationship between individuals and the state goes, this understanding of the right to work as a programmatic provision seems to be shared among Japanese academic labour lawyers.[5] In particular, it is understood that the right to work as a provision in the Constitution of Japan does not give individuals the concrete right to claim against the state, but requires the state not to interfere with the ability to work of individuals, and also requires the state to take such steps as necessary to realise the right to work. The state therefore has two obligations. The first is a duty to intervene in labour markets so as to enable people (workers) to obtain employment consistent with their occupational abilities. The second is to guarantee the livelihood of those people (workers) who do not have an opportunity to obtain such employment.[6]

But, as we will see in the next section, regarding the issue of whether or not the right to work can require employers to do something as a norm of the Constitution, which would differ from the theory of the right to work as a programmatic provision because that denies any horizontal effect of the right to work on employers, shortly after the Second World War there has been a theory of the right to work which affirms its horizontal effect.

ii The Theories of the Right to Work in a State of Working

In contrast to the theory of the right to work as a programmatic provision, Numata proposed the theory of the right to work in a state of working.[7] Although he recognised that, in principle, the right to work provided in Article 27, paragraph 1 of the Constitution of Japan was the above incomplete concept of the right to work, he did not think that only the unemployed could assert politically the right to work, because the right to work should not only apply in the context of unemployment, but should also apply to people in a state of doing work. According to this view, the reason why the right to work in a state of doing work should be recognised is not only that it is supported by dominant norm consciousness, but also that the Constitution of Japan itself in its Article 27, paragraph 2 provides that '[s]tandards for wages, hours, rest and other working conditions shall be fixed by legislation'. So, the right to work should be understood in a way that secures lives worthy of human beings (right to life) through maintaining jobs worthy of human beings (right to work) and by being primarily embodied in protective labour law.

[4] ibid, 302.

[5] S Nishitani, *Jinken Toshiteno* (*Decent Work as a Human Right*) (Tokyo, Junposha, 2011) 44.

[6] K Sugeno, *Japanese Employment and Labor Law*, trans L Kanowitz (Durham NC, Carolina Academic Press, 2002) 16. In one case, the Osaka High Court expressed the same opinion (23 January 1963) 14 Gyosyu 131.

[7] I Numata, 'Danketsuken Yogoron Jo' ('Theories of Defending the Right to Organise') in I Numata, *Numata Inajiro Chosakusyu* (*Collection of Inajiro Numata's Works*) Vol 7 (Tokyo, Rodo Junposha, 1976, first published 1948) 23–24.

Some scholars today ascribe to the above theory of the right to work in a state of doing work. Satoshi Nishitani argues that employers are required to endeavour not to make workers whom they employ leave their employment, because employers should be required to cooperate in the realisation of the right to work, from the viewpoint of the idea of a right to work which seeks to secure opportunities of employment for workers and jobseekers as much as possible.[8] Hajime Wada argues that, since working itself brings a worker the realisation of a personal interest, it is a constitutional value not to become unemployed rather than merely a guarantee of the livelihood of the unemployed, so that the regulation of dismissal is based on the right to work.[9] Furthermore, Nishitani argues that, since Article 27, paragraph 1 of the Constitution guarantees the right to work on the basis of viewing it not as a means of livelihood but as one which has a value in itself, the worker's right to obtain and to keep a job against the employer is based on the right to work.[10]

Thus, whether the effect of the right to work provided in Article 27, paragraph 1 should be understood in a narrow way, ie, as only existing between the state and the people, or in a broader way, for example as a normative basis of the regulation of dismissal since it can require the employer to do something as a constitutional norm, is an important point of disagreement.

B The Theory of the Right to Work as a Theory of a System of Labour Law

A different theory of the right to work from the viewpoint of the effect of Article 27, paragraph 1 of the Constitution of Japan emerged from theories of a 'system' of labour law. Seisho argues for a theory of the right to work as a right to security of employment and a right to fair standards at work.[11]

According to this view, since labour law should be conceptualised as a system of rights, it should be systematised in line with the structure of workers' fundamental rights, which provide the basis of labour law. The workers' fundamental rights consist in the right to organise in a broad sense and the right to work. And

[8] Nishitani, *Jinken Toshiteno*, above n 5, 44.

[9] H Wada, *Jinken Hosyo to Rodoho* (*Securing Human Rights and Labour law*) (Tokyo, Nihonhyoronsha, 2008) 206. In some cases the lower courts referred to the right to work as one of the normative bases of regulation of abusive dismissal: *Karisyobun Koso* case, Tokyo High Court (24 April 1968) 19 Rominshu 571; *Shokusan Jutaku* case, Tokyo District Court (21 March 1972) 147 Rohan 42; *Wotaman* case, Osaka District Court (28 September 1982) 396 Rohan 76. However, in the two Supreme Court cases which endorsed and formulated the doctrine of abusive dismissal created by judicial precedents in lower courts, the Supreme Court did not refer to the right to work as a normative basis of doctrine of abusive dismissal: *Nihon Shokuen* case, Supreme Court (25 April 1975) 29 Minshu 456; *Kochi Hoso* case (31 January 1977) 268 Rohan 17.

[10] Nishitani, *Jinken Toshiteno*, above n 5, 226; S Nishitani, *Rodoho* (*Labour Law*) (Tokyo, Nihonhyoronsha, 2008) 26.

[11] H Seisho, *Koyo Hoshoho no Kenkyu* (*The Study of Employment Security Law*) (Kyoto, Horitsubunkasha, 1987) 20–27.

the right to work provided in Article 27 of the Constitution should be understood as a right which consists of the right to employment security and the right to a guarantee of fair standards in work. Then, the legal domain which is normatively based on the right to work is divided into two sub-domains. The first is employment security law and the second is labour standards law. Labour law therefore consists of three systems: employment security law; labour standards law; and union security law based on the right to organise.

The right to work normatively requires that labour conditions in individual labour relations based on labour contracts should be worthy of human beings. And the right to employment security consists of the right to maintain the state of working (employment relations) and the right of the unemployed against the state.

The 'freedom to choose suitable employment' or the 'right to choose suitable employment' is derived from the 'freedom to choose employment' which is the main content of the right to work. This 'right to choose a suitable job', which is included in the right to work, sets the duties of the state and the employer to secure suitable employment and, especially in the sphere of compensation for unemployment, it means that unsuitable job offers or refusal of unsuitable vocational training shall not be the reason for restriction of unemployment benefits. In other words, workers shall not be subject to disadvantage by reason of their refusal of unsuitable job offers or vocational training.

C Recent Theories on the Right to Work

i The Theory of the Right to a Career

Just like the strategy of 'a job is property' during the nineteenth century, as the end of the twentieth century approached, the strategy of 'employment is property', which sought to guarantee current employment at one's company, ran headlong into the incisive question of whether, in an age of change, it was possible to continue to maintain this stable employment and whether it was appropriate to do so. This is the theory of the increasing mobility of employment. On the above mentioned understanding, Suwa argues for the theory of the right to a career as follows.[12]

According to this view, the nature of the right to a career is that it is a right that integrates the freedom to choose an occupation and the right to an education, centred on the right to work. Given that a concept of labour without the formation and development of a career is poor and unattractive, it is appropriate to understand the substantive content of the right to work as containing the right to

[12] Y Suwa, 'Kyaria Ken no Koso womeguru Ichi Shiron' ('One Tentative Theory concerning the Concept of the Right to a Career') (1999) 41 *The Monthly Journal of the Japan Institute of Labour* 54; see also, Y Suwa, 'The Concept of the Right to a Career: How to Protect the Careers of Workers' (2011) 8 *Japan Labor Review* 6.

a career.[13] With regard to what the right to work should guarantee, it must guarantee not only the opportunity to work, which should be secured in quantitative terms, but also the opportunity to work that includes qualitative factors that take into consideration the skill, aptitude and willingness to work of the worker.[14] Then, with regard to the effect of the right to a career, we should concretise the right to a career as a standard. For example, as a means of hedging against the risk of unemployment in times of change, the accumulation of a career that will be the 'property' (human capital) of workers cannot be downplayed. Therefore, it may be possible that personnel policies that prioritise only the needs of the organisation and which conspicuously ignore the career of individual workers could, depending on the circumstances, be deemed to constitute an abuse of right over personnel issues (Article 1, paragraph 3 of the Civil Code). And it is also believed that consideration of such matters as education, placement, changes in placement, secondment, promotions and pay increases and employment requests by workers will need to be approached from a different angle from that employed hitherto.[15]

ii The Theory of the Micro Right to Work and Macro Right to Work

Viewing the above theories of the right to work, Araki argues that the right to work consists of (1) a 'micro right to work' that requires security of good employment opportunities for individual workers, and (2) a 'macro right to work' that requires security of good employment opportunities for society as a whole.[16] According to this view, fixing the direction of labour market policy towards greater labour movement between jobs, a policy developed in the wake of the changes to the structure of industries, may cause conflict with the micro right to work. Thus, the state's labour market policy should be achieved by way of inducements and in a form that does not infringe the realisation of the right to work of the individuals.

This view appears to be based on the basic understanding of labour law regulation, namely that in the wake of changes in the structure of the population, the diversification and individualisation of workers, the slowing down of economic growth and the globalisation of business, which create the context for the change of the environment of employment and the labour market, new labour law must search for harmonisation between the needed legal intervention and the individ-

[13] Suwa points out that even if we understand part of the specific content of the right to work as incorporating the right to a career, it is not the case that the legal nature of the right to work will change significantly, that is to say that there is no change in the basic nature of social rights as a programme provision. Suwa, 'One Tentative Theory', above n 12, 58; Suwa, 'The Concept of the Right to a Career', above n 12, 13.

[14] Suwa, 'One Tentative Theory', above n 12, 57–58; Suwa, 'The Concept of the Right to a Career', above n 12, 8.

[15] Suwa, 'One Tentative Theory', above n 12, 61; Suwa, 'The Concept of the Right to a Career', above n 12, 13.

[16] T Araki, 'Rodo Shijo to Rodoho' ('Labour Market and Labour Law') (2001) 97 *Nihon Rodoho Gakkaishi* (*Journal of Labor Law, Japan Labor Law Association*) 55, 73.

ual's own choice. It must also properly control the function of the labour market in coping with the diversification of workers, and if it is possible to effectively use the function of labour market, then it must include the system of using it.[17]

iii Theories of the Right to Work as Securing Decent Work

Attaching great importance to the aspect of quality in securing the right to work, another theory of the right to work insists that its normative content should include Article 13 (respect for individuals), Article 14 (equality under the law and no discrimination in political, economic or social relations because of race, creed, sex, social status or family origin) and Article 25 (the right to a minimum standard of living) of the Constitution of Japan. This is akin to the idea of 'decent work', that the International Labour Organization (ILO) proposes. Work that complies with the right to work on this view consists of suitable work, within the social security framework, and work that permits the development of workers' abilities, social dialogue and participation and sex equality.[18] Wada argues for this theory of the right to work as securing decent work.[19] According to this view, decent work means the 'standard labour relation and its radiated state', in which diverse types of jobs will be established and amalgamated, to which measures of equal treatment (and parity of treatment) and mutual transferability are taken, all in accordance with the ideal model of the labour relation, on which the traditional labour law and social security law have been based. In other words, the law should ensure that all labour law and social security law is applicable to all workers, so that everyone works full-time and for standard working hours, is paid on a monthly basis and is employed on indeterminate contracts without a fixed term and with protection against unjust dismissal. The right to work should secure the above concept of decent work.

Another theory of the right to work as securing decent work is argued by Nishitani.[20] He sets up the right to decent work as a superordinate normative concept, and sees the right to work as securing decent work under the above right to decent work. According to this view, it can be said that the Constitution of Japan, which secures both civil liberties and various social rights, also secures the right to decent work for all, and that the right to work is one of the things that realise it.

D Conclusion

We can summarise the above outline of the development of theories of the right to work in Japan as follows.

[17] ibid, 79–82.

[18] As to the concept of 'decent work', which the ILO proposes, see D Ghai (ed), *Decent Work: Objective and Starategies* (Geneva, International Labour Office, 2006) especially 1–30 (D Ghai).

[19] Wada, above n 9, 282–83.

[20] Nishitani, *Jinken Toshiteno*, above n 5, 42 ff.

In Japan, theories of the right to work started as theories relating to the effect of the right to work provided in Article 27, paragraph 1 of the Constitution of Japan. It then became the almost common understanding that the right to work is a 'programmatic provision' governing only the relations between the state and the people. However, it is an important point of disagreement whether the effect of the right to work provided in Article 27, paragraph 1 should be understood in such a way that it can form the normative basis of regulation, such as the regulation of dismissal, since that would require the employer to do something as a constitutional norm. Differing from the above theories which discuss the effect of the right to work, theories of the right to work, which are grounded in the sphere of employment security law as a system of labour law have developed. These have argued that the normative content of the right to work includes the right to choose a suitable job, and an awareness that the problem of the quality of work which the right to work secures should be discussed. Following that development, this awareness appears to have led to the recent theory of the right to work as securing decent work. Taking a serious view of the problem of quality in securing the right to work, the normative content of this right must include the constituents of Article 13, Article 14, paragraph 1 and Article 25 of the Constitution of Japan. It is the same decent work concept as that proposed by the ILO, the contents of which include suitable jobs, inclusion in social security, the development of workers' abilities, social dialogue and participation and sex equality.

Differing from these theories of the right to work, theories of the right to work based on the understanding that the functions of the labour market should be used, have developed in recent years. In the wake of fixing a course of labour market policy towards labour movement between jobs, the theory of the right to a career, which is based on the strategy of 'a career is property', considers the impact of the external labour market. This theory of the right to work argues for a tension between the micro right to work, which requires security of good employment opportunities for individual workers in the labour market, and the macro right to work, which requires security of good employment opportunities for society as a whole.

II Recent Theories of the Right to Work in the Western World and the United Nations

A Theories of the Right to Work in the Western World

i The Significance of the Right to Work

As to the background need and significance of securing the right to work, Collins points out that 'jobs are a vital necessity for citizens, both to provide the means of subsistence and to enable social inclusion and personal fulfilment' and that, '[a] right to work can be regarded as necessary to secure dignity for individuals'.[21] The understanding that the right to work is essential to secure dignity for individuals can also be seen in the development of the theories of the right to work in Japan. Thus, there seems to be a common understanding as to the significance of the right to work.

ii The Effect of the Right to Work

As to the effect of the right to work, Vigneau argues that there are two effects of the right to work.[22] The first is 'vertical direct effect' and the second is 'horizontal direct effect'.

According to Vigneau, the former vertical direct effect means that the right to work is interpreted as a political commitment by the state to develop an active employment policy, to guarantee the freedom of work and require the state to organise a functioning free labour market. This vertical direct effect seems to be similar to the effect of the right to work for which the theory of the right to work as a programmatic provision of the Constitution of Japan argues.

Horizontal direct effect means that the right to work may have legal relevance as between individuals. Vigneau states that, in countries where such a right is recognised by the constitution, the right to work may be invoked by courts in giving judgment in various situations. For example, discrimination or unreasonable restrictions on entering into a work relationship, or provisions that oblige a person to accept a job could be challenged by invoking the right to work. Even in countries where the right to work is not recognised by the constitution (such as the United Kingdom and Ireland), the horizontal direct effect of the right to work has been invoked.

In this regard, according to Collins, the idea of the right to work may influence the interpretation of contracts of employment in the United Kingdom.[23] He gives an example. In some contracts of employment involving the exercise and development of specialist skills, for the sake of conserving the workers' employability in the labour market, courts may require the employer either to permit the employee to perform any work there is to be done or to go to work for a competitor.[24] He explains that in such cases, which might involve actors hired to perform in a play or journalists hired for a special assignment, the idea of the right to work is used rhetorically to ensure that the interpretation of the contract of employment secures a fair balance of interests between the employer and the employee. This horizontal direct effect of the right to work seems to be similar to the effect of

[21] H Collins, *Employment Law*, 2nd edn (Oxford, Oxford University Press, 2010) 253. See also H Collins in this volume, chs 2 and 13.

[22] C Vigneau, 'Freedom to Choose an Occupation and Right to Engage in Work (Article 15)' in B Bercusson (ed), *European Labour Law and EU Charter of Fundamental Rights* (Baden-Baden, Nomos, 2006) 175–77.

[23] Collins, *Employment Law*, above n 21, 254–55.

[24] *William Hill Organisation Ltd v Tucker* [1999] ICR 291 (CA).

the right to work for which the theory of the right to work in a state of working in Japan argues.

Besides the above mentioned points, there are some arguments presented by some scholars that the right to work provides grounds for justifying other social rights, such as the right not to be unfairly dismissed.[25] Vigneau argues that the right to work appears to be a principle or the concept behind much of modern legislation on training, dismissals, transfer of undertakings and so on.[26] According to Harvey,[27] the right to work occupies a particularly important position because of the role it plays in supporting efforts to secure other economic and social rights. This effect of the right to work stems in part from the breadth of the right to work itself, and in part from its effect on both the level of unmet social needs in society and the level of resources available to meet those needs. Because of this 'dual effect' (reducing unmet needs while simultaneously increasing social resources), a society that is successful in securing the right to work is likely to have a relatively easy time securing other economic and social rights recognised in the Universal Declaration of Human Rights (for example, the right to adequate food, decent housing, adequate health care, a good education, income security for persons who are unable to be self-supporting and so forth). From this viewpoint, the right to work seems to occupy a central position among economic and social rights.

iii The Normative Contents of the Right to Work

Some academics' structural analyses of the right to work argue that it has the following components. According to Mundlak, there are three components in the right to work, and they are intertwined and inseparable.[28] The first is the liberty component. The flipside of the freedom to work is the guarantee against coerced work, namely slavery. The second is the right to have work and the corresponding duty of the state or of employers to provide work to individuals. Mundlak formulates this into the right to an opportunity to gain work as a compromise, which does not grant individuals a subjective right that is enforceable in court, but which is not only a moral right but also one that can place an obligation on the state, and perhaps even on private employers. But this formulation does not resolve the dilemma of how to place this right on a continuum going from the moral claim to the individual, subjective claim. The third is the right to dignified work. It includes a general guarantee of 'fair working conditions' or, more concretely, a guarantee for remuneration, leisure and occupational health and safety, prohibiting child labour, and promoting profit-sharing and co-management. Mundlak points out that beyond the three components mentioned above, it is important to emphasise

[25] B Hepple, 'A Right to Work' (1981) 10 *Industrial Law Journal* 65, 82; Collins, *Employment Law*, above n 21, 253–54.

[26] Vigneau, above n 22, 177–78.

[27] P Harvey, 'Benchmarking the Right to Work' in S Hertel and L Minkler (eds), *Economic Rights* (Cambridge, Cambridge University Press, 2007) 118.

[28] G Mundlak, 'The Right to Work: Linking Human Rights and Employment Policy' (2007) 146 *International Labour Review* 189, 192–94.

that the right to work is inseparable from several other rights: the right to equality in general and in the context of employment in particular, the right to free artistic expression and creation and the right to social security, as well as broader rights, such as the right to human dignity.[29]

According to Harvey's structural analyses, the right to work is a multidimensional entitlement, which has four aspects.[30] The first relates to the 'quantitative' aspect of the right to work. This aspect of the right to work is intended to protect the right of jobseekers to actually be employed in freely chosen jobs, and requires the condition where the so-called 'full employment' is achieved in the labour market. The second relates to the 'qualitative' aspect. This aspect of the right to work includes those factors that determine whether a particular job qualifies as decent work in the sense in which the ILO uses the term. These factors include things such as pay, fringe benefits, hours of work, working conditions, workplace governance, employment security and so on. For the right to work to be secured, not only must the number of jobs available in an economy exceed the number of jobseekers or persons wanting employment, but those jobs must also provide decent work. And because securing the right to work itself is instrumental to the broader goal of ensuring that all members of society have the opportunity to freely develop their personhood, the employment opportunities that a society provides to secure the right to work must also be of sufficient variety and type to fulfil that role. Accordingly, the qualitative features that employment opportunities must possess to satisfy the right to work depend on the development needs of the population as well as certain absolute quality requirements. The third element relates to the 'distributive' aspect of the right to work. Since the right to work must reflect the commitment of the Universal Declaration of Human Rights to the equal worth and equal rights of all persons, it is essential for securing the right to work to achieve equal employment opportunities and equal conditions of employment for all persons. This is the proper object of policies designed to overcome or eliminate 'structural' barriers to employment. The fourth element relates to the 'scope' of the right to work. Although the right to work was originally conceived, in the Universal Declaration, as a right to a paying job, the language defining the right to work in the Declaration does not limit its scope to wage employment, and a large population of the world's population work in capacities other than that of a wage labourer. Therefore, the question arises as to whether and how the right to work applies to non-wage employment.[31]

Differing form the above mentioned structural analysis theories of the right to work, Freedland et al demonstrate an awareness of the problem caused by the 'workfarist' tendency in government policies that develop active labour market

[29] See also V Mantouvalou in this volume, ch 3.

[30] Harvey, 'Benchmarking the Right to Work', above n 27, 123–25.

[31] This aspect relates to the theory of 'basic income' and is an important theme to be considered. On this issue, see P Harvey, 'The Right to Work and Basic Income Guarantees: Competing or Complementary Goals?' (2005) 2 *Rutgers Journal of Law & Urban Policy* 8.

policies (ALMPs).[32] They have put forward a theory of a series of narrower rights to work, stemming from the right to refuse a specific job offer on a number of grounds without suffering any negative consequence on the social security side of the equation, and bridging the regulation of the labour market on the one hand, and social security legislation on the other.[33] According to this view, first, at the very least, every democracy respectful of fundamental rights and freedoms of the individual and of social groups should grant jobseekers the right to choose 'decent' employment, which means work that respects at least three rights and values: health and safety, fundamental human rights and conscientious objection and, as a consequence, the right to be able to refuse lawfully any job offer that does not match this definition without risking the loss of their social security entitlements.[34] However, it is arguable that respect for fundamental human rights and liberties cannot be the one and only concern of a democratic legal system when regulating the labour market. When balancing the freedom to work in the labour relationship sphere against the duty to work in the sphere of social security, other rights and claims of a social and economic character should also be taken into account. Second, in addition to having a right to choose decent work, jobseekers should have the right to choose 'suitable' work.[35] Where the right to choose suitable work is secured, the state should not threaten to deprive a jobseeker of his or her social security entitlements when the job offered would jeopardise the worker's acquired professional, personal and family life.

However, Freedland et al argue that these elements are not sufficient for the normative content of the right to work. When the standard, full time and open ended, employment relationship based on the contract of employment was the paradigm in the labour market, career progression occurred within the employment relationship. But as that model is being replaced by a more fluid one, it becomes more cogent to claim that the regulation of the labour market should provide workers with the possibility of career advancement between different and successive jobs. From this perspective, Freedland et al argue that the normative content of the right to work is the right to choose decent, suitable and 'rewarding' work, so workers might be allowed to refuse a job offer which would not help them in their career progression, in improving their job prospects and in elevating their personal skills and endowments.[36]

B The Recent Theory of the Right to Work in the United Nations

The United Nations (UN) as an international organisation has given its opinion about the right to work in recent years. The International Covenant on Economic,

[32] See also A Paz-Fuchs in this volume, ch 10.

[33] M Freedland et al, *Public Employment Services and European Law* (Oxford, Oxford University Press, 2007) 225.

[34] ibid, 227.

[35] ibid, 228–29.

[36] ibid, 229–30.

Social and Cultural Rights (ICESCR), which Japan has ratified, protects the right to work in its Article 6. The Committee of Economic, Social and Cultural Rights (CESCR) issued General Comment No 18 (GC No 18) on Article 6 of the ICESCR, adopted at its thirty-fifth session, on 24 November 2005.[37] GC No 18 considers the normative content of the right to work, the obligations of states, the implementation of the right at national level and the obligations of actors other than state parties.

i The Significance and Structure of the Right to Work

GC No 18, first, affirms that the right to work is essential for realising other human rights, and forms an inseparable and inherent part of human dignity.[38] Second, GC No 18 articulates the structure of the right to work as follows. The ICESCR proclaims the right to work in a general sense in its Article 6 and explicitly develops the individual dimension of the right to work through the recognition in Article 7 of the right of everyone to the enjoyment of just and favourable conditions of work, in particular the right to safe working conditions. The collective dimension of the right to work is addressed in Article 8, which enunciates the right of everyone to form trade unions and join the trade union of their choice, as well as the right of trade unions to function freely.[39] Therefore, the right to work is an individual right that belongs to each person and is at the same time a collective right.[40] GC No 18 grasps the structure of the right to work as one that has both an individual and a collective dimension.

ii The Normative Content of the Right to Work

GC No 18 mentions and considers the normative content of the right to work as follows.[41] First, the right to work encompasses all forms of work, whether independent work or dependent wage-paid work. Second, the right to work includes the right of every human being to decide freely to accept or choose work. This implies not being forced in any way whatsoever to exercise or engage in employment and the right of access to a system of protection guaranteeing each worker access to employment. It also implies the right not to be unfairly deprived of employment. Third, the right to work is a right to decent work. This is work that respects the fundamental rights of the human person, as well as the rights of workers in terms of conditions of workplace safety and remuneration. It also provides an income allowing workers to support themselves and their families, as highlighted in Article 7 of the Covenant. These fundamental rights also include

[37] Committee on Economic, Social and Cultural Rights, General Comment No 18: The Right to Work, Article 6 of the International Convention on Economic, Social and Cultural Rights, UN Doc E/C.12/GC/18 (6 February 2006).

[38] GC No 18, para 1.

[39] ibid, para 2.

[40] ibid, para 6.

[41] ibid, paras 6–18.

respect for the physical and mental integrity of the worker in the exercise of his or her employment. And since Articles 6, 7 and 8 of the Covenant are interdependent, the characterisation of work as decent presupposes that it respects the fundamental rights of the worker.

iii Obligations of States

GC No 18 affirms that the principal obligation of states is to ensure the progressive realisation of the exercise of the right to work, and emphasises that specific measures to increase the flexibility of labour markets must not render work less stable or reduce the social protection of the worker.[42]

GC No 18 indicates that states should develop and maintain mechanisms to monitor progress towards the realisation of the right to freely chosen or accepted employment, to identify the factors and difficulties affecting the degree of compliance with their obligations and to facilitate the adoption of corrective legislative and administrative measures.[43] GC No 18 also indicates that any person or group that is a victim of a violation of the right to work should have access to effective judicial or other appropriate remedies at the national level, that judges and other law enforcement authorities are invited to pay greater attention to violations of the right to work in the exercise of their functions and that trade unions and human rights commissions at the national level should play an important role in defending the right to work.[44]

iv Obligations of Actors other than States

GC No 18 indicates that, while only states are parties to the Covenant and are thus ultimately accountable for compliance with it, all members of society – individuals, local communities, trade unions, civil society and private sector organisations – have responsibilities regarding the realisation of the right to work. GC No 18 affirms that private enterprises in particular – national and multinational – while not bound by the Covenant, should conduct their activities on the basis of legislation, administrative measures, codes of conduct and other appropriate measures promoting respect for the right to work, agreed between the government and civil society. Last but not least, trade unions play a fundamental role in ensuring respect for the right to work at the local and national levels and in assisting state parties to comply with their obligations under Article 6.[45]

[42] ibid, paras 19, 25.
[43] ibid, para 45.
[44] ibid, paras 48, 50.
[45] ibid, paras 52, 54.

III Conclusion – The Right to Work as a Comprehensive Basic Right (a Tentative Argument)

Comparing the development of theories of the right to work in Japan with the development of theories of the right to work in the Western world and the UN, I conclude this chapter by considering their meaning and points, and then by presenting a tentative argument about the right to work.

It is the almost common understanding in Japan, the Western world and the UN, that the effect of the right to work is 'programmatic' insofar as it applies to the relations between the state and the people. However, it is an important point of difference that, in Japan, there is a disagreement about whether the effect of the right to work provided for in Article 27, paragraph 1 of the Constitution of Japan should be understood as a normative basis of regulation, such as the regulation of dismissal and so on, since that would require the employer to do something because of a constitutional norm. As mentioned above, such an effect seems to be commonly recognised in the Western world and the UN.

In the theories of the right to work in the Western world and the UN in recent years, there seems to be a common understanding that the right to work provides grounds for justifying other social rights, such as the right not to be unfairly dismissed. There also seems to be a common understanding in those theories that, through a structural analysis, a qualitative aspect of the right to work is identified, under which the goal of the right to work must be to secure decent work. This includes things such as pay, fringe benefits, hours of work, working conditions, workplace governance, employment security and so forth. There are common understandings like that in Japan.

Extracting some points in common from those arguments would support the right to work as a 'comprehensive basic right' which gives comprehensive ground for labour law regulation. It is possible to say that labour law regulation is needed to achieve the right to work as the right to decent work. I think that the reconstruction of the right to work as a comprehensive basic right provides the normative basis by which labour law regulation today, even as it becomes more complicated and multipolar, may become generally and coherently systematised.[46] For example, the right to work as a comprehensive basic right seems to make it possible to adopt a coherent position in the system of labour law regulation as to why the sphere of discrimination law is expanding into labour law regulation. I think that such an interpretation of the right to work as a comprehensive basic right could be valid as the understanding of the constitutional norm in Japan.

[46] See H Karatsu, 'Rodoho Paradaimuron no Genkyou to Rodoho Kisei no Tagensei' ('Present Situation of the Paradigm of Labour Law and Multipolarisation of Labour Law Regulation') (2009) 1700 *Rodo Horitsu Junpo* 6ff, which argues that the normative ground of multiple regulation of labour law lies in the provision of fundamental rights in the Constitution.

As to the problem of the promotion of labour market flexibility, which has caused the development of the theories of the right to work in recent years, and of the way labour law should regulate the labour market, there is an issue to be considered to which Joseph refers in respect of GC No 18.[47] It is the following. GC No 18 simply asserts that Article 6 (right to work), Article 7 (right to just and favourable conditions of work) and Article 8 (right to join effective trade unions) are interdependent, but it does not address the perceived dissonance between Article 6 rights and the rights enshrined in Articles 7 and 8. In the globalised economy, a state will arguably lose jobs to offshore competition if its labour market is too costly or inflexible. This issue is also not addressed at all in GC No18. It only asserts that states must not only strive for full employment, but also decent employment.

According to my tentative view, the problem to which Joseph points is perceived as the problem of coordinating among those rights which are constituents of the right to work as a comprehensive basic right, namely the right to work, the right to just and favourable conditions of work and the right to join effective trade unions. In other words, the problem is how states should strike a balance between their duty to achieve full employment and their duty to secure decent work (ie, how much states could lower standards regarding labour conditions in order to achieve full employment). The view that poor working conditions can cause low productivity and consequent business failure, thus leading to more unemployment, which Hepple and Joseph point out, seems to provide a guide for that problem.[48]

Last, I consider the issue of the mobilisation of the labour market by ALMPs. According to the theory of the micro right to work and macro right to work, fixing a course of labour market policy towards labour movement between jobs, in accordance with government policy in the wake of business restructuring, may cause conflict with the micro right to work. The theory of the right to a career may present one possible answer to that problem. The theory of the right to a career seems to be a theory which finds its rationale in securing the careers of workers on the premise that the labour market is mobilised. However, such an understanding presented by the theory of the right to a career is criticised by Wada, who points out that ALMPs premised on the mobilisation of the labour market themselves destroy jobs and the goals of human dignity and self-determination supported by employment.[49] Regarding this point, according to the view of Freedland et al, mentioned earlier, which attaches importance to securing a career as well, the normative content of the right to work is the right to choose decent, suitable and rewarding work, so workers might be allowed to refuse a job offer which would not help them in their career progression, in improving their job prospects and

[47] S Joseph, 'UN Covenants and Labour Rights' in C Fenwick and T Novitz (eds), *Human Rights at Work: Perspectives on Law and Regulation* (Oxford, Hart Publishing, 2010) 340–41.

[48] ibid, 341; B Hepple, *Labour Law and Global Trade* (Oxford, Hart Publishing, 2005) 14.

[49] Wada, above n 9, 282.

elevating their personal skills and endowments.[50] I think that we should deal with that issue by understanding the construction of the right to work as a multilayered one, like Freedland et al[51]

I only present very roughly the above mentioned tentative theory of the right to work with a comprehensive basic right as its skeleton. The detail of it remains to be considered in the future.

[50] Freedland et al, above n 33, 229–30.

[51] See also K Arita, 'Rodo Shijo no Ryudoka to Kyaria Keisei no Hoseisaku' ('Mobilisation of Labour Market and Legal Policies on Career Development') (2003) 75 *Horitsu Jiho* 30.

13

Progress towards the Right to Work in the United Kingdom

HUGH COLLINS

Introduction

In 1981, Bob Hepple asked to what extent the law in the United Kingdom protects a 'right to work'.[1] At that time, the question seemed especially pertinent: in the previous year, about a million workers had lost their jobs, elevating the level of unemployment in the United Kingdom from about 6 per cent to 10 per cent of the labour force. Today, with Britain having recently been subject to a recession of nearly equal proportions, with unemployment rising by a million people between 2008 and 2009, peaking at above 8 per cent of the labour force,[2] it seems appropriate to return to the same question. What progress has been made in securing a legal right to work in the United Kingdom?

Labour law as a whole has changed considerably in the intervening three decades. On the one hand, the imposition by successive governments of individualistic, market-oriented policies on the labour market has deregulated employment relations in many respects, especially in connection with support for trade union organisation and collective bargaining, thereby diminishing effective protections for job security and related rights;[3] on the other hand, the combined influence of the European Union's (EU) social policies and the enactment of legally enforceable charters of fundamental rights has revised the legal framework in potentially radical ways. Labour lawyers can more readily perceive the subject now as comprised of a series of individual employment rights such as a minimum wage, maximum hours and protection from discrimination and unfair dismissal. Furthermore, the sources of law now derive from many levels, not only UK statutes, but also treaties and legislation of the EU and the European Convention on

[1] B Hepple, 'A Right to Work?' (1981) 10 *Industrial Law Journal* 65.

[2] G Clancy, 'The Labour Market and the Economy: Twenty Years Reviewed' (2009) 3 *Economic & Labour Market Review* 17 (Office of National Statistics).

[3] PL Davies and MR Freedland, *Labour Legislation and Public Policy: A Contemporary History* (Oxford, Clarendon Press, 1993).

Human Rights (ECHR), incorporated into national law by the Human Rights Act 1998 (HRA).

The first question to consider is whether these new transnational sources of labour law include to any extent a legally enforceable right to work. Having concluded that there is at least indirect support for a right to work in both the ECHR and the Treaties of the EU, which may in the long term have a significant impact on labour law, we consider the current law of the United Kingdom with respect to the main contexts in which a legally recognised right to work may influence the development of legal regulation: hiring decisions by employers, an obligation placed on an employer to provide work to perform, termination of employment and regulatory restrictions on access to work or particular professions.

I A Legal Right to Work?

The absence in the United Kingdom of a written constitution and a Bill of Rights has the effect that there is no formal enactment of any statement upholding the right to work. However, support for the existence for a right to work can be discovered in the common law, in the ECHR through incorporation by the HRA and in the Treaties establishing the EU. The common law has tackled regulatory and contractual restrictions to the right to work primarily through the restraint of trade doctrine. The ECHR does not explicitly protect the right to work, but some of its provisions, especially the right to respect for private life in Article 8, have been interpreted by the European Court of Human Rights (ECtHR) to include some protection for access to the labour market. Both the common law and the scope of the ECHR will be considered in detail in section IV below in the context of regulatory and contractual restrictions on access to the labour market. We should concentrate here on potentially the most important legal protection for a right to work, which is found in the legally binding Treaties of the EU.

As a result of revisions to the Treaties of the EU, for the first time in the United Kingdom, there is a legally binding right to work. Article 15 of the Charter of Fundamental Rights of the EU (CFREU) states:

1. Everyone has the right to engage in work and to pursue a freely chosen or accepted occupation.
2. Every citizen of the Union has the freedom to seek employment, to work, to exercise the right of establishment and to provide services in any Member State.[4]

Although the Charter does not confer rights on individuals that are directly enforceable in the courts, it has the legal status of a treaty within the EU,[5] so that

[4] Charter of Fundamental Rights of the EU (CFREU), [2007] OJ C303/5.

[5] Treaty on European Union (TEU), Art 6, [2010] OJ C83/13.

it has potential effects on the interpretation of labour laws. When applying EU laws such as directives concerned with employment relations, courts are required to interpret those laws in a manner that is compatible with the rights, freedoms and principles of the CFREU. Given the wide influence of EU law on labour law today through numerous directives, the potential 'radiating effect'[6] of Article 15 CFREU on labour law is considerable. Article 15 is itself based upon prior declarations of rights: paragraph 1 draws upon Article 1(2) of the European Social Charter, 1961, ratified by all the Member States, which has been interpreted on numerous occasions by the European Committee of Social Rights during its work of assessing country reports;[7] paragraph 2 expresses in summary form three of the fundamental economic freedoms protected in the Treaty on the Functioning of the European Union (TFEU),[8] namely freedom of movement for workers, freedom of establishment and freedom to provide services.[9] These interlocking legal protections for the right to work seem destined to raise its profile in legal consciousness and to steer legal reasoning towards more careful assessments of justifications for restrictions on the freedom to work.

Nonetheless, this legal embodiment of the right to work in Article 15 CFREU needs to be read circumspectly. The wording does not confer a right to a job, but merely the right to engage in any opportunities afforded to individuals by the labour market. In that sense, nothing much has changed since Hepple wrote in 1981: in modern times, governments in Western market societies have never promised actual jobs for everyone. Article 15 protects a freedom to enter the labour market, but it does not protect a social right to work in the sense of requiring a government to provide everyone who wants one with a job. Although employment is generally recognised as the best route out of poverty and social exclusion, European governments do not believe that it is possible within the normal fiscal constraints to provide everyone with some form of paid employment. Levels of unemployment can be reduced by governments indirectly through capital infrastructure projects paid for by government borrowing or more directly by rather inefficient and not very effective temporary employment subsidies paid to employers,[10] but the bulk of the unemployed must still rely on welfare benefits to provide financial support until the economy begins to grow again. During the past 30 years Western governments seem to have become more convinced of the folly of public job creation programmes funded by the enlargement

[6] This is the phrase used in some German constitutional theory to describe the influence of the Basic Law (and its rights) on all aspects of the legal system: see: M Kumm, 'Who is Afraid of the Total Constitution? Constitutional Rights as Principles and the Constitutionalization of Private Law' (2006) 7 *German Law Journal* 341; J Fedtke, 'Germany: Drittwirkung in Germany' in D Oliver and J Fedtke (eds), *Human Rights and the Private Sphere: A Comparative Study* (London, Routledge–Cavendish, 2007) 125.

[7] These are examined by C O'Cinneide in this volume, ch 6.

[8] Treaty on the Functioning of the European Union (TFEU), [2010] OJ C83/47.

[9] TFEU, Arts 45, 49 and 56.

[10] eg Employment Subsidies Act 1978. P Davies and M Freedland, *Labour Law: Text and Materials*, 2nd edn (London, Weidenfeld and Nicolson, 1984) 27–37; H Collins, KD Ewing and A McColgan, *Labour Law: Text and Materials* (Oxford, Hart Publishing, 2001) 1002.

of government debt. Instead, the emphasis has been on making welfare benefits contingent on active jobseeking by the unemployed.[11] In the United Kingdom claimants for Jobseeker's Allowance (the principal welfare benefit paid to the unemployed) have to wait a week for any benefits, during which time they will be assisted and required by government jobcentres to apply for jobs using new Internet search techniques, with follow-up required weekly visits to the jobcentre until work has been acquired.[12] More intensive scrutiny of the claim occurs after 13 weeks. It is reported that in the last three months of 2013, 227,629 lost their Jobseeker's Allowance for failure to comply with these conditions.[13] Far from there being a claim against the government for a paid job, the contingent benefits of the welfare system place considerable economic pressure on the unemployed to seek work, to acquire work experience and training and to take pretty much any job they are offered.

Article 15 CFREU should also be interpreted cautiously because it is merely one right amongst many, which may compete with each other in a particular concrete case. In particular, in jurisdictions such as France where versions of Article 15 in earlier international conventions have been acknowledged by domestic courts as having a binding effect, protection for the right to work has to be balanced against the freedom of employers to run their business and to engage in enterprise. This principle is also stated in Article 16 CFREU: 'The freedom to conduct a business in accordance with Union law and national laws and practices is recognised'. Whenever it is claimed that EU law confers a right on a worker that is inspired by Article 15, an employer can almost certainly match that claim by the competing argument that enforcement of the proposed interpretation of EU law would disproportionately interfere with the employer's freedom to conduct a business under Article 16. For example, in *Alemo-Herron*,[14] the Court of Justice of the European Union (CJEU) rejected a particular interpretation of the Acquired Rights Directive that would have protected the employee's interests in continuing to benefit from the application of a collective agreement following the transfer of the business to a new employer on the ground that such an interpretation of the Directive would disproportionately interfere with the new employer's freedom to conduct a business.

Although there is no legal right to an actual paid job, the idea of the right to work nevertheless does influence many aspects of the regulation of employment. Hepple divided his examination of the effects of the idea of the right to work into

[11] J Fulbrook, 'New Labour's Welfare Reforms: Anything New?' (2001) 64 *Modern Law Review* 243. *cf* A Paz-Fuchs in this volume, ch 10.

[12] HM Treasury, Spending Round June 2013 (Cm 8639, 2013) 7, citing an expected annual saving of £350m.

[13] P Wintour, 'More Sanctions Imposed on Jobseeker's Allowance Claimants' *The Guardian* (14 May 2014).

[14] Case C-426/11 *Alemo-Herron and others v Parkwood Leisure Ltd*; S Weatherill, 'Use and Abuse of the EU's Charter of Fundamental Rights: On the Improper Veneration of "Freedom of Contract"' (2014) 10 *European Review of Contract Law* 167; J Prassl, 'Freedom of Contract as a General Principle of EU Law? Transfers of Undertakings and the Protection of Employer Rights in EU Labour Law' (2013) 42 *Industrial Law Journal* 434.

two categories: claims brought by employees against their employers, and claims brought by workers against trade unions. With respect to the latter subject of claims against trade unions, however, the influence of the right to work in the context of debates about the closed shop has greatly diminished as a result of decisions by the ECtHR. Relying on Article 11 ECHR, the protection for freedom of association, and not mentioning the idea of the right to work, the ECtHR has both protected the right to be a member of a trade union,[15] and reasserted the right not to be a member.[16] In the United Kingdom, an amended Trade Union and Labour Relations (Consolidation) Act 1992 (TULRCA), Part III gives effect to this legal framework and has effectively outlawed the closed shop by providing a compensatory remedy for anyone denied a job as a result of a requirement to be a member of a trade union.[17] Although these judicial decisions and statutes have largely settled controversies regarding the application of the right to work in relation to trade unions and closed shops, the relevance of the right to work with respect to claims against employers remains a live issue. Following Hepple's structure, claims against employers involving the right to work will be examined under three headings: the employer's decision whether or not to hire a worker; the decision whether or not to give an employee work to perform; and the decision to terminate employment.

In a departure from Hepple's earlier framework, however, a contemporary account of the right to work in the United Kingdom also needs to consider more extensively those regulatory controls imposed by governments that are designed to restrict the access of individuals to the labour market as a whole or to a particular trade or profession. Under the common law developed by judges, the restraint of trade doctrine protected individuals against unreasonable restrictions on their ability to ply their trade or profession arising either from private agreements or business regulation. But it is the government itself that is responsible for the most stringent contemporary controls over access to work. The variety of these regulations that interfere with the rights and freedoms set out in Article 15 CFREU above range from clear interference through immigration controls and the regulation of professions and other kinds of occupational licensing, to more indirect types of interference such as those arising from planning laws that prevent someone exercising a trade or profession in a particular location.[18] Although these regulations are likely to serve worthwhile and legitimate policy goals, they will require justification before the courts to the extent that they interfere with the fundamental economic freedoms guaranteed under EU law (free movement of workers, freedom to provide services and freedom of establishment) or rights protected under the CFREU, the ECHR and the HRA 1998. A modern survey of the right to

[15] *Wilson and Palmer v United Kingdom* [2002] ECHR 552.

[16] *Young, James and Webster v UK* (1982) 4 EHRR 38; *Sigurjonnson v Iceland* (1993) 16 EHRR 462; *Sorenson and Rasmussen v Denmark* (2008) 46 EHRR 29, [2006] ECHR 24; V Mantouvalou, 'Is there a Human Right Not to be a Trade Union Member?' in C Fenwick and T Novitz (eds), *Human Rights at Work: Perspectives on Law and Regulation* (Oxford, Hart Publishing, 2010) 439.

[17] TULRCA 1992, ss 137–43, 152–67.

[18] eg Case 44/79 *Hauer* [1979] ECR 3727.

work under UK law therefore needs to examine, at least briefly, how various aspects of the right play a part in challenging the way in which the government regulates the labour market.

II Employers' Control Over Access to Work

Under the common law, an employer's freedom of contract permitted free choice of contractual partner by reference to any criteria, no matter how arbitrary and capricious. That freedom has now been substantially curtailed by the anti-discrimination laws. Building on the prohibitions against sex and race (including nationality) discrimination already enacted by 1981,[19] the consolidated legislation contained in the Equality Act 2010 includes protection against discrimination by employers in hiring decisions on the further grounds of numerous protected characteristics including age, disability, gender reassignment, marriage and civil partnership, pregnancy and maternity, religion or belief and sexual orientation.[20] This legislation has not, however, been generally described as an aspect of the right to work, but rather it has been presented as a broader implementation of ideas of equality, human rights and civil liberties. Nevertheless, it is possible to find strong historical linkages between anti-discrimination legislation and the idea of the right to work.

Some political justifications for the legislation are framed in the language of social inclusion, where a central idea is that access to work, and not merely welfare benefits, is a crucial ingredient for individual well-being, justice as fairness and social cohesion.[21] Similarly, many of the original political claims for anti-discrimination laws were framed in the United States (US) by reference to the right to work.[22] The primary claim of black activists was for the right to work, the right to choose an occupation and the removal of colour bars from the better jobs. It was only after the Supreme Court in *Brown v Board of Education*[23] relied on the equal protection clause in the Constitution to justify the constitutional invalidity of race segregation laws that the value of equality became the dominant political and legal value governing discrimination claims. Without a constitution to hand, however, in the United Kingdom Lord Denning MR had to rely on a common law

[19] Sex Discrimination Act 1975; Race Relations Act 1976; Equal Pay Act 1970.

[20] Equality Act 2010, s 4.

[21] H Collins, 'Discrimination, Equality and Social Inclusion' (2003) 66 *Modern Law Review* 16, 21–26.

[22] J Shim, 'Equality or the Right to Work? Explaining and Justifying Employment Discrimination Law' (PhD, London School of Economics, 2008) ch 6, which examines the history of measures, such as HR 7142, 'A Bill To Prohibit Discrimination In Employment Because Of Race, Color, Creed, Religion, National Origin, Or Citizenship' (20 July 1942, referred to the House Committee of the Judiciary) placed before the US House of Congress prior to the Civil Rights Act 1964, in which the right to work rather than the idea of equality was presented as the justification for the legislation.

[23] *Brown v Board of Education* 347 US 483 (1954).

right to work to create an incipient anti-discrimination law. He relied on the idea of the right to work at common law in the law of restraint of trade to invalidate the bylaws of the Jockey Club, which had prevented a woman from becoming a racehorse trainer.[24] Although he took some of the shine off this decision by insisting that women were still unsuited for certain kinds of jobs – he mentioned the occupations of jockey and speedway rider – the decision signalled the beginning of the construction of an anti-discrimination rule under the common law on the foundation of the right to work. The subsequent anti-discrimination legislation in the United Kingdom borrowed notions of equal treatment from the United States, though its focus in its early versions still lay on the right to work in the sense that discrimination in employment was the key target. One possible historical interpretation of the genesis of this legislation is that, in order to justify the imposition of mandatory anti-discrimination laws on private employers, at least initially, the principle of equality was not thought sufficient to overcome the basic liberty of employers to manage their business, and that what was required in addition was the moral force of the idea of the right to work.

Some further aspects of the modern anti-discrimination legislation itself also reveal a concern for the right to work. In the case of disability discrimination, for instance, the legislation does not require parity of treatment with non-disabled persons, but rather requires an employer to make reasonable adjustments in favour of the worker.[25] For example, in *Archibald v Fyfe Council*,[26] the employee suffered complications from a surgical operation and was unable to continue to work at her manual job as a street cleaner. The Council tried to make reasonable adjustments for her disability by giving her training for a clerical job and placing her on the shortlist for more than a hundred clerical posts. But she was unsuccessful, so the question became whether the Council's policy of requiring appointments to be made on merit, based on statute,[27] should be waived in this case. The House of Lords allowed an appeal by the employee and remitted the case to a tribunal, suggesting strongly that, on further investigation of the facts by the tribunal, it would probably be reasonable in all the circumstances to make an adjustment by appointing her directly to a clerical post. This interpretation of the employer's duty to make adjustments was guided by the underlying European Union Directive 2000/78/EC,[28] which establishes a general framework for equal treatment in employment and occupation. In Article 5 of the Directive, it explains the purpose of the obligation of reasonable accommodation: 'This means that employers shall take appropriate measures, where needed in a particular case, to enable a person with a disability to have access to, participate in, or advance in employment'.[29] Although the idea of a right to work is not mentioned in the

[24] *Nagle v Feilden* [1966] 2 QB 633 (CA).

[25] Equality Act 2010, s 20.

[26] *Archibald v Fyfe Council* [2004] UKHL 32, [2004] ICR 954.

[27] Local Government and Housing Act 1989, s 7(1) requires appointments to be made 'on merit'.

[28] Council Directive 2000/78/EC of 27 November 2000 establishing a general framework for equal treatment in employment and occupation [2000] OJ L303/16.

[29] Cited by Lady Hale in *Archibald*, above n 26, [60].

Directive,[30] the purpose of the duty to make reasonable adjustments appears to be strongly directed towards enabling disabled workers actually to obtain a job, not just to be treated equally and fairly. The applicant in *Archibald* had probably been treated equally and fairly by the Council, but that was almost certainly not enough, because they had not given her what she wanted and needed – a job.

With respect to discrimination against members of a trade union by employers, as mentioned earlier, the ECtHR has insisted that Article 11 ECHR provides strong protection for guaranteeing an individual's right to be a member of a trade union (and not to be a member). Since the enactment of the Employment Act 1990, UK law provides explicit protection for trade union members against discrimination by employers at the point of hiring:

It is unlawful to refuse a person employment –

a. because he is, or is not, a member of a trade union, or
b. because he is unwilling to accept a requirement –
   i. to take steps to become or cease to be, or to remain or not to become, a member of a trade union.[31]

It is also automatically unfair to dismiss an employee because of trade union membership or activities.[32] As well as bare membership of a trade union, following the decision of the ECtHR in *Wilson and Palmer v United Kingdom*,[33] the right to membership also includes the right to proper representation of the interests of the member through collective bargaining or some other mechanism for representation. This decision has led to the prohibition of inducements designed both to discourage trade union membership and also to discourage the use of a trade union for the purpose of representation through collective bargaining or otherwise.[34] Although there are some gaps in the legislative protection of workers against anti-union discrimination,[35] legal protections are stronger today than at any time in the past. For example, when ASDA offered its workforce located at Washington, Tyne and Wear, a pay rise of 10 per cent if they agreed to abandon collective agreements in favour of individual contracts to set pay, 340 applicants to a tribunal were each awarded compensation of £2500 for this anti-union action.[36] A worker is therefore entitled to participate in the labour market free from any discrimination based upon membership of a union or a wish for the union to represent his or her interests.

[30] The Directive rather uses the language of social inclusion through work: 'Employment and occupation are key elements in guaranteeing equal opportunities for all and contribute strongly to the full participation of citizens in economic, cultural and social life and to realising their potential'. Preamble, para (9).
[31] TULRCA 1992, s 137(1).
[32] TULRCA 1992 s 152; *Fitzpatrick v British Railways Board* [1992] ICR 221 (CA).
[33] *Wilson and Palmer*, above n 15.
[34] TULRCA 1992, ss 145A and 145B.
[35] CEM 466–68.
[36] Case no 2501510/05 *Davies v ASDA Stores Ltd* (13 February 2006).

One gap in the protection against anti-union discrimination that has been recently uncovered is the use by employers of 'blacklists' of union activists, which are compiled by independent organisations. Blacklists pose a threat to the right to work because a person on the list will not be hired by any employer that pays for a subscription to the list. The workers concerned will almost certainly be unaware of the true reason for the refusal of employment or indeed the very existence of the secret blacklist and their inclusion on it. In those circumstances, it will be difficult to prove the elements of the legal claim for refusal of employment on the ground of trade union membership. A further complication is that the blacklists were used extensively in the construction industry, where workers are often classified as self-employed, which normally takes them outside the statutory protection against anti-union discrimination.[37] The Blacklists Regulations 2010[38] tackle the source of the problem by making it unlawful to compile, use, or supply such a list of names that can be used to discriminate against trade union members or participants in trade union activities. As well as making it unlawful to refuse to employ someone for a reason related to such a prohibited list,[39] with a remedy of compensation for the individual before an employment tribunal,[40] it is also possible to make a complaint against the compiler or user of the list in the ordinary civil courts, where the remedies include a restraining order against the use of the list and damages for breach of a statutory duty with the possibility of compensation for injured feelings.[41]

One last major change in the anti-discrimination laws that deserves special mention in the context of the right to work concerns the introduction of the prohibition on unjustifiable age discrimination. Before the advent of that legislation, it was typical for employers to dismiss a worker who reached the contractual retirement age and it was usually extremely difficult for the older person to find other regular employment. Although compulsory retirement is not absolutely prohibited by the legislation,[42] to avoid claims for unfair dismissal and age discrimination an employer will need to be able to justify having a retirement age, to justify the selection of a particular age and be willing to listen to an employee who has reasons for continuing in work and is able to do so.[43]

[37] KD Ewing, *Ruined Lives – Blacklisting in the UK Construction Industry* (Liverpool, Institute of Employment Rights, 2009).
[38] Employment Relations Act 1999 (Blacklists) Regulations, SI 2010 No 493.
[39] reg 5.
[40] reg 8.
[41] reg 13.
[42] C-159/10 *Fuchs (Social Policy)* [2012] ICR 93 (CJEU).
[43] *Seldon v Clarkson Wright & Jakes* [2012] UKSC 16, [2012] ICR 716; *Homer v Chief Constable of West Yorkshire* [2012] UKSC 15; [2012] ICR 704.

III A Right to be Given Work to Do?

In the wage-work bargain of the contract of employment, does the employer promise to provide work and does the employee have a correlative right to perform work? This question may be answered by reference to the express terms of the particular contract of employment. In the absence of express terms that address the issue, how far do the default rules of the common law support a right to work? The normal interpretation placed on contracts of employment by the courts is that the employer does not promise to provide work to be done, but merely promises to pay wages.[44] The consideration that supports the contract of employment, viewed as an executory contract, is that in return for the worker's promise to be ready and able to perform work under the direction of the employer, the employer promises to pay the agreed wages. This default rule should normally place the risk of the absence of work to be done on the employer, so that the employee receives wages provided they are ready and willing to perform work when called upon to do so. If there is work to be done and the employer prevents the employee from performing any, as in the case of suspension, normally wages should remain payable as well, and in some cases there may be the slight possibility of obtaining an injunction to prevent the employer from denying the employee access to the workplace.

A Casual Work and Zero Hours Contracts

Using the express terms of the contract, however, the employer may shift the risk of the absence of work back onto the employee by inserting a condition that the employee will be paid only when required, not for a regular number of hours. Such contracts can take the form of 'zero hours contracts' or 'casual work contracts'. Under the express terms of such contracts, the employee is paid only for those hours that are actually worked, and the employer determines unilaterally when work is required. There are two possible forms of this contractual arrangement. Under what may be termed a zero hours contract, the employee promises to be ready and available for work during set hours ('on call'), but the employer merely promises to pay for work actually performed according to the requirements of the employer. These contracts may lead to the abuse that workers can be kept hanging around but not actually working, and therefore possibly earning no money or only the national minimum wage if the worker is required to be physically located at or near the place of work.[45] Under arrangements for casual work, the second form taken by such contracts, again the employer does not promise to offer any work, but equally in this case the employee does not promise to be avail-

[44] *Turner v Sawdon & Co* [1901] 2 KB 653 (CA).

[45] National Minimum Wage Regulations 1999, 1999/584, reg 15(1).

able when required by the employer. Such arrangements may not amount to binding contracts at all; rather they comprise 'umbrella agreements' about the terms of employment when and if the employee is called upon, and agrees to perform work.[46] Under both of these forms of employment relation, the employer obtains the advantage of allocating the risk of the lack of work to be performed onto the employee, thereby permitting the employer to adjust labour costs precisely to its needs at any particular time. For casual workers, like zero hours employees, their income is precarious, but they are subject to the additional risk of almost complete exclusion from employment protection rights because they lack any kind of long-term binding contract to perform work personally.

In the context of zero hours contracts and casual work contracts, the question arises whether the courts will imply a term into the contract that requires the employer to provide some work with the consequence that the employee should receive some wages. Such a term will be difficult to imply if the written contract expressly negatives any duty to offer work at all. But it may be possible to imply a term that restricts the employer's choice whether or not to offer work based upon the oral negotiations between the parties or on the basis of some other implicit understanding. In *Carmichael v National Power Plc*,[47] which concerned casual worker guides for groups of tourists around a nuclear power plant, the House of Lords rejected such an implication of terms imposing a duty upon the employer to provide work. Lord Irvine observed: 'The parties incurred no obligations to provide or accept work but at best assumed moral obligations of loyalty in a context where both recognised that the best interests of each lay in being accommodating to the other'.[48] The reference to an obligation of loyalty reflects the finding of the tribunal that the guides felt obligated to the manager and could not let him down by not being available to take a tour. In this evidence, there is recognition of the long-term economic interest that in practice binds the parties together in such casual work arrangements, but Lord Irvine insists that this creates merely a moral obligation, not a legal one.

In contrast, in the Court of Appeal in *Carmichael*, Ward LJ held that the agreement included an implied obligation on the company to provide a reasonable share of work for each guide whenever the company had work available and on the guides to take a reasonable amount of work.[49] Chadwick LJ formulated the implied term slightly differently: a promise by the guides to provide the service on being given reasonable notice, and a promise by the employer that any work available would be offered first to the trained guides before anyone else.[50] Either version of this implied term could be justified on the ground of business efficacy since it corresponded to the long-term economic interest of both parties, and

[46] H Collins, KD Ewing and A McColgan, *Labour Law* (Cambridge, Cambridge University Press, 2012) 179.

[47] *Carmichael v National Power Plc* [1999] ICR 1226.

[48] ibid, 1229E.

[49] *Carmichael* [1998] ICR 1167, 1187.

[50] ibid, ICR 1194, 1196.

deviation from it would probably provoke termination of the arrangement. Freedland supports this kind of approach as consonant with a relational approach to the contract of employment,[51] and it also fits a systems theory approach that emphasises the importance of both the long-term economic interests of the parties and the psychological dimensions of the contract of employment.[52] In the absence of the implication of such terms promising work to be performed, the risk for employees is that they will not be asked to perform any work, with the consequence that they will receive no wages and even be excluded from protection under employment law generally on the ground that they lack a contract of employment altogether.

B Payment by Results

An alternative way in which the risk of the absence of work can be shifted onto the employee is to use the express terms of the contract to make payment of wages contingent on the completion of a task, as in the case of piecework and commissions on sales, without any express obligation on the part of the employer to supply opportunities to satisfy those conditions. Such an arrangement relies on the absence of a default obligation on the employer to provide work, but replaces the duty to pay wages when the employee is ready and willing to perform work with a duty to pay wages only when work has actually been performed.

Devonald v Rosser Sons[53] illustrates the reluctance of courts to interpret contracts of employment in a way that imposes all risks of the absence of work onto the employee. The plaintiff worked as a rollerman in the defendant's tinplate factory. Under the express terms of his contract, the employee was required to perform those tasks directed by the employer and both parties were entitled to 28 days' notice of termination of employment. The employer used a piece-rate payment system for each completed box of 112 tin plates, though this payment mechanism was not specified in the written contract of employment. Following a decline in demand for its product, the employer closed the plant and two weeks later gave the employee notice of dismissal. The question before the court was what payment, if any, fell due during the six-week period between the plant closure and the expiration of the notice period, during which time the employer had not provided the employee with any work to perform. The Court of Appeal awarded the employee a sum equivalent to his average earnings prior to the plant closure for a period of six weeks. This result was achieved in part by regarding this particular contract of employment as a 'time-service contract' under which the employee should be paid when ready and willing to work, despite the payment mechanism of piece-rates. The Court distinguished between the continuing exis-

[51] M Freedland, *The Personal Contract of Employment* (Oxford, Oxford University Press, 2003) 104.

[52] H Collins, 'The Contract of Employment in 3D' in D Campbell, L Mulcahy and S Wheeler (eds), *Changing Concepts of Contract* (Basingstoke, Palgrave MacMillan, 2013) 65.

[53] *Devonald v Rosser Sons* [1906] 2 KB 728 (CA).

tence of the contract, which was determined by the operation of its notice provision, and its mechanism for determining the amount of pay due. According to the Court, as long as the contract persists and the employee is able and willing to work, the employer must either provide a reasonable amount of work to be performed, so that the employee may complete the required pieces, or pay compensation instead. Another line of argument endorsed by the Court was that, on a proper construction of the contract and giving it business efficacy, although the employee bore the risk of lack of work as a result of some contingencies such as breakdown of the machinery, an employee did not bear the risk of absence of work due to plant closure. The decision in *Devonald v Rosser Sons* therefore provides support for the idea that a court may imply a duty to pay some wages when the payment mechanism adopted is based upon outputs and as a result of a decision by the employer there is no work to be done, provided that the employee is also under an obligation to be ready and willing to work and under a duty to give notice of unavailability. This is not a right to work, but a right to be paid even if there is no work to be done. Furthermore, express terms of the contract may succeed in rebutting any such implication.

C Suspension

An employer may decide not to require the employee to perform any work while continuing to pay wages. There are a number of reasons why an employer may decide to suspend performance of work: as a disciplinary measure, perhaps pending a proper investigation of allegations of misconduct that have been made against an employee; as a response to redundancy in the sense that there is no available work of the kind that the employee was contracted to perform; or during the course of termination of the contract under a long period of notice when the employer does not want the employee to have continuing access to the information and knowledge generated within the business. Under the traditional interpretation of the contract of employment, the employer is not usually in breach of contract for failing to provide work provided that the wages continue to be paid.[54] This view is justified by the argument that the consideration to be provided by the employer under the contract is not to make work available but merely to pay wages. In the absence of express terms dealing with the matter, suspension without pay should therefore normally be regarded as a breach of contract.[55] But this traditional stance of the common law is surely incomplete, because it ignores various aspects of the performance of work that are highlighted by the idea of the right to work.

In the case of suspension on full pay as a disciplinary measure, though the employer may need to protect its interests or those of its customers or clients by taking such disciplinary action, there may come a point where the continuing

[54] *Turner*, above n 44.
[55] *Hanley v Pease & Partners Ltd* [1915] 1 KB 698.

suspension is disproportionate and unnecessary. At that point, the continuing suspension may be regarded as a breach of the implied term of mutual trust and confidence. The employee should then be entitled to resign and claim compensation for constructive dismissal.[56] Similarly, an employee who is ready and able to work, having been absent from work owing to illness from which he has now recovered, should be entitled to wages.[57] Suspension without pay may be permitted, however, as a disciplinary sanction where it is an authorised deduction under the express terms of the contract of employment. Again, misuse of this power in a disproportionate manner is likely to comprise a breach of the implied term of mutual trust and confidence.

In the case of redundancy, where there is no longer an appropriate job to be performed but the employer continues to pay wages, the traditional view is that the employer has not committed a breach of contract by failing to offer any work to be performed. But that view may have to be qualified where a skilled employee can establish that actual performance of work is important, because the employee needs to 'keep his hand in' by practising his skills.[58] A similar argument regarding an obligation to provide work to be performed applies where the opportunity to perform the job will potentially enhance the employee's reputation or standing in the profession, such as the opportunity to perform a leading role in a theatrical production.[59] It may also be qualified if the court finds an implied term in the particular circumstances of the case that the employer would provide suitable work for that employee.[60] Such a finding may have been the basis for the decision in *Collier v Sunday Referee Publishing Co*,[61] where the employee had a two-year fixed-term appointment as a sub-editor on a particular Sunday newspaper. The employer sold the newspaper and therefore no longer required his services. The court held that even though the employer offered to continue to pay wages, the absence of work to be performed constituted a fundamental breach of contract. The employee was therefore entitled to claim damages for wrongful dismissal. The issue between the parties was more complex, however, since the amount of wages for the fixed term of employment and the measure of damages would in principle be the same. The employer argued that the employee, by purporting to terminate the contract and seeking work elsewhere, was in breach of contract himself and not entitled to any more wages or damages. But Asquith J decided that the employee had merely accepted the employer's repudiatory breach of contract, and therefore could claim full compensatory damages for wrongful dismissal (subject to the duty to mitigate loss). The employer's breach of contract was the failure to provide the work envisioned in the contract as sub-editor of a

[56] *Gogay v Hertfordshire County Council* [2000] IRLR 703 (CA).

[57] *Beveridge v KLM UK Ltd* [2000] IRLR 765 (EAT).

[58] Suggested but not found applicable in the particular case in *Langston v Amalgamated Union of Engineering Workers* [1974] IRLR 182 (NIRC).

[59] *Fechter v Montgomery* [1863] 33 Beav 22; *Marbe v George Edwardes (Daly's Theatre) Ltd* [1928] 1 KB 269; *Herbert Clayton and Jack Waller Ltd v Oliver* [1930] AC 209.

[60] *Breach v Epsylon Industries* [1976] IRLR 180 (EAT).

[61] *Collier v Sunday Referee Publishing Co* [1940] 2 KB 647 (QB).

newspaper. It was not enough that the employer merely required the employee to hold himself ready and willing to perform work, when there was no prospect of such work arising.

The *Collier* case is hard to reconcile with the earlier authorities, because it suggests that some jobs may have special features that entitle the employee to expect work of a particular kind actually to be offered. Those jobs are presumably relatively high status positions; the job of 'sub-editor' is described as an 'office'. Freedland doubts whether it is satisfactory to identify jobs where the employer is under an obligation to provide work to be performed on the basis of 'this rather suspect typology of contracts and of workers'.[62] He argues instead that the issue should be regarded rather as whether the employer has misused its managerial powers so as to violate the implied term of mutual trust and confidence. In the *Collier* case, for instance, Freedland suggests that the employers may have hoped that the employee would resign in response to the absence of work, thereby avoiding any obligation to pay wages for the remainder of the fixed-term contract.[63] But it is hard to describe the employer's behaviour in this case as an abuse of managerial power, for it consisted only in continuing to pay wages when the editor was redundant. Another solution is to recognise, using the vehicle of an implied term, that at least in some jobs the performance of work of the particular kind promised will be important to the employee for reasons of gaining experience, know-how and fulfilment, and that deprivation of that opportunity (even though wages are being paid) would constitute a breach of that implied term. For example, if a person were appointed to be the Vinerian Professor of English Law at the University of Oxford, but then was instructed not to perform any of the duties of the post such as giving lectures, it could be argued that the University would have committed a breach of an implied term of the contract that the professor should be able to profess her field of expertise.

In the case of termination of contract by notice, either at the initiative of the employer or the employee, the question may arise whether the employee should be permitted to continue to work until the expiration of the notice period so that the employee can exercise a calling or profession. The employer may decide that the interests of the business are best served by excluding the employee during the period of notice while continuing to pay wages. At the same time, however, the employer may want to prevent the employee from resigning and working for a competitor. In effect, the employer may try to ensure that the employee remains at home, 'on garden leave', idle, but on full pay. This period of enforced rest may be challenged by the employee on the ground that it is unreasonable and unnecessary to protect the employer against unfair competition arising from the employee working for a competitor. If that claim is successful, the employer will be unable to win an injunction to prevent the employee from working for a competitor. Another ground on which it may be possible for an employee to challenge the

[62] Freedland, above n 51, 489.
[63] ibid, 490.

enforced idleness of garden leave during the period of notice is a claim that the employee needs to 'keep his hand in' by keeping up to date through work. In *William Hill Organisation Ltd v Tucker*,[64] a senior dealer in a betting business resigned in order to take a job with a competitor. His work involved the complex calculation of the determination of betting odds in a new market known as 'spread betting'. Under the terms of his contract, he was required to give six months' notice of termination. Although the contract did not contain an express 'garden leave' clause forbidding work for a competitor, the employer insisted that the employee should not work for a competitor during that period, but instead should remain at home and continue to receive his wages. The employer sought an injunction to restrain the employee from working for a competitor, but the injunction was refused. The Court of Appeal construed the contract to provide that, if the job is there to be done and the employee was appointed to do it and is ready and willing to do so, then the employer must permit him to do so. The employee needed to be able to exercise his skills and keep abreast of this rapidly developing specialist market. If the employer failed to provide suitable work during a lengthy notice period, the employee should be free to exercise his skills and maintain his employability by working for another employer. This decision does not give the employee the right to perform the job itself, but merely forbids attempts by the employer to prevent the employee from exercising their talents and skills for another employer where the employee has an interest in being able to perform work of this kind.

IV Termination of Employment

Legal protections for employees against dismissal without cause, or against dismissal for economic and business reasons, may be regarded as partly inspired by the right to work. An employee who is dismissed and becomes unemployed is deprived, if only temporarily, of the freedom to work. More seriously, dismissal for reasons of individual fault may damage an employee's career plans and employability, perhaps irretrievably. For example, a hospital consultant working for the NHS is likely to find it almost impossible to obtain another post as a consequence of having been dismissed for serious misconduct or incompetence. If those charges turn out to be false or misconceived, the doctor's right to work in the sense of freedom to pursue a profession may be severely damaged without justification. These severe consequences for the right to work will not occur in most instances of unfair dismissal or dismissal for redundancy. After a period of search for a job, most dismissed employees will be able to obtain equivalent jobs in their chosen line of work. In the majority of cases of unfair dismissal, therefore, the main justification for legal protection lies not so much in protection of the

[64] *William Hill Organisation Ltd v Tucker* [1999] ICR 291 (CA).

right to work, but in the protection of employees against injury to their dignity and self-respect by unfounded charges and unfair treatment by employers and also to provide some protection for job security and the opportunity to make plans for one's life. Even so, the deprivation of employees from substantial protection from unfair dismissal that has resulted from the introduction of a two-year qualifying period[65] and from exorbitant charges for bringing a claim before a tribunal[66] certainly undermines the right to work.

In the case of economic dismissals, the argument in favour of requiring employers to pay some compensation is probably more concerned with minimising social costs than with protecting the right to work and job security. A possible exception arises under the Transfer of Undertakings Regulations 2006,[67] Regulation 7(1), which renders a dismissal in connection with a relevant transfer automatically unfair. The aim of this provision is to keep employees in their jobs despite the sale of the business to a new employer. However, this protection is substantially weakened by the further provision that the new employer can make dismissals for economic, technical or organisational reasons, though it will be required usually to make a redundancy payment. It is rare that a finding of unfair dismissal will result in an order of reinstatement, which further supports the view that the legal framework is not focused on the right to work as much as other values and principles. These connections between the right to work and the law of dismissal and reinstatement are considered in more detail below in the chapter by Joanna Howe.[68]

Here the focus will be on those uncommon cases where dismissal from a job has the consequence of effectively denying an individual the right (in the terms of Article 15 CFREU) 'to pursue a freely chosen or accepted occupation'. As well as the hospital doctor mentioned above, other individuals who might find themselves in such a situation may include workers in the financial and banking sector, where dismissal for dishonesty or serious breach of financial regulations is likely to preclude future employment in that sector, and workers whose jobs involve contact with children such as teachers or youth club leaders, where the reason for the dismissal is some kind of inappropriate sexual or violent conduct towards the children. Assuming that the allegations against the employee are false or mistaken, the question arises whether UK law affords the individual effective protection for the right to work.

In principle, such an employee may bring a statutory claim for unfair dismissal and seek either reinstatement or compensation. The test of fairness includes a requirement placed on the employer to follow a fair procedure and for the

[65] Unfair Dismissal and Statement of Reasons for Dismissal (Variation of Qualifying Period) Order 2012, SI 2012/989.

[66] The Employment Tribunals and the Employment Appeal Tribunal Fees Order 2013, SI 2013/1893.

[67] Transfer of Undertakings (Protection of Employment) Regulations (SI 2006/246), which implements Council Directive 2001/23/EC of 12 March 2001 on the approximation of the laws of the Member States relating to the safeguarding of employees' rights in the event of transfers of undertakings, businesses or parts of undertakings or businesses ('Acquired Rights Directive') Art 4.

[68] J Howe in this volume, ch 14.

employer to have acted reasonably in all the circumstances. Provided the employer carries out a fair investigation of the circumstances and has acted within the range of reasonable responses to the circumstances of the case, the dismissal will be regarded as fair, even though the case against the employee may not be proven.[69] Even if the dismissal is found to be unfair, an employment tribunal is unlikely to order reinstatement as the employer may argue that in the circumstances, such as where there persists a residue of suspicion against the employee, it would not be 'practicable' to reinstate the employee.[70] A tribunal will award 'just and equitable' compensation to the employee for the losses caused by the unfair dismissal,[71] but that amount is constrained by a fixed upper limit,[72] so that the loss of a career in a particular profession will not be fully compensated. The statutory protection of the law of unfair dismissal is therefore unlikely to provide an adequate remedy for the wrong of damaging the right to work in the sense of an unfair exclusion from a chosen career or profession.

An alternative course of action available to the employee is to claim breach of contract under the common law. This is an area of considerable complexity and confusion. Compensatory damages for the wrongful dismissal itself are strictly limited to the wages due under the period of notice to which the employee is entitled. But under the normal principles of the common law of contract an employee should be able to claim damages for breach of another term of the contract apart from the duty to give notice. In *Mahmoud v Bank of Credit and Commerce International SA*,[73] for instance, which concerned banking staff, the House of Lords accepted that the employer had broken the implied term of mutual trust and confidence by operating a corrupt business with the consequence that the employee's reputation and employability in a particular line of work may have been harmed. If the stigma was demonstrated to have damaged career prospects in banking, it was held that it would be possible to claim damages for the economic loss caused by that stigma. Similarly, if in breach of contract an employer negligently writes an inaccurate and damaging reference for an employee that significantly harms his job prospects in a particular line of business, in this case finance and insurance, it was decided in *Spring v Guardian Assurance plc* that in principle the employee should be able to recover compensation for the economic losses caused by the damage to reputation.[74] This claim for the economic loss resulting from damage to reputation faces great obstacles in practice, however, because the employee will have to prove the causal link between the stigma and his failure to obtain future employment in a particular profession. The employee may need to bring evidence from prospective employers her job application was rejected owing to the cloud of suspicion caused by the employer's

[69] *Post Office v Foley; HSBC v Madden* [2000] ICR 1283 (CA).
[70] Employment Rights Act 1996, s 116(1)(b).
[71] ibid, s 123.
[72] ibid, s 124.
[73] *Mahmoud v Bank of Credit and Commerce International SA* [1998] AC 20 (HL).
[74] *Spring v Guardian Assurance plc* [1994] ICR 596 (HL).

misconduct or negligent and inaccurate reference, and that this cause of rejection was weightier than other considerations such as qualifications and experience.[75]

A possible alternative way of presenting such a case would be to claim damages for the stigma itself on the ground that the distress and psychological injury of the dismissal, together with damage to personal reputation, represent losses that should be compensated. Claims of this kind at common law appear to be foreclosed by *Addis v Gramophone Co Ltd*,[76] where the House of Lords appears to have disallowed an award of damages by a jury that could only be explained by their concern for the damage to the reputation of the employee arising from the summary dismissal. A similar restriction has been applied under the statutory claim for unfair dismissal, though it may be possible to claim a larger amount of compensation for economic loss if it can be demonstrated that the stigma has affected job prospects following the dismissal. In contrast, the ECtHR has been more attentive to psychological damage and injury to reputation resulting from an unfair dismissal. In a case where a senior policeman was dismissed amid much attendant publicity for condoning the torture of suspects under interrogation, following his reinstatement when it emerged that the claims were untrue (or at least not proven), he unsuccessfully sought compensation for the 'moral damage' arising from the dismissal. The peremptory rejection of this claim by the Cypriot Supreme Court was found by the ECtHR to have unjustifiably interfered with his right to respect for his private life under Article 8 ECHR, a provision that includes respect for a person's reputation.[77] Although this was a very severe case, the similar peremptory rejection of such claims for damage to reputation arising from dismissal under UK law must also be vulnerable to challenge under the ECHR.

Moreover, the courts have demonstrated a steadfast resistance towards awarding substantial damages at common law for loss of a career. One reason given for this resistance is that a substantial award of damages would circumvent the upper limit on compensation provided for claims for unfair dismissal.[78] That argument should not apply to claims regarding a breach of contract that has damaged a career and that occurred prior to termination of the contract,[79] but in practice it is hard to disentangle such claims since an employee who is subjected to such unfair treatment is likely to regard himself accurately as having been constructively dismissed. Perhaps the most effective way in which an employee can obtain legal protection against an unjustified dismissal that damages career prospects is to obtain terms in the contract of employment that require the employer to follow a fair procedure that is likely to make an accurate assessment of the employee's fault. It is likely that an employee would be able to obtain an interim injunction against breach of that procedure, thereby preventing in the short term the

[75] eg, *Bank of Credit and Commerce International SA v Ali* [1999] IRLR 508 (ChD).
[76] *Addis v Gramophone Co Ltd* [1919] AC 488 (HL).
[77] *Kyriakides v Cyprus* [2008] ECHR 1087.
[78] *Johnson v Unisys Ltd* [2001] UKHL 13, [2001] ICR 480 (HL).
[79] *Eastwood v Magnox Electric plc* [2004] UKHL 35, [2005] AC 503 (HL).

dismissal from taking place.[80] Indeed, this appears to be the employee's only remedy for breach of a contractual procedure, since a majority of the Supreme Court in *Edwards v Chesterfield Royal Hospital Trust* and *Botham v Ministry of Defence* rejected any claim for career damages at common law for breach of a contractual disciplinary procedure.[81]

This restriction on claims for damages for breach of a contractual disciplinary procedure removes a crucial ingredient in protection for the right to work. In *Edwards*, for instance, a consultant surgeon employed by the defendant NHS Trust was summarily dismissed for gross professional and personal misconduct. He asserted that the defendant had not followed the correct contractual disciplinary procedure, and that, if the employer had followed the correct procedure, he would not have been found guilty and would not have been dismissed from his position. He claimed compensation in the sum of £4.3 million for loss of income until the age of retirement, plus an additional sum for loss of an occupational pension, on the basis that this amount represented his loss of earnings for the remainder of his career, because in the circumstances the dismissal for misconduct would prevent him from ever obtaining a permanent consultant position in the NHS again. This claim for breach of the contractual disciplinary procedure was rejected and so his compensation was confined to his wages during his notice period, assuming that the dismissal was wrongful, plus possibly a further amount representing his wages during his suspension during the period of time that the correct procedure would have taken to complete.[82] In the *Botham* case, a youth worker whose dismissal seemed certain to disbar him from working with young people again was equally unsuccessful on the ground that his losses were caused by the dismissal itself rather than the defective procedure, so that his only claim (which had been successful) lay under the statutory claim for unfair dismissal. These decisions restrict the protection afforded by the common law against dismissals or breaches of contract that seriously damage an employee's career prospects. While there may be a need to restrict the total amount of damages in such cases, a significant reduction can usually be achieved by an application of the duty to mitigate loss. It is unnecessary and a disproportionate interference to disallow altogether any compensation for injury to the right to work.

V Regulatory Restrictions on Access to Work

Governments have good reasons to regulate access to particular kinds of work. Consumers need protection against those who falsely claim professional skills such as those of doctors, pharmacists, lawyers and dentists. As well as occupa-

[80] *West London Mental Health NHS Trust v Chhabra* [2013] UKSC 80.

[81] *Edwards v Chesterfield Royal Hospital NHS Foundation Trust, Botham v Ministry of Defence* [2011] UKSC 58, [2012] ICR 201.

[82] *Gunton v Richmond-upon-Thames London Borough Council* [1980] ICR 755 (CA).

tional licensing schemes, recent legislation has developed the regulatory technique of blacklists under which persons included on a list are prevented from working with groups such as children and vulnerable adults.[83] In the public sector, some parts of government require security clearances and nationality qualifications that restrict the freedom to work. Governments also seek to control access to the domestic labour market. Some measures, such as those applicable to school age youth in order to protect their education and safety, seem fully justifiable.[84] Others, such as the controls over the absolute numbers of immigrants and the imposition of selective entry requirements provoke political controversy.[85] However they may be justified, all these regulatory restrictions on access to work interfere with the right to work in the sense of the freedom to pursue a freely chosen occupation.

A Common Law

While various regulatory controls over access to work have existed for centuries, since the seventeenth century the starting point of the common law seems to have been vigorous support for freedom of access to work. At the beginning of the seventeenth century, the Corporation of the Tailors of Ipswich, a town in Suffolk, was a guild incorporated under a charter from the king, which granted the corporation general authority to regulate their trade. The guild barred anyone from practising as a tailor in Ipswich, unless they had served an apprenticeship for seven years (a statutory requirement) and had been approved by its master and wardens. William Seninge moved to Ipswich and practised as a tailor in the service of a gentleman, and did not seek approval from the guild for 20 days. The guild sued Seninge in debt under its ordinance, seeking £3 13s 4d. In 1614, the Court of Common Pleas declared that the common law will not allow a man to be prohibited from a lawful trade. The protections of quality in services afforded by the guild system were applicable to sales to the general public, not within a household. Furthermore, someone who purchased defective work would have a remedy in an action on the case, so that the guild's restraint on trade was unnecessary. But more fundamentally, beyond the argument that the guild had exceeded its authority to regulate the trade, the Court upheld a general protection for freedom of access to work:

> At the Common Law no man might be forbidden to work in any lawful Trade, for the Law doth abhor idleness, the mother of all evil, . . . and chiefly in young men, who ought to their youth, (which is the time of their sowing) to learn lawful Sciences and Trades, which are profitable to the Commonwealth, and whereof they might gather the

[83] Safeguarding Vulnerable Groups Act 2006, as amended by Protection of Freedoms Act 2012, Part V.

[84] Council Directive 94/33/EC of 22 June 1994 on the protection of young people at work [1994] OJ L216/12.

[85] Immigration law as a restriction on the right to work is considered by V Mantouvalou in this volume, ch 3.

> fruit in their old age, for idle in youth, poor in age; and therefore the Common Law doth abhor all Monopolies, which forbid any one to work in any lawful Trade.[86]

As well as applying to delegated legislation such as the ordinances of the Taylor's Guild, the freedom also applied to contractual covenants in restraint of trade. Even in an otherwise binding contract a promise not to work in a particular trade for a period of time in a particular location could be invalid under the doctrine of restraint of trade. For instance, in the second year of the reign of Henry V, a dyer was subject to a contractual requirement that he should not use the dyer's craft for two years. Hull J declared that the obligation was against the common law and that if the plaintiff (who was trying to enforce the covenant) had been in court he would, by God, have sent him to prison.[87] Without going into detail about the restraint of trade doctrine and its application to non-competition clauses in contracts, the mandatory prohibition against covenants in restraint of trade and other terms that are functionally equivalent such as garden leave clauses remains applicable, so that restrictions on access to work imposed by statutes and contract will require strong justification. It is true that restraints can in principle be justified, either on the ground of reasonableness as between the parties or in the public interest, but any term that imposes a significant restraint on the right to work is unlikely to satisfy those requirements.

Under British constitutional conventions, it seems unlikely that the common law could be invoked as a means of challenging parliamentary primary legislation that imposes regulatory restrictions on the right to work. Challenges to such restrictions would therefore have to rely on either the supremacy of EU law or on the HRA 1998, which permits domestic legal enforcement of the ECHR.

B EU Law

As well as the common law, EU law places controls over the extent to which a national government may lawfully restrict access to work. The free movement of workers is guaranteed by Article 45 TFEU, and this freedom extends to the self-employed and businesses that are service providers.[88] At their inception these measures were regarded as serving the economic aim of permitting migration in order to reduce unemployment in the internal market and to match skills to the needs of each home state. More recently, the right of workers to freedom of movement has been conceived as an aspect of their rights to EU citizenship, so that as citizens they have the right to move themselves and their families to another Member State.[89] The protected status of worker includes those seeking

[86] The Case of the Tailors of Habits &c. of Ipswich (1614) Michaelmas Term, 12 James 1. *Coke's Reports,* vol 11, 53a (KB).

[87] 2 Hen 5 5b.

[88] TFEU, Arts 49 and 56.

[89] Directive 2004/38/EC of 29 April 2004 on the right of citizens of the Union and their family members on the right of citizens of the Union and their family members to move and reside freely within the territory of the Member States [2004] OJ L158/77 ('Citizens Rights Directive').

work.[90] Workers exercising their right to freedom of movement are protected against direct or indirect discrimination in the labour market on the basis of nationality,[91] and can work in any Member State and remain in that state after having been employed.[92] These treaty rights are directly effective, so that applicants can rely on them against the host government[93] and a private employer.[94] For the UK government or an employer to try to reserve jobs for British workers would therefore breach these free market provisions.

Furthermore, even non-discriminatory national measures that substantially impede access to the labour market may also breach the market freedoms protected by TFEU unless they can be objectively justified.[95] It is here that EU law presents its severest challenge to those national regulations over access to employment and pursuit of an occupation that may serve entirely legitimate purposes such as consumer protection. For example, an application by a Greek lawyer to become a *Rechtsanwalt* – German lawyer – was refused by a German Ministry of Justice on the grounds that she had neither completed the First State exams, nor studied law at a German university for two years, nor undergone the relevant period of training in Germany, though she had in fact worked for a German law firm for five years. She successfully argued that the German regulations violated Article 49 TFEU, the right to freedom of establishment including the right to take up and pursue activities as a self-employed person, as no account was taken under those regulations of her Greek legal qualifications or her work experience in Germany.[96] This decision indicates that restrictions on the freedom to pursue an occupation or a profession that are based upon formalities and formal qualifications will always be vulnerable to claims for their invalidity under EU law unless the regulations also permit substitutes such as other qualifications and experience. To overcome the complexity of this standard, EU law tries to facilitate cross-border movement of the employed and self-employed by providing a general scheme for mutual recognition of professional qualifications between Member States.[97] In assessing whether or not such restrictions in national regulations regarding the right to work will be regarded by EU law as justifiable, it is important to recall that EU law must be interpreted in the light of the CFREU, including Article 15, which presents the right to work as a fundamental right. In addition, the right to respect for private life in CFREU Article 7 (which repeats Article 8 ECHR) may be invoked when national regulations block the pursuit of a

[90] Case C-85/96 *Martinez Sala v Freistaat Bayern* [1988] ECR I-2691; Case C-138/02 *Collins v Secretary of State for Work and Pensions* [2003] ECR I-2703.

[91] reg 492/2011.

[92] TFEU, Art 45(3).

[93] Case 41/74 *Van Duyn* [1974] ECR 1337.

[94] Case C-281/98 *Angonese* [1998] ECR I-4139.

[95] Case C-415/93 *Union Royale Belge des Sociétés de Football Association ASBL v Jean-Marc Bosman* [1995] ECR I-4921; Case C-379/09 *Casteels v British Airways* [2011] ECR I-1379.

[96] Case C-340/89 *Vlassopoulou v Ministerium fur Justiz Bundes- und Europeaangelegenheiten Baden-Wurtemberg* [1991] ECR I-2357.

[97] Directive 2005/36/EC of 7 September 2005 on the recognition of professional qualifications [2005] OJ L255/22.

professional career, especially when an individual has already been permitted to embark on such a career, as where a Russian national had been permitted to have a training contract with a law firm and to take the professional examinations, only then to be excluded from the profession by the Greek Order of Advocates.[98]

Article 45 TFEU provides an important exception for employment in the public service. It permits discrimination on the ground of nationality for jobs that 'involve direct or indirect participation in the exercise of powers conferred by public law and duties designed to safeguard the interests of the State or of other public authorities'.[99] The European Commission suggests that this exception would normally apply only to the police, armed forces, the judiciary, tax authorities and the Diplomatic Service.[100] The free movement of workers protects the right to work in the sense of access to the labour market only for EU citizens. These measures do not protect the right to work of third-country nationals from outside the EU,[101] and indeed EU law requires Member States to have minimum standards on sanctions against employers of illegally staying third-country nationals.[102]

C Human Rights Act 1998

A second route by which national primary and secondary legislation that restricts access to work may be challenged is under the Human Rights Act 1998. Although the ECHR rights that are protected under the Act do not explicitly mention the right to work, that does not mean that the right to work is unimportant in the judicial interpretation of the protected rights. On the contrary, notions related to the right to work may influence the interpretation of the scope and meaning of a particular right and they may also play a role in the application of the test of proportionality when considering whether an interference with a right is justifiable.[103]

With respect to the interpretation of the protected rights, for instance, one issue before the Supreme Court has been whether the right to a fair trial in the determination of disputes regarding civil rights, under Article 6 ECHR, requires public authorities to have an elaborate quasi-judicial procedure prior to the dismissal of a public sector worker. Such a procedure might require a hearing before an independent disciplinary panel with the possibility of legal representation.

[98] *Bigaeva v Greece* [2011] ECHR 2164.

[99] Case 149/79 *Commission v Belgium* [1982] ECR 1845, [7].

[100] Notice no 88/C [1988] OJ C72/02.

[101] Though EU law does provide some protection for third-country nationals who have been admitted lawfully by a Member State: S Inglesias Sánchez, 'Free Movement of Third Country nationals in the European Union? Main Features, Deficiencies and Challenges of the New Mobility Rights in the Area of Freedom, Security and Justice' (2009) 15 *European Law Journal* 791.

[102] Directive 2009/52/EC of 18 June 2009 providing for minimum standards on sanctions and measures against employers of illegally staying third-country nationals [2009] OJ L168/24. The United Kingdom is not taking part in this Directive, though UK law probably exceeds its minimum standards.

[103] R O'Connell, 'The Right to Work in the European Convention on Human Rights' (2012) 2 *European Human Rights Law Review* 176.

While denying that consequence of Article 6 – since public sector workers in general have the same right to bring a statutory claim for unfair dismissal before a tribunal as private sector workers – the Supreme Court has applied Article 6 requirements where the dismissal and associated administrative procedures involve more than the loss of a particular job, because it interferes with the right to work in the sense of the right to pursue one's chosen occupation. The ECtHR has held that the 'right to practice a profession' is a civil right, and the Court will uphold the right even though national law does not expressly provide such a civil right in the circumstances.[104] Usually, however, the dismissal by an employer from a particular job and the administrative or professional banning from employment in a particular sector are separate procedures. Where the dismissal by the employer does not determine the outcome of the administrative blacklisting, the formal requirements of Article 6 do not apply to the employer's dismissal procedure, but solely to the administrative decision.[105] The test is whether the decision to dismiss has 'a substantial influence or effect' on the administrative decision to blacklist.[106] This distinction is not entirely convincing, since it seems likely that in many circumstances an employer's dismissal of an employee for gross misconduct will influence considerably the outcome of the administrative blacklisting. Where there is no administrative blacklist, but where a dismissal on grave charges seems likely to deprive an individual of the opportunity to pursue his or her chosen career, it seems possible that Article 6 may be engaged – at least to the extent of permitting the individual to have legal representation.[107]

Regarding the operation of the administrative procedure itself, in *R (Wright) v Secretary of State for Health*,[108] following dismissal for gross misconduct from a care home, a registered nurse looking after vulnerable adults was included on a statutorily authorised blacklist as someone unsuitable for that kind of work,[109] thereby preventing her from getting any other such employment in the future.[110] Although she had the right to appeal to a tribunal against the listing – an appeal that was successful after several years had passed – she complained that her rights under Articles 6 and 8 ECHR had been unjustifiably breached on the ground that there had been no formal procedure by which to contest the listing of her name prior to its 'provisional listing'. The Supreme Court accepted that there had been a breach of Article 6, because the procedure did not provide for a fair hearing

[104] *Le Compte, Van Leuven and De Meyere v Belgium* [1981] ECHR 3, (1982) 4 EHRR 1.

[105] *R (on the application of G) v Governors of X School* [2011] UKSC 30, [2012] 1 AC 167. A Sanders, 'Does Article 6 of the European Convention on Human Rights Apply to Disciplinary Procedures in the Workplace?' (2013) 33 *Oxford Journal of Legal Studies* 791.

[106] *R(G) v Governors of X School*, ibid [69], [90], [104].

[107] *Kulkarni v Milton Keynes Hospital NHS Trust* [2009] EWCA Civ 789, [2010] ICR 101; this position has been doubted in *Mattu v Univ Hospitals of Cov & Warw NHS Trust* [2012] EWCA Civ 641, [2013] ICR 270, but seems to be supported by decisions of the ECtHR such as *Le Compte*, above n 104, where the emphasis is on the effects on a professional career in fact. See Sanders, above n 105, 807–08.

[108] *R (Wright) v Secretary of State for Health* [2009] UKHL 3.

[109] Care Standards Act 2000, ss 80–82.

[110] Care Standards Act 2000, s 89 apparently authorises summary dismissal and makes it a criminal offence for a listed care worker to apply for a job in the sector.

prior to an inclusion on the blacklist, which might do irreparable damage to a person's employment or prospects of employment.[111]

In addition, the Supreme Court was inclined to take the view that the listing procedure violated Article 8, the right to privacy, because the low threshold and weak procedure for listing posed a potential risk of a major impact on personal relationships that might interfere with the right to respect for private life.[112] In *Sidabras v Lithuania*,[113] the ECtHR had concluded that the legislation that banned former KGB officers not only from public sector employment, but also from large swathes of private sector jobs interfered with the right to privacy. The law 'affected [their] ability to develop relationships with the outside world to a very significant degree, and has created serious difficulties for them as regards the possibility to earn their living, with obvious repercussions on the enjoyment of their private life'.[114] Given the discriminatory stigma attached to having been a former KGB officer, the ECtHR concluded that the legislation fell within the ambit of Article 8 for the purpose of the prohibition of discrimination in the enjoyment of Convention rights protected in Article 14. This decision suggests strongly that the right to work in the sense of the freedom to pursue one's chosen profession falls within the scope of Article 8, so that any legal restrictions on the freedom will need to be justifiable under a strict test of proportionality, and in addition the formal requirements of a fair trial under Article 6 will also have to be satisfied. That view of the scope of Article 8 was confirmed in *Campagnano v Italy*,[115] where a bankrupt person who was automatically excluded from a large number of types of work and professions for a period of five years persuaded the Court that this was a disproportionate interference with the right to respect for private life. Article 8 was also used by the ECtHR as the successful ground for challenging the UK's policy of a complete ban on gay men and lesbians from serving in the armed forces.[116]

With regard to the use of the right to work in assessing the proportionality of an interference with a protected right, the ECtHR has observed on many occasions that dismissal or exclusion from the labour market is a severe penalty that requires a strong justification.[117] Rules that require dismissal or managerial decisions to dismiss a worker in circumstances that involve an interference with a Convention right must therefore be appropriate and necessary. In particular, the Court will assess whether a lesser disciplinary sanction would have served the legitimate aim of the employer. In *Obst v Germany*,[118] the applicant was dismissed from his position as director of public relations for the Mormon Church for hav-

[111] Para [28].

[112] *R (Wright)*, above n 108, para [36].

[113] *Sidabras v Lithuania* (2004) 42 EHRR 104.

[114] ibid, para [48].

[115] *Campagnano v Italy* (2006) 48 EHRR 43.

[116] *Lustig-Prean v UK* (1999) 29 EHRR 548; *Smith and Grady v UK* (1999) 29 EHRR 493.

[117] *Fuentes Bobo v Spain* (2001) 31 EHRR 50; *Redfearn v UK* [2013] IRLR 51 (ECtHR); *Pay v UK* [2009] IRLR 139 (ECtHR).

[118] *Obst v Germany* App no 425/03 (ECtHR, 23 September 2010).

ing an extramarital affair. In this case, the dismissal was justifiable despite an interference with Article 8, because the applicant had been raised as a member of the Mormon Church and was aware that his conduct would be contrary to its beliefs, which he (as a person responsible for its public relations) represented. By signing his contract with the Mormon Church, he had consented to respect marital fidelity as a central tenet of the Church. In contrast, in *Schuth v Germany*,[119] the ECtHR found a breach of Article 8 when the German labour court declined to find that a dismissal was unfair in the circumstance that the organist and choirmaster of a Catholic church was dismissed for having an extramarital affair. The Court held that the dismissal and interference with Article 8 did not satisfy a test of proportionality, because the affair had not be publicised in a way that could harm the image of the Roman Catholic Church and because (unlike in *Obst*) it would be hard for the applicant to find another employer given the specialised nature of his work. Here, the right to work in the sense of being able to pursue one's chosen occupation of being an organ player in a church was threatened, so the dismissal could not eventually be justified as proportionate.

VI Conclusion

This exploration of the contemporary protection of the right to work in UK law demonstrates the existence of a thorough and almost comprehensive protection for the freedom to work in the sense of the removal of unjustifiable restrictions on the pursuit of employment or a career. This assertion of a free market for labour has been achieved to a considerable extent as a result of the EU's measures designed to facilitate the free movement of workers within the single market and to embrace a strong principle of equal opportunities in the labour market. Fundamental rights protected under the CFREU and the ECHR also play a vital role in providing grounds for challenging rules and procedures that tend to exclude jobseekers from finding jobs and pursuing a calling. To a considerable extent these measures have met Hepple's hopes – expressed in his 1981 article – that the law would guarantee the fundamental right of individuals to equal treatment and equal respect.[120]

On the other hand, UK law has arguably reduced its protection for job security in the intervening years. The decline in effective union representation combined with such legal measures as the extension of the qualifying period for unfair dismissal to two years, and the fees charged by tribunals that obstruct access to justice have rendered all jobs more precarious. The policy goal of encouraging flexibility in labour markets has in the United Kingdom led to a decline in jobs that fit the old standard model of permanent full-time employment. The idea of

[119] *Schuth v Germany* App no 1620/03 (ECtHR, 23 September 2010).
[120] Hepple, above n 1, 82.

job security has been replaced with the idea of employability as the preferred way of supporting a right to work. In this realm of job security, the EU lacks general competence to regulate dismissals though it has provided stronger protection in the event of economic dismissals. The ECtHR has also provided modest support for job security against dismissals by employers that interfere with the Convention rights of employees. Perhaps the strongest decision in that vein was *Redfearn v UK*,[121] where a majority of the Court held that the qualifying period for unfair dismissal had to be excluded where the employee claimed that the reason for dismissal involved an interference with an ECHR right.[122] The ECtHR also regards dismissal by an employer as a severe measure, so that under the test of proportionality an employer must have powerful reasons for dismissal and should consider other less harsh disciplinary measures.

None of this legal framework addresses directly the idea of a social right to work, under which the state would guarantee all workers a job. Of course, the government invests considerable resources in facilitating job search through the provision of jobcentres and in offering training in skills through the education system. But the emphasis in recent years of these arrangements has been to challenge 'welfare dependency' by a combination of deprivation or reduction of benefits and the provision of incentives to work such as the possibility of in-work benefits to supplement low pay. Although work is vital to social inclusion and the pursuit of meaning in our lives, governments either lack the tools or the will to ensure that everyone has a job.

[121] *Redfearn*, above n 117; H Collins and V Mantouvalou, '*Redfearn v UK*: Political Association and Dismissal' (2013) 76 *Modern Law Review* 909.

[122] The decision required a new exclusion from the qualifying period: Enterprise and Regulatory Reform Act 2013, s13, amending Employment Rights Act 1996 s 108.

14

Why Do So Few Employees Return to their Jobs? In Pursuit of a Right to Work Following Unfair Dismissal

JOANNA HOWE

Introduction

The centrality of work to a person's life has long been accepted.[1] Work provides us with the economic means to live. Other benefits also ensue: a framework for acquiring and practising skills, a chance to develop friendships and networks, an impetus to refrain from idleness and the opportunity to find meaning and purpose for one's existence through contribution to a larger good, such as the success of the business or the well-being of the community. When an employee is dismissed without just cause, all this is unfairly taken away. Thus, a 'right to work', which is enforceable against the employer, can be realised if a worker who has been unfairly dismissed can insist upon returning to his or her job. Of course, the notion of a right to work is much broader than this and its other dimensions are explored elsewhere in this book. In particular, the contribution of Bob Hepple in developing the notion of a right to work in his seminal piece in the *Industrial Law Journal* provides the inspiration for this chapter, which focuses specifically on a right to work in the context of unfair dismissal. Although Hepple's article explores the idea of a right to work more generally, he explores the meaning of 'a right to work' as being a right against the employer. In his view, this encompasses 'a right to remain continuously employed, including the right to be reinstated in the event of unjustified termination'.[2] This chapter draws upon the limited extent to which reinstatement is awarded in the unfair dismissal systems of Australia and Britain,

[1] eg, see J Budd, *The Thought of Work* (New York, Cornell University Press, 2011); F Meyers, *Ownership of Jobs: A Comparative Study* (Los Angeles, University of California Press, 1964); W Njoya, *Property in Work* (Aldershot, Ashgate Publishing, 2007); B Hepple, 'A Right to Work' (1981) 10 *Industrial Law Journal* 65; R Owens, J Riley and J Murray, *The Law of Work* (South Melbourne, Oxford University Press, 2011) ch 1.

[2] Hepple, 'A Right to Work', above n 1, 73.

to argue that neither jurisdiction presently fully recognises a right to work.[3] This is contrasted to the historical situation in both jurisdictions, where reinstatement was achieved more regularly, albeit not as a universal entitlement, for it existed predominantly in unionised workplaces. The final part of this chapter explores reasons why reinstatement has become such a marginalised remedy under British and Australian unfair dismissal laws and suggests alternatives as to how to ameliorate the status quo.

I The Treatment of Reinstatement in Legislation and Case Law

Statutory protection against unfair dismissal is accorded in both Britain and Australia. In the former, a right against unfair dismissal was introduced in the Industrial Relations Act 1971 (UK) and enabled an individual employee to query the employer's decision of dismissal before an employment tribunal. Over three decades later, unfair dismissal protection was introduced in the Australian federal system in the Industrial Relations Act 1993 (Cth), which provided independent adjudication of the fairness of an employee's dismissal. From the beginning, both unfair dismissal systems permitted either compensation or reinstatement to be awarded.

In Australia and Britain there is a disjuncture between the legislative provision, whereby reinstatement is the primary remedy for unfair dismissal and the practical reality, which is that neither jurisdiction awards it to any significant degree. In Australia, the preference for reinstatement over compensation has been present in the architectural foundation of Australia's federal unfair dismissal system since its inception in 1993, although its status has ebbed and flowed over time. Section 170EE of the Industrial Relations Act 1993 (Cth) indicated plainly that 'it was Parliament's intention that the primary remedy for unlawful termination should be reinstatement and that compensation should be available only where this was impracticable'.[4] However, in the Workplace Relations Act 1996 (Cth) this was amended so that reinstatement was the 'primary' remedy under the Act, but only in the sense that reinstatement must be considered *first*. There was no overriding presumption in favour of reinstatement under section 170CH.[5] This was changed in 2009 under the Fair Work Act 2009 (Cth) with the insertion of section 390(1), providing reinstatement as the presumptive remedy when dismissal has been

[3] Other limitations on unfair dismissal law also exist in both jurisdictions, eg, the two-year qualifying period in the UK before an application can be made and the imposition of filing costs. In Australia, there is a six-month qualifying period before an unfair dismissal application can be made, and for employees of a small business this period is 12 months.

[4] *Liddell v Lembke* (1994) 127 ALR 342, 360 (Wilcox CJ and Keely J).

[5] *Newtronics Pty Ltd v Salenga*, Print R4305, 29 April 1999, Polites SDP, Acton DP, Smith C, 6, affirming the decision of the Full Bench in *Australia Meat Holdings v McLaughlan* (1998) 84 IR 1.

deemed to be unfair. The intention of legislators that an unfairly dismissed worker should be able to return to her job is also evident from the Explanatory Memorandum[6] and the objects of the unfair dismissal provisions contained in section 380(1)(c), which requires that the system provides remedies for an unfair dismissal with 'an emphasis on reinstatement'.

In Britain, legislators initially favoured the remedy of compensation following the advice of the Donovan Commission.[7] This policy was changed with the Employment Protection Act 1975 (UK), expressly providing that reinstatement was to be the primary remedy. To encourage more orders of reinstatement, the legislation was amended again in 1978 to make it clear that if an employee wished to be reinstated the tribunal must make an order to this effect, unless it was satisfied by the employer that it was 'impracticable for him to comply with an order, or that it would not be just to make an order because the employee caused or contributed to his own dismissal'.[8] This legislative preference for reinstatement has continued to the present day, and is now encapsulated in section 116 of the Employment Rights Act 1996 (UK). However, this provision operates on a more qualified basis than in Australia, as 'it is necessary nevertheless to appreciate the form in which that intention, or presumption, is enacted. It consists simply in providing that those remedies be considered first'.[9]

Yet, despite the intentions of legislators, in both jurisdictions reinstatement is very much the exception and has always been so. In Britain, as far back as 1973, only 4.2 per cent of cases settled through conciliation resulted in the worker returning to their job and by 1979 this had fallen to 1.8 per cent.[10] Of those who went to a tribunal hearing, 2.3 per cent were recommended to be given their job back in 1973, but by 1979 only 0.8 per cent were awarded reinstatement orders.[11] Freedland and Davies noted that the commitment to reinstatement by Labour during its term in government between 1974 and 1979 was limited at best:

> [T]he crucial point, however, is that the 1970 Bill, 1971 Act and 1975 reforms all protected the freedom of the employer to buy its way out of an award of reinstatement upon payment of a relatively modest additional lump sum.[12]

[6] Fair Work Bill 2009 (Cth), Explanatory Memorandum, paras 1555–56.

[7] Britain's unfair dismissal law was introduced in the Industrial Relations Act 1971; the Donovan Commission was the colloquial name given to the Royal Commission on Employers and Trade Unions, which conducted a significant study into British industrial relations in the late 1960s. One of the questions they considered was whether Britain should introduce a statutory unfair dismissal system. For their final report see, 'Report of the Royal Commission on Trade Unions and Employers' Associations' (Cmnd 3888, 1969). For a comprehensive history of British unfair dismissal law, see: PL Davies and MR Freedland, *Labour Legislation and Public Policy: A Contemporary History* (Oxford, Clarendon Press, 1993); see also: S Deakin and G Morris, *Labour Law*, 6th edn (Oxford, Hart Publishing, 2012).

[8] These provisions were introduced in the Employment Protection (Consolidation) Act 1978, ss 68–71.

[9] *Oasis Community Learning v Wolff* (2013) UKEAT/0364/12/MC, para 10 (*Oasis*).

[10] B Hepple, 'Individual Labour Law' in GS Bain (ed), *Industrial Relations in Britain* (London, Blackwell Publishing, 1983) 409.

[11] ibid.

[12] Davies and Freedland, above n 7, 210.

The marginalisation of reinstatement as a remedy has continued: whilst there were over 40,000 unfair dismissal claims before the Tribunal in 2010–11, only eight cases concluded with orders from the Tribunal reinstating the claimant; the result was similar in 2011–12 with five awards of reinstatement out of 46,100 unfair dismissal applications made to the Tribunal.[13] A similar narrative can be told of Australia, where the remedy of reinstatement has never been awarded to any significant degree. Of the 774 applications disposed of by arbitration in 1997–98, 17 resulted in an order for reinstatement and 403 resulted in compensation orders.[14] More recently, between 2011 and 2012 only 17 reinstatement orders and 85 compensation orders were made out of 525 unfair dismissal applications which proceeded to arbitration.[15] Of the 81 per cent of claims that were settled at the conciliation stage in 2011–12, 1.4 per cent received reinstatement, 59 per cent received compensation and 20.6 per cent received a non-monetary benefit, with the remaining 19 per cent receiving no outcome from the conciliation.[16]

That not every applicant seeks reinstatement is an important qualification upon the preceding statistics. Given that in neither jurisdiction statistics are compiled on the intentions of applicants, it is difficult to properly evaluate whether the fact that there have been few orders of reinstatement in either jurisdiction is attributable to the applicant's lack of interest in this remedy or because of an unwillingness of the Commission or the Tribunal to award it. As such, in this section I have chosen to focus on a number of cases from each jurisdiction to identify principles relating to reinstatement that govern when and how it is awarded.

The case law from both jurisdictions sheds some light as to why reinstatement is so infrequently awarded. Even assuming that not many employees request reinstatement, when they do, employer opposition may be anticipated given that the employer is likely to want to stand by its original decision to dismiss the worker. The employer's assertion that there is no longer the necessary trust and confidence in the worker to maintain the employment relationship often is a powerful persuasive factor constraining the award of reinstatement. Whilst in both jurisdictions reinstatement is rarely granted, in Australia there exists a more favourable legislative framework and, consequently, the Commission[17] has been more willing than in Britain to look behind the employer's argument to see whether the employment relationship can be repaired if an order of reinstatement is made. The cases discussed below reveal how the Australian and British courts approach reinstatement in practice.

[13] Ministry of Justice, *Employment Tribunals and EAT Statistics, 2011–12: 1 April 2011 to 31 March 2012* (20 September 2012), available at: www.gov.uk/government/uploads/system/uploads/attachment_data/file/218497/employment-trib-stats-april-march-2011-12.pdf.

[14] GM Giudice, *Annual Report of the President of the Australian Industrial Relations Commission and Annual Report of the Australian Industrial Registry, 1 July 1997 to 30 June 1998* (25 September 1998) table 9, available at: www.airc.gov.au/about/annual/ar1998/chapter1.htm.

[15] Fair Work Australia, *Annual Report 2011–2012: 1 July 2011 to 30 June 2012* (2012) 29, available at: www.fwc.gov.au/documents/documents/annual_reports/ar2012/FWA_Annual_Report_2011-12.pdf.

[16] ibid, 92.

[17] The 'Commission' refers to the Fair Work Commission. This was formerly known as Fair Work Australia. This body replaced the Australian Industrial Relations Commission.

A Australia

Although reinstatement is rarely ordered in Australia, when it is, judicial treatment of the remedy recognises the importance of placing the employee back into an employment situation no less favourable than the one he or she previously enjoyed. In *Blackadder v Ramsey Butchering Services Pty Ltd*[18] the High Court found it to be a violation of a reinstatement order when a meat worker was asked to sit a medical examination as a precondition of returning to work. When the worker declined to undergo the medical test the employer did not reinstate the worker, as he was deemed unable to return to his particular job boning meat. In this case, McHugh J said:

> To reinstate means to put back in place. In this context, it means that the employment situation as it existed immediately before the termination must be restored. It requires restoration of the terms and conditions of the employment in the broadest sense of those terms. It empowers the Commission to do more than restore the contract of employment. So far as practicable, the employee is to be given back his 'job' at the same place and with the same duties, remuneration and working conditions as existed before the termination.[19]

In a recent case applying *Blackadder*, the Fair Work Commission ordered reinstatement of a worker for whom there was no valid reason for dismissal, in the face of significant employer opposition.[20] In this case, the employer had actually tendered evidence to suggest that even if the worker was reinstated he would not be allowed entry into the construction site on which he had previously worked. The Commission was critical of the employer's position and the reinstatement order made it clear that reinstatement means 'the same place, duties, remuneration and conditions of employment'.[21]

In Australia, the concept of 'a fair go all round' is used by the Commission to determine remedies in unfair dismissal cases.[22] The Commission has emphasised, however, that 'the *fair go* object does not constitute a basis for ignoring, or for rolling into one amorphous act of judgment, the procedures or conditions associated with the powers and discretions to determine remedies'.[23] An example of how the 'fair go all round' principle impacts upon the Commission's approach can be seen in *Brooks v Australian Dried Fruit Sales Pty Ltd*.[24] There the Commission found that the termination of two employees on the grounds of redundancy was harsh, unjust or unreasonable, but only one employee was reinstated. In deciding that reinstatement was not appropriate for the other employee, Commissioner Simmonds took into account the low score that the employee had achieved on a

18 *Blackadder v Ramsey Butchering Services Pty Ltd* (2005) 215 ALR 87.
19 ibid, 90–91.
20 *John Dalziel v Bilfinger Berger Services (Australia) Pty Ltd* [2010] FWA 1129 *(Dalziel)*.
21 ibid, 53.
22 Fair Work Act 2009 (Cth), s 381.
23 *Sprigg v Paul's Licensed Festival Supermarket* (1998) 88 IR 21, para 31.
24 *Brooks v Australian Dried Fruit Sales Pty Ltd* (1998) 84 IR 33, para 50.

competency test, which was 17 per cent below the lowest person retained by the company during the redundancy process. He considered that in these circumstances 'there are insufficient grounds for me to conclude that reinstatement is appropriate as it would not provide the company with a "fair go all round"'.[25]

This application of the 'fair go all round' principle in taking into account the employer's interest in justifying a decision not to award reinstatement is perhaps at odds with the traditional idea of a 'fair go all round' which recognised the employee as the 'underdog'. In the entry under the 'fair go' in *The Oxford Companion to Australian History*, there is reference to the 1964 writings of influential Australian public intellectual and journalist David Horne that 'fair-goes', are not only for oneself, but for underdogs and a recognition that the concept might be used to justify assistance for less gifted students or pensions for the old.[26] The term is identified as originating from the British expression 'a fair show' and to give a person a 'fair go' was to give them a reasonable opportunity or to ensure that the rules of competition were fair to all. Thus, in his seminal work, Hancock identified it as 'the popular refrain of Australian democracy, repeated incessantly in pleas and judicial decisions, in statutes, Parliamentary debates, trade union conferences and platform orations'.[27] The term was introduced into the specific context of Australian arbitration and conciliation by Higgins J, who sought to identify what was 'fair and reasonable' in determining wages and conditions.[28]

However, when applied to the unfair dismissal context, the notion of 'a fair go all round' does not seek solely to protect the employee as the underdog, but is about according fairness to both parties in the employment relationship. This principle allows the tribunal to scrutinise the dismissal decision in order to counterbalance the employer's managerial prerogative and assess whether the decision to fire was unjust given the subordinate status of the employee. The origin of the arbitral principle of 'a fair go' in the unfair dismissal context is the judgment of McKeon J in *Western Suburbs District Ambulance Committee v Tipping*.[29] Whilst this was a dissenting opinion, the statement of principles contained within the judgment has been widely regarded as authoritative.[30] McKeon J characterised the employer's right to dismiss as clear and fundamental and placed the burden on the individual employee to prove the unfairness of the dismissal. He suggested that in deciding whether to order reinstatement, the question the Court should ask is whether there has been oppression, injustice, or unfair dealing on the part of the employer. This discussion of justice in dismissal is extended by the significant decision of the NSW Industrial Relations Commission in *Loty & Holloway v*

[25] ibid, 51.

[26] G Davison, 'Fair Go' in G Davison, J Hirst and S Macintrye (eds), *The Oxford Companion to Australian History* (South Melbourne, Oxford University Press, 2001).

[27] W Hancock, *Australia* (London, Ernest Benn, 1930).

[28] K Hancock and S Richardson, 'Economic and Social Effects' in J Isaac and S Macintrye (eds), *The New Province for Law and Order* (Cambridge, Cambridge University Press, 2004) 146–47.

[29] *Western Suburbs District Ambulance Committee v Tipping* (1957) NSW AR 273.

[30] See *North West County Council v Dunn* (1970) CLR 247, 263 (Walsh J); see also *In Re Coccia and Australian Iron and Steel Pty Ltd* (1971) NSW AR 111, 115 (Sheldon J).

Australian Workers Union[31] which concerned an application for reinstatement of two employees dismissed from their positions in a union after a change in the composition of the union executive. In determining whether to make awards providing for their reinstatement, Sheldon J asked whether the employees had 'received less than a fair deal'.[32] Sheldon J also referred to the objective of the unfair dismissal jurisdiction as being to provide 'industrial justice' by reference to a number of factors, including the inviolability of the right of the employer to manage his business, the nature and quality of the work in question, the circumstances surrounding the dismissal and the likely practical outcome if an order of reinstatement was made. Sheldon J affirmed an earlier statement of a Commissioner that the purpose of the exploration into the individual's dismissal by the NSW Commission is to ascertain whether there has been a 'fair go all round'.[33]

After 1996 the Coalition Government imposed the principle of a 'fair go all round' into the jurisdiction of unfair dismissal. In determining whether a dismissal is harsh, unjust or unreasonable, section 170CA(2) contained an express statement of legislative purpose as being to provide a system to ensure a 'fair go all around' to the employer and the employee. The use of this specific phrase in the Act arose out of significant debate over the predecessor Act, which did not include this phrase. In the Second Reading debates over the 1995 amendments, Peter Reith referred to the judgment of Gray J of the Commission and stated:

> [Labour's unfair dismissal laws] proved to be totally biased against employers. Honourable members do not have to accept my view of that. Justice Gray, in one of the very many court cases we have had on these provisions, said, 'The former South Australian and the present State Act, like their counterpart in New South Wales, operate in the realm of the 'fair go all round' . . . This is not a realm that this Court inhabits. The provisions of division 3 of part VIA of the federal Act are not directed to achieving some balance between the interests of employers and employees in particular cases. They constitute a charter of rights for employees. They are directed towards the protection of the existing jobs of employees.[34]

Once elected, the Coalition Government moved quickly to amend the unfair dismissal laws so that the principle of a 'fair go all round' was inserted into the Act. Almost 20 years on, Australia's current statutory unfair dismissal laws have retained this reference to 'a fair go all round' in the working out of remedies.[35] Whilst the traditional understanding of 'a fair go' was to protect the employee because of their disadvantaged position in the employment relationship, this principle has been applied to the statutory unfair dismissal context since 1996 and has evolved into allowing a justification *against* the award of this remedy because of an employer's need to have trust and confidence in her staff.

[31] *Loty & Holloway v Australian Workers Union* [1971] AR (NSW) 95.
[32] ibid, 99.
[33] ibid.
[34] Commonwealth of Australia, *Parliamentary Debates*, House of Representatives, 30 August 1995 (Peter Reith, Minister for Workplace Relations).
[35] Fair Work Act 2009 (Cth), s 381(2).

Despite the number of reinstatement orders remaining low, the Fair Work Commission has been willing to order reinstatement in the face of employer opposition. Two recent cases evince that relationship breakdowns need not be fatal to an order for reinstatement.[36] In the case of *Stutsel* the employee was dismissed because of negative comments about two managers which he had posted on his private 'Facebook' page and which the company argued breached its equal opportunity and diversity policies. Although this was deemed to be a valid reason for the dismissal, Commissioner Roberts held that the employee's particular factual circumstances meant that the dismissal was unfair and ordered reinstatement. This included the employee's 22-year history with the company, his extremely good employment record, his age, his limited future employment prospects and his incomplete understanding as to the privacy of Facebook communications.[37] On appeal, the Full Bench of the Commission rejected the company's argument that there had been such a significant breakdown in the employment relationship as to render reinstatement inappropriate. The company claimed that it had lost trust and confidence in the employee because he had been initially reticent as to his authorship of the Facebook comments. During an investigation of the incident Stutsel denied making the Facebook comments when his manager first asked him about them; however when he was shown printouts of the specific statements he conceded to making them. The Full Bench said that the Commissioner had considered a range of matters concerning the appropriateness of a reinstatement order, including the fact that on his return to work Stutsel was unlikely to be in contact with the two managers who were the subject of the Facebook post. The Full Bench supported the Commissioner's finding that there clearly 'had not been any such conduct on the part of the Applicant which was so destructive of the employment relationship as to make reinstatement inappropriate'.[38]

Similarly, in the case of *Bellia* the Full Bench quashed an earlier ruling that reinstatement was inappropriate on the basis that there was no evidence to support the decision at first instance by Commissioner Ryan that the employer would act unprofessionally or unfairly towards the employee if he was reinstated. The Full Bench said that the breakdown in the relationship between Bellia and his employer was entirely because of the poor conduct of two other employees, one of whom was on the board that employed Bellia. Given there was no valid reason for dismissal in the first place, the Full Bench said there was no justification for a finding that it was inappropriate to reinstate Bellia, particularly as the decision had

[36] The two cases explored in this section are the Full Bench decisions of *Linfox Australia Pty Ltd v Glen Stutsel* [2012] FWAFB 7097 (*Stutsel*) and *Fr Andrea Bellia v Assisi Centre Aged Care* [2011] FWAFB 5249 (*Bellia*). Other recent cases where reinstatement has been awarded are: *Frank Moretti v HJ Heinz Company Australia Ltd* [2012] FWA 1016; *Dalziel*, above n 20; *Boom Logistics Limited v Bell Mackay* [2013] FWC 1017; *Lawrence & Coal Allied Mining Services Pty Ltd v Lawler* [2011] FCAFC 54; *Holcom (Australia) Pty Ltd v* Serafini [2011] FWAFB 7794; *Cliff Jones v BHP Billiton Iron Ore Pty Ltd* [2010] FWA 6959; *Neil Evans v Coles Group Supply Chain Pty Ltd T/A Supply Chain* [2010] FWA 6454.

[37] *Glen Stutsel v Linfox Australia Pty Ltd* [2011] FWA 8444.

[38] *Stutsel*, above n 36, 41.

exonerated Bellia in all respects.[39] The Full Bench stated that the two employees who were responsible for the machinations leading to Bellia's removal from his post had

> an obligation to behave properly [following a reinstatement order] and the Board has an obligation to ensure [this] . . . The finding that the Board would fail to behave fairly and professionally is unsupported by the evidence and is a significant error of fact.[40]

These two Full Bench decisions demonstrate that in Australia there is some preparedness to look behind the employer's allegation that the employment relationship has irrevocably deteriorated and to order reinstatement despite employer opposition.

B Britain

The preference for the remedy of reinstatement is expressed in more qualified terms in British legislation and awarded even less frequently than in Australia. In terms of the legislative framework, section 112 of the Employment Rights Act 1996 requires the tribunal to explain to the complainant that he or she can request reinstatement once a finding has been made that the unfair dismissal application was well founded. According to the Employment Appeal Tribunal (EAT), 'compliance with section 112 is a valuable discipline for the purpose of ensuring that important issues relating to reinstatement and re-engagement are not overlooked'.[41] Section 113 empowers the Tribunal to award either reinstatement or re-engagement and section 116 provides guidance about the discretion whether to order either of these remedies with particular emphasis placed on the practicality of returning a complainant to work for their employer and consideration of whether the employee's conduct contributed to his or her dismissal. Two early British authorities provide guidance on the correct approach to the question of practicality of reinstatement, namely *Coleman v Magnet Joinery Limited*[42] and *Meridian Ltd v Gomersall.*[43] In *Coleman*, the Court of Appeal emphasised that 'practicable' meant not just 'possible' but 'capable of being carried into effect with success'[44] and that reinstatement would not be practicable in that sense if it would lead to the reinstated employee's colleagues taking industrial action. In *Meridian*, the EAT endorsed 'a broad commonsense view of what was practicable' and found that practicality of reinstatement is determined at the date it is to take effect and not at the date of dismissal or the date of the unfair dismissal application.[45]

[39] *Bellia*, above n 36, para 12.
[40] ibid, para 13.
[41] *King v Royal Bank of Canada Europe* Ltd [2011] UKEAT.0333.10.DM 17, para 55.
[42] *Coleman v Magnet Joinery Limited* [1975] ICR 46.
[43] *Meridian Ltd v Gomersall* [1977] ICR 597.
[44] Stephenson LJ, 52 B-C.
[45] *Great Ormond Street Hospital v Miss Patel* [2007] UKEAT/0095/07/LA, para 27(1); *Rembiszewski v Atkins Ltd* [2012] UKEAT/0402/11/ZT, para 39.

Although reinstatement is very rarely awarded in Britain, a recent case where re-employment was awarded provides an interesting example of how this remedy can be used to reconstruct the employment relationship. This case is rather unusual in that the tribunal took a rather interventionist approach in its judgment and was perhaps more favourably disposed towards ordering reinstatement than another tribunal may have been facing the same situation. This case concerned a British schoolteacher dismissed because of a substantial number of allegations of misconduct against him. He in turn made a number of serious allegations of misconduct on the part of other employees of the school authority. The teacher sought the remedy of re-employment with the same school authority, largely because of a desire not to have an unexplained gap on his curriculum vitae. Upon making a finding of unfair dismissal, the Tribunal turned to the question of which remedy it was appropriate to award and made the following observations:

> Whilst as we have indicated, very few successful claimants nowadays seek re-employment orders, the relevant legislation, setting out the primary remedies of reinstatement/re-engagement is now some forty years old. It has not been substantially amended during that period. It remains the intention of Parliament that a successful claimant should be reinstated or re-engaged if he so wishes. The only relevant circumstance in which that will not occur is if it is not practicable . . . It seems to us that [both sides asserting substantial allegations of misconduct] is not an uncommon situation in unfair dismissal claims involving professional people. It is notoriously the case that complex allegations and counter-allegations are made in such cases and Tribunals frequently spend weeks, rather than days, in analyzing and deciding the contention of those parties . . . We consider that if we were to accept [the employer's] argument that re-employment is not practicable, the more bitter the dispute between the parties and the more serious the allegations and counter-allegations that had been made, that approach would have the effect of emasculating the remedy of re-employment. We do not regard that as the intention of Parliament.[46]

In making an order for re-engagement the Tribunal identified the bitterness of the dispute between the parties as the primary barrier in terms of practicality. To rectify this the tribunal took the rather unusual step of including in its order a clause which it had initially asked the complainant to draft, which stated that he would treat all disputes as resolved and that he would comply with the employer's procedures relating to disciplinary and grievance matters, whistle-blowing policies and reasonable management direction pertaining to his employment.[47] The Tribunal's decision to award the remedy of re-employment by requiring that the teacher be posted to a different school overseen by the school authority was appealed by the latter on the basis that the original decision overstated the primacy of reinstatement as a remedy for unfair dismissal and that the Tribunal erred in its finding that re-employment was practicable given the severity of the allegations made by the parties. The EAT rejected the appellant's case, stating that 'the Tribunal's mood music was rather more favourable to re-engagement than

[46] The Tribunal's reasons are set out in full in the appeal decision at para 24: *Oasis*, above n 9.

[47] ibid, para 25.

that is generally heard; but that cannot amount to an error of law'.[48] The EAT was satisfied that the Tribunal had addressed the difficulties raised by the school authority in re-engaging the school teacher and had made a considered judgment on the facts. It noted the willingness of the teacher to make a fresh start and that the rehiring would be at a different school with 'a wholly new set of colleagues and no history to live down'.[49] Finally in its conclusion, the EAT noted that 'no general conclusions about the readiness which reinstatement or re-engagement orders should be drawn from our decision, except perhaps that every case depends on its facts'.[50]

We can see from this recent case the substantial hurdles an applicant has in making an argument for reinstatement. Here the teacher was fortunate that the school authority had a different workplace in which he could be placed; however most applicants would not have this option available to them. Furthermore, the tribunal in this case was willing to take a rather interventionist role in mending the relationship between the parties by including in the order a stipulation that the teacher, whilst recognising him to be a strong-minded 'man of principle', be cognisant of his responsibility to obey the employer's reasonable directions going forward.[51] As the EAT noted, not all tribunals would be so inclined to award the remedy of reinstatement in circumstances such as these, given the bitterness of the dispute and the existence of allegations of misconduct by both parties. Furthermore, given the time-consuming nature of pursuing an unfair dismissal application and the increasing incidence of the parties making 'complex allegations and counter-allegations' as identified in the original decision, reinstatement remains an unlikely outcome of a British unfair dismissal dispute.

II A Historical Contrast with a Time when Reinstatement was More Frequent

It was not always so that reinstatement was such a marginalised remedy. In previous incarnations of the labour laws of Australia and Britain, unfairly dismissed workers were more likely to return to their jobs. In both jurisdictions, the state relied upon collective organisation to protect workers' interests and unions had a pivotal role in securing job security. Reinstatement was more regularly achieved despite the fact that in neither traditional system did an individual worker have a statutory right to unfair dismissal. This is revealed in the ensuing exploration of Britain's system of 'collective laissez-faire'[52] prior to the enactment of the

[48] ibid, para 33.
[49] ibid, para 36.
[50] ibid, para 44.
[51] ibid, para 15.
[52] Otto Kahn-Freund coined the term 'collective laissez-faire' to describe the British system of industrial relations prior to 1971. Recently, Alan Bogg revisited the question of the usefulness of this

Industrial Relations Act 1971 and the traditional New South Wales[53] model for dealing with unfair dismissal prior to the Industrial Relations Act 1991 (NSW). Both the aforementioned Acts provided a break with the traditional approach of collective protection of job security, in favour of a statutory individual right safeguarding against unfair dismissal. The more frequent achievement of reinstatement of unionised employees in both jurisdictions under their traditional models compared with under the current unfair dismissal laws, provides ammunition for the school of thought identified by Hepple in 1981 that the 'legislation on dismissals has simply put a price on jobs and weakened workers' protective attitudes to their jobs in return for cash and procedural fairness'.[54]

A Australia

Prior to 1991, New South Wales's (NSW) traditional model for resolving unfair dismissal disputes did not allow individual workers to initiate an unfair dismissal claim without collective support. Unlike other Australian state jurisdictions where provision was made for individually initiated dismissal disputes,[55] in NSW unions retained their right to act as gatekeeper to the conciliation and arbitration system for every industrial dispute, including disputes relating to individuals. An individual employee was not able to initiate proceedings without the support of a union, or alternatively, a group of aggrieved fellow workers.[56] The rationale for union monopoly was a way of ensuring that only dismissals that could give rise to industrial disruption were dealt with. It was thought that the best way to guarantee industrial peace was through unions vetting unfair dismissal applications and only pursuing those of merit. This had the practical effect, however, that if an individual had a legitimate unfair dismissal claim but was unable to secure union support because pursuing the individual's claim did not complement the union's broader agenda or undermined their relationship with the employer, then that individual had no opportunity for redress. In contrast, dismissal of a union official was much more likely to receive adjudication by the conciliation and arbitration system: as such, a claim would naturally attract union support.[57] The only remedy the NSW Industrial Relations Commission could award in arbitration

theory in aiding understanding of British labour law and assessed the validity of the main critiques of collective laissez-faire which have emerged, namely the absentionist, neutrality and coherence critiques. He concluded that each of these critiques is somewhat misplaced and that 'collective laissez-faire still offers the most compelling theoretical rationalisation of the pattern of auxiliary intervention in the post-war period': A Bogg, *The Democratic Aspects of Trade Union Recognition* (Oxford, Hart Publishing, 2009) 3.

[53] New South Wales is a state within the Australian federation.

[54] Hepple, 'A Right to Work', above n 1, 68.

[55] See, eg, South Australia, Victoria and Western Australia. For more on the systems existing in the Australian states, see A Stewart, 'Employment Protection in Australia' (1989) 11 *Comparative Labor Law & Policy Journal* 1, 27.

[56] *Roberts v Mona Vale District Hospital* [1975] 2 NSWLR 132, para 138 (CA); Industrial Arbitration Act 1940 (NSW), s 74.

[57] Stewart, 'Employment Protection in Australia', above n 55, 27.

was reinstatement. Whether this remedy was awarded depended more upon maintaining industrial peace than achieving justice for the individual concerned. As Stewart observes, 'the likelihood of a remedy being secured is often directly related to the industrial muscle of the relevant union and to its willingness to act as an enforcer of any order made'.[58] This is because the primary task of the NSW Industrial Relations Commission was to settle collective disputes in order to promote industrial harmony. The Commission applied this task to its adjudication of individual dismissal disputes, which meant that remedies were often awarded to avoid sympathy strikes rather than addressing whether the dismissal itself was unfair. Stewart notes that the emphasis on industrial peace led to the elevation of conciliation as the primary method of resolving dismissal disputes, and resulted in the resolution of the vast majority of disputes at this stage either through the remedy of reinstatement, or through an agreed monetary amount reflecting the merits of the applicant's case, as indicated informally by the Commission.[59]

The more frequent achievement of reinstatement under the NSW model, prior to 1991, reveals the importance of union presence in the workplace for securing a right to work. Union support for a reinstated worker helped in monitoring subsequent events and in dissuading the employer from any retaliatory action against the worker.[60] A study comparing the incidence of reinstatement in NSW as opposed to two other state jurisdictions in Australia – which had no such requirement that a union be supportive of an individual's unfair dismissal claim – provides evidence for this.[61] Between 1980 and 1984, over half of adjudicated settlements in NSW resulted in reinstatement, whereas in Western Australia it was 2.7 per cent with 38 per cent receiving compensation. In South Australia the reinstatement rate was 25.5 per cent but this remedy was almost three times as likely to be achieved if the individual's worker was sponsored by a union.[62] This study also suggested that unfair dismissal disputes were more expediently resolved in NSW as opposed to under Western Australia's and South Australia's individual rights-based model.[63] This may be a reason why reinstatement was more frequently achieved in the former jurisdiction. A study of the NSW system showed that when there was more delay in proceedings reinstatement was less likely to be achieved.[64] Stewart suggests that involving unions means that a right not to be unfairly dismissed becomes 'infinitely more valuable' when supported by the collective and leads to the realisation of 'a more meaningful remedy'.[65] Because of the

[58] ibid.
[59] ibid, 27–28.
[60] For more, see A Stewart, 'A Quiet Revolution: Unfair Dismissal in New South Wales' (1992) *Australian Journal of Labour Law* 69.
[61] MR Sherman, 'Unfair Dismissal and the Remedy of Re-employment' (1989) 31 *Journal of Industrial Relations* 212.
[62] ibid, 221.
[63] Sixty-nine days to reach a decision in NSW, as opposed to 214 days under individual jurisdictions in Australia such as Western Australia and South Australia: Sherman, above n 61, 221.
[64] Sherman, above n 61, 221.
[65] A Stewart, 'And (Industrial) Justice for All? Protecting Workers Against Unfair Dismissal' (1995) 1 *Flinders Journal of Law Reform* 85, 93.

institutional support it provides within the workplace, a union can ensure the reinstatement order is complied with through monitoring of the employer's conduct towards the reinstated worker so that he or she is not dismissed for another reason or is constructively dismissed because of substandard treatment.[66]

B Britain

Prior to 1971, the British system of 'collective laissez-faire' was characterised by a reliance on the collective organisation and, as such, industrial action was used as the primary tool to deal with unfair dismissal. The mobilisation of the workers as a collective tended to be effective in achieving a speedy return of the dismissed individual to their job. In Britain, the Whitley Committee's First Interim Report in 1917 recommended

> the establishment for each industry of an organisation representative of employers and workpeople, to have as its object the regular consideration of matters affecting the progress and well-being of the trade from the point of view of all those engaged in it.[67]

According to Clay, this amounted to a 'public and official recognition of trade unionism and collective bargaining as the basis of industrial relations'.[68] In this way, the British 'collective laissez-faire' system prioritised the achievement of union security over other industrial relations goals, because it was believed that collective bargaining would lead to the orderly resolution of industrial conflict and thereby bring about industrial peace.[69]

Unions preferred to use industrial tactics rather than the law to secure the return of an unfairly dismissed employee to her job. In 1961, the Trades Union Congress (TUC)[70] questioned officials of its affiliated unions about their attitude towards the introduction of legislation providing protection against unfair dismissal. The majority of respondents – 44 out of 57 unions – said they preferred the matter to be dealt with through collective bargaining.[71] This view was, of course, in keeping with the 'voluntarist' tradition, whereby it is thought that workers can best achieve their goals by relying upon their own organisation. The traditional strategy employed by unions to protect individual employees facing dismissal they deemed to be unreasonable was to threaten the employer with industrial action in order to secure the individual's reinstatement. From the union's perspective, this situation was mainly satisfactory as the union could use

[66] ibid.

[67] The Whitley Committee, 'Interim Report on Joint Standing Industrial Councils' (Cd 8606, 1917) para 5.

[68] H Clay, *The Problem of Industrial Relations: And Other Lectures* (London, Macmillan & Co, 1929) 154, 177.

[69] For more, see A Flanders, 'The Tradition of Voluntarism' (1974) 12 *British Journal of Industrial Relations* 352.

[70] The Trades Union Congress (TUC) is the peak body for British trade unions, equivalent to the Australian Council of Trade Unions (ACTU) in Australia.

[71] 'Protecting Against Unjustified Dismissal' *The Times* (London, 15 March 1965).

its industrial leverage to enable an unfairly dismissed employee to get their job back. This was an industrial tactic unions were not afraid to use. Unofficial dismissal-related strikes were a well-known phenomenon of British collective laissez-faire. For example, between 1964 and 1966 there were 276 strikes resulting from dismissal.[72] Furthermore, it was not high on the unions' agenda to secure statutory unfair dismissal protection for workers in non-unionised industries, as it was perceived that the first priority for these workers was to achieve unionisation. It was believed that this would then result in greater all-round protection for these workers, including protecting their right to job security by using industrial tactics rather than legal measures. The union's position is aptly summated by the following submission from a union representative to the Donovan Commission:[73]

> I do not think there is any one on the TUC side who would argue against the rights of the worker to be protected equally with the rights of the employer, but we are facing the law as it stands and what we are saying is, do we want the court to protect it or do we want the ordinary industrial machinery to protect it? *The evidence of the TUC has been in favour of the strengthening of the industrial machine* . . . it is not an argument as to whether we think the worker is entitled to the protection, but the method by which the protection is given.[74]

It was not just unions that were reluctant to lobby for the introduction of statutory unfair dismissal protection, but employers too. The principle of industrial autonomy meant it was unlikely that employers would press for any limit on their contractual right to dismiss employees. Whilst the high incidence of dismissal-related strikes was an issue of potential concern for employers, the prevailing attitude amongst employer groups was that a statutory scheme protecting an individual from unfair dismissal would lead to a greater number of contested dismissals. It was believed that unions acted as a filtering mechanism, weeding out weak complaints, as they only resorted to industrial action for dismissals they genuinely disagreed with.[75] When employer groups raised this concern about a statutory scheme with the Donovan Commission, Professor Kahn-Freund of the Commission responded to this argument by suggesting that the Confederation of British Industry (CBI) should consider the American model where the union decides whether or not to take the unfair dismissal case to the arbitrator as a mechanism for preventing vexatious litigation. However, Mr Taylor of the CBI

[72] Report of the Royal Commission on Trade Unions and Employers' Associations (Cmnd 3888, 1969), para 528.

[73] The Donovan Commission was a government-established Royal Commission investigating the question of how to reform British labour law. One of the areas they focused their attention on was the feasibility of introducing a statutory unfair dismissal system in Britain. For more on the Donovan Commission, see: Davies and Freedland, above n 7.

[74] Royal Commission on Trade Unions and Employers' Associations, Minutes of Evidence of 29 November 1966 and 31 January 1967 (London, Her Majesty's Stationery Office, 1967), para 10402, Mr Cousins (emphasis added).

[75] Royal Commission on Trade Unions and Employers' Associations, Minutes of Evidence of 23 November 1965 and 7 December 1965 (London, Her Majesty's Stationery Office, 1966), para 1529, Mr Taylor.

rejected this approach arguing that under collective laissez-faire the union recognises that to take on an unfair dismissal claim it may ultimately have to call upon industrial action, whereas a union is more likely to support a claim if the union is only responsible for pursuing a case before a tribunal instead of organising a strike.[76] The CBI also argued that the statutory scheme would favour compensation over reinstatement and that the advantage of encouraging voluntary procedures is that they allow for reinstatement which 'goes to the heart of what an unjustly dismissed worker wants'.[77]

Another British employer group strongly advocating the traditional system was the Engineering Employers' Federation (EEF), which believed that its procedure, graduating from informal to formal mechanisms for dealing with unfair dismissal, was more flexible and responsive to employee needs than a statutory scheme.[78] In providing evidence before the Donovan Commission, the EEF was extremely critical of a statutory scheme as it thought it unlikely that reinstatement would be awarded, unlike under its scheme, where reinstatement was regularly achieved.[79] In response to the criticism of Professor Kahn-Freund that it would be more just and forward-thinking to develop a statutory scheme, the EEF's view was that its system, predicated upon the collective laissez-faire notion of industrial autonomy, afforded more justice to the worker. Mr Brown stated that

> we believe that the unions and the employee is much more concerned with getting his job back than with monetary compensation. Our figures show in a surprising number of cases he does in fact get his old job back which shows that we do not favour the employer in dealing with these cases.[80]

C Conclusion

In both the traditional labour law systems of NSW in Australia and Britain, there was greater opportunity for workers to be reinstated if they were dismissed without cause. However, there is an important caveat to this analysis: only unionised workers were able to achieve this, as they were able to rely upon the union's support to place industrial pressure on the employer to overturn their dismissal decision. In Britain, this issue of unequal access to collective protection was one of the reasons for the introduction of an unfair dismissal scheme according a statutory right to individuals to challenge their employer's dismissal decision.[81] In Australia,

[76] ibid.

[77] Royal Commission on Trade Unions and Employers' Associations, Minutes of Evidence of 12 December 1967 (London, Her Majesty's Stationery Office, 1968), para 11357, Mr Taylor.

[78] Royal Commission on Trade Unions and Employers' Associations, Minutes of Evidence of 1 February 1966 (London, Her Majesty's Stationery Office, 1967), para 3069.

[79] Donovan Commission, above n 72, para 3958.

[80] ibid, para 3072.

[81] The majority of the Donovan Commission was of the view that the introduction of a statutory scheme would lead to an immediate raising of standards to a more satisfactory level as employers would seek to comply with the legislative framework governing dismissal procedures. They also argued that a statutory scheme would protect workers in non-unionised industries and would greater protect

an individual statutory right not to be unfairly dismissed was developed in the NSW state system in 1991.[82] This meant that unions no longer acted as the gatekeeper to the bringing of an unfair dismissal claim. The benefit of achieving reinstatement more frequently under the traditional models has to be counterbalanced against the reliance upon union coverage in order to protect job security.

III Future Directions for the Remedy of Reinstatement

This chapter has contrasted the normative idea of reinstatement with the status quo in both Australia and Britain, where it is (and has always been since the introduction of statutory unfair dismissal schemes) an exceptional remedy rather than the norm. Need it necessarily be so? Is there a way unfair dismissal law can more meaningfully achieve a right to work enforceable against the employer, if the content of this right is defined as the extent to which an unfairly dismissed worker can insist upon returning to her job?

It is possible that more expedient processing of unfair dismissal applications could produce a greater frequency of reinstatement orders. The rationale being that if less time lapses between when an employee is dismissed and the finalisation of her unfair dismissal claim, she will be more inclined to want to return to her previous job and will be less likely to have secured new employment. In Australia there has been an increasing emphasis on resolving unfair dismissal claims in a 'quick, informal and flexible' fashion, with key performance indicators (KPIs) introduced to the work of the Commission in order to try and secure prompter processing of claims.[83] There is a KPI of 34 days for the lodgement of claims until the first conciliation conference. In 2011–12 this was nearly reached, with 90 per cent of unfair dismissal applications reaching conciliation within 36 days.[84] In fact, the average time taken from lodgement to finalisation of the application is currently 49 days, although when a decision proceeds to tribunal determination this increases significantly to an average length of 171 days.[85] In the United Kingdom, where an unfair dismissal application is often part of a multiple claim involving a dispute relating to another individual employment right, the average

workers in unionised industries, as even in the latter situation, 'employer procedures tend to leave the final decision on dismissal in the hands of management and this cannot be accepted as sufficient to ensure that an employee both has fair treatment and is seen to have it': Report of the Royal Commission on Trade Unions and Employers' Associations (Cmnd 3888, 1969), para 542.

[82] Industrial Relations Act 1991 (NSW), Part 8, ch 3.

[83] Fair Work Australia, *Annual Report 2011–2012*, above n 15, 27. For the increasing emphasis of the current system on inducing fast settlements, see A Stewart, 'Fair Work Australia – The Commission Reborn?' (2011) 53 *Journal of Industrial Relations* 563, 572.

[84] ibid.

[85] B O'Neill, *General Manager's Report into the operation of the first three years of the Fair Work Act 2009 (Cth) unfair dismissal system* (Commonwealth of Australia, December 2012) 20, available at: www.fwc.gov.au/documents/documents/UDS.pdf.

time it took to resolve an employment tribunal case was 560 days. Although this figure is distorted because of the high proportion of multiple claim cases, 50 per cent of employment tribunal claims are resolved in 217 days or less. In both jurisdictions, but particularly in the United Kingdom where the case load of tribunals is significantly higher, it takes a fairly long time to resolve an unfair dismissal claim. Timeliness, in and of itself, will not result in more frequent reinstatement – arguably it is necessary but not sufficient. Of course, when unfair dismissal claims take a long time to process, it is hardly surprising that reinstatement is not a common outcome.

Other than timeliness, another factor that could lead to a more frequent award of reinstatement is if the Commission or tribunal was prepared to take a more interventionist approach to reconstructing the employment relationship. In the case of *Oasis*, described earlier in this chapter, the Tribunal took the unusual step of drafting an agreement between the parties that would govern their conduct going forward. This included requiring both parties to acknowledge that all disputes were to be treated as resolved and that there was to be a fresh slate going forward. In Australia, there has been increasing reliance on the use of 'enforceable undertakings' to require employers to make commitments as to how they will improve behaviour.[86] If enforceable undertakings were applied to the unfair dismissal scheme, an employer involved in an unfair dismissal could be required to make a public admission of contravention, to apologise to the employee and accept ongoing monitoring and training. This approach could have lasting benefits for workplace culture by educating employers about their dismissal obligations. The enforceable undertaking would also be useful in providing ongoing reassurance for the reinstated employee that she had a defined set of yardsticks with which to measure the employer's treatment of her. In the absence of union monitoring, which was described in section II of this chapter, an enforceable undertaking could assist in ensuring that an employee's job security was protected subsequent to the reinstatement order. In his seminal work, *Justice in Dismissal*, Collins recognises supervision of the employer's conduct as necessary in order to make the remedy of reinstatement a meaningful one: 'Reinstatement without subsequent official monitoring to ensure that the employer does not victimize the employee through the almost invisible operation of the internal labour market for promotion and betterment seems to be an almost useless remedy'.[87] It is to be expected that an order of reinstatement, even with an enforceable undertaking, will necessarily involve some resultant disharmony or interpersonal tensions in the workplace. The dismissal, the lengthy litigation and the consequences for the morale of the workforce will affect both parties. Whilst reinstatement will bring closure to an unfairly dismissed employee, the irony is that it is usually only an employee with a particularly 'thick skin' who could cope with being reinstated after the employment relationship has broken down to the extent of a dismissal, a

[86] Fair Work Act 2009 (Cth), s 175.

[87] H Collins, *Justice in Dismissal* (Oxford, Clarendon Press, 1992) 215.

lengthy hearing and an order forcing continuation of the employment relationship.[88] Given this, if it is likely that the remedy of reinstatement is never going to be frequently requested by applicants or awarded by a tribunal, perhaps another option would be for the statutory schemes to enable more meaningful compensation to be awarded to applicants. Wanjiru Njoya has recently developed this notion in her influential work on job security and job property.[89] Whilst Frederick Meyers advocated reinstatement as the remedy for unfair dismissal in his conception of job property,[90] Njoya proposes a more nuanced version of job property that accepts the contemporary dominance of compensation payments as the primary remedy in many national unfair dismissal systems. Njoya states that the idea of job property is 'not simply on trying to keep one's job at all costs, but on drawing attention to the true value involved when the job was lost'.[91]

However, Njoya's view of compensation is of monetary payments that compensate for the 'true value' of the loss of the job in cases where an employee has been arbitrarily deprived of it; this is different from the current unfair dismissal schemes of Britain and Australia where of the small number of claims that proceed to arbitration, only a modest amount of compensation is awarded. In Britain, the median award made by way of compensation for unfair dismissal was just £4591 in 2010–11,[92] or roughly double the amount that the average claimant spends on legal fees (£2493).[93] In Australia, 82 per cent of claimants who settle their claim at conciliation and 55 per cent who are awarded the remedy of compensation by the Commission receive less than A$8000.[94] If the compensation amount was increased and came closer to reimbursing the worker for the true value of the job that was lost, this could mean an employer would be more willing to contemplate supporting an order of reinstatement, as this would enable an employer to benefit from an employee's productive effort rather than being burdened with a significant financial payout. It would also mean that, if it were ordered that a payment be made in lieu of reinstatement, it would more properly account for the value of the right to work to an employee.

In his seminal article that is the inspiration for this book, Hepple proposed the Swedish model whereby an employee's dismissal could not take place until any unfair dismissal application had been resolved. It is unlikely this type of restraint on managerial prerogative would be perceived as politically possible in either Australia or Britain today; however, there could be a movement towards an automatic right for the employee to elect reinstatement in the case of a finding of unfair dismissal. Employers would of course oppose this, but it would provide a

[88] H Meggiorin, 'Reinstatement under the Workplace Relations Act (Cth): Is it Practicable, Appropriate or Just Plain Speculative?' (1999) 27 *Australian Business Law Review* 438, 453.

[89] Njoya, above n 1, 63.

[90] Meyers, above n 1.

[91] ibid.

[92] *Employment Tribunals and EAT Statistics 2010–2011*, above n 13, 10.

[93] Department of Trade and Industry, *Better Dispute Resolution: A Review of Employment Dispute Resolution in Great Britain* (London, DTI, 2007) 22.

[94] O'Neill, above n 85, 58.

concrete rejection of the common law doctrine of specific performance and a realisation of an employee's right to work enforceable against an employer. If an employer desired to extinguish this right, there could be a significant additional monetary award that was payable that could seek to achieve meaningful compensation.

Perhaps the final observation to be made is this: whilst unfair dismissal law in its present form does not greatly achieve a right to work, acknowledging this is not to diminish its significance. Although in neither system reinstatement or meaningful compensation is largely achieved, a statutory right not to be unfairly dismissed provides a worker with acknowledgment by an independent body that the dismissal was unfair. This provides satisfaction to the worker and – combined with the opportunity for a remedy (however limited) – provides an incentive for employers to dismiss their workers according to a fair process and with a valid reason. The presence of unfair dismissal law provides an important check on managerial prerogative and accords workers with a greater sense of security about their jobs. Without unfair dismissal law a worker could be dismissed for no good reason and be powerless to challenge an employer's decision. This statutory right is vital given the more vulnerable position of an employee in unfair dismissal disputes. After all, it is a worker's livelihood that is at stake, whereas in most instances an employer can more readily replace one worker with another.

15

A Right to Work in the United States: Historical Antecedents and Contemporary Possibilities

KATHERINE VW STONE

Introduction

Progressive scholars and social activists often advocate the creation of a 'right to work' either under domestic law or by means of international treaties or conventions. However, the concept of a right to work in the United States is problematic. Indeed, in the United States, the notion of a right to work has a negative connotation amongst progressives because it is associated with the National Right to Work Committee (NRWC), an association formed in 1955 with the objective of weakening the power of labour unions.[1] The NRWC promotes right to work laws – laws that prohibit unions from negotiating arrangements by which employers promise to hire or retain only employees who pay union fees or their equivalent for representation services.[2] These fees are necessary to pay unions' expenses for grievance handling, collective bargaining negotiations and contract administration services. US labour law requires unions to provide services to all employees in the bargaining unit regardless of union membership. As a result, right to work laws deprive unions of the funds they need to perform their representation functions. Right to work laws also permit some employees to enjoy the benefits of union representation without paying for them. Because of the NRWC's aggressive anti-union campaigns, 24 states have enacted right to work laws.[3] Union supporters consider the

[1] According to the NRWC web page, 'The National Right to Work Committee ... is a single-purpose citizens' organization dedicated to the principle that all Americans must have the right to join a union if they choose to, but none should ever be forced to affiliate with a union in order to get or keep a job'. Its objective is to 'combat[] compulsory unionism through an aggressive program designed to mobilise public opposition to compulsory unionism and, at the same time, enlist public support for Right to Work legislation'. National Right to Work Committee, 'About Us', available at: nrtwc.org/about-2.

[2] ibid.

[3] Section 14(b) of the National Labor Relations Law, the provision that permits states to enact right to work laws, was inserted into the statute in the 1947 Taft–Hartley amendments, 29 USC §164(b).

term 'right to work' a dangerous misnomer, and claim that right to work laws are actually 'right to starve' or 'slave labour laws' that authorise, validate and even celebrate union-busting tactics and substandard labour conditions.[4]

Leaving aside the misleadingly termed 'right to work' promoted by the NRWC, there have been several attempts in the United States to articulate and promote a progressive vision of a right to work. In this chapter I explore and contrast two proposals for the creation of a right to work in the United States that have been advocated in the past. An examination of these proposals reveals both the potential of and the obstacles to the creation of a right to work in the United States. Moreover, by contrasting the two, I show that we can imagine a third proposal for a right to work that is better suited to our time.

At the outset, it is necessary to clarify what a right to work in the United States might look like. As the legal theorist, Wesley Hohfeld teaches, a right is a legal claim possessed by one party that gives rise to a legal duty for another.[5] If an individual has a right to work, then it follows that some entity has a duty to provide that individual with work. Therefore, a conception of a right to work requires the specification of who has a duty to provide work and what kind of 'work' will satisfy it.

Presumably a right to work envisions work that is freely chosen – ie, not coerced – and that provides terms and conditions that exceed some bare minimum. That is to say, a right to work must be a right to voluntary employment under minimally adequate terms. A more capacious right to work might mean that some entity has a duty to provide individuals with 'decent work' – work that pays a living wage, has safe and healthy working conditions and offers pensions, vacations and other social benefits. Or, it might further require that some entity provides individuals with 'meaningful work', ie, work that utilises the individual's skills, engages her intellect, increases her human capital and/or is compatible with her values.

Once the right to work is stated in this Hohfeldian form, it is obvious that there is no such right in the United States. No entity has a duty to give anyone a job, no less a decent or meaningful job. We might be tempted to restate the question as, not whether there is a right to work, but whether there is a Hohfeldian 'privilege' to work, ie, a regime in which no one can stop someone from working if that person has an entity willing to hire them. In this sense, there is such a legal privilege to work in the United States, subject to the not insignificant caveats that (1) one has to find work in order to exercise it; (2) one has to be of legal age; and (3) one has to have the requisite citizenship and/or immigration status. The conception of a right to work restated as a 'privilege to work' does not ensure that individuals

[4] See, eg, J Schaubach, 'Right to Work: Get the Facts', Minnesota AFL-CIO, available at: www.mnaflcio.org/news/right-work-laws-get-facts. For a critical analysis of the economic impact of right to work laws, see D Madland, 'Right to Work 101', Center for American Progress, available at: www.americanprogressaction.org/issues/labor/report/2012/02/02/11103/right-to-work-101.

[5] W Hohfeld, 'Some Fundamental Legal Conceptions as Applied in Legal Reasoning' (1913) 23 *Yale Law Journal* 16.

have work, no less decent or meaningful work. Hence, it is a very thin notion and does not address the aspirations that are evoked by advocates of a right to work.

There is a narrower conception of a right to work that could have attracted more support amongst some social reformers. That conception defines a right to work not as a right to a job, but rather as a right that becomes operative once one has a job. A right to work becomes a 'right to job security', ie, a right not to be fired without good cause. In this sense, the 'right' would mean that the employer has an ongoing obligation to retain employees, barring serious misconduct or true economic exigency. Many industrial countries provide some version of a right not to be fired unfairly, or a right to job security, through statutory or constitutional provisions. However, the United States does not.

Nevertheless, by restating a right to work as a right to job security, it becomes clear that there have been some examples of such a right in the United States arising from legislation, judicial application of common law principles, industrial custom and collective contract. However, many of these practices, customs and legal developments are in decline.

Below I explain the US approach to job security that prevailed widely, although not universally, for much of the twentieth century. I then explore two different notions of a more robust right to work that have been advocated in the United States. Each one attempts to answer the question of who has the duty to provide work, and what kind of work satisfies the duty. I show that each view embodies a different conception of the relationship between the state and the economy. Although neither one is politically feasible at the present time, they point towards a third and more relevant conception of a right to work that might have political traction in the current era.

I Is There a Legally Enforceable Right to Work in the United States Today?

The dominant form of employment in the United States is 'at-will' employment. The American at-will rule holds that an employee who is employed for an indefinite period of time can be dismissed at any time for any reason. In addition, the terms of at-will employment can be changed at any time because the employment contract is completely performed at each moment, subject to the possibility of renewal, but also subject to momentary cancellation. In an employment contract for an indefinite term contract, no one has a right to a job or the continuation of an existing job, only a right to be paid for time already worked.[6] Because most

[6] For a detailed exposition of the nature of the at-will employment contract under US law, see KVW Stone, 'Revisiting the At-Will Employment Doctrine: Imposed Terms, Implied Terms, and the Normative World of the Workplace' (2007) 36(1) *Industrial Law Journal* 84.

employment in the United States is for an indefinite term, the at-will rule governs most employment relationships.

Despite the at-will rule, however, there are some statutory exceptions that provide protection against unjust dismissal in some narrow circumstances. For example, anti-discrimination laws make it unlawful for an employer to fire an employee on the basis of their race, gender, age, ethnic origin, nationality or disability. Moreover, labour law makes it unlawful to fire someone for engaging in concerted protected activities such as union organising. And some statutes prohibit employers from firing employees in retaliation for exercising other statutory employment rights. But these are all narrowly defined protections that do not constitute a full-blown right to job security. In addition, since the mid-1970s, some state courts have developed exceptions to the at-will rule for specific types of dismissals. For example, some state courts have held it is unlawful to fire someone if the dismissal contravenes a specific public policy, such as firing someone for serving on a jury.[7] Some have held it is unlawful to dismiss someone in a way that breaches an implied covenant of good faith and fair dealing, such as firing a salesman just before their commission becomes due.[8] And some state courts began to enforce promises of job security when companies made such promises sufficiently concrete in their own personnel policies. [9] But these exceptions were few and far between, and have been narrowed in subsequent cases. Also, firms have learned that they can avoid any implicit contractual obligation of job security by making it explicit to their employees that their employment is at-will. Thus, these developments do not alter the essential at-will nature of most employment in the United States.[10]

Apart from the statutory and judge-made exceptions to the at-will rule, until recently many employers gave their employees implicit promises of job security. For most of the twentieth century in the United States, large industrial firms gave their employees considerable de facto job security, not under compulsion of law but by virtue of management practice. The practice of implicitly promising job security had its origins in early twentieth century approaches to industrial relations, embodied in scientific management and personnel management. These practices were reinforced by the industrial unions that emerged in the mid-twentieth century.[11]

By the mid-twentieth century, the United States, like most other advanced countries, developed what is called a 'standard contract of employment' – a widespread employment arrangement in which employees had long-term relationships with a particular employer who provided them with job security, income stability, promotion possibilities and social insurance for retirement and medical

[7] *Needs v Hocks*, 536 Pd 2d 512 (Or 1975).

[8] *Foley v National Cash Register Co*, 364 NE 2d 1251 (Mass 1977).

[9] *Pugh v See's Candies*, 171 Ca Rptr 917 (CA Ct App, 1981).

[10] See KVW Stone, *From Widgets to Digits: Employment Regulation for the Changing Workplace* (New York, Cambridge University Press, 2004) 85–86.

[11] ibid, 26–62.

needs.[12] Unlike most of Europe, where the standard contract of employment was embedded in statutes, in the United States the standard contract of employment was a social practice. And it was never a universal practice; it was primarily found in large manufacturing firms, and made available usually only to male employees. Nonetheless, it was widespread, and served as the template on which most of the twentieth century labour laws were built.[13]

This American right to job security – or what might better be termed the 'implicit contract for long-term employment' – was a customary norm, rather than a legal obligation. As such, it was difficult for individuals to enforce. For some, it was enforced by unions, which put dismissal protection into their collective bargaining agreements and created grievance and arbitration systems for resolving disputes. But for non-union workers, there was no comparable mechanism for enforcing employers' implicit promise of long-term employment.

Beginning in the late 1970s, employers retreated from the standard contract of employment. Firms started utilising more temporary work, independent contractors, sub-contractors and others who lacked long-term attachment to the employing entity. They also began to repudiate any promise of long-term employment and to deny any such expectation on the part of their regular employees. Since the mid-1980s, with the advent of new human resource theories, particularly strategic human resource management (SHRM), employers have attempted to foster a culture of flexibility and impermanence, in contrast to the earlier culture of stability they had previously sought to create.[14]

In sum, today in the United States, there are pockets of limited purpose dismissal protection found in a few specific federal statutes, some state common law doctrines and union collective bargaining agreements. However, these pockets have never coalesced into a general right to work. Moreover, in the United States, as in many other parts of the Western world, unionism has been declining and over the past three decades the standard contract of employment has been disappearing.[15] Thus, to the extent that there might have been a minimal and spotty right to job security in the United States at one time, it no longer exists.

[12] KVW Stone, 'The Decline of the Standard Contract of Employment in the United States: A Socio-Regulatory Perspective' in KVW Stone and H Arthurs (eds), *Rethinking Workplace Regulation: Beyond the Standard Contract of Employment* (New York, Russell Sage Foundation Press, 2013).

[13] Stone, *From Widgets to Digits*, above n 10, ch 3.

[14] Stone, 'The Decline of the Standard Contract of Employment', above n 12.

[15] KVW Stone and H Arthurs, 'The Transformation of Employment Regimes: A Worldwide Challenge' in KVW Stone and H Arthurs (eds), *Rethinking Workplace Regulation: Beyond the Standard Contract of Employment* (New York, Russell Sage Foundation Press, 2013).

II Two Proposals for a Right to Work in the United States

Although there is no right to work in the United States in the strong sense, and any enforceable right to job security is vanishing, it is worthwhile examining two conceptions of a robust right to work that have been advocated by prominent theorists and policymakers in the past. Specific proposals for a right to work were devised by John R Commons, the pioneer of American industrial relations, in the late nineteenth century, and by a group of prominent Keynesian policymakers immediately after the Second World War. Below I describe each of these proposals, compare them and distil lessons from each one. I then suggest that we draw on the insights each offered to formulate a right to work that is appropriate to the current era. I conclude that we need to redefine a right to work not as a right to job security or an employment guarantee, but as a right to 'livelihood security'. Livelihood security, as I define it, involves public policies that enable individuals to move in and out of the labour market throughout their lives, providing opportunities for training, retooling and skill upgrading, as well as protection for the inevitable gaps in the employment experience today.

A John R Commons' Conception of the Right to Work

John R Commons was the most important theoretician of American labour of the twentieth century. He was both a scholar and an activist, an empiricist and a theoretician, a friend of the labour movement and an inspiring teacher. In his 60-year career, Commons produced dozens of books on labour history, economic theory, social policy and public administration.[16] He was instrumental in founding the fields of American labour history, institutional economics, labour sociology and industrial relations. At the same time, Commons was active in public affairs, ceaselessly advocating the interests of labour in arenas such as the Wisconsin legislature, the Wisconsin state house, the National Civic Federation, the Department of Labor and the President Wilson's Industrial Commission. He created the Wisconsin Industrial Labor Commission – the first of its kind in the country – and he drafted numerous pieces of labour legislation, including the Wisconsin unemployment insurance law and the Wisconsin workmen's compensation laws,

[16] Commons is best known for two monumental labour history works that he produced in the early twentieth century. His ten-volume work, *A Documentary History of American Industrial Society* contains documents about customs, practices, organisations and daily life of the multitude of craft workers existed throughout American history: JR Commons et al (eds), *A Documentary History of American Industrial Society (1910–1911)* (Cleveland, The Arthur H Clark Company, 1910). Commons followed up the *Documentary History* in 1918 with another classic, the multi-volume, *The History of Labor in the United States*, comprised of essays by his students and edited by Commons: JR Commons (ed), *The History of Labor in the United States* (New York, Macmillan, 1918).

both of which were also the first of their type in the United States. Commons also had a gift for teaching his graduate students to talk to working people and learn all the minutiae of their working lives, trades, practices, customs and aspirations. [17] Many of Commons' students became the architects of the labour policies of the 'New Deal'.[18]

Commons developed his concept of a right to work early in his career, when he was a young political economist studying with Richard Ely at Johns Hopkins University. Ely himself had studied under the German historical economists. In 1893, Commons published his first book, entitled *The Distribution of Wealth.*[19] The book was a frontal attack on nineteenth century classical political economy, using both Austrian marginal utility theory and the German historical approach that Commons had studied in graduate school.[20] However, the book added something that was not part of either school: it tried to integrate economic theory with a theory of law in order to advocate a state-created right to work.

Commons' book emphasised the role of law in establishing and maintaining the distribution of income. It began with the proposition that the distribution of income is a function of economic exchanges and is determined by the ratio by which goods and services are exchanged. This was not a novel idea at the time. However, unlike his peers, Commons did not treat the conditions of supply and demand as determined solely by natural physical scarcity and therefore as fixed. Rather, while acknowledging that natural scarcity is one factor that limits supply and hence creates value, Commons contended that legal rules that create monopolies, protect property and restrict supply are equal, if not more important, determinants of value.

Commons claimed, for example, that government creates private property and monopoly privileges, both of which limit supply. Patents, copyrights, trademarks and franchises, he argued, are 'public grants of *exclusive privileges of selling goods or services*'.[21] He said of patents that:

> The right is in itself valuable because it gives its owner power to limit the production of the article patented relatively to the demand for it. In this way he can keep up the marginal utility and the price of the article at some point above its cost of production, so that in selling it, he may receive a surplus, or monopoly profit, on each unit of the article. This principle underlies the value also of copyrights, trade-marks, and franchises.[22]

Commons contended that most commodities are produced under monopoly conditions. Therefore, he concluded, the value of most commodities is a product of legal rules. Thus, to Commons, the state – and specifically law embodied in

[17] G Korman, 'John R Commons' in ET James (ed), *Dictionary of American Biography 1941–1945: Supplement Three* (New York, Macmillan, 1977).

[18] KH Parsons, 'John R Commons: His Relevance to Contemporary Economics' (1985) 19 *Journal of Economic Issues* 755, 759–60.

[19] JR Commons, *The Distribution of Wealth* (New York, Macmillan, 1893).

[20] J Dorfman, 'Introduction: The Foundations of Commons' Economics' in JR Commons, *The Distribution of Wealth*, reprinted (New York, Augustus M Kelly, 1965) viii.

[21] Commons, *The Distribution of Wealth*, above n 20, 101–02, emphasis original.

[22] ibid, 102.

statutes and common law – is the primary factor that determines income distribution.[23]

Commons presented a lengthy discussion of the nature of legal rights, and argued that the manner in which rights are defined and protected determines the distribution of income. In keeping with the legal theorists of his day, Commons divided legal rights into two types, personal rights and rights of property.[24] He identified four types of personal rights which he claimed were fundamental: the rights to life, liberty, employment and marriage. He showed that, in each case, the content of the right is a product of government action and, moreover, that the content of each right is not fixed, but has changed over time. Rights can be defined in a variety of ways and the manner in which the rights are defined determines the distribution of income. For example, in discussing the right to employment, he said:

> If labourers . . . can limit their numbers in any given industry, [by means of collectively restricting apprentices and excluding nonunion men from trades] . . . they can each obtain individually a larger share of the social product than when they have no control over their numbers.[25]

That is, the existence *vel non* of a legal right to organise and take collective action determines the ability of a worker to obtain 'a surplus of the social product over his minimum of substance'.[26]

Commons did not merely analyse the role of legally defined rights in the then existing distribution of income. He also advocated government creation and protection of rights for wage-earners in order to improve their economic position. To this end, Commons concluded that government should recognise a right for workers to organise. He acknowledged that, while such a right would enable organised workers to raise their wages, it could depress the wages of the unorganised. To combat this potential negative result, Commons argued that government should assist workers in their efforts to find new employment opportunities by facilitating movement and providing education and public services.[27]

Commons further argued that government should create a 'right to employment' that would guarantee to all people the right to work.[28] This right, he argued, should consist of two distinct rights: a right to *job security* and a right to *guaran-*

[23] ibid, 107. Commons illustrated his point in his Appendix, where he showed that of the 4000 millionaires in the United States at the time of his writing, 78 per cent derived their fortunes from monopoly privileges, and in terms of sheer size, 95 per cent of the value of the fortunes were the product of government-bestowed monopolies.

[24] Commons relied heavily on TE Holland for his claims about the legal system. Holland, together with Austin, constituted the school of legal positivism at Oxford in the late nineteenth century. See, J McLean, *Searching for the State in British Legal Thought* (Cambridge, Cambridge University Press 2012) 62–66; D Kennedy, *The Rise and Fall of Classical Legal Thought* (Washington DC, Beard Books, 2006) 180–92.

[25] Commons, *The Distribution of Wealth*, above n 20, 74–75.

[26] ibid, 76.

[27] ibid, 76–79.

[28] ibid, 66–70.

teed employment. Commons described the first of these as 'the right to security in the tenure of employment against arbitrary discharges, so long as one proves efficient and honest'.[29] The second was 'the right of the unemployed to have work furnished by government'.[30] He urged that these new rights of employment be enforced in publically-created 'courts of arbitration, created by government, and empowered to compel employers to submit to investigation and to suffer punishment for violating the right of employees to work'.[31] In Commons' vision, 'work will be constant and regular for those who work at all'.[32] Those displaced by technology will be employed by government, which will use public works projects to take up the slack in the private employment system. Commons hypothesised that once a system of guaranteed employment is in effect, labour will be in short supply, and thus his proposals 'would raise the marginal utility of the marginal labourers, thus raising the wages of all'.[33]

Commons' book was greeted with contempt and anger by leaders of the economics profession. Commons was personally attacked as unprofessional in reviews by Yale Professor Arthur Hadley, president of the American Economic Association, and by Columbia Professor Richmond Mayo-Smith (who had formerly been Commons' friend). University of Chicago Professor AC Miller accused Commons of surreptitiously promoting socialism. John Bates Clark – after whom the most prestigious prize in the economics profession is named – apparently thought the book to be so inconsequential that, when he published a book on the same subject in 1899, he called his book *The Distribution of Wealth*, without so much as referring to the fact that Commons had published a book with practically the same title six years earlier. After Commons' book was thoroughly excoriated, it was banished from economics bibliographies and reading lists. Professor Edwin Seligman of Columbia did not even mention Commons' book in his extensive bibliography of economic theory entitled *Principles of Economics*, published in 1905.[34] Thus, to Commons' deep disappointment, the book had no influence on the economics profession.[35]

Elsewhere I have recounted the story of Commons' dismissal from his university position as a result of the book, and his re-entry five years later as a much chastened but nonetheless passionate social reformer.[36] The relevant point here is not that his ideas were attacked and that he was banished, but that his ideas have relevance today. For while Commons' 'right to work' might sound hopelessly idealistic to the contemporary ear, his underlying point – that the government

[29] ibid, 81.
[30] ibid.
[31] ibid, 82–83.
[32] ibid, 84.
[33] ibid, 84–85.
[34] ERA Seligman, *Principles of Economics* (New York, Longmans, Green & Co, 1905) xli–xliii.
[35] LG Harter, *John R Commons: His Assault on Laissez-Faire* (Oregon State University Press, 1962) 37 (reporting on an interview between the author and Selig Perlman conducted in 1952).
[36] KVW Stone, 'The Other Tragedy of the Commons' in D Hamilton and A Brophy, *Transformations in American Legal History*, vol II (Cambridge MA, Harvard Law School, 2011).

creates the distribution of income and thus government can and should create a more equitable distribution by revising the laws regulating the labour market – is one that we need to revive and implement today. Before developing this point, however, it is useful to describe a competing conception of a right to work that has been advocated more recently in US policy circles.

B The Keynesians and the (Full) Employment Act of 1946

Another concept of a right to work in the United States first surfaced in policy debates in the 1940s. During the Second World War, John Maynard Keynes' ideas about the role of macroeconomic policy in redressing unemployment gained strength within the American economics profession and policy community. Towards the end of the Second World War, many feared that the end of the war and cessation of wartime production would trigger massive unemployment on the scale of the Great Depression. Economists in the Roosevelt Administration, armed with Keynes' recently published *General Theory of Employment, Interest, and Money*, argued that the economic system was not automatically self-adjusting. Rather, they warned, unemployment was caused by insufficient aggregate demand, and massive unemployment could not be rectified by the 'normal' operation of the private economy. These economists believed that government action was necessary when there was a threat of massive unemployment in order to bolster aggregate demand and counter the downward spiral that would otherwise result from natural economic cycles. They argued that remedial government action should take the form of deficit spending and other efforts to raise output to the level of full employment.[37]

In 1943, President Roosevelt sent Congress a report entitled *Security, Work and Relief Policies* that had been prepared by the National Resources Planning Board, an executive agency that had become a centre of Keynesian thinking within the Administration. The Report called for a 'New Bill of Rights', that included a right to work, a right to fair pay, a right to security in old age, a right to medical care and a right to equality before the law.[38] President Roosevelt echoed the Report in his annual message to Congress in 1945, where he called for a 'new Economic Bill of Rights that would include the right to a useful and remunerative job'.[39] Shortly thereafter, Senator James Murray introduced the Full Employment Act of 1945, embodying Roosevelt's proposal and setting out the contours of a general right to work. Section 2 of the proposed Act declared that 'all Americans . . . are entitled to an opportunity for useful, remunerative, regular, and full-time employment'. It also stated that it was the responsibility of the federal government to assure con-

[37] S Kemp Bailey, *Congress Makes a Law: The Story Behind the Employment Act of 1946* (New York, Columbia University Press, 1950); GJ Santoni, 'The Employment Act of 1946: Some History Notes', Federal Reserve of St Louis paper, November 1986, 7–9; BL Jones, 'The Role of Keynesians in Wartime Policy and Postwar Planning, 1940 – 1946' (1972) 62(2) *American Economic Association* 125.

[38] Kemp Bailey, *Congress Makes a Law*, above n 37, 26–27.

[39] ibid.

tinuing full employment for all Americans. The Act further provided that it was the obligation of the federal government to provide the necessary investments and expenditures to assure 'continuing full employment'.[40]

The right to work embodied in the 1945 legislation and advocated by the New Deal Keynesians was progressive and idealistic. It sought to provide a job for everyone who wanted one, and called upon the federal government to make the right to work a reality by creating jobs when the private sector did not produce full employment. The result, proponents claimed, would be a virtuous cycle in which employed workers would purchase more goods, and manufacturers would need more workers to keep up with the increased demand for their products. Under the statute, government intervention, while costly, would serve the public good three times over. It would provide jobs to people who needed them, thus helping to keep millions out of poverty. It would stimulate demand by augmenting buying power. And it would employ people to build needed infrastructure or provide useful public services.

The Full Employment Bill passed the Senate in September 1945, but it ran into trouble in the House of Representatives. Conservative members decried it as a socialist measure that would undermine the free enterprise system. The National Association of Manufacturers, the Chamber of Commerce and other leading business organisations lobbied intensely against the Bill.[41] The *Wall Street Journal* warned that it led to the very type of collectivism that Fredrich Hayek had warned against in his influential libertarian polemic, *The Road to Serfdom*.[42]

In conference, the Bill was amended and diluted. The language establishing a right to work was changed to read that,'[t]he Congress hereby declares that it is the continuing policy and responsibility of the Federal Government to promote maximum employment, production, and purchasing power'. In addition, the provision requiring federal investment and expenditure at a level that would maintain full employment was eliminated. The Act's title was also changed so that the words 'Full Employment' were dropped, and the Act was renamed the Employment Act of 1946.[43] As amended, it passed and was signed by President Truman in 1946.

The 1946 Employment Act did not create the right to work that its advocates had hoped for. Rather, its primary accomplishment was to establish two institutions, the President's Council of Economic Advisors and the Congressional Joint Economic Committee, that were charged with the preparation of regular reports of macroeconomic indicators and forecasts of economic trends. Some have surmised that the Act had an additional salutary impact: it made the federal government responsible for the overall performance of the American economy and

[40] Santoni, above n 37, 9.
[41] Kemp Bailey, above n 37, 129–49.
[42] ibid, 54–55.
[43] Santoni, above n 37, 12; L Fisher, 'Employment Act of 1946', available at: www.encyclopedia.com/topic/Employment_Act_of_1946.aspx.

embodied a symbolic commitment to full employment.[44] But it did not come close to creating a right to work in any meaningful sense.

The idea of a federally created right to work was revived in Congress in 1976, amid a period of high unemployment and inflation. Senator Hubert Humphrey and Representative Augustus Hawkins introduced a statute that would have reinstated the original 1945 Act, ensuring every American a job and making the federal government the employer of last resort. The Humphrey–Hawkins Bill suffered a fate similar to that of its predecessor. It was mutilated by numerous amendments so that, in addition to promoting the goal of full employment, it contained a grab bag of competing and conflicting policy goals including promoting 'balanced growth, a balanced federal budget, growth in productivity, an improved balance of trade, and price stability'. After two years of debate, the Full Employment and Balanced Growth Act of 1978 was enacted but, in its final form, it was so diluted that it barely addressed the goal of full employment at all and totally eliminated any language concerning the creation of a right to work.[45]

III Comparing the Visions

Although neither Commons nor the post-war Keynesians were successful in their attempts to create a right to work, both advocated similar policies. They both advocated that the government should guarantee employment to all who wanted to work. Despite their similarities, however, there is a significant difference between the two. Each is built upon a different view of the role of the state in economic life, and each contains a different implicit theory of political economy.

The Keynesians sought to create a right to work by means of a government programme to supplement the market and correct market failures. In their view, unemployment is an unfortunate by-product of capitalist markets, one that can be avoided through the intervention into the private economy of an exogenous force – the government. The state-created and state-guaranteed right to work is seen as medicine to be administered when the economy becomes ill. The medicine might be costly in terms of tax dollars, but in the long (and medium) run, it is better to pay for the cure than to let the patient die.

Commons did not view the right to work as an add-on to an otherwise neutral and autonomous, though sometimes errant, private market economy. Rather, to Commons, the market itself is a product of government action. By granting some

[44] See M Weidenbaum, 'The Employment Act of 1946: A Half Century of Presidential Policymaking' (1996) 26 *Presidential Studies Quarterly* 880.

[45] Title II of the 1978 Act contained provisions that 'permitted the president to establish "reservoirs of employment", if he found that other policies were failing to achieve full employment goals', and 'required that any such reservoir job be "on the lower ranges of skill and pay" . . . so as not to draw workers from the private sector'. Title IV required that such reservoir jobs be paid no less than the federal minimum wage and that there be equal pay for equal work. Other than this weak and purely discretionary language, the 1978 Act failed to create a right to work.

firms monopolies and protecting certain forms of private property (for example, intellectual property) the government gives some people great wealth. The government also maintains and enforces rules that enable some people to employ others at low wages and in poor conditions, such as through the prohibitions of secondary boycotts or by failing to protect union organising efforts.[46]

To Commons, the right to work should not be conceived as an adjustment to the market, but rather as an aspect of the market that progressives should advocate. His vision is that the market itself is a political creation, and it should be revised to provide more equitable outcomes. Commons does not call for abolition of the market, but he does call for restructuring the market with due regard to the distributional consequences of market-defining rules.

Both the Commons and the Keynesian conceptions of a right to work achieve important policy goals that would be constructive in the current recession. It is a tragedy of immeasurable dimensions that the US political elite rejected even a rhetorical commitment to full employment in 1946 and 1978. Today there are tens of millions of unemployed Americans who might have jobs if the 1945 Full Employment Act, or its attempted resurrection in 1978, had been enacted. A return to a Keynesian full employment agenda would be an important step in creating a more adequate social safety net and a more equitable distribution of income in the United States.

Commons' approach would go further along two dimensions. Commons' right to work is directed not merely at macroeconomic trends in unemployment; it also aims to empower workers in their own right. Thus Commons would add, as one of the essential elements of the right to work, that workers have legal protection against unfair dismissal. He contends that dismissal protection would enhance workers' bargaining power, and thus enable them to achieve better labour market outcomes for themselves. He also conceives of the government guarantee of employment as a worker empowering reform because it would tighten the labour supply and thereby give workers as a group more bargaining power.

The other respect in which the two approaches differ is more profound. For Commons, the government is not separate from the market – the market is a creation of the state, and market outcomes are the concrete manifestation of government action. Hence, the reforms he advocates are not merely, or even primarily, about correcting market failure – they are about restructuring the market itself. His is therefore a deeper critique of the existing economic order, and hence a more far-reaching vision of what a right to work would entail.

[46] Using Commons' analysis today, we could add that the government enables some people to amass large fortunes by making bets with other people's money, knowing they will be bailed out by government if those bets go sour.

IV What Should a Right to Work Entail Today?

The two theories discussed above suggest two different rights to work – a right to work as government-guaranteed employment and a right to work as job security in a specific job. The Keynesians advocated only the first of these, and Commons advocated both. I contend that neither one is a realistic aspiration today, due to changes in firm-level practices that have resulted from globalisation and technological change.[47] However, I suggest that we should adopt Commons' implicit political economy, even though we cannot adopt his proposals wholesale today because they grew out of a particular historical moment that no longer exists.

A right to job security made sense in an era when firms utilised long-term employees. During much of the twentieth century, large firms constructed internal labour markets in order to generate employee loyalty and ensure intergenerational transmission of skills. Today firms no longer seek loyalty, long-term commitment, or a fixed set of skills from their employees. Pressures from the global economy force today's firms to adapt quickly to changing technologies, markets for materials and consumer preferences.[48] Thus, firms have changed their human resource practices, trading stability for agility. Firms need flexibility to utilise different employees, with different skills, as market conditions change. Hence, dynamic firms utilise project work and hire workers with specific skills on an as-needed basis rather than committing to long-term employment. In this environment, any effort to enact legislation to require employers to offer indefinite job security to everyone would certainly be doomed.

The second aspect of a right to work – the right to a guaranteed government job – is also laudable but problematic in era of fiscal austerity and an increasingly globalised world. The idea of the government as the employer of last resort requires that there be both economic growth to provide the requisite demand and tax revenue, and a clear definition of who is entitled to government-provided or government-subsidised jobs. With increasing immigration, a right to a government-assured job would have to specify who counts as a right-holder. Any effort to delineate right-holders would generate bitter controversy about such issues as whether newly arrived immigrants or undocumented workers were included. This does not make it impossible to create such a right, but it does show that such a right would be politically explosive in the United States. Denmark has addressed the issue by requiring that a person lawfully reside in Denmark for seven years before they become eligible for participation in their active labour market programmes.[49] In the United States, a similar kind of time requirement would be necessary if we were to create a right to government-created or subsidised jobs.

[47] These changes are described in detail in Stone, *From Widgets to Digits*, above n 10, ch 5.

[48] See Stone and Arthurs, 'The Transformation of Employment Regimes', above n 15, 3–5.

[49] A Daguerre, *Active Labour Market Policies and Welfare Reform* (London, Palgrave Macmillan, 2007) 96–98.

However, recent immigration reform debates demonstrate that any move to offer social benefits to immigrants, even after a lengthy waiting period, would be extremely controversial.

I suggest we rethink the concept of a right to work in light of current employment practices. Drawing on Commons' insight that a right to work is not separate from the operation of the private market but is instead a potential aspect of the private market, we should situate a right to work in a larger analysis of the role of the state in the private sector. Because the state upholds the system of rules and constraints that define the private market, we can imagine a different set of rules that produces different results.

In today's labour market, firms are constantly changing their product and resource mix, and as a result jobs are always in a state of flux. In this world, we should advocate not a right to job security, but focus instead on the problem of support during life–work transitions. We need to devise programmes that help facilitate workers' movement between jobs, and transitions in and out of the labour market, throughout their working lives. Workers need to be able to learn new skills, weather periods of unemployment, retool, devote time to care work, engage in entrepreneurial activity and transition from school to work and from work to retirement. Fluidity and transitions in and out of the labour market are a fact of life for workers today, and social policies need to address the burdens these transitions entail.

Currently our social programmes are structured in a way that assumes long-term job attachment. Yet workers today are in transition. As such, they have different needs from workers in the past. They need measures such as lifetime learning opportunities, relocation assistance, childcare, portable benefits, transitional income maintenance and housing policies that suspend mortgage payments during periods out of the labour force. We need a social safety net that does not draw a sharp line between employment and unemployment, but that recognises that individuals should have the ability to move between labour market statuses without risking financial ruin.[50] However, we also need to take seriously the concern about empowerment that underlies Commons' vision. While Commons emphasised the impact of state action on the private sector outcomes, he failed to consider the role of private sector action on state policy. That is, he did not consider the problem of an empowered and wealthy elite – an elite which gained their wealth and power as a result of government action – acting

[50] I have proposed some of these in in the US context in Stone, *From Widgets to Digits*, above n 10, 282–88. There are currently policies under discussion in Europe that would address these challenges, including the Supiot Commission's proposal for social drawing rights, See *A Supiot, Beyond Employment: Changes in Work and the Future of Labour Law in Europe* (New York, Oxford University Press, 2001) 56; the Danish 'flexicurity' model, see, T Bredgaard, 'Flexibility and Security in Employment Regulation: Learning from Denmark' in KVW Stone and H Arthurs (eds), *Rethinking Workplace Regulation: Beyond the Standard Contract of Employment* (New York, Russell Sage Foundation Press, 2013); and proposals for a guaranteed basic citizen wage, see, G Standing (ed), *Promoting Income Security as a Right* (London, Anthem Press, 2005).

systematically to shape government policy to their needs. Yet this is the fundamental political problem in the United States today.

In the United States, income distribution has become so imbalanced and the super-rich have become so wealthy that they have been able to influence not only the results of elections through campaign contributions, but they have also reshaped the labour laws in ways that disempower unions. Corporations spend more on lobbying for regulations and laws they like than they spend on political campaigns.[51] In the past, when incomes were not so divergent, unions empowered workers not only in the workplace, but also in the political process. But now, any illusion of parity of political power between labour and large corporations has vanished. Hence, in recent years, Congress has enacted many reforms to the rules of the market that have exacerbated inequality and diminished social justice. For example, welfare reform and immigration non-enforcement has swelled the low-wage labour market, depressing wages for large segments of the working population. The recent cutbacks in unemployment benefits and the defunding of food stamps have devastated the unemployed. The reforms we see today are generating more wealth for the few and imposing more burdens on the middle and lower income groups. Even more insidious, the super-rich are rewriting the rules of elections to their benefit.[52] Therefore, we are in a pernicious spiral – as more and more income is funnelled upwards to the top of the income distribution, the more power those at the top use to escalate that trend.

The challenge for today is not only to conceive of what a newly imagined right to work might look like, but how it can be achieved. I propose that we build on reformers of the past and advocate a right to work reformulated to provide the right to livelihood security that would provide a sustainable, secure and dignified life for all members of our community.

[51] JS Hacker and P Pierson, *Winner-Take-All Politics: How Washington Made the Rich Richer – and Turned its Back on the Middle Class* (New York, Simon & Schuster, 2011).

[52] eg, in a recent election law case, the Supreme Court held that corporations can spend unlimited amounts on communications and other efforts to influence political elections. *Citizens United v Federal Election Commission* 130 S Ct 876 (S Ct, 2010). The case was brought and financed by brought by the multi-billionaire Koch brothers.

16

Working Out the Right to Work in a Global Labour Market

GUY MUNDLAK

Introduction

In the state of Nirvana, the economy was flourishing, and other than frictional unemployment, people at the age of employment enjoyed many employment opportunities. When the adjacent country of Paradisia offered huge tax breaks to foreign capital investments, many manufacturing enterprises crossed the border from Nirvana, speeding economic growth and boosting employment levels in Paradisia. Some of the prosperous urban centres in Nirvana experienced rapid deterioration. Attempts by Nirvana's government to correct the situation were only partially successful. Unemployment surged and many jobs that were opened were in low-waged occupations, part-time arrangements and offered limited employability horizons. Poverty and despair on one side of the border; growth and rewarding employment standards on the other.

This stylized example, albeit not far removed from more complex realities in an ever-growing globalized labour market, suggests a major challenge for thinking about respecting, protecting and fulfilling the right to work (RTW). The RTW, which is on shaky grounds to begin with, encounters a global reality in which there is a disparity between the scope of the political agents' impact on the distribution of valuable work, and the scope of the labour market that abandons the confines of the nation state. In this process many questions need to be posed: whose work should be promoted? Who can and should be held responsible for the absence of jobs? Who can draw on the subjective RTW and make the moral and legal claims? And where can such claims be made? Moreover, if we move away from a simplistic assumption that the number of jobs in the world is fixed and that the movement of jobs creates a zero-sum-game of winners and losers, what kind of policy measures are expected to be taken in fulfilment of the right to work?

In the following chapter I seek to address these challenges to the RTW. Section one commences with a summary of some observations on the RTW, its particular difficulties and the reasons it should be endorsed as a fully-fledged right among the roster of human rights generally, and social rights in particular. The section concludes with a proposal that extends beyond the specific context of the RTW, advocating a judicial review that is based on assessing the process of policymaking in the complex system of labour relations. The second section develops the layering of challenges for the RTW in the process of globalization and its impact on the world of work. The third section suggests that globalization also affects the feasibility of a process-based review. Nevertheless, I advocate this solution as the best option to maintain a focus on the crisis of work in the global village, and as a way to encourage innovative experiments and solutions to the problem, while ensuring that the labour problem remains on political benches as one of the crucial components for an agenda of development, dignity and equality in the distribution of fair and rewarding employment opportunities.

I The Ambiguities of the Right to Work – Established Territory

Work is central to human experiences, both good and bad. It is an integral part of personal development and a central axis of the social order. For the individual it is a choice that celebrates liberty, a place that satisfies various needs – income to provide for one's material needs, a sense of security that is associated with the stability of daily routines and lifelong career patterns, a circle of friends and colleagues, an important anchor of social status and a source of recognition and, ideally, a place for developing a higher level of self fulfilment.[1] Each of these can be achieved outside work, but it is the integrative effect that pulls them all together, which makes work so meaningful. For society, work is a source of generating order, forging a sense of community, facilitating mobility between classes and a meeting place that brings together people from all walks of life. Admittedly, it is also a source of individuals' frustration, fatigue, subordination and low self esteem. Societies also draw on work to entrench and legitimize patterns of social and economic stratification, discrimination, discipline and order, and even exclusion.[2] The pile of expectations built around work is also the source of work's intolerable negative effects. Nevertheless, those who believe in work's potential for individual and collective growth, seek to improve its redeeming features and eliminate, or at least attenuate its negative aspects. Those who believe in work's

[1] The various virtues are sorted according to Maslow's theory of needs and motivation: A Maslow, *Motivation and Personality* (New York, Harper, 1954). Its application to the world of work was indirectly developed through his vision of humanistic management, in A Maslow, *Eupsychian Management: A Journal* (New York, Richard Irwin, 1965).

[2] For a critical view of work that highlights its centrality but also its 'darker' sides: R Muirhead, *Just Work* (Cambridge MA, Harvard University Press, 2004); SP Vallas, *Work* (Cambridge, Polity, 2012); K Weeks, *The Problem of Work: Feminism, Marxism, Antiwork Politics and Postwork Imagineries* (Durham, Duke University Press, 2011).

potential must realize that its brighter prospects should be a central pillar in our vision of humanity, community and solidarity and therefore the RTW must be part of the human rights roster.

In previous articles I lamented the multiple sources of disadvantage suffered by the right to work. First, as part of the cluster of social and economic rights, some question its ideological thrust as well as the possibility to operationalize the right.[3] Second, as noted at the outset, work, unlike other social goods that are promoted by social rights (such as housing, education and health) is a good we tend to feel ambivalent about.[4] Third, addressing and fulfilling the RTW requires drawing on labour market strategies that often tend to be dialectical in their implications, leading to a horizontal internal pressure in the operationalization of the right. Otherwise stated, the RTW of some may, in practical terms, imply the denial of the RTW of others.[5] It is therefore not surprising that even staunch labour advocates are suspicious about the RTW.[6] Despite the importance of recognizing the RTW, perhaps the right presents too many hurdles to be taken seriously as a subjective right – a right that private citizens (and groups) can effectively make a claim to have, with a clear addressee who is expected to fulfil their claim.

Although these problems may account for the thin body of jurisprudence on the RTW, the centrality of work urges for solutions. First and foremost, the easiest task is to do away with the general claims against social and economic rights. The point of departure for the following discussion is that all rights are interdependent and that social–economic rights can and must be pursued just as much as civil and political rights.[7] Subsets of the general claim are therefore also rejected in their various forms. For example, the arguments that social rights are difficult to operationalize because they are positive rights (require to do, rather than abstain from doing), or the claim that social rights are intrinsically vague, or that a unique expertise is required to evaluate infringement of social rights, should all be dismissed.[8]

A less common approach to address the arguments against social and economic rights, suggests the possibility of relocating the RTW as part of the political rights, ie, the rights necessary to participate in the exercise of political power.[9] Admittedly this approach does not resonate with the historical roots of the right, but the

[3] On the problems associated with economic and social rights, see generally C Gearty and V Mantouvalou, *Debating Social Rights* (Oxford, Hart Publishing, 2010).

[4] G Mundlak, 'The Right to Work – The Value of Work' in D Barak-Erez and A Gross (eds), *Exploring Social Rights: Between Theory and Practice* (Oxford, Hart Publishing, 2007) 341.

[5] G Mundlak, 'The Right to Work: Linking Human Rights and Employment Policy' (2007) 146 *International Labour Review* 189.

[6] B Hepple, 'A Right to Work?' (1981) 10 *Industrial Law Journal* 65.

[7] Proclamation of Teheran, International Conference on Human Rights, 22 April–13 May 1968, 13, UN Doc A/CONF.32/41 (1968), available at: www.unhchr.ch/html/ menu3/b/b_tehern.htm. Also see IE Koch, *Human Rights as Indivisible Rights* (Leiden, Martinus Nijhoff Publishers, 2009).

[8] See Gearty and Mantouvalou, above n 3.

[9] This definition of political rights draws on TH Marshall, *Citizenship and Social Class* (Cambridge, Cambridge University Press, 1950).

relationship between work and political rights should be recognized.[10] Such a connection is most visible when political rights are denied from working people (as was the case in the Athenian democracy),[11] or when political rights are conditioned on earnings and income, as were the census suffrage forms that tied the level of tax with the weight of voting (hence granting more weight to high earners and minimizing the political power of the unemployed). Even if those who do not work are accorded formal voting rights, as is universally true today, work remains a ticket to the enjoyment of other rights. For example, in corporatist (conservative) welfare regimes, some social rights are linked with access to work.[12] In caste systems, access to work, or forms of work, are interrelated with other forms of rights and social privileges. Just as citizenship is considered to be the right to enjoy rights, work is de facto a form of activity that is a precondition to realization of some rights, such as the right to forge personal relationships.[13] There is an affinity between work and citizenship that underscores the political nature of the RTW, leading some to argue that state-based citizenship should be substituted with work-based criteria of belonging.[14] None of these connections allow the fully-fledged categorization of the RTW within the domain of political rights, but they strengthen the argument that drawing the line between the political or civil rights on the one hand, and the social–economic rights on the other, is a tilted constitutive effort that purposefully seeks to undermine social rights generally and the RTW in particular. Instead, the option of viewing all rights as interrelated presents an alternative in which citizenship and human rights are necessary for constituting a shared community of virtue.

Unlike the problems associated with the *right* to work and its jurisprudential aspects, the problems of *work* pose a greater challenge. These include dilemmas regarding both the means (policy instruments) and the ends (values). There are two general ways to address these problems. The first is to minimize the scope of the RTW, hence eliminating some of its more controversial components. The second is to reconsider the objectives of human rights' *telos* and the institutional practices associated with the field.

With regard to the former strategy of minimizing the scope of the right, it is important to note that the RTW can be evoked in some cases with no particular problems. These situations are more likely to be related to one of three categories:

[10] Historically the RTW is part of the 'third generation' social rights, as described by Marshall. Other classifications designate social rights as second generation. See K Vasak, 'Human Rights: A Thirty-Year Struggle: The Sustained Efforts to give Force of Law to the Universal Declaration of Human Rights' (1977) 30 *UNESCO Courier* 11.

[11] J Shklar, *American Citizenship: The Quest for Inclusion* (Cambridge MA, Harvard University Press, 1991).

[12] GE Andersen, *Three Worlds of Welfare Capitalism* (Princeton NJ, Princeton University Press, 1990).

[13] R O'Connell, 'The Right to Work in the European Convention on Human Rights' (2012) 2 *European Human Rights Law Review* 176.

[14] J Gordon, 'Transnational Labor Citizenship' (2007) 80 *Southern California Law Review* 503; J Fudge, 'After Industrial Citizenship: Market Citizenship or Citizenship at Work?' (2005) 60 *Relations industrielles/Industrial Relations* 631.

(a) *the negative dimension* of the right: denying convicts who served their term, people with HIV or asylum seekers the opportunity to work is an infringement of the (negative) right to work;[15] (b) *individual circumstances*: instances in which an individual is denied access to the employment bureau, or does not receive positive aid to find a job; or (c) *concerns about equality*: imposing entry requirements into a profession or a job that have a disparate impact on ethnic minorities or restricting access of some groups (the elderly or people with disabilities) to the labour market. These do not need to be 'easy' cases, in the sense that they provide unequivocally right or wrong answers. Many issues that concern rights require balancing between rights (for example, between managerial rights and work-related rights) and between rights and social interests (for example, security or fiscal related interests). However, the legal toolbox is well equipped to deal with such matters.

Outside the negative, individual and discriminatory nexus of cases, the RTW presents more thorny issues. Some of them concern dilemmas regarding internal conflicts within the RTW.[16] For example, should the RTW be extended to non-waged work, including household labour? [17] Should the RTW be used to uphold the right to be employed in degrading work?[18] Similarly, the RTW may require compromising rights *at* work – ie, the right to work in decent working conditions or the right not to be discriminated against. For example, flexible employment contracts that seek to incorporate young workers into the labour market in exchange for lesser working conditions, wages and benefits,[19] or special arrangements that seek to incorporate people with disabilities into the labour market by lowering their wages.[20] The positive duty on the state (as well as on private agents where applicable) to expand employment opportunities raises similar problems. For example, is the state always responsible if high levels of unemployment persist? Can and should the RTW be constructed as requiring the benchmark of full employment?[21] Such problems attract a particular type of response that seeks to place them outside the sphere of human rights, moving them into the sphere of

[15] *IB v Greece* App no 552/10 (ECtHR, 3 October 2013).

[16] See, generally, Mundlak, 'The Right to Work, The Value of Work', above n 4.

[17] ND Zatz, 'The Impossibility of Work Law' in G Davidov and B Langille, *The Idea of Labour Law* (Oxford, Oxford University Press, 2011).

[18] See Muirhead, above n 2.

[19] eg, in France, there was an attempt to introduce the *contrat première embauche* in 2006, whereby employers were encouraged to hire young employees (under the age of 26) by subsidies and ensured easier dismissals procedures. Followed by strong public critique the arrangement was abolished. See O Kaufmann, 'Weakening of Dismissal Protection or Strengthening of Employment Policy in France?' (2007) 36 *Industrial Law Journal* 267.

[20] eg, in Israel special provisions were enacted allowing people with disabilities to apply for a certificate that allows them to be hired for work with exemption from the prevailing minimum wage. Minimum Wage Bylaws (Adjusted Minimum Wage for People with Disabilities and Reduced Working Capacity) (2002).

[21] For arguments in favour of matching the RTW with full employment policies, see P Harvey, 'Human Rights and Economic Policy Discourse: Taking Economic and Social Rights Seriously' (2002) 33 *Columbia Human Rights Law Review* 363.

industrial policy. For example, some claim that the RTW does not include the right to be provided with work.[22]

The desire to leave out the RTW's contested zones from the scope of human rights, relegating it to the domain of policy is explicable, but misconceived. The rise, by 2012, of unemployment in Spain to the level of almost a quarter of the workforce, and approximately half of the young (under 25) workers is a matter of crucial importance for the unemployed individuals and the community alike.[23] Detroit's bankruptcy in 2013 is a derivative of the fact that Detroit lost a huge share of jobs that made it a flourishing city in the past.[24] For those who are involuntarily unemployed, the impact of 'policy' is no less than an infringement of their civil and political rights. Stating that their problems are merely a matter of policy and not of human rights does not really respect the stated values of the RTW. Holding that the RTW is limited to negative, individual and discriminatory cases actually misses the *core* of the right, and not its periphery. What significance has a human right if it can only address the anecdotal prevention of occupational opportunities from an individual, but cannot be relevant to the masses of unemployed people who are gradually being marginalized in the political, economic and social spheres, and to disintegrating communities? Can the moral core of the right be made into a policy matter because we are uncertain about the correct means to fulfil it?

Hence, the second approach that can be taken to deal with the challenges posed by the RTW is to relieve the sphere of human rights from the expectation to provide clear-cut solutions to every problem. Human rights, or their translation into constitutional rights, provide a focal point, a form of discursive space. Rather than assuming that the RTW can prescribe precise policy instruments to increase decent work to all, it should serve as a benchmark that public (and private) agents must pursue. Together with the requirement for decent work and freedom of association, public (and private) agencies must consider the implications of policy (or lack of) to achieve the progressive realization of the right.[25] The legislature and the executive branches should be critically scrutinized with regard to their

[22] K Drzewicki, 'The Right to Work and Rights in Work' in A Eide, C Krause and A Rosas (eds), *Economic, Social and Cultural Rights*, 2nd edn (Leiden, Martinus Nijhoff, 2001) 235. UN Committee on Economic, Social and Cultural Rights, General Comment No 18: The Right to Work, Article 6 of the International Covenant on Economic, Social and Cultural Rights, UN Doc E/C.12/GC/18 (6 February 2006) – takes an ambivalent view on this matter. It clarifies in para 6 that the RTW should 'not be understood as an absolute and unconditional right to obtain employment', but also requires in para 19 that 'the principal obligation of States parties is to ensure the progressive realization of the exercise of the right to work. States parties must therefore adopt, as quickly as possible, measures aiming at achieving full employment'.

[23] I Baviera, 'Employment Stability in Spanish Labor Law: Between Regulatory Tradition and Social Reality' (2013) 34 *Comparative Labor Law and Policy Journal* 655.

[24] J Stiglitz, 'The Wrong Lessons from Detroit's Bankruptcy' *New York Times* (11 August 2013).

[25] To emphasize, I am *not* arguing that the negative, individual instances are the 'core' of the right, while employment creation is its periphery. There are various considerations – including quantitative ones – that should aid in distinguishing core from periphery. Extensive unemployment among youth may be core, while restrictions on any one individual may take place for reasons that are at the periphery. The difference is that some aspects – collective, positive and substantive matters – may require instruments that are too complex to be prescribed by a human rights discourse.

performance on employment matters, because decent and dignified work is central to humanity and to the integrity of the community. Some considerations can be weighed differently in different societies, or may need to be developed over time until a moral consensus evolves. For example, the matter of recognizing household labour as work, equal in value and deserving recognition just like waged labour is currently controversial.[26] This should not prevent deliberations in the sphere of human rights. Mandatory retirement was considered an acceptable and even desirable policy in the past, and is currently coming under attack and being reformed in many states.[27] Ideas of how human rights should be fulfilled change over time, through the process of social deliberations.

Shifting from clear-cut assignment of practices that infringe human rights towards a deliberative method should not be confused with an argument of 'non-justicability'. Judicial review can be a catalyst for the deliberative process.[28] Courts can ask to review benchmarks, monitoring efforts and the considerations underlying recognized trade-offs. They do not need to establish the policy themselves. This is what I designate as process-based judicial review.[29]

What do I think about when thinking about process-based constitutional review:

Assume that towards elections, parties envision that the "hot topic" affecting the electorate's preferences choices is a solution to youth (entry–level, after high school) unemployment. The reigning coalition comes up with a programme for prioritizing youth in the labour market. An NGO representing the elderly (over 40) in the labour market files a petition in the court for a violation of the 'elderly's RTW'. Another individual may join such a petition, demonstrating that the conditions for receiving priorities disadvantage a certain minority, or have a gendered tilt. Small and medium sized employers may file an amicus curiae, demonstrating that the new policy imposes on them an undue burden.

[26] See above, n 17.

[27] For a comparative overview, see A Wood, M Robertson and D Wintersgill, *A Comparative Review of International Approaches to Mandatory Retirement* (UK, Department for Work and Pensions, 2010).

[28] In the words of Roberto Gargarella – 'When we accept that judges are subordinate to, indeed – servants of public debate, then we may begin to see the judiciary as a crucial engine of public debate'. See R Gargarella, 'Theories of Democracy, the Judiciary and Social Rights' in R Gargarella, P Domingo and T Roux (eds), *Courts and Social Transformation in New Democracies: An Institutional Voice for the Poor* (Aldershot, Ashgate, 2006) 28.

[29] There is no fixed concept of a procedural method of constitutional review. For a relevant example of a procedural approach in the related area of social security, see the German approach that was deployed in what is known as the 'HartzIV case' of the German Constitutional Court – BVerfG, 1 BvL 1/09, Judgment of 9 February 2010 (Hartz IV). English translation available at: www.bverfg.de/entscheidungen/ls20100209_1bvl000109en.html. For a commentary on the case, see IT Winkler and C Mahler, 'Interpreting the Right to a Dignified Minimum Existence: A New Era in German Socio-Economic Rights Jurisprudence? (2013) *Human Rights Law Review* 388; for a comparative view, see DM Davis, 'The Relationship Between Courts and the Other Arms of Government in Promoting and Protecting Socio-Economic Rights in South Africa: What About Separation of Powers?' (2012) 15(5) *PER, Potchefstroom* 638.

A narrow substantive approach may claim that the RTW does not seek to extend work opportunities and therefore no one can make such a claim. A more expansive substantive approach may dismiss the claim because the policy was aimed to advance work opportunities and is therefore within the clear boundaries of the RTW.

By contrast, a process-based approach acknowledges that the benefits to some may require assessing their effects on others. The court is not the appropriate branch to even out the policy. However, the court may require the state to demonstrate the empirical assumptions underlying the policy and the ethical trade-offs the state considered.

In some cases, the forcing of information may enable a substantive response (for example – denying a formulation holding that "people who immigrated in the last decade should move to the end of the queue"). Other times, forcing such information may disclose the state's lack of concern for some groups, poor judgment, contested empirical basis, or the invisibility of some groups. On the positive side, the debate may disclose reasonable sequencing of priorities for fighting unemployment. Such debates may reveal policy options that were disregarded. Alternatively, they may require the state to ensure a monitoring system that measures and reports changes in the participation rates of elderly workers in the labour market; define a threshold level in which the policy should be re-considered and identify means that are taken to reduce the pressure from the elderly workers.

In such a process, the RTW serves as a focal point that illuminates empirical knowledge, strategies, values, interests, alternative options and the prices that were paid. It views the courts as catalysts of democratic deliberations. It is entrusted with ensuring that the political process realizes that access to adequate/decent/rewarding work is in the realm of human rights and not just a matter of political preference. It does not bracket the political process from the constitutional debate, but it does not prescribe the 'proper' policy in a manner that trumps the political process.

Rethinking the role of the constitutional process should be favoured over the option of narrowing the scope of the RTW. The values underlying the RTW and its sister-rights to decent and dignified working conditions and the right of association should not be diluted for reasons of convenience. Admittedly, a process-based view of human rights has its vices and virtues, and these were discussed elsewhere.[30] For the sake of this introductory part, I take this as my point of departure to explore new territories.

The process-based framework is inseparable from aspects of citizenship. It requires that all those who are affected by policy trade-offs should be involved in

[30] See above, n 5.

the process.[31] Involvement extends beyond voting rights, and should include active participation in trade unions, employers associations and organizations in civil society.[32] It requires access of multiple agents to where law-making actually takes place – parliamentary committees, regulatory bodies and the courtroom, and should also include mobilization of interests in the streets and the media. Labour market policy intrinsically involves trade-offs in the allocation of power, privileges and resources among different workers (and the unemployed as well).[33] These should be encouraged to surface, rather than simplified and concealed. This form of radical democracy is essential to airing the many layers of the RTW, as well as to all other rights. As noted at the outset, advocating the fulfilment of human rights generally, and the RTW in particular, is tightly linked with active political participation. The social and the political are inseparable.

The feasibility of the process-based solution to the difficulties associated with the RTW rests on the assumption that the political community is well defined. Outside the boundaries of the political community, the process-based construct of human rights may lose its coherence, moral strength and political legitimacy. The labour market is no longer confined to the boundaries of the nation state. Allegedly, human rights are as stated – the rights of humans and should not be affected by the globalization of markets. However, the process-based construct is embedded in a political community. Can the process-based solutions identified for advancing the RTW within the political community (usually the nation state) apply in a global community? Or perhaps globalization requires sufficing with a shrunk and modest version of the RTW?

II New Territories to Explore – The Right to Work in a Global Labour Market

Human rights are those that enjoy universal application, reflecting our sense of humanity regardless of national boundaries. Constitutional rights often reflect the list of human rights, although they provide a more cultural or national-sensitive list of rights, and provide the development of a local jurisprudence that adapts the dictates of universal rights. Moreover, national recognition of human rights provides new forums for litigation and other forms – legal and non-legal – of claiming rights.

[31] RA Dahl, *A Preface to Economic Democracy* (Berkeley, University of California Press, 1986).

[32] A Bogg and C Estlund, 'Freedom of Association and the Right to Contest: Getting Back to Basics' in T Novitz and A Bogg (eds), *Voices at Work* (Oxford, Oxford University Press, 2014); G Mundlak, 'Workplace – Democracy: Reclaiming the Effort to Foster Public-Private Isomorphism' (2014) 15 *Theoretical Inquiries in Law* 159.

[33] G Mundlak, 'The Third Function of Labour Law: Distributing Labour Market Opportunities among Workers' in G Davidov and B Langille (eds), *The Idea of Labour Law* (Oxford, Oxford University Press, 2011).

The nation state remains a central player responsible for respecting, protecting and fulfilling human rights. It incorporates human rights into its domestic legislation, whether at the meta-normative constitutional level or at the statutory level;[34] it responds to claims that it violated human rights in international fora; it adjudicates claims that arise domestically. While private agents and corporate bodies assume some level of responsibility in international law as well, it is secondary to that of the state.[35] Potentially, unemployment in a given state may raise an a priori claim against the state, which failed to adopt the means necessary to ensure the RTW of its citizens. This claim can be made internally (in a constitutional court) or externally (for example, in a shadow report that is submitted to the Committee on Economic, Social and Cultural Rights). The state is regarded as the primary – albeit not the sole – holder of duty that corresponds to the right.

In this state-centred framework, the problems underlying the operationalization of the RTW become all the more visible. The main reason is that labour markets are no longer confined to the nation state's boundaries. Consequently, there is a mismatch between our state-based perception of the RTW ('the state must ensure work opportunities to its citizens') and the labour market that no longer operates according to the dictate of any single state.

States can be held responsible for the way in which they address domestic problems in their labour markets. Most actions that correspond to the 'simple' dimension of the RTW – individual, negative and discriminatory – are those in which the state's actions can be connected with the action (or omission) of the state. For example, the denial of work opportunities from an individual for security reasons, or even a policy decision that youth should receive priority in new jobs while the elderly must be regarded as residual claimants.

However, many matters that are decided by the state may have implications on citizens and workers of other states. The opposite holds true as well. Some problems in the labour market are the result of competition from workers and business in other countries. The assumption of an overlap between the state, its citizens and economic activity was never perfectly correct, but it is remote from the reality of globalized labour markets at present.[36]

Consider the following problems. First, states may advance employment guarantees that are important for the progressive realization of fulfilling rights at work, but may experience the flight of capital to other states. (This is in essence the contested globalized process of 'race to the bottom'.) A different strategy to protect the RTW of workers within the state is to impose tariffs that protect domestic industry. Similarly, states may attempt to establish preferences, for example in public tender offers, for employing local workers rather than 'foreign workers' or

[34] Over 130 countries extend constitutional protection to the RTW to some degree or another. See the comparison between constitutions at the Constitute Project, available at: www.constituteproject.com.

[35] D Lustig and E Benvenisti, 'The Corporation as the Good Despot' (2014) 15 *Theoretical Inquiries in Law* 125.

[36] An extended discussion of this argument appears in G Mundlak, 'De-Territorializing Labor Law' (2009) 3 *Journal of Law and Ethics of Human Rights* 188.

to manufacture domestically rather than offshore.[37] Such barriers to trade and competition may have an impact on the RTW of workers in other countries. A third strategy to protect workers domestically is to seal the border to migrant workers or impose severe restrictions on entry and the employment conditions of migrant workers. Refusing employment opportunities for work seekers who may not have recourse to a job in their state of citizenship may be an infringement of their RTW. Alternatively, the state may decide to extend equal rights to migrant workers, to deter employers from preferring undocumented migrant workers. However, even when equal treatment is applied, states generally do not assume responsibility for these workers once they leave the territory of the state. Their connection to the state is temporary, instrumental in nature and so is the state's responsibility to their RTW.

In addition to states' strategies internally, in response to strategies of other states, or affecting the rights of workers in other states, states also influence the development of international standards and norms that in turn affect the rights of workers in the global labour market. For example, states may take a position in global debates on trade law, advancing their rent-seeking interests in the enjoyment of trade's benefits, even if it is at the expense of workers in other countries.

At least some of these problems, if not all, are not unique to a globalized labour market and variations appear in domestic (national) regulatory dilemmas. Such is the case when municipalities or provinces compete for business and employment opportunities.[38] However, the process-based solution that was proposed in the introductory section, assumes a political community in which deliberations take place. If an argument is made that a given employment standard (or policy) may have adverse consequences on the level of employment in other localities, trade-offs can be discussed under the umbrella of the right to work in decent working conditions. The state should establish benchmarks and monitor performance, trade unions should negotiate rewards and sanctions, NGOs should contest the state's priorities. The state remains as the broker of competing demands.

But how should such deliberations take place when the boundaries of the political community are permeable, losing their importance to economic activity that takes a much lesser concern for national boundaries?[39] This is in essence the general dilemma posed by globalization. Dani Rodrik designates this to be a trilemma, because any attempt to reconcile intense globalization, democracy and the power of the nation will require some kind of a compromise.[40] Consider the

[37] C Barnard, 'Procurement Law to Enforce Labour Standards' in G Davidov and B Langille, *The Idea of Labour Law* (Oxford, Oxford University Press, 2011).

[38] Y Blank, 'Spheres of Citizenship' (2007) 8 *Theoretical Inquiries in Law* 411.

[39] For a comprehensive discussion of these questions with regard to economic and social rights generally, see M Langford, W Vandenhole, M Scheinin and W van Genugten, 'Introduction: An Emerging Field' in M Langford et al (eds), *Global Justice, State Duties: The Extraterritorial Scope of Economic, Social and Cultural Rights in International Law* (Cambridge, Cambridge University Press, 2012).

[40] D Rodrik, *The Globalization Paradox: Democracy and the Future of the World Economy* (New York, Norton, 2011).

problem of structural unemployment that denies people of their RTW. Nation states may opt for job creation programmes, preventing relocation of industry, and giving preference to localized production and workers (drawing on nationalist hyperboles such as 'buy stuff that is made in your own country'; 'employ your own country(wo)men'). A globalized order may imply a supranational agency that considers just allocation of work, whether by means of tweaking trade law or advancing global job creation programmes and migration. Democracy requires that those who may pay the price of allocating work should be able to have a say in the decision-making process. In the deliberative framework suggested earlier, the democracy principle is more familiar in the national context. However, the globalization of the labour market sheds doubt on whether national solutions are adequate.

Consider the aforementioned dilemmas. In the context of capital's movement and forum shopping, nation states impose trade barriers to prevent the dislocation of local industry. These can take the form of, for example, conditioning trade on raising labour standards, or by imposing tariffs on imports. The former is demonstrated by increased use of social clauses in bilateral and regional trade agreements, as well as in unilateral general systems of preferences.[41] The latter is demonstrated in cases concerning anti-dumping measures.[42] Both types of instrument may have implications on the distribution of work opportunities in a global labour market. The requirements derived from a social clause may resonate and even be mandated by the human right to decent and fair working conditions. At the same time, countries that compete globally by offering cheap labour costs may lose out in the competition.[43] Similarly, the use of tariffs has an indirect implication on workers' opportunities and working conditions, because their employers may lose their niche in the global labour market. There is nothing intrinsically wrong with the attempt to raise wages and improve working conditions abroad, and such actions may be warranted by the RTW. However, if these actions also carry a price in terms of employment opportunities, who should determine the proper balance? Deliberations *within* one state intrinsically exclude the interests of those who are residents and workers of another country, even if they are affected by the outcomes.

In the context of workers' movement across borders, the RTW appears to be in tension with immigration policy. One of the most difficult areas in the regulation of migration is that of labour migration. Clearly, arguments about the RTW in the context of labour migration are in fully-fledged tension with immigration policy and the state's power of sovereignty at the borders. Allowing wholesale claims of

[41] On the increasing use of social clauses in unilateral, bilateral and regional agreements, see B Hepple, *Labour Laws and Global Trade* (Oxford, Hart Publishing, 2005) 89–150.

[42] See, eg, the case of Chinese-made tyres imported into the United States, discussed in J Fudge and G Mundlak, 'Justice in a Globalizing World: Resolving Conflicts Involving Workers Rights Beyond the Nation State' in Y Dahan, H Lerner and F Milman-Sivan (eds), *Global Justice and International Labour Rights* (Cambridge, Cambridge University Press, 2014, forthcoming).

[43] GW Seidman, 'Labouring Under an Illusion? Lesotho's "Sweat-Free" Label' (2009) 30 *Third World Quarterly* 581.

migrants workers (and those who would like to migrate if restrictions are removed) to a RTW would merely be a way of circumventing the nation state's policy on labour migration. There are however instances in which work is not the reason for entry, in which the RTW would raise different concerns. The rights of refugees include the RTW.[44] However, there are asylum seekers whose status is unclear, and people seeking citizenship rights for reasons of family unification, for whom a RTW claim would suffice and make other status-related conditions less important. Hence, the RTW serves as a positive incentive for crossing borders at times when nation states tighten immigration controls. It is also important to note that in many states, advancing the RTW of the citizens may entail programmes for deporting undocumented and even documented migrant workers.[45]

A third category in which global problems emerge is the movement of services. This category can be viewed as a combination of the other two or as a distinct third category. Contractors who provide services and bring their workers to perform the work raise the problem of dislocating jobs to employers outside the territory (like in the movement of capital) and to their workers who come into the nation state (who are in a situation that is similar to that of migrant workers). Such problems were raised in the European Union with regard to the Posted Workers Directive but are also triggered by the GATT IV and in regional arrangements.[46]

In all these contexts, national solutions may come at the expense of people outside the confines of the state and its citizens. Tariffs ignore the question of job creation in other countries; migration policy ignores the basic need to migrate to find gainful work; imposing local standards on foreign service providers may affect the work and business opportunities that are available to citizens of other states. Who will speak for Chinese workers affected by American tariffs? For African asylum seekers who encounter high entry barriers to Europe? For Latvian workers who are claimed to be taking jobs from developed European countries? Who will compare and prioritize the claims of local communities in developed countries and those of the international 'reserve army of labour'? At the empirical level – is the loss of one the gain of the other? At the moral level – is there an agreed upon criterion for comparing the loss of one with the gain of the other? If the answer to the empirical question is 'yes' and even a 'maybe', and the answer to the second question is that no such moral consensus exists, then the RTW is in a deep state of crisis.

To emphasize, the argument is not merely that when moving from the national to the global level, the RTW becomes vague and difficult to operationalize. The argument is a stronger one: decisions that are commonly taken by the nation state

[44] UN General Assembly, Convention Relating to the Status of Refugees (adopted 28 July 1951, entered into force 22 April 1954) UNTS vol 189, 137, Arts 17–19.

[45] On the relationship between job creation and proposals to limit migration, see OECD, 'The Employment of Foreigners: Outlook and Issues in OECD Countries' (2001) *OECD Employment Outlook*, ch 5.

[46] Fudge and Mundlak, above n 42.

to advance the RTW (of its citizens), may have negative repercussions on the RTW of people who have no political power to affect the decision-making process; the outsiders of the polity.

It is also important to state that questioning policies that seek to conserve work for the 'insiders' does not imply advocacy of unfettered global markets to be the most just distributive arrangements. There is nothing intrinsically just in the outcomes of unrestricted movement and the elimination of labour market institutions and intermediaries. The argument merely states that *sometimes* there *may* be trade-offs and that such trade-offs must be resolved in a process that corresponds to democratic precepts.

If the RTW could be confined to its negative, individual and discriminatory dimensions, the problems illustrated here are easier to reconcile.[47] They will be regarded to be outside the confines of the human right. However, if we insist that lack of opportunities for meaningful jobs is a problem of human rights, then the global dimension severely aggravates the problem and sheds a strong shadow over (democratic) process-based solutions as was previously suggested.

To conclude and summarize the argument – the vagueness of the RTW can elicit two types of 'easy' responses. The first is to restrict the meaning of the right and to assume that the RTW is not really about job creation. The second is to simply identify the RTW with full employment policies. An attempt to present a middle ground that is based on process requires some form of adherence to the principles of a democratic process. These are difficult to implement when decisions are made at the national level but their impact at the global level may be detrimental to the effort to uphold the RTW.

III National and Global Process-Based Solutions – An Expedition

The difficulty in implementing democratic process-based processes to mediate conflicting claims on the RTW at the global level can be somehow resolved if we relax the requirement for democracy and substitute it with experts or philosophers. Experts may substitute deliberations if they can clearly account for empirical evidence and 'neutral' benchmarks. Philosophers may substitute other aspects of the deliberative process by posing normative moral criteria for distributing jobs.

Experts can provide different economic accounts of job creation. However, not all matters lend themselves to easy formulas. The creation of jobs in one country does not imply the immediate loss of jobs in another country. There are many factors that affect that aggregate number of jobs. For example, the race-to-the-

[47] See Langford et al, above n 39, 19–20.

bottom thesis is empirically contested.[48] Other consequences of diverging production and services from one country to another are even more difficult to measure, as trade can increase economic activity or merely divert economic activity.[49] Migration provides a solution to jobless horizons in developing countries, but efforts at increasing development propose the option of investing in the developing country, forcing job creation and preventing the 'brain-drain'. Moreover, the empirical data do not provide moral guideline for trade-offs or distribution of jobs. There is no reason to assume that growth in itself (general economic growth or trade growth) will ultimately benefit everyone with more and better jobs, or necessarily will be channelled to those who are most deserving of new jobs.[50]

Philosophers can also contribute to the understanding of how we need to consider the advancement of the RTW. However, at this stage, political theory continues to provide two dominant strands – the nation-centred liberal view and the cosmopolitan view.[51] The former adheres to the traditional priority given to the needs and interests of the nation state's citizens, while the latter requires abandoning such priorities and seeking universal goals for the people of the global village. For each strand there are different types of argument – for example: are there meaningful institutions that actually forge a global community? Do communitarian ideals justify recognizing priority to those who are members in the closely-knit community? I believe that recognition of the RTW across borders requires a more cosmopolitan approach, particularly because the labour market is not confined to the nation state, and the beneficiaries of one's labour are dispersed in many countries.[52] However, I do not assume that any one political theory can adequately resolve the problems of implementing the RTW. Moreover, the list of human rights cannot (and should not) eliminate moral debates. Selecting only some human rights, and restricting their scope to those segments that are uncontroversial, may constitute a thin list of human rights and an even thinner vision of humanity.

Empiricists on the one hand and philosophers on the other can make an important contribution to the deliberations over the distribution of employment opportunities in a global labour market, but neither can conclude the debate and settle controversies, nor replace the deliberative aspect of process-based protections.

[48] OECD, *International Trade and Core Labour Standards* (Paris, OECD, 2000); D Drezner, *All Politics is Global: Explaining International Regulatory Regimes* (Princeton NJ, Princeton University Press, 2007).

[49] J Viner, *The Customs Union Issue* (New York, Carnegie Endowment for International Peace, 1950). For linking the distinction between trade creation and diversion with the question of job creation, see K Kolben, 'Trade, Development, and Migrant Garment Workers in Jordan' (2013) 5 *Middle East Law and Governance* 195.

[50] J Stiglitz, *Globalization and its Discontents* (New York, Penguin, 2002).

[51] For variants of a cosmopolitan approach in this context, see T Pogge, *World Poverty and Human Rights: Cosmopolitan Responsibilities and Reforms* (Cambridge, Polity Press, 2002); P Singer, *One World: The Ethics of Globalization* (New Haven CT, Yale University Press, 2002).

[52] Y Dahan, H Lerner and F Milman-Sivan, 'Labor Rights as Duties of Justice: A Cosmopolitan Approach' in Y Dahan, H Lerner and F Milman-Sivan (eds), *Global Justice and International Labour Rights* (Cambridge, Cambridge University Press, 2014, forthcoming).

Consequently, we are left with the realization that while global processes trumpet the trade-offs inherent in the RTW, they render the preferred method of process-based solutions particularly difficult to administer.

Attempts to promote employment policy within the European Union, even if in the form of soft law instruments, demonstrate the potential for deliberating over the RTW across borders. Policies devised under the auspices of the European Employment Strategy (EES) pay attention, among other issues, to the expansion of the European Union and to matters of distribution of resources and opportunities across borders.[53] The EES draws on the method of Open Method Coordination and is a form of 'soft law' coordinating mechanism. Established by the Treaty of Amsterdam, it creates a mechanism in which the Member States of the European Union bring to the attention of the centralized bodies needs and problems from the field. Together they coordinate priorities and benchmarks, which are then translated by the Member States into policies, the results of which are monitored, reported and then serve as the basis for future guidelines. It is an iterative process, in which exchange of information, prescription of interests and experimentation in implementation move cyclically from the bottom up and then down again. It involves both the representatives of the Member States and the European social partners, as well as additional agents at the Member State level.

Arguably, the EES serves as a transnational forum that demonstrates the feasibility of developing process-based solutions for addressing the RTW. It sets employment creation and the quality of work as goals that instruct nation states, sets goals that resonate with the formulation of 'progressive realization' and requires demonstration of compliance that extends beyond the level of 'just plain policy'. At the same time the EES also indicates the limits of such solutions and is suggestive of how deep is the problem of addressing and promoting the RTW beyond borders. The lessons are at several dimensions. First, replicating the EU's experience to other regions, and even more so, to the global level, faces the absence of a sense of shared polity, akin to that which exists at the European level. Moreover, like other cardinal issues of European integration, such as immigration policy, the integration within comes in tandem with the heightened boundaries that surround the EU.[54] Together, these claims point at a concern regarding the territorial scope of political deliberations. Second, it is possible to argue that the soft law nature of EES is ill-adapted to fulfilling the ideal of human rights and is far removed from familiar legal responses to violations of human rights, by means of adjudication and 'hard law' sanctions. This claim is of a different sort, as it raises concerns about the relationship between ends and means in the context of human rights praxis.

[53] D Ashiagbor, *The European Employment Strategy: Labour Market Regulation and New Governance* (Oxford, Oxford University Press, 2005); M Heidenreich and J Zeitlin (eds), *Changing European Employment and Welfare Regimes: The Influence of the Open Method of Coordination on National Reforms* (London, Routledge, 2009).

[54] Symbolic in this sense is the move from the emphasis on 'the strengthening social cohesion and *inclusion*' (2003) to 'strengthening social and *territorial* cohesion' (2005–08).

I will address the two concerns separately, and then look at their interaction and its impact on our understanding of the RTW as a universal human right.

A Extending Territoriality

Regional coordination exists in several other regions beyond the EU (North American Free Trade Agreement (NAFTA); Organization for the Harmonization of African Business Law (OHADA); Asia-Pacific Economic Cooperation (APEC), El Mercado Común del Sur (MERCOSUR) and more).[55] Although the EU faces significant challenges from within, none of these regions provides a sense of shared polity that is even remotely similar to that of the EU. These regions take different approaches for addressing matters that are associated with rights at work and the freedom of association. These range from obligations to uphold each country's labour laws (NAFTA), to avoidance of employment issues altogether (APEC). The RTW itself is less commonly addressed, mechanisms for deliberating over the relocation of jobs are not available and the general assumption that seems to prevail is that regionalism, which is devised to foster free trade, will indirectly secure the just allocation of jobs and lead to job creation.

The growing number of bilateral trade agreements similarly address, at most, rights at work, usually listing a narrow list of employment standards. Like regional arrangements, they do not directly discuss questions of work allocation. Indirectly, such agreements may contain provisions with regard to anti-dumping measures, which are strongly related to labour costs in the two countries.[56] Regional arrangements and bilateral agreements regarding migration are even less common than those governing trade and investment.[57] Like trade agreements, they prescribe, at best, some rules regarding the rights of migrant workers. They may also include references to arrangements that discuss particular forms of rights, such as relaxed rights of entry in circular migration schemes, or even a guarantee of quotas.

Regional and bilateral arrangements bring with them various forms of dispute resolution mechanisms. These are mostly nation-based and provide voice to the interests of the nation states. They accord lesser opportunities for comprehensive deliberations between those whose employment opportunities are affected. Moreover, the lessons of the EES remind us that drawing new boundaries around partial transnational regimes or partnerships merely shifts the boundaries of inclusion and exclusion. Even to the extent that such agreements would venture into the domain of job creation within the region or in the contracting states, then

[55] D Ashiagbor, 'Embedding Trade Liberalization in Social Policy: Lessons from the European Union?' (2011) 32 *Comparative Labor Law & Policy Journal* 373.

[56] See, eg, Art 10 of the US–Jordan trade agreement (2009), available at: www.ustr.gov/trade-agreements/free-trade-agreements/jordan-fta/final-text.

[57] J Gordon, 'People Are Not Bananas: How Immigration Differs from Trade' (2011) *Northwestern University Law Review* 1109; G Mundlak and H Shamir, 'The Global Governance of Domestic Care' in B Anderson and I Shutes (eds), *Care and Migrant Labour: Theory, Policy and Politics* (Basingstoke, Palgrave Macmillan, 2014).

such decisions would most likely implicate the RTW of people outside the territorial confines of the arrangement. Otherwise stated, the fundamental problem that was highlighted in the previous section – that advancing the RTW within the nation state has implications on the RTW outside it – remains. It may be relocated to an extra-national level, but it remains.

Drawing on Rodrik's trilemma, it is possible to remedy some of the shortcomings of regional and bilateral arrangements by strengthening the 'global'.[58] Labour markets are not confined to any one state, just as they are not confined to the region. The arguments favouring a global regime tend to criticize the move to the regional and bilateral arrangements because these carry with them a 'spaghetti bowl effect' – unsynchronized arrangements. The critique often highlights the uneven arrangements that are created across the globe, but the focus on the RTW also highlights that the problem is not merely that of complexity. Strengthening alliances in one corner may weaken opportunities in another. Just as agreements between two municipalities within one country that seek to attract capital from other regions in the country have an inclusive effect for some and exclusionary for others, regional and bilateral arrangements shift the opportunities for work from one place to another. Unlike the nation state that can democratically mediate conflicting claims by various communities, the emerging spaghetti bowl of arrangements defies the deliberative response.

Intense globalization can therefore serve as a solution. However, turning to the global relieves some problems but accentuates others. The WTO's law-making and dispute resolution processes are indicative of the difficulty in establishing global governance mechanisms. With regard to law-making, the debate over the recognition of social matters within international trade law reflects the political and rent-seeking interests involved.[59] These difficulties are in fact reflective of the impact that trade law has on the progressive realization of the RTW. The World Trade Organization's (WTO) dispute resolution mechanism provides limited avenues for individuals, collectivities and non-state agents to make claims, and particularly claims that are not related specifically to trade effects.[60] As demonstrated at length elsewhere, in a US–China trade dispute that centres on the movement of industry from the United States to China, the lengthy and detailed decision of the Appellate Body hardly refers to the employment question at all. While an American trade union initiated the process in quest of preserving jobs within the United States, no agency voiced concerns of Chinese workers or workers in the sector who are affected by the process in other countries.[61]

Side by side with the global trade regime, there are also direct interventions by the International Organization for Migration (IOM) and the International Labour

[58] See Rodrik, above n 40.

[59] On the debate over the social clause, see A Blackett, 'Whither Social Clause? Human Rights, Trade Theory and Treaty Interpretation' (1999) 31 *Columbia Human Rights Law Review* 1.

[60] MA Orellana, 'WTO and Civil Society' in *The Oxford Handbook of International Trade Law* (Oxford, Oxford University Press, 2009) 671-694; W Davey, 'The Limits of Judicial Processes', in *The Oxford Handbook of International Trade Law* (Oxford, Oxford University Press, 2009) 460-478.

[61] Fudge and Mundlak, above n 42.

Organization (ILO). The former does not make its own norms, but is entrusted with advancing the migration policies and rights established in other international and regional instruments.[62] The ILO has been known for years to be a forerunner in developing an international codex of norms. There is a flourishing debate over the norms-setting function of the ILO, as well as the attempt to overcome the critique by the Declaration on Fundamental Principles and Rights at Work.[63] However, only a small number of ILO conventions and recommendations deal with employment creation.[64] The ILO's focus on employment creation should therefore be sought under the auspices of the Decent Work Programme, where job creation is one of the four pillars.[65]

B From Hard to Soft Measures

The shift from standards setting, that resonates with a command and control form of global governance, to the operations of international agencies by means of advice, support and on-the-ground implementation of globally defined trajectories, is indicative of the way international labour (and migration) law is being reconsidered. Rather than preventing a race-to-the-bottom, there is an attempt to induce a race-to-the-top.[66] Rather than finding the highest common denominator that can apply to all countries (which is rather low), there is an attempt to take a developmental approach that seeks to progressively advance decent work and fair rules for migration in hyper-global markets.[67] Rather than seeking an agency with a 'bite' to enforce conventions, which are not ratified by countries that wish to avoid the little force such conventions have, there is a move to seek integration of local (national-based) NGOs, INGOs, national and international trade unions

[62] K Newland, 'The Governance of International Migration: Mechanisms, Processes, and Institutions' (2010) 16 *Global Governance: A Review of Multilateralism and International Organizations* 331.

[63] ILO Declaration on Fundamental Principles and Rights at Work (1998, updated 2010); ILO Declaration on Social Justice for a Fair Globalization (2008). The 1998 Declaration stirred a debate regarding its strategic and conceptual underpinnings. On the debate, see P Alston, 'Core Labour Standards and the Transformation of the International Labour Rights Regime' (2004) 15 *European Journal of International Law* 457; BA Langille, 'Core Labour Rights – The True Story (Reply to Alston)' (2005) 16 *European Journal of International Law* 409; A Hyde, 'The International Labor Organization in the Stag Hunt for Global Labor Rights' (2009) 3 *Law and Ethics of Human Rights* 154; J Murray, 'Taking Social Rights Seriously: Is There a Case for Institutional Reform of the ILO?' in C Fenwick and T Novitz (eds), *Labour Rights as Human Rights* (Oxford, Hart Publishing, 2010) 359.

[64] See, eg, ILO Convention 168 on Employment Promotion and Protection Against Unemployment (1988) with eight ratifications, or ILO Convention 122 on Employment Policy (1964) with a significant ratification rate of 104 (a priority convention). Numerous other conventions and recommendations deal with matters that are highly significant to the RTW, and all conventions that deal with rights at work and the freedom of association are inseparable.

[65] On the Decent Work Agenda, see P Egger, 'Perspectives: Towards a Policy Framework for Decent Work' (2002) 141 *International Labour Review* 161; LF Vosko, 'Decent Work – The Shifting Role of the ILO and the Struggle for Global Social Justice' (2002) 2 *Global Social Policy* 19.

[66] Hepple, *Labour Laws and Global Trade*, above, n 41.

[67] K Kolben, 'Development Approach to Trade and Labor Regimes' (2010) 45 *Wake Forest Law Review* 355; J Murray, above n 63.

and multiple levels of engagement with rights.[68] In this diffuse notion of global intervention to advance labour and migration rights, the turn to human rights, as a supportive mechanism, is important.

The turn to human rights does not necessarily assume that global human rights forums are 'harder', or better in reclaiming the command and control vision that launched the project of international labour law. The Committee on Economic, Social and Cultural Rights does not have power bites that exceed by far those of the ILO.[69] Neither are the complaints procedures that appear in various human rights documents translated into a spontaneous transformation of practices in the various countries.[70] Instead, the growing integration between labour, migration and human rights allows the entry of more agents who can participate and rely on diverse soft mechanisms in the global regime.

This view responds to the second critique of soft law as a means that is suitable to accommodate human rights. We need to observe the emerging global regime, the growing reliance on a developmental approach and the multiplicity of agents and venues for addressing the objectives of the RTW, none of which is significant as a stand-alone player. Shedding doubt on the possibility of 'hard enforcement' of the RTW in a global labour market cannot be used as a real claim against the validity of a broad RTW. For better or for worse, the use of hard enforcement as a litmus test for human rights, seems oblivious to a much broader institutional framework for addressing human rights; *all* human rights.

C Extending Process-Based RTW Across Borders

The EES serves as a model for a process-based method for protecting, respecting and fulfilling the RTW. Without over-idealizing its accomplishments, it also has several features that make it difficult to generalize. The most fundamental challenge is the problem of territorial spillovers. Opting for global solutions allows overcoming the problem of spillovers but augments the problem of implementing process-based mechanisms. This in turn gives more emphasis to soft measures of activism that fall significantly short of process-based solutions that can be developed within the nation state.

At this stage, the argument may reach its limits, and actually be used to prove that the RTW should be read narrowly, or even removed from the roster of human rights. However, there can be means in which a process-based approach can introduce the global into the local. The examples are embryonic, but they are present. Consider, for example, the option of recognizing claims by, and interven-

[68] G Seidman, *Beyond the Boycott: Labor Rights, Human Rights, and Transnational Activism* (New York, Russell Sage Foundation, 2007).

[69] UN General Assembly, International Covenant on Economic, Social and Cultural Rights (adopted 16 December 1966, entered into force 3 January 1976) UNTS, vol 993, 3. For a description of the monitoring system, see: Committee on Economic, Social and Cultural Rights, Report on the 46th to 47th sessions (2012) 6–15.

[70] Mundlak and Shamir, above n 57.

tions of non-citizens (migrants or workers abroad) in processes exploring the effects of the RTW on employment policy. For example, in a legal process that emerges from community employment-preserving policies (such as the right to strike in the *Laval* case, or in procurement procedures that seek to guarantee jobs for local workforce), individuals, NGOs and states may seek to insert a claim regarding the effects of such policy on outsiders.[71]

It is also possible to consider incremental improvements in global forums that affect the RTW. The recent flexibilization of the WTO's dispute resolution process, whereby the panel agrees to receive amicus curiae from NGOs and non-state entities can force considerations related to the RTW.[72] Strengthening the role of NGOs and non-union representation of multiple interests in the ILO can similarly achieve a broader spectrum of opinions and reveal trade-offs that are currently being taken into consideration.[73] Advancing methods for voicing the interests of the migrant workers themselves, in the process of designing and implementing bilateral and regional migration agreements may also advance the agency of migrant workers in tuning the policies that affect them to their RTW.[74]

Respecting the RTW has a radical potential, even if not by means of hard law. Surfacing competing claims *within the* RTW is likely to reveal its complexities. Admittedly, many voices may accumulate to a cacophony that will merely serve as an obstacle to promoting the hope that human rights should designate a clear and unequivocal position on the needs of humanity. However, this argument assumes that the alternative is to crystallize a lucid core of the RTW that will enable hard action and tough responses. The stuttering of the international community even in response to the worst employment-related infringements of human rights sheds doubt on this alleged trade-off.

IV Summary

The RTW was dormant for many years. Partially it was tucked under the blanket of suspicion covering all social and economic rights, and partially it suffered from particular sources of disadvantage. The fact that tribunals are now experimenting with its individual, negative and discriminatory aspects, suggests an interesting awakening but it should not prescribe the right's limits. Whether in soft law, hard law or process-based governance, the RTW should be viewed as advancing one of the important, albeit difficult to govern, aspects of human experience. It is an experience many people struggle for; it is also a relationship many people seek to

71 See Fudge and Mundlak, above n 42.

72 See above, n 60.

73 On the need for pluralist representation see F Milman-Sivan, 'Representativity, Civil Society, and the EU Social Dialogue: Lessons from the International Labor Organization' (2009) *Indiana Journal of Global Legal Studies* 311.

74 Gordon, 'Transnational Labor Citizenship', above n 14.

avoid, at least when in excess and in unrewarding conditions. The RTW is not the right to any kind of work, nor is it a duty. The RTW should be framed as a means of deciphering work's rewarding aspects from its laborious and exploitative ones.

The globalization of markets aided the constitutional rights and rights-claims of capital – it increased the freedom of movement and expanded the freedom to choose. By contrast, the RTW, coupled with rights at work and the right to organize, only suffered additional drawbacks. For some people, globalization expands choices, for others it removes access to rewarding employment opportunities. Freedom of movement is easier to secure than the right to access work. However, in response to this state of affairs, rather than organizing and simplifying, I argued the need to force the debate and reveal its problematic aspects.

This approach requires us to reconsider our telos in labour law as well as the praxis of human rights. Labour lawyers deal with employment standards or freedom of association. Labour academics rarely teach about job creation. Restricting the scope of the RTW to the negative, individual and discriminatory, seems to be a solution that embraces the right as long as it is on our own turf. Instead, taking the RTW seriously should actually bring us to reconsider the mission and the means to obtain it. For advocates of human rights, the RTW similarly challenges fundamental premises of universal goals that should be equally applied and provided to all members of humankind. There is something about work that forces to consider trade-offs *within* the domain of the right, and not merely between the right and other rights and interests. Expanding the mission of human rights praxis should be driven by questions regarding the achievements of past attempts to protect human rights, just as much as to envision new ways to achieve progressive realization of rights.

The global challenge to the RTW outlined in this chapter indicates new challenges, and should not undermine whatever achievements have been made thus far with the integration of work into the roster of human rights. At the outset I argued that some claims against the RTW, namely those that criticize the feasibility of economic and social rights generally, can be easily dismissed. This can be attributed in large part to the continuous conceptualization of economic and social rights in international jurisprudence since the 1980s.[75] Only recently has this body of jurisprudence started to address the questions of extraterritorial obligations. The Preamble to the Maastricht Principles on Extraterritorial Obligations of States in the Area of Economic, Social and Cultural Rights, states:

> The human rights of individuals, groups and peoples are affected by and dependent on the extraterritorial acts and omissions of states. The advent of economic globalization

[75] UN Commission on Human Rights, Note verbale dated 5 December 1986 from the Permanent Mission of the Netherlands to the United Nations Office at Geneva addressed to the Centre for Human Rights ('Limburg Principles'), 8 January 1987, E/CN.4/1987/17; International Commission of Jurists (ICJ), Maastricht Guidelines on Violations of Economic, Social and Cultural Rights (26 January 1997). Also see the General Comments that are written by the Committee on Economic, Social and Cultural Rights in the UN, available at: tbinternet.ohchr.org/_layouts/treatybodyexternal/TBSearch.aspx?Lang=en&TreatyID=9&DocTypeID=11.

> in particular, has meant that States and other global actors exert considerable influence on the realization of economic, social and cultural rights across the world.[76]

Coupling the embryonic attempt to identify an appropriate framing of extraterritorial obligations, with the particular problems that are attributed to the dialectics of work and the nature of the labour market, indicates that the road is long and haphazard, but prior achievements of clarification should also encourage the journey forward.

[76] International Commission of Jurists (ICJ), Maastricht Principles on Extraterritorial Obligations of States in the Area of Economic, Social and Cultural Rights (29 February 2012).

17

The Right to Work and Labour Market Flexibility: Labour Market Governance Norms in the International Order

KERRY RITTICH

Introduction

The 'right to work' can be approached as a question of first principles, identified in such classic sources as constitutions, conventions and human rights treaties[1]; elaborated in the jurisprudence of courts and other tribunals[2]; and analyzed within scholarly and expert commentary.[3] Yet rather than begin with the legal norm, we might reverse the direction of enquiry and take the right to work as the end point or product of social and economic processes, conflicts and circumstances. For the right to work emerged at a specific historical juncture, and it was deeply connected to a set of shared normative, political and theoretical commitments of its time. Attention to its origins also makes clear that, in practice, the right to work was embedded within a thick set of other institutional norms, practices and understandings. The right to work was also the product of a particular philosophy regarding the organization of social and economic relations in market-based economies. In some places, it was largely a matter of informal norms and customs: in locales such as the United States, it is even possible to speak of a right to work that existed as a matter of human resources policy completely apart from any supporting legal entitlement.[4]

[1] See, eg, the International Covenant on Economic, Social and Cultural Rights Art 6, available at www.ohchr.org/EN/ProfessionalInterest/Pages/CESCR.aspx.

[2] For a discussion of the jurisprudence of the European Court of Human Rights interpreting the European Convention on Human Rights so as to extend protection to some aspects of the right to work, see R O'Connell, 'The Right to Work in the European Convention on Human Rights' (2012) 2 *European Human Rights Law Review* 176.

[3] UN Committee on Economic, Social and Cultural Rights (CESCR), General Comment No 18: The Right to Work, Article 6 of the International Covenant on Economic, Social and Cultural Rights (6 February 2006), UN Doc E/C.12/GC/18, available at: www.refworld.org/docid/4415453b4.html.

[4] See KVW Stone, 'The Decline of the Standard Contract of Employment in the United States: A Socio-Regulatory Perspective' in KVW Stone and H Arthurs (eds), *Rethinking Workplace Regulation: Beyond the Standard Contract of Employment* (New York, Russell Sage Foundation, 2013).

The 'effective' right to work, then, might be imagined as a product of a range of rules, policies and philosophies, both formally and informally inscribed, that operate on labour markets and the wider economy, some of which aim to directly regulate work and labour markets and others which are either collateral to or even at some remove from them. Viewed from this perspective, the right to work requires attention to both the direct and ancillary rules and policies that organize work and labour markets and to the forces that move those rules and policies in one direction or another.

Here, I use this reversal of optics to get at the following questions: what purchase might the right to work possess once the interconnected set of rules, policies and philosophies that originally gave it shape and meaning has been hollowed out, or simply turned in a different direction? How might the right to work be interpreted once the objectives that animated it have been repudiated and the rules to which it was connected placed in question? One thing that follows, I suggest, is that the meaning of the right to work is subject to change and reinvention as the background normative and institutional structure in which it is situated shifts. Freed from its traditional context, the right to work points in different directions: rather than a single set of work-related objectives, with relatively clear institutional implications, it might support a range of decisions and policy choices at both the adjudicative and legislative levels. One possible result, one in evidence now, are labour market regimes that, in operative terms, negate or reject a central aspiration of social rights, the decommodification of work.[5] Rather than enable free choice concerning work, they induce or simply compel the acceptance of work on whatever terms are on offer.

I propose to illustrate this claim by situating the right to work within mainstream norms about good labour market governance, taking as a marker of those norms the policy and regulatory projects of the international economic and financial institutions, the Organisation for Economic Co-operation and Development (OECD), the World Bank and the International Monetary Fund (IMF) in particular. At first glance, this may seem like an odd starting point. These institutions neither speak of, nor appear to recognize, a right to work as such; nor do they have direct jurisdiction over labour policy or questions of workers' and human rights at the international level. Nonetheless, as those institutions that *are* charged with oversight of the right to work have recognized, financial and economic institutions may have a deep impact on the realization of social and economic rights.[6] Their most immediate link with the right to work lies in the power to mandate reforms to workers' rights and labour market institutions, as well as other economic policies of crucial importance to work and workers, in exchange for release of funds; as described below, this power is clearly in evidence in their response to

[5] International Labour Conference, 'Declaration Concerning the Aims and Purposes of the International Labour Organization' (Philadelphia PA, 1944) available at: www.ilo.org/public/libdoc/ilo/1944/44B09_10_e_f.pdf.

[6] CESCR, 'Report on the Eighteenth and Nineteenth Sessions – Globalization and its impact on the enjoyment of economic, social and cultural rights' (E/1999/22-E.C.12/1998/26, ch VI, para 515) 93.

the current financial crises in Europe. Yet another conduit or connection with the right to work resides in their authorship and support of a powerfully transformative normative vision of the relationship between markets and social progress, one in which a broad range of social as well as economic goals are conceptualized, pursued and realized through participation in markets.[7] This commitment to the achievement of social as well as economic goals through market participation is programmatic as well as normative and methodological. In practice, it is constructing a parallel duty to work in which fewer resources and entitlements are available to workers and citizens as of right and more are dependent on demonstrable engagement in labour markets.[8]

A number of shifts and complexities emerge when the right to work is considered from this institutional standpoint. The first is that the right to work as classically understood and realized within the frameworks of human rights and social rights appears to be in headlong opposition to the dominant paradigm of labour market governance of the day: labour market flexibility. The management of financial crises provides an unusually sharp window on this conflict, confirming across a range of contexts a repudiation of the post-war conception of the right to work at the most fundamental level that was already under way before the crisis itself. The second is that a broad range of legal and economic policies effectively bear on the right to work. Changes to the manner in which those policies are conceived and designed can be expected to produce effects on workers and labour markets; they may also fundamentally destabilize the right to work. The third is that embedded within the right to work are internal tensions and instabilities around the design of labour standards and labour market institutions, tensions which the new labour market governance paradigm is bringing more clearly into view.

Section I situates the right to work in the post-war social contract, identifying the wide range of legal, policy and institutional commitments that gave it shape and force. Section II examines the norm of labour market flexibility, discussing its implications for two dimensions of the right to work: access to work and better terms and conditions of work. Focusing on fiscal and monetary policy, section III describes the financial crises and crisis management strategies on the right to work, identifying their impact on labour law and on both access to, and conditions of, work. Section IV reviews the implications of this *tour d'horizon* for the right to work, identifying the challenges to be overcome if the normative aspirations of the right to work are to be recuperated.

[7] K Rittich, 'The Future of Law and Development: Second Generation Reforms and the Incorporation of the Social' in DM Trubek and A Santos, *The Future of Law and Development: Second-Generation Reforms and the Incorporation of the Social* (Cambridge, Cambridge University Press, 2006).

[8] See also A Paz-Fuchs in this volume, ch 10.

I The Right to Work and the Post-War Social Contract

The right to work can be read first and foremost as the expression of a social, political, even cultural[9] commitment to the centrality and importance of work, normativized in the most powerful form available in the contemporary liberal legal imaginary, that of constitutional and human rights. For related reasons, it has also been described as the foundational right in the European Social Charter.[10]

Rather than an individual right, the right to work is best understood as a programmatic commitment.[11] The right to work is indelibly connected to the post-war social contract, itself part of the embedded liberal compromise around which the international economic and political order was reconstructed in the post-Second World War era.[12] It crystallized the consensus view of a particular historical moment, one grounded in experience of widespread economic privation as well as destabilizing and destructive political conflict, that work is not only central to personhood and individual dignity. Work is also fundamental to social inclusion and social cohesion and, ultimately, to political stability and security, both domestic and international.

Because labour markets are subject to periodic disruptions that, in their extreme as in the 1930s, can lead to massive deficits in the demand for work, a central objective of the right to work was the commitment to full employment. It is important to note that full employment was achieved not merely through labour policy or rights at work; it was also a macroeconomic objective pursued through fiscal and monetary policy. And while access to work and employment levels are crucial concerns, not just any work will do: because work is a principal means of participating in society as well as processes of economic growth, the right to work also encompasses the goal of 'better' work, not simply as a matter of economic circumstances or individual fortune but as a basic entitlement of citizenship.[13]

The right to work reflects the understanding, grounded in both theory and historical experience, that market processes do not automatically produce good, or even any, work. To the contrary, bargaining asymmetries, resource disparities and what we now identify as market failures and collective action problems are structural features of labour markets that routinely produce employment contracts with terms and conditions of work that are disadvantageous for workers. It has

[9] T Judt, *Postwar: A History of Europe Since 1945* (New York, Penguin Press, 2005).

[10] See C O'Cinneide in this volume, ch 6.

[11] See also H Collins in this volume, ch 2.

[12] JG Ruggie, 'International Regimes, Transactions, and Change: Embedded Liberalism in the Postwar Economic Order' (1982) 36 *International Organization* 379; D Ashiagbor, 'Embedding Trade Liberalization in Social Policy: Lessons from the European Union?' (2011) 32 *Comparative Labor Law & Policy Journal* 373.

[13] V Mantouvalou in this volume, ch 3, argues that we should understand the right to work as a right to non-exploitative work.

long been understood that the labour contract is subject to a systemic imbalance in bargaining power of a particularly marked sort. Rather than the product of negotiation among equals that reflect mutual input, interest, assent and benefit, the terms of the employment contract are typically established unilaterally by the employer: the absence of real alternatives often means that they are effectively imposed by the employer as well.[14] For this reason, enabling or actively promoting the construction of a countervailing source of power through collective action on the part of workers has been the heart of the enterprise of labour law.[15]

In the post-war era, the objectives of access to work and better terms and conditions of work were reflected in the recognition of a series of rights at work, realized through a complex of legal entitlements as well as social and economic policies. Although the legal regimes in which rights at work manifested took a variety of forms,[16] the general objectives were widely shared. A measure of job and income security was secured for many workers through the labour law systems operating within the different models of welfare state capitalism. Better terms and conditions of work were buttressed by minimum employment standards, whether legislated or determined through collective bargaining. Employment insurance, income transfers and other forms of social protection bridged periods of unemployment and ensured that where work itself could not be provided, the worst economic consequences of the shortfall in jobs – namely, lack of income – could be mitigated.

But access to work was also supported by fiscal and monetary policy that, in the initial years and for a substantial period afterwards, was informed by Keynesian macroeconomic theory and a broadly shared belief in its utility in managing the adverse consequences of cyclical downturns in the economy. Workers' effective or social wage was a function of public services and income transfers supported by steeply progressive taxation rates, as well as income garnered in the labour market. Falling demand for jobs in the private sector, for example, was routinely met by increased demand in the public sector and/or mitigated through increased access to unemployment benefits and other social transfers. Monetary policy was also part of the policy arsenal: most central banks had dual mandates – growth *and* welfare enhancement through employment creation – ensuring that jobs and labour market consequences remained part of the policy calculus when it came to the setting of interest and exchange rates. Even in 'normal' times, employment levels could be managed to some degree, with the perceived trade-off between jobs and inflation or price stability calibrated by attention to the non-inflation

[14] M Cohen, 'Property and Sovereignty' (1927) 13 *Cornell Law Quarterly* 8; R Hale, 'Coercion and Distribution in a Supposedly Noncoercive State' (1923) 38 *Political Science Quarterly* 470.

[15] O Kahn-Freund, *Labour and the Law* (London, Stevens, 1977); K Klare, 'Countervailing Workers' Power as A Regulatory Strategy' in H Collins, P Davies and R Rideout, *Legal Regulation of the Employment Relation* (London, Kluwer Law International, 2000).

[16] PA Hall and D Soskice, *Varieties of Capitalism: The Institutional Foundations of Comparative Advantage* (Oxford, Oxford University Press, 2001); G Esping-Andersen, *The Three Worlds of Welfare Capitalism* (Princeton NJ, Princeton University Press, 1990).

rate of unemployment.[17] This attention to employment was also inscribed as a foundational purpose in the Articles of Agreement of the international financial institutions.[18] In short, the right to work operated within a matrix of rules and institutions that was, in turn, informed by a conjoined political–economic vision in which support for high levels of employment and some degree of redistribution of power and resources within labour markets were imagined as a matter of economic rationality as well as political necessity.

The question is what happens when this supporting structure around the right to work falls away. Although formally unchanged, the right to work may be infused with different social and political visions; it may be (re)interpreted on the basis of new legal and economic theories; and it may be institutionalized within a changed policy and regulatory framework. It is these altered visions, theoretical understandings and institutional frameworks, I suggest, that are most pertinent to the right to work now. As described in part II, in the discussion on the rise of flexibility norms and in part III, in the context of the financial crisis management strategies, labour market governance norms manifest a rejection of the right to work, at least insofar as it is conceptualized in terms of obligations by the state to directly provide opportunities for work or to backstop rising incomes and better terms and conditions of work.

II The Right to Work Within Flexible Labour Markets

Recall that the right to work manifests both as a question of the adequacy and security of work opportunities and as a matter of the quality of work and the adequacy of income. The right to work thus raises fundamental questions of labour market dynamics: how to explain processes of employment creation; how to account for processes of labour market inclusion and exclusion; and how to identify the forces behind rising and falling income levels and changes in the terms and conditions of work. It is at this level that we can see the extent to which the meaning or substance of the right to work depends on the wider ideational and institutional matrix in which it operates. Changing narratives about labour market processes and dynamics and new, or newly hegemonic, theories about the rules and policies that generate desirable labour market outcomes can fundamentally alter the normative and institutional content of the right to work.

[17] See R Schettkat and R Sun, 'Monetary Policy and European Unemployment' (2009) 25 *Oxford Review of Economic Policy* 94.

[18] See Art I of the Articles of Agreement, International Bank for Reconstruction and Development, available at: web.worldbank.org/WBSITE/EXTERNAL/EXTABOUTUS/0,,contentMDK:20049563~menuPK:63000601~pagePK:34542~piPK:36600~theSitePK:29708~isCURL:Y,00.html; Art I of the Articles of Agreement of the International Monetary Fund identifies one of the purposes of the fund to contribute to 'the promotion and maintenance of high levels of employment and real income', available at: www.imf.org/External/Pubs/FT/AA/index.htm#art1.

The original aspirations behind the right to work remain quite recognizable and entrenched from the vantage point of the human rights treaty bodies;[19] they also continue to animate many initiatives within the International Labour Organization (ILO), the campaign to promote 'decent work' in particular.[20] Elsewhere within the international order, however, the picture looks quite different.

In the 1980s, Keynesian economic policies, as well as a large measure of respect for the autonomy of states when it came to managing internal questions of social policy, were challenged and partly displaced by a comprehensive vision of good economic management and governance based largely on neoclassical and institutional economic theories.[21] By the 1990s, this vision included a stylized picture of good labour market governance, one that originated in a comparison of Anglo-American versus continental labour markets[22] but quickly assumed the status of more general wisdom about good labour market governance.[23] For the purposes of the right to work, note, in contrast with the vision associated with embedded liberalism, first the representation of the problems of work and labour markets; second, their sources; and third, their cures.

The basic narrative goes as follows.[24] Access to work is fundamentally a matter of calibrating supply and demand in the labour market through the price mechanism, while wages and other terms and conditions of work are ultimately a function of workers' marginal productivity or contribution to output. Thus, at the level of positive state action, the right to work is something to be secured primarily through the establishment of rules, norms, policies and institutions that promote well-functioning labour markets. Whether or not labour markets are well functioning, however, is not approached as an empirical, sociological or historical question; nor is it something that depends on local contexts and varies with national systems and institutions of labour law. Rather, it is, in the first instance, a matter of theory: it involves ensuring that markets are free from the distorting effects of state 'interventions' which, under the received understanding of neoclassical and new institutional economics, are thought to produce a cascade of undesirable effects, from the exclusion of labour market outsiders to lost jobs.

[19] CESCR, General Comment No 18, above n 3. For a discussion, see C O'Cinneide in this volume, ch 6.

[20] The promotion of 'decent work' lies at the core of the ILO's current activities around work and labour markets. For a discussion of the four pillars of the decent work agenda, see ILO, *Decent Work*, available at: www.ilo.org/global/topics/decent-work/lang--en/index.htm.

[21] For a more detailed discussion, see K Rittich, 'Rights, Risk and Reward: Governance Norms in the International Order and the Problem of Precarious Work' in J Fudge and R Owens (eds), *Precarious Work, Women, and the New Economy: The Challenge to Legal Norms* (Oxford, Hart Publishing, 2006).

[22] OECD, *Jobs Study* (1994), available at: www.oecd.org/employment/emp/1941679.pdf.

[23] World Bank, *World Development Report: Workers in an Integrating World* (1995), available at: wdronline.worldbank.org/worldbank/a/c.html/world_development_report_1995/abstract/WB.0-1952-1102-2.abstract1.

[24] This is elaborated in detail in Rittich, 'Rights, Risk and Reward', above n 21, and K Rittich 'Global Labour Policy as Global Social Policy' (2008) 14 *Canadian Labour and Employment Law Journal* 227.

Thus, persistently high levels of unemployment are due to excessive labour market 'rigidity' which, in turn, is associated with mal-adapted labour market institutions, if not the introduction of labour market rules and standards tout court. Adding to their deficiencies, labour market institutions introduce distributional perversities into labour markets, privileging labour market insiders at the expense of those with a marginal position in the labour market. While these institutions may ensure that workers in protected sectors enjoy enhanced job security and better terms and conditions of work, those benefits come at the inevitable expense of other workers who either have no jobs at all or who can, at best, attain tangential and episodic connections with the labour market on much less favourable terms.

The stock solution, introduced in the early 1990s and continuing up to the present moment, has been structural reforms to ensure more flexible labour markets. In general, structural reforms aim to reduce job security provisions, limit access to income replacement schemes and decentralize the process of collective bargaining through the weakening, repeal or deinstitutionalization of worker rights and employment protections. Post structural reforms, the legal structure of labour markets emerges as something that does not differ substantially from that of commercial markets. The basic requirements remain well ascertained and secure property rights and enforceable contract rights, all lodged within a general regulatory climate conducive to attracting investment and facilitating exchange.[25]

Structural reforms represent a generational effort to globalize an idealized model of Anglo-American labour market governance. But structural reforms might also be understood as a project to transform, if not dismantle, the post-war social contract by altering labour market institutions and turning social rights away from the aspiration to 'decommodify' work and towards the objective of more intense and productive participation in market.[26] Replacing 'passive' with 'active' labour market measures, a central aim is to nudge, even compel, workers to become more responsive to market signals by rendering alternatives to market work less attractive or simply closing them off entirely.[27] Rather than constrain the economic forces that operate on workers, the aim is to mobilize those forces in the service of higher levels of growth and reduced levels of 'dependency' on the state. So central is this objective, and so thoroughly is it buttressed by policy and regulatory shifts, that labour market activation might be called the keystone of contemporary labour market governance and social policy.

Where are workers' rights located in this narrative? In the first place, they are simply the rights shared with other individuals as citizens and commercial actors, located in private law rights of contract and property as well as human and other

[25] World Bank, *Doing Business* (various years), available at: www.doingbusiness.org.

[26] J Fudge, 'The New Discourse of Labor Rights: From Social to Fundamental Rights?' (2007) 29 *Comparative Labor Law & Policy Journal* 29; K Rittich, 'Making Natural Markets' (2014) 65(3) *Northern Ireland Legal Quarterly* 323–43.

[27] OECD, *Jobs Study*, above n 22; OECD, *Boosting Jobs and Income* (2006), available at: www.oecd.org/els/emp/36889821.pdf; Rittich, 'Global Labour Policy', above n 24.

fundamental rights. These rights may be supplemented by express references to workers' rights. For example, as a result of pressure to accommodate human rights and social concerns, many international organizations and institutions, along with an increasing number of commercial actors and industry groups, now recognize the 'core' labour standards articulated in the ILO Declaration on Fundamental Principles and Rights at Work.[28] Nonetheless, flexibility is still thought to be essential to the proper functioning of labour markets, something of benefit, on balance, to workers as well as the economy as a whole.[29]

What about labour standards and the objective of decent or better work? Here, workers' rights beyond the core remain a fundamental challenge. Poor terms and conditions of work may surface as a topic of interest because they are a marker of low worker productivity and low levels of growth.[30] As far as labour policy is concerned, there may well be a case for initiatives to increase skill and the acquisition of human capital.[31] But the idea that access to work and better substantive terms and conditions of work are a matter of fundamental *right*, something to be directly ensured or promoted through positive law and state policy, is a proposition that runs counter to the organizing narrative about labour market governance. This, to repeat, is that such ends are best produced, and if perverse outcomes are to be avoided *only* produced, when employers have relatively unconstrained latitude to deploy labour resources as commercial necessities dictate, and policymakers set regulatory and macroeconomic conditions to ease transactions and investment and ensure financial stability.

On the basis of these assumptions, the question of the right to work can only be asked, and assessed, in very limited terms. There can be no right to access work of any given quality, on any specific terms, or under any particular conditions. Simply put, a few minimal framework conditions of contracting aside, there is no concept of 'adequate' or 'decent' work or its correlative, inadequate or unacceptable work, beyond that established by market forces and sustained by the productivity of the worker or workforce in question. Indeed, expressed and institutionalized in its post-war form, the right to work would provoke a classic response in the mode of the rhetoric of reaction: it threatens to both jeopardize economic growth – itself the goose that lays the golden egg of more and better

[28] International Finance Corporation, *Performance Standard 2: Labor and Working Conditions* (1 January 2012), available at: www.ifc.org/wps/wcm/connect/2408320049a78e5db7f4f7a8c6a8312a/PS2_English_2012.pdf?MOD=AJPERES.

[29] See 'Protecting Jobs, Enhancing Flexibility: A New Look at Employment Protection Legislation' in *OECD Employment Outlook 2013*, available at: www.oecd-ilibrary.org/employment/oecd-employment-outlook-2013/protecting-jobs-enhancing-flexibility-a-new-look-at-employment-protection-legislation_empl_outlook-2013-6-en.

[30] GE Perry et al, *Informality: Exit and Exclusion* (Washington DC, World Bank, 2007), available at: web.worldbank.org/WBSITE/EXTERNAL/COUNTRIES/LACEXT/0,,contentMDK:21345369~pagePK:146736~piPK:146830~theSitePK:258554,00.html.

[31] World Bank, *World Development Report 2013: Jobs* (Washington, DC, World Bank, 2012). See S Deakin and F Wilkinson, *The Law of the Labour Market: Industrialization, Employment and Legal Evolution* (Oxford, Oxford University Press, 2005) for a justification of labour rights rooted in Amartya Sen's theory of development as freedom and capabilities.

work – ultimately producing perverse results for workers. So understood, the right to work is both a destructive and an inherently futile exercise.[32]

It is at this point that we can begin to see not only how established conceptions of the right to work might seem problematic, but also how competing ideas, with quite different regulatory and institutional implications, might be defended. Under a labour market flexibility paradigm, the right to work could be understood, for example, as the right to be 'free' of labour standards and collective bargaining rights, on the basis that they constitute an interference with freedom of contract; this is, of course, a long familiar objection to workers' rights and labour market institutions.[33] The right to work could also be grounded in an ideological objection to legal protections that give material or political support to unions. Indeed, this *is* the popular meaning of the right to work in the United States[34] and Canada.[35]

The right to work could also be detached from its traditional linkage to labour market institutions and workers' rights, both collective and individual, through a consequentialist argument rooted in claims about ensuring regulatory quality. One element of the right to work is the obligation to take measures aimed at achieving full employment.[36] Following the received mainstream understanding about their (negative) effects on employment levels, the elimination of labour standards, as well as changes to collective bargaining rights designed to reduce the power of unions, might be grounded in the argument that such a regulatory environment *is* actually the best way to promote opportunities to work.

Parallel arguments have already been formulated in debates about the causes and consequences of labour market informality.[37] Human rights bodies have traditionally identified labour market informality as being at odds with the right to work as, by definition, informal sector workers are excluded from the protection of the rule of law.[38] However, an alternative diagnosis advanced by the World Bank locates the cause of informality not in workers' exclusion from rights and labour standards, but in their decisions to 'exit' the formal sector due to dissatisfaction with the labour market rules and social protections on offer.[39] This alternative reading is itself grounded in another touchstone of mainstream governance norms, which is that licensing requirements and excessive regulation constitute an invitation to corruption as well as an impediment to full economic participa-

[32] A Hirschman, *The Rhetoric of Reaction: Perversity, Futility, Jeopardy* (Cambridge, Belknap Press, 1991).

[33] *Lochner v New York* 198 US 45 (1905).

[34] There are now 23 'right to work' states the United States in which measures requiring non-members to contribute dues to unions are illegal; as a result, there is virtually no collective representation of workers in those states. For further discussion, see K Stone in this volume, ch 15.

[35] D Doorey, 'Reflecting on the Rand Formula as Ontario's Tories Target Their Union Foes' (25 January 2013), available at: lawofwork.ca/?p=6147.

[36] CESCR, General Comment No 18, above n 3, para 19.

[37] See K Rittich, 'Modeling Informal Labour Markets and Development', draft.

[38] CESCR, General Comment No 18, above n 3, para 10.

[39] Perry et al, above n 30.

tion, especially for those at the bottom of the market.[40] One result of the latter, 'exit' diagnosis is an inversion of the traditional remedy for informality: rather than the extension of labour market protections to those outside their ambit, the solution may be to redesign or even eliminate those protections to increase participation in the formal sector. It is but a short step to defend the right to work in precisely these terms.

Notice what has transpired with the right to work under these changed labour market norms and paradigms. In this post-Washington consensus world,[41] the commitment to work remains as strong as ever, perhaps stronger. However, the legal entitlements and obligations surrounding work have been profoundly transformed if not simply inverted, with predictable effects on the quality of work as well as workers' real capacity or freedom to decline as well as to accept work. As job security is reduced, workers assume greater risk, including for economic events and circumstances that lie entirely beyond their control. Yet the state need not prioritize employment creation over other policy objectives; indeed, where there is any perceived conflict, the obligation is to set macroeconomic policy in ways that supports price stability even if that reduces the number of jobs.[42] Nor need the state cushion the loss of work through insurance schemes that permit unemployed workers to seek work suitable to their skills and circumstances; instead, prevailing wisdom holds that these entitlements should be reduced or eliminated to promote labour market participation and 'make work pay'.

Second, note the fate of efforts to improve the terms and conditions of work, whether directly through labour standards or indirectly through the institutions that organize collective bargaining. Under current labour market governance norms, the state is actively discouraged from adopting measures like non-waivable minimum terms that protect job security or directly improve workers' wages and working conditions. At the same time, the decentralization of collective bargaining – another current governance nostrum – also weakens workers' and unions' capacity to prevail in direct contract negotiations with employers. Thus, the major devices for rebalancing the process of labour contracting have been either weakened or repudiated outright.

Third, and relatedly, notice the elimination of bargaining power as part of the regulatory calculus. Under a flexibility paradigm, no problems or properties – or even market failures or imperfections – specific to labour markets are recognized. Thus, the traditional rationales for regulatory 'interventions' in freedom of contract in respect of work – namely, to put a floor under the labour contract or to

[40] H de Soto, *The Other Path: the Invisible Revolution in the Third World* (New York, Harper & Row, 1989). As Hugh Collins (this volume, ch 2) has described, confiscatory licensing and corruption by the police, leading to denial of economic freedom and livelihood, is also the dominant reading of Mohamad Bouazazi's decision to set himself on fire, the event that triggered the uprising in Tunisia and the broader 'Arab Spring' of 2011.

[41] JE Stiglitz, 'Is There a Post Washington Consensus Consensus?' in N Serra and JE Stiglitz (eds), *The Washington Consensus Reconsidered: Towards a New Global Governance* (Oxford, Oxford University Press, 2008).

[42] See discussion in section III.

rebalance bargaining power among workers and employers – disappear. At the same time, support for freedom of association can be detached from institutionalized support for collective bargaining or other forms of collective action on the part of workers.

Finally, note the way that labour market activation policies elide any meaningful distinction between choice and coercion at work. The right of workers to engage in freely chosen and accepted work is a central element of the right to work.[43] Yet labour market flexibility and activation policies may, as a practical matter, reduce or eliminate any real choice on the part of workers concerning their work options, while the 'passive' policies classically associated with the right to work often provide a genuine measure of freedom in respect of those choices.[44]

On the one hand, the flexibility paradigm looks completely consistent with the aspirations of the right to work. For example, reductions in 'rigidities' introduced by job security and other limits on employment contracting promise to reduce the penalties experienced by labour market outsiders, while labour market activation policies focus attention on increasing access to employment, surely now a critical issue given the very high levels of youth unemployment. On the other hand, flexibility arguably produces a 'bad double' of the right to work, even an effective 'duty' to work, compelling workers to labour under reduced job security and on whatever terms and conditions are generated by market forces. And despite the apparent focus on labour market inclusion, as reinvented, this right to work also imposes significant penalties – ranging from labour market marginality and low wages to complete exclusion – on those who fail to measure up by market metrics. Under a flexibility paradigm, lack of relevant skills, significant non-market obligations around care or unpaid work, for example, or any other condition that impedes responsiveness to market signals become difficult to address, even to see.

The flexibility optic does, however, bring potential tensions within the right to work to the surface.[45] Because of the assumption that legislative mandates to advance collective bargaining or employment standards cost jobs, any effort to promote better work risks operating at cross-purposes with the promotion of access to work. For this reason, the old normative content of the right to work appears incoherent if not unintelligible, as access to work is set at odds with efforts to ensure improved quality of work. Such claims need not be accepted in any categorical or simple way. The identification of labour market policies historically associated with better work with the exclusion of labour market outsiders is certainly overstated, if not simply wrong in some cases. Neither firms nor workers necessarily benefit from the unconstrained disposability of workers.[46] Flexibility

[43] CESCR, General Comment No 18, above n 3.

[44] G Standing, 'Globalization: Eight Crises of Social Protection' in L Beneria and S Bisnath (eds), *Global Tensions: Challenges and Opportunities in the World Economy* (New York, Routledge, 2004).

[45] See also A Bogg in this volume, ch 9 and M Freedland and N Kountouris in this volume, ch 7.

[46] W Njoya, 'Job Security in a Flexible Labor Market: Challenges and Possibilities for Worker Voice' (2012) 33 *Comparative Labor Law & Policy Journal* 459.

itself can be both conceptualized and pursued in different ways;[47] as conventionally understood, flexibility simply introduces one-time efficiency gains, leaving aside the far more important challenge of addressing dynamic efficiency in the new economy.[48] Nonetheless, the design of labour market institutions may still engage real distributive conflicts among workers, and wrestling with such conflicts, the conundrums they raise for the design of workplace rules in particular, is an essential part of thinking intelligently about the laws regulating work after the decline of the standard employment relationship.[49]

To what extent does the right to work help us sort out these questions? For example, does it help order the relative priority of access to work and better terms of work? Can it assist in striking the balance that should be struck when labour market policies and institutions benefit some classes or groups of workers but disadvantage others? And to what extent can it serve to counterbalance the policy advice generated by neoclassical economists and mainstream financial and economic institutions, not only in respect of labour policy, but fiscal and macroeconomic policy too?[50]

III The Right to Work in Times of Crisis[51]

A Labour Market Flexibility and Crisis Management

While flexibility norms have been in circulation for the better part of two decades, the ongoing financial crises have presented unparalleled occasions to further their adoption, allowing policymakers to circumnavigate obstacles that have prevented their acceptance within periods and processes of 'normal' politics. Even though excessive rigidity in labour markets has little, if anything, to do with the origins of the crises, and even where the reductions in workers' incomes and aggregate demand provoked both by labour law reforms and broader fiscal policy arguably impair prospects for restoring economic growth, the reconfiguration of workers' rights has been at the centre of mandatory conditions for the release of funds to both public and private entities on both sides of the Atlantic. Indeed, financial

[47] See S Fredman, 'Precarious Norms for Precarious Workers' in J Fudge and R Owens (eds), *Precarious Work, Women, and the New Economy: The Challenge to Legal Norms* (Oxford, Hart Publishing, 2006).

[48] Deakin and Wilkinson, above n 31.

[49] See Stone and Arthurs, above, n 4.

[50] D Elson, R Balakrishnan and J Heintz, 'Public Finance, Maximum Available Resources and Human Rights' in A Nolan, R O'Connell and C Harvey, *Human Rights and Public Finance: Budgets and the Promotion of Economic and Social Rights* (Oxford, Hart Publishing, 2013).

[51] This analysis in this section rests on a more detailed consideration of the impact of the financial crisis on both labour law and macroeconomic policy in K Rittich, 'Fragmented Work and Multilevel Labour Market Governance: Informality, Crisis Policy and an Expanded "Law of Work"' in G de Búrca, C Kilpatrick and J Scott (eds), *Critical Legal Perspectives on Global Governance: Liber Amicorum David M Trubek* (Oxford, Hart Publishing, 2013).

crisis management has now emerged as the most important catalyst for the adoption of Anglo-American style labour market norms. A central reason is that internal devaluation via wage and price repression has become the preferred, even normal, mode of restoring competitiveness and resolving debt and balance of payments crises, particularly in Europe.

Begin with Europe: as a condition of financing, the 'troika' – the European Commission, the European Central Bank and the International Monetary Fund – required Greece to cut its minimum wage by 22 per cent, 32 per cent in the case of youth below the age of 25, with an expected reduction in real wages from 22 to 40 per cent; renegotiate existing collective agreements or simply give up contractually negotiated terms such as wage increases pension entitlements; and terminate the positions of 150,000 public employees.[52] Ireland, too, cut its minimum wage and agreed to roll back collective agreements, including those of low-wage workers, in exchange for access to funds to service newly nationalized private bank debt;[53] parallel stories can be told for other countries in the periphery. The immediate price was cuts in jobs, incomes and pensions; the ongoing effect has been a deeply depressed labour market and, almost certainly, the growth of labour market informality as well. In the countries of the European periphery – Ireland, Greece and Spain most immediately – the effects can only be described as catastrophic, evident in unemployment rates among youth which are now at almost unimaginably high rates.[54] The deeper, and more enduring, consequence however may be the official sanction of weakened labour market norms and institutions: that is, the deliberate decision to drive down the terms and conditions of work as part of the mandate to take all measures necessary to foster the objectives of competitiveness, employment, the sustainability of public finances and financial stability.[55] Despite concerns about the incursion into national sovereignty over labour market policy, official recognition of the effects of these concessions on workers' rights has been muted at best. The primary focus has been on whether it constitutes good *policy*, understood first and foremost in terms of the action necessary to lower debt levels and restart economic growth.

In North America, the assault on jobs and workplace norms took place in the private sector as well as the public. While levels of public employment plummeted in the United States during the financial crisis as states struggled to balance their

[52] For a discussion, see C Barnard, 'Financial Crisis and the Euro Plus Pact: A Labour Lawyer's Perspective' (2012) 41 *Industrial Law Journal* 98; A Koukiadaki and L Kretsos, 'Opening Pandora's Box: The Sovereign Debt Crisis and Labour Market Regulation in Greece' (2012) 41 *Industrial Law Journal* 276, 286–301.

[53] See the 'Memorandum of Understanding of the EU/IMF Programme of Financial Support for Ireland' (16 December 2010), available at: www.finance.gov.ie/documents/publications/reports/2011/euimfrevised.pdf; '2011–2014 National Recovery Plan, 36–37', available at: budget.gov.ie/RecoveryPlan.aspx; N Hardiman and A Regan, 'The Politics of Austerity in Ireland' in 'Austerity Measures in Crisis Countries – Results and Impact on Mid-term Development' (2013) 48 *Intereconomics* 4.

[54] Recent statistics put them at 62.9% for Greece, over 56% for Spain and 28.6% for Ireland. See: www.finfacts.ie/irishfinancenews/article_1026472.shtml.

[55] Barnard, above n 52.

budgets,[56] significant modifications to collectively negotiated terms of work were the price of a raft of financial and policy supports designed to relieve debt levels in the auto sector and ensure that both General Motors and Chrysler survived the financial crisis.[57] In both firms, labour contracts were renegotiated to ensure that wages were reduced to match those of non-union plants, and two-tier labour contracts were introduced that set wages for new workers at 50 per cent of existing wages in order to significantly reduce wages and wage growth in the future. All these concessions were accompanied by massive job cuts; between 2005 and 2009, the North American auto sector lost 50 per cent of its jobs.[58] There are reasons to think that, rather than isolated events, these concessions may serve as catalysts for broader labour market reform and restructuring; as the EU recognized in the Euro Plus Pact, public sector agreements – or, as here, publicly mandated changes to private sector agreements – can be expected to have a signalling effect in the broader private sector. Whatever the causal relationship, collective bargaining in the public sector has been under unrelenting siege in the United States since the crisis, and pressure to save money by reducing wages through the contracting out of public services continues.

Even assuming that financial crises and other emergencies provide some margin of manoeuvre, these actions represent a massive assault on rights at work, undermining workers' bargaining power, collective labour rights and ultimately the terms of work themselves. As was the case in Europe, no concept of workers' fundamental rights such as the right to collective bargaining restrained these concessions. When it came to collective agreements, even respect for acquired contractual rights had little purchase; instead, contracts were redrawn and pension rights impaired simply as a matter of business or financial expediency. This is not, however, because the concept of fundamental rights was missing entirely from debates about the status of employment contracts during the bail outs. At the same time as collective agreements in the auto industry were subject to mandatory renegotiation, the suggestion to reopen the contractually-guaranteed bonuses of bankers was met with the response, *pacta sunt servanda*. Although the firms that employed those workers received, and continue to receive, subsidies that dwarf those of the auto industry, when it came to private employment contracts, respect for existing contractual terms was even defended in terms of respect for the rule of law itself.[59] These differences in the conceptualization of employment contracts and workers' rights surely bear the imprint of economic and political

[56] D Cooper, M Gable and A Austin, 'The public-sector jobs crisis' (2 May 2012), available at: www.epi.org/publication/bp339-public-sector-jobs-crisis.

[57] These supports ranged from new vehicle rebates to debtor-in-possession financing, loan guarantees and equity investments totalling US$81 billion in the United States; the support was even greater, on a proportionate basis, in Canada. For a detailed discussion, see J Stanford, 'The Geography of Auto Globalization and the Politics of Auto Bailouts' (2010) 3 *Cambridge Journal of Regions, Economy and Society* 383, 396.

[58] Stanford, above n 57.

[59] See the statement by Larry Summers, then chair of the President's Council of Economic Advisors in the United States, available at: emac.blogs.foxbusiness.com/2009/03/16/781.

power – both the evident influence of the banks and its lack on the part of unions – that has marked the course of financial negotiations throughout the crisis. However, they also reveal, I suggest, the presence of normative shifts as well as analytic assumptions that are relevant to the right to work. First, they mark a return to the primacy of private contractual rights and the further retreat of social rights, always confined and weakly institutionalized in the United States in any event. Second, they indicate an increased resistance and, in the United States, a marked hostility, to unions and collective bargaining. Third, and relatedly, they reflect a set of assumptions about the legal and institutional character of 'normal' markets. The baseline assumption animating all these policies, the express use of non-union agreements as the benchmark for revised labour contracts in particular, is that undistorted markets are those in which the price of labour is structured by private rights.

However, different assumptions concerning workers' rights seemed to obtain elsewhere. In Germany, for example, tripartite negotiations in the auto sector at the beginning of the crisis led to the implementation of short-time agreements that were supplemented by additional state unemployment benefits, a strategy that both avoided layoffs and ensured the retention of jobs but also enabled employers to quickly resume full production and maintain market share once the initial stages of the crisis were past. Rather than mere differences in economic calculation and industrial strategy, might the response in Germany reflect the enduring normative pull of the right to work, as well as the persistence of the broader social contract in which it is embedded? There seems little question that the institutionalized structures of dialogue and consultation among the social partners facilitated the implementation of responses that would, in North America, be difficult if not impossible to contemplate, in large part because those structures are missing even in those (diminishing) sectors of the economy where workers are still represented. However, temporary, contract and agency workers lost their jobs in large numbers in Germany at the same time, as employers took advantage of the flexibility enabled by these workers' employment status to downsize their workforces. Moreover, it is clear that the suppression of wages has been a key element of the German strategy to retain and expand its competitive position in both Europe and the global economy for the last decade.[60] Even where the concept of the social market is strongest, then, the status of the right to work appears to be uncertain if not eroding.

B Economic Policy and Crisis Management

Employment in the public and para-public sectors is typically important to the level of work opportunities even in normal times. It is also, historically, a source

[60] T Niechoj, 'Does Supranational Coordination Erode its National Basis? The Case of European Labour Market Policy and German Industrial Relations' (2009) 13 *European Integration online Papers* art 10, available at: eiop.or.at/eiop/texte/2009-010a.htm.

of 'better' work, particularly for women and others who have traditionally experienced discrimination and disadvantage at work in the private sector. Terms and conditions of work in the public sector may also serve as a benchmark for those in the wider economy; thus, cuts to wages and benefits and the unravelling of collective agreements on the part of public employers may license or presage similar changes in the private sector. In combination, then, the reforms to labour and employment laws, the rewriting of labour contracts and the retrenchment of employment in both the public and private sectors, represent a direct, and highly visible, assault on the normative aspirations behind the right to work.

However, related economic policy decisions operate directly and indirectly on labour markets, both during the crisis and during normal times. And what has come most sharply into focus during the current crises is the significance of fiscal and monetary policy. Their evident impact on opportunities to work and workers' bargaining power and, by extension, the terms and conditions of work, arguably makes them central to any assessment of the state of the right to work.

Decisions about fiscal policy – taxation and the allocation of state resources – are directly relevant to workers' income and bargaining position in a variety of ways. The progressivity of the tax rate structure helps determine how much of the general burden of financing government falls on labour, and on what sectors of the labour market that burden falls. Public services, income transfers and social protection programmes are crucially important to social or effective wage: depending on their quality, extent and design, they ensure the delivery of some goods and services either for free or at subsidized rates, making workers less dependent on wage income and insulating them from some of the effects of cyclical variations in the labour market. They may even affect workers' reservation wage, generating exit options from the labour market where they are sufficiently generous and closing them off where they are not. Apart from their immediate and intrinsic value to workers' standard of living and freedom of choice in respect of work, they also have a potentially significant impact on workers' bargaining power.

All these are affected by the broader approach to fiscal policy, as are levels of employment. Two features of the post-industrial economy – the phenomenon of 'jobless' growth and the paradox that increases in productivity may reduce as well as increase the number of jobs – mean that neither access to work nor better work tracks economic growth in any automatic way. Nonetheless both are, in the first instance, profoundly affected by levels of growth. Simply put, if the economy is not growing, the number of jobs is unlikely to grow either; in general, slack labour markets reduce workers' bargaining power while tighter ones increase it. The willingness to address the shortfall in private demand by engaging in macroeconomic demand management, then, can be crucial both to access to work and to the presence of good, or at least better, work, particularly in times of recessions or outright crisis.

Yet macroeconomic policy informed by a rejection of Keynesianism in favour of monetarism[61] tilted fiscal policy in ways adverse to the interests of workers and, in combination with decisions about debt management, created intense pressure to reform labour law and reduce workers' rights. Despite the adoption of fiscal stimulus at the beginning of the crisis, 'anti-deficit radicalism', already entrenched as a governance norm,[62] constrained both the depth and duration of stimulus measures; by 2010, the principal concern became, once again, the state of public finances.[63] In the EU, the Stability and Growth Pact already restricted the extent to which states in the eurozone could adopt counter-cyclical fiscal measures; agreements concluded since the onset of the crisis such as the Euro Plus Pact have only increased those constraints.[64] And in states experiencing sovereign debt crises, the absolute priority of debt servicing mandated by the troika in exchange for debt relief meant that public resources were channelled not towards enhanced social programmes, public employment, lower taxes or other measures to support economic demand, but in large part to banks and foreign creditors instead, ensuring enormous sums in foregone investments and costs to workers and citizens at large.[65]

Pro-cyclical fiscal policies and the decisions to prioritize debt servicing over economic expansion have suppressed growth and, by extension, employment, reducing tax receipts and increasing the likelihood that debt ratios will stagnate, if not worsen, through the process of contraction that fiscal austerity or 'consolidation' inevitably provokes.[66] Rather than a commitment to full employment, a central obligation of the right to work,[67] states and, more importantly, international institutions, are demonstrating the capacity to tolerate distressingly high levels of unemployment.

However powerful the effects of fiscal decisions on work – labour markets as well as labour law – monetary policy may be equally significant, to growth rates, to access to work and to the distribution of the benefits of productive activity even though its impact may not be immediately visible. [68] Interest rates affect the availability of credit, and hence decisions about expansion and hiring especially within small and medium-sized enterprises. Changes in exchange rates can both fuel and depress external demand for products and services; at the margins, they can represent life or death for firms or entire industries and of course the jobs of the

[61] F Scharpf, 'Monetary Union, Fiscal Crisis and the Preemption of Democracy' (2011) Max Planck Institute for the Study of Societies Discussion Paper 11/11, available at: www.mpifg.de/pu/dp_abstracts/dp11-11.asp.

[62] AK Sen, 'Human Development and Financial Conservatism' (1998) 2 *World Development* 742.

[63] ETUI, *Benchmarking Working Europe 2014*, available at: www.etui.org/Publications2/Books/Benchmarking-Working-Europe-2014.

[64] For a detailed discussion, see Barnard, above n 52.

[65] See Hardiman and Regan, above n 53.

[66] P Krugman, *End This Depression Now!* (New York, WW Norton, 2012); J Quiggin, 'Expansionary Austerity' in J Quiggin, *Zombie Economics: How Dead Ideas Still Walk Among Us* (Princeton NJ, Princeton University Press, 2010).

[67] CESCR, General Comment No 18, above n 3.

[68] Scharpf, above n 61.

workers they employ.[69] Wages and benefits, too, may be affected by credit and interest rates because of their effects on the competitiveness of firms and industrial sectors. These decisions, moreover, may be extremely important for workers at the bottom of the income distribution, as there is evidence that their incomes are more variable and sensitive to such decisions while those at the top are far less affected.[70]

A critical issue for workers is the balance that is struck between price stability and growth and job creation in the setting of interest rates. Despite the dual mandate of most central banks, monetary policy now persistently favours inflation control over economic expansion and employment creation;[71] in the case of the European Central Bank, the priority of price stability is specified in the Maastricht Treaty itself.[72] The structure of monetary unions is also crucial, given that union implies the loss of the exchange rate as a mechanism of rebalancing. As the crisis in the eurozone has disclosed, peripheral states within currency unions may have very different stakes in the direction of interest rate changes than those in the centre. In the absence of transfer mechanisms to adjust for these differences, states on the losing end of those decisions are effectively compelled to pursue enhanced competitiveness through internal devaluation of wages, a compulsion that itself puts downward pressure on labour standards.

Even the adoption of extraordinary monetary policy may have ambiguous effects when it comes to work and workers. There seems little doubt that quantitative easing (QE) – the decisions on the part of a number of central banks to engage in regular, announced bond purchases – helped forestall the collapse in private demand that would otherwise have followed in the wake of the crisis, abating the jobs crises in measurable ways.[73] However, the main beneficiaries of QE may be the banks which enjoy expanded, virtually costless, access to funds; QE may also disproportionately benefit upper income earners.[74] Whether such policies are the best or the only way to ensure the protection of jobs and decent work is, in the wake of the crisis, surely an open, and important, question.

[69] ibid; LM Bartels, 'Partisan Politics and the US Income Distribution' (2004) Russel Sage Foundation Working Papers Series, available at: www.russellsage.org/sites/all/files/u4/Bartels_Partisan Politics.pdf.

[70] Bartels, above n 69.

[71] J Singleton, 'Inflation Targeting: The Holy Grail?' in J Singleton, *Central Banking in the Twentieth Century* (Cambridge, Cambridge University Press, 2011).

[72] Scharpf, above n 61.

[73] JC Williams, 'The Federal Reserve's Unconventional Policies', available at: www.frbsf.org/publications/economics/letter/2012/el2012-34.html

[74] L Elliot, 'Britain's richest 5% gained most from quantitative easing – Bank of England' *The Guardian* (23 August 2012), available at: www.theguardian.com/business/2012/aug/23/britains-richest-gained-quantative-easing-bank.

IV The Future of the Right to Work?

Well before the crisis, the compulsion to engage in labour market work had been intensifying. Post-crisis, continuing high levels of unemployment and/or declining labour force participation rates in many countries indicate that work is becoming both more difficult to access and less attractive in substance. What is the place of the right to work in such a context? Can it serve as a normative counterweight to policy, legislative and institutional reforms that reduce or eliminate employment opportunities, worsen the terms and conditions of work and/or compel the rewriting of labour and employment contracts? Although initial efforts to challenge the employment reforms mandated in the financial crisis by reference to the European Court of Justice were unsuccessful,[75] such reforms may – in some contexts, at least some of the time and at least at the margins – be restrained by the invocation of workers' rights. Another, perhaps equally likely scenario, however, is the defence or reinvention of the right to work in ways that support the policy, legislative and legal transformations which are already under way.

Whatever the future, it seems clear that the right to work on its own cannot do the heavy lifting. This discussion has suggested some of the ways in which arguments associated with labour market flexibility might generate an alternative vision of the right to work; indeed such arguments are already being used to help justify or support legal regimes and policy environments that, for all practical purposes, create an obligation to accept work on whatever terms are available. What the crisis has revealed above all however, is the extent to which the right to work hangs on the vision of political economy that informs it, the theoretical paradigm through which it is refracted, the institutional structure that gives it life, and the knowledge claims through which it operates.

The right to work now sits in the midst of an ideological and programmatic commitment to the transformation of labour market governance and social protection in ways that intensify rather than restrain the effects of market forces on workers. At the same time, fiscal, monetary and a host of other economic policies are themselves generating significant downward pressure on the terms and conditions of work. If the outcome, so far, seems clearly adverse to the interests of workers, new recognition of workers' rights in the abstract could only be the first step in restaging this relationship. Different narratives about the connections between markets and welfare will have to be part of the story: at both the legislative and adjudicative levels, social and political sensibilities about solidarity, the importance of equality and distributive justice, as well as the benefits and drawbacks of risk mutualization can be expected to play decisive roles in the development of law and policy around the right to work.

[75] See N Countouris and M Freedland, *Resocialising Europe in a Time of Crisis* (Cambridge, Cambridge University Press, 2013).

Interpretations of rights and support for legal institutions more favourable to the interests of workers appear now to require more work at the mid-level as well, through engagement with the theories, epistemes and logics of market dynamics and market governance.[76] If the norms, rules and policies traditionally associated with the right to work are to recover from their current status as suboptimal or second best strategies and, just as important, if *other* legal institutions that might advance the normative aspirations of greater freedom and choice at work are not to be ruled out of order ex ante, then the regulation of labour – and other – markets needs to be recuperated as a matter that is at once normative, ideological and political rather than merely technical.

The crisis has exposed key disputes among economists and public policymakers about what contributes to an expanding economy and the growth of jobs and, by extension, improvements in general social welfare. Does full employment entail support for Keynesian demand management, or is it better served by policies of fiscal austerity and monetarism? When assessing the state of employment, do we focus on declining rates of unemployment which may indicate progress or declining rates of labour force participation which may point in the opposite direction?[77] And what happens to the calculus when changes of the quality of work are factored in?

Whatever the work-related objective, further excavation and unsettling of reigning assumptions about the nature and effects of legal institutions is needed, particularly concern the neutrality and efficiency of labour markets in the absence of workers' rights and labour market institutions.

One way to challenge the tendency to implicate workers' rights and labour standards in both labour market inefficiencies and distributive inequities is to endorse the general enquiry into efficiency and distributive justice but refuse its special, and motivated, application to labour law and workers' rights. Yes, questions of rights and their consequences for efficiency and distributive justice are relevant to work and to labour markets, and yes we should think hard about the design of labour law from these angles. However, this is also true of other legal rules and institutions. Labour laws and workers' rights do not, either uniquely or disproportionately, disturb an otherwise stable and neutral market; nor do they alone determine the position of disadvantaged workers within labour markets. Rather, a wide range of rules, from private law to international law, operate on labour markets, imposing costs and risks, conferring powers and immunities and entitling, or disentitling, parties to call on the state to back up their claims and demands. These rules also operate as bargaining endowments,[78] and for that reason may be important to the distribution of market returns as well as the extent and character of economic growth.

[76] See also Elson et al, above n 50.

[77] C Rampell, 'Soft Jobs Data Not Expected to Deter Fed' *New York Times* (6 September 2013), available at: www.nytimes.com/2013/09/07/business/economy/us-economy-adds-169000-jobs-as-unemployment-rate-falls.html.

[78] R Mnookin and L Kornhauser, 'Bargaining in the Shadow of the Law: The Case of Divorce' (1979) 88 *Yale Law Journal* 950.

What those insights imply in terms of workers' rights and labour market institutions in different contexts is surely open to debate; there is no single, best way to organize workers' rights or labour market institutions, nor is there any neutral legal or normative baseline from which to assess the rules that structure labour markets.[79] But if this enquiry is central to labour law, then it is also central to decisions about other rules, including the many laws that structure the powers and freedoms of employers. Given the extent to which the realization of the normative aspirations of the right to work – both free choice of work and access to better work – are tied to the bargaining asymmetries that pervade both the labour contract and the employment relationship as a whole, it is hard to imagine a legal strategy to advance the right to work *now* that does not involve more systematic and far-reaching engagement with the links between legal rules, market power and labour market outcomes.

[79] See DK Tarullo, 'Beyond Normalcy in the Regulation of International Trade' (1987) 100 *Harvard Law Review* 546, eg, in respect of trade law.

INDEX

Introductory Note

References such as '178–9' indicate (not necessarily continuous) discussion of a topic across a range of pages. Wherever possible in the case of topics with many references, these have either been divided into sub-topics or only the most significant discussions of the topic are listed. Because the entire work is about the 'right to work', the use of this term (and certain others which occur constantly throughout the book) as an entry point has been restricted. Information will be found under the corresponding detailed topics.

www.ingramcontent.com/pod-product-compliance
Ingram Content Group UK Ltd.
Pitfield, Milton Keynes, MK11 3LW, UK
UKHW020133290926
15471UKWH00003B/454

9 781509 913787